BTEC NATIONAL
Public Services (Uniformed)
Book 1

Debra Gray, Boris Lockyer, John Vause

www.heinemann.co.uk
✓ Free online support
✓ Useful weblinks
✓ 24 hour online ordering

01865 888058

Heinemann
Inspiring generations

Heinemann Educational Publishers
Halley Court, Jordan Hill, Oxford OX2 8EJ
Part of Harcourt Education

Heinemann is the registered trademark of
Harcourt Education Limited

First published 2004

08 07 06 05 04
10 9 8 7 6 5 4 3 2 1

British Library Cataloguing in Publication Data is available
from the British Library on request.

ISBN 0 435 45659 8

Websites
Please note that the examples of websites suggested in this book were up to date at the time of writing. It is essential for tutors to preview each site before using it to ensure that the URL is still accurate and appropriate. We suggest that tutors bookmark useful sites and consider enabling students to access them through the school or college intranet.

Edited by Rosalyn Bass
Designed by Artistix
Typeset and illustrated by J&L Composition

Original illustrations © Harcourt Education Limited, 2003

Printed by The Bath Press Ltd

Cover photo: © Getty Images

Acknowledgements
Every effort has been made to contact copyright holders of material reproduced in this book. Any omissions will be rectified in subsequent printings if notice is given to the publishers.

Tel: 01865 888058 www.heinemann.co.uk

Contents

Acknowledgements

I would like to thank the following:

Colleagues at Dearne Valley College: Christine Rawson (without whom none of this would be possible – you are an inspiration to me!), Dave Stockbridge, Barry Pinches, Paul Meares, Geoff Smales, Lynn Harris, Colin Parrish.

Members of the public services and others who have helped me: South Yorkshire Police – PC Surinder Dev, Inspector Ian Cox, Inspector Mick Venables, PC Ian Saunderson, PC Paul Sherridan, 124 Army Youth Team, Major Keith Tomlinson, 64th (City of Sheffield) Signal Squadron, Signaller Kelly Stevens.

Debbie Rowe for being the best typist in Chesterfield (and understanding my handwriting)! Pen Gresford and Rosalyn Bass and Dave Smith at Heinemann for all of their inspiration and support, Iris Stevens the best mum in the world, but most especially to my husband Ben and my daughter India who have often had to play in the park alone while this book was being written, thank you for your love and patience.

Debra Gray

I would like to thank my wife, Lynne, for her immeasurable patience and understanding and Christine for her support, guidance and for being so lovely.

John Vause

I would like to thank Cheryl McCanaan, Christine Rawson, Paul Meares, Geof Smails, Barry Pinches and Garry Barrs.

Boris Lockyer

Photo acknowledgements

We are grateful to the following for permission to reproduce photographs:

Alamay page 185
Corbis page 185, 258, 259
Corbis/Harcourt Index pages 136, 138
Corbis/Rupert Horrox page 16
Empics pages 146, 148, 150
Gareth Boden pages 134, 140
Getty Images/Alexander Joe/AFP page 77
Getty Images/Graeme Robertson page 5
Getty Images/Ian Waldie page 58
Getty Images/Royal Navy page 95
Hulton Archive pages 74, 76, 80
Hulton Archive/Archive Photos page 79
Motorola page 240
PA Photos pages 18, 19, 100, 143, 210, 212, 216, 222, 257, 261, 262, 267 278, 281
PA Photos/Andrew Parsons pages 42, 96, 127
PA Photos/Ben Curtis page 81
PA Photos/Chris Young page 103
PA Photos/David Cheskin page 7
PA Photos/EPA pages 98, 122
PA Photos/Matthew Fearn page 18
PA Photos/Phil Noble page 101
PA Photos/S.J Lewis/Ministry of Defence/Crown Copyright page 95
Rex Features/Sipa Press page 78
The Defence picture Library page 220, 241

INTRODUCTION

This textbook is designed to help you achieve the National Award in Public Services, but it also covers many units which are essential for completion of the Certificate and Diploma.

The National Award in Public Services is designed primarily for adult learners who wish to follow a shorter programme of study because they are considering a career change or adults who are already in the public services and who may wish to enhance their career prospects and improve their knowledge of the sector. However, many colleges are offering it to students aged 16–19 either as a prelude to completion of the National Certificate or Diploma in Public Services or as an additional programme to support other qualifications such as A-levels, AVCEs or GNVQs.

Structure of the Public Services National Qualifications		
Award – 6 units	**Certificate – 12 units**	**Diploma – 18 units**
Core – All 3 units must be studied: 03 – Leadership 08 – The Uniformed Services 09 – Physical Preparation for Uniformed Services	**Core – All 5 units must be studied:** 01 – Understanding the Public Sector 02 – Law and the Legal System 03 – Leadership 04 – Citizenship and Contemporary Issues 08 – The Uniformed Services	**Core – All 8 units must be studied:** 01 – Understanding the Public Sector 02 – Law and the Legal System 03 – Leadership 04 – Citizenship and Contemporary Issues 05 – Diversity and the Public Services 06 – International Perspectives 07 – Data Interpretation 08 – The Uniformed Services
Options – 3 units must be studied from the following list: 02 – Law and the Legal System 11 – Expedition Skills 14 – Understanding Discipline 16 – Dealing with Accidents 22 – Signals and Communication Systems 24 – Major Incidents	**Options – 7 units must be studied from the following list:** 07 – Data Interpretation 09 – Physical Preparation for Uniformed Services 10 – Democratic Processes 11 – Expedition Skills 12 – Human Behaviour 13 – Media and the Public Services 14 – Understanding Discipline 15 – Public Services in Europe 16 – Dealing with Accidents 17 – Teamwork in the Public Services 18 – Health and Fitness 19 – Nautical Studies 20 – Outdoor Activities 21 – Criminology 22 – Signals and Communication Systems	**Options – 10 units must be studied from the following list:** 09 – Physical Preparation for Uniformed Services 10 – Democratic Processes 11 – Expedition Skills 12 – Human Behaviour 13 – Media and the Public Services 14 – Understanding Discipline 15 – Public Services in Europe 16 – Dealing with Accidents 17 – Teamwork in the Public Services 18 – Health and Fitness 19 – Nautical Studies 20 – Outdoor Activities 21 – Criminology 22 – Signals and Communication Systems 23 – Custodial Care 24 – Major Incidents

Structure of the Public Services National Qualifications

If you are studying the National Award then this is the only book you will need. However, if you are studying the National Certificate or Diploma then this book should be used in tandem with the second textbook in this series. Each textbook covers a different set of units:

Book One – Award
Leadership
The Uniformed Services
Physical Preparation for the Uniformed Services
Law and the Legal System
Expedition Skills
Understanding Discipline
Signals and Communications Systems
Major Incidents

Book Two – Certificate
Understanding the Public Sector
Citizenship and Contemporary Issues
Diversity and the Public Services
International Perspectives
Democratic Processes
Human Behaviour
Media and the Public Services
Health and Fitness
Criminology

In addition, Unit 07 Data Interpretation and Unit 23 Custodial Care are available in a web-based format.

How to use this book

This book is designed to operate on a unit by unit basis which means you don't need to read all of the book in order to find the information you need. Simply look in the contents, choose the unit you need and go to the appropriate page. If you are looking for a specific topic within a unit then go to the index and find the topic with its appropriate page number. Sometimes if a unit has strong links with another you may find information is cross referenced. Examples of units with strong links are:

Unit 02 – Law and the Legal System and Unit 21 – Criminology

Unit 09 – Physical Preparation for the Public Services and Unit 18 – Health and Fitness

You can use this book for a whole range of purposes including background reading for a particular unit, help with your assignments, understanding a topic that you missed or didn't understand in class, completion of the activities to reinforce what you already know or to improve your broader general public service knowledge so that you are a better employment prospect for the public services.

This book is written at the level of an A-level text book as the National Award qualification is equivalent to an A-level qualification. However, it is written in a friendly and accessible style.

How this book is designed to help you

Each chapter contains many or all of the following elements.

Think about it

These are points designed to provoke classroom discussion or discussion in your study group or even just to get your mind working by considering something from a different point of view. This is important because many of the public services could ask you spot questions in your interviews and prior discussion will ensure you will be much better prepared to tackle them if and when they occur.

Case studies

The case studies in the chapters are a mixture of real life events and realistic simulations. They are designed to give you an insight into potential problems or controversial issues which can arise in the public services.

Completing the case studies may involve you critically considering the actions or inactions of the public services, commenting on their positive and negative conduct and putting yourself in the shoes of serving officers and deciding what you would have done in their place. The use of role-play and case studies is on the increase in public service recruitment procedure and is seen as a valuable tool in assessing your potential.

Case studies also allow you to put the subject knowledge you have learned in the chapters to practical application. This will ensure you retain more of the information you need to learn.

Theory into practice

Activities are included throughout the units to provide you with the opportunity to work with others and implement the knowledge you will learn during the chapter.

Assessment

At the end of each unit you will find a series of assessment activities which are based around the assessment criteria set by EDEXCEL. Any assessment you are set by your own college will be based around exactly the same questions, so if you complete the assessment activities provided you will have a head start on how to approach your real assignment. In addition, each assessment activity tells you how to obtain the higher grades of merit and distinction as well as the basic pass criteria.

Completing your assignments

As the National Award/Certificate and Diploma are based on coursework, it is extremely important that you are disciplined and organised with your time to enable you to meet deadlines and have a better chance of getting higher grades.

It is important that you understand and comply with the key words specified in the grading criteria. An understanding of the key words will enable you to achieve merits and distinctions with greater ease. For example: 'Explain how courts deal with three types of criminal offence'. Below is a description of some of the most common action words found in your assignments.

Analyse – this means to examine something in great detail or to break something down into its essential parts. For example, if you were asked to analyse the role of a police officer, you would not just say that a police officer was someone who wore a uniform. This is not an analysis – it is one particular feature and a feature that fits many other professions. To analyse the role of a police officer you must state everything that fulfils the role of being a police officer and in doing so separates a police officer from other professions.

Identify – this means to recognise, select or establish something. For example, if you were asked to identify three qualities needed for self-discipline, then you would merely state what they are, just as you would state that a certain item belonged to you.

Describe – if you were asked to describe three qualities needed for self-discipline, then you would give a descriptive account of them just as you would an item of property that belonged to you.

Examine – this means to look at something very closely and in detail – to subject something to close scrutiny. It differs from 'analyse,' though it is very similar in meaning, in that you are not necessarily breaking it down into its essential parts. For example, a doctor may examine a patient to see what is wrong with them but she doesn't have to analyse the patient in order to do so.

Investigate – this is similar to 'examine' in that they both involve studying something very carefully, though they do have different meanings. To investigate something is to ask questions and have an inquiring mind so that we may find answers to the questions or put forward a theory based on the information that has been gathered. For example, when a police officer investigates a crime, he or she gathers clues and information so that he or she can form a picture (or a theory) of why and how the crime was committed. However, if we examine something, we do not necessarily have to ask questions about something, we merely give a true account of what happens to be the case. For example, a scene of crime or a fingerprint could be examined without the need for forming an opinion.

Evaluate – this means to assess something or to appraise it – to balance the good points against the bad points and then give a reasoned opinion. It does not mean, merely, to describe or summarise something, though you may have to do this before you evaluate it. For example, if you were asked to evaluate the role of discipline in the public services, you would firstly have to say why discipline was necessary and what its effects were. This could include the negative and positive effects of blind obedience. You would then have to weigh up the positive effects against the negative effects and give an opinion as to whether discipline was, overall, a good or bad thing.

What can I do with a National Award/Certificate/ Diploma in Public Services

The course you have chosen to study is not only a superb introduction to the working and organisation of the public services, it is also an excellent general education course as well. If you complete the National Diploma in Public Services

you will have studied eighteen different subjects and gained the equivalent of three A-levels. This means that in addition to joining a public service or any other form of employment you also stand a very good chance of being accepted into higher education institutions such as universities and HE colleges. As many public services such as the police prefer recruits to have some life experience and be a little older than the lowest age of entry which is eighteen, many students feel that a university education makes them more employable to the services and provides them with life experience such as living independently.

If you want to go to university your college will be able to advise you on the procedure and help you select the right course for your career aspirations. See your tutor or careers advisor if you feel this is the right option for you. If you want to join a public service straight away the main thing to remember is that the majority of the services are highly competitive and they have more people applying than they can take on. This means that if you want to be employed, you must be better than the other candidates. This is not easy when you consider you could be up against people who have more experience and qualifications than you do. However, there are some things you can do to make yourself more attractive to the services.

Complete your public services qualification

The services like to see commitment to a project as they are not looking for people who change their minds frequently about what is right for them. It costs a great deal of money to train a public service recruit and they will not be willing to spend that money on someone with a track record of not completing tasks they have undertaken.

Be punctual and reliable at college

Your public service application could depend on the reference of a tutor who has known you for a long period of time. Your tutor must be honest in any reference they give, which means that if you have repeated absence, sickness and lateness your reference will not make particularly good reading. The services require you to be punctual and reliable so it is best to get into the habit at college and allow your tutors to be able to pass on your good conduct to the service of your choice.

Hand your coursework in on time

Once again, this is directly related to references. If you regularly fail to meet set deadlines it does not speak well of your management and organisational skills and your tutor will write this in a reference. The services will be less likely to recruit someone who has a track record of poor self discipline.

Take part in college and community activities

Many students simply attend college and go home which does not add to their CV or their value to the services. All public service employers want team players who show an active interest in their community. If you are serious about a public service career then join some college clubs such as sports or martial arts clubs or consider giving a couple of hours voluntary work to a local charity. Not only will this make you much more employable, it will also help you understand your public services qualification to better effect.

Wear your uniform smartly

Many public services courses have a uniform as a requirement, such as a college tracksuit, a particular colour polo shirt or a full police style uniform with epaulettes. Uniforms are worn to get you into the habit of being different from other students (just as you will be different from members of the public if you join a service) and it is also used to teach you self discipline. If your uniform is untidy, it does not give a good impression and if you can't take this small amount of discipline in college are you likely to be able to cope with a large amount of discipline in the line of duty?

LAW AND THE LEGAL SYSTEM

Introduction to Unit 2

This unit introduces a range of different types of law including; public service law, common law, statute law, civil law and criminal law as well as different legal institutions including the magistrates and crown courts. These institutions are examined and comparison made with other legal systems. It describes the role of the public services in upholding and delivering the law and how legal powers are granted and the constraints that are placed upon them as they fulfil their duties.

Assessment

Throughout the unit, activities and tasks will help you to learn and remember information. Case studies are included to add industry relevance to the topics and learning objectives. At the end of each unit, end of unit questions test your knowledge and assessment tasks outline the evidence requirements required for assessment in order to obtain a Pass, Merit or Distinction as well as suggesting ways of providing assessment evidence. This unit is internally assessed. You are reminded that when you are completing activities and tasks, opportunities will be created to enhance your key skills evidence.

After completing this unit you should have an understanding of the following outcomes.

Outcomes

1 Examine the key features of **public service law**.

2 Examine English **legal institutions** and compare them with other national legal systems.

3 Examine the **legal process** in England in relation to different types of law.

4 Examine the **role of the public services** in the English legal system.

Public service law

The public services derive their power from a variety of sources, but like any ordinary citizen they are also subject to the law and can be held accountable for their actions and misconduct by both the people and the government.

Police and the law

The police have legal powers as well as legal controls on their activities as shown in Figure 2.1.

Police powers

The Terrorism Act 2000

This legislation is designed to give the British government and public service organisations increased powers to monitor and control potential or actual terrorist threats. The Act has been criticised by civil liberties groups who claim that it is an assault on personal privacy and freedom and gives the public services a great deal of power which could be open to abuse.

The Criminal Justice and Police Act 2001

This Act provides legislation which enables the public services to work towards the primary goals

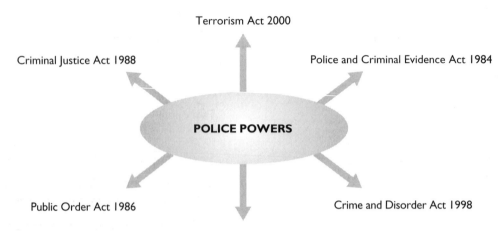

Figure 2.1 The police have legal controls on their activities

of The Home Office: to reduce youth crime, to reduce the fear of crime and to ensure public order. It includes measures to combat alcohol related disorder, police training and organisation and police powers of seizure.

The Protection From Harassment Act 1997

This Act is often referred to as the 'Stalkers Act'. However it is designed to help combat many forms of harassment, not just stalking. It includes provisions to deal with issues such as neighbourhood disputes, racial hatred, bullying at work and nuisance tenants.

The Police and Criminal Evidence Act 1984

This is a major piece of law governing the actions and conduct of the police. It defines powers such as stop, search, entry and seizure and also provides guidance on how these powers should be used.

The Crime and Disorder Act 1998

This act places a duty on local authorities and public services to operate in partnership with local businesses, charities and schools to reduce crime and disorder in local areas. It requires local problems to be analysed and then strategies to combat the problems implemented in a multi-agency manner. This means many organisations working together towards the same goal of a safer community.

The Criminal Justice Act 1988

This Act governs the admissibility of evidence in criminal cases and has an impact on how the police can conduct investigations and collect evidence.

Theory into practice

Describe how these acts confer powers onto the police.

There is a great deal more legislation that has an impact on the role of the police, but the laws listed are those which may be more commonly used in day-to-day operations.

Police conduct

The police also have to adhere to laws which regulate and monitor their conduct. Some of these acts are the same as the ones above, the primary example being the Police and Criminal Evidence Act (PACE) 1984.

PACE is a key piece of legislation which provides the police with powers and creates safeguards on misuse of these powers. PACE provides guidance on several key areas of policing practice as shown in Figure 2.2.

Other examples of laws that govern how the police conduct themselves are:

- Human Rights Act 1998
- Police Act 1996
- Police Act 1997.

Key concepts

1 The public services are like ordinary citizens in that they are accountable for their actions.

2 There are laws which give them their powers and laws which regulate their powers.

3 One of the most important pieces of law which provides the police with powers is PACE 1984.

4 PACE governs areas such as stop and search, arrest, seizure and detention.

Police And Criminal Evidence Act 1984	
Area of law	**Details of the powers and safeguards**
Stop and search	Introduced a general power of stop and search for persons or vehicles on the basis of reasonable suspicion of finding stolen or prohibited articles. The suspect has to be informed of the reasons for the search and accurate written records must be kept.
Entry, search and seizure	Premises may be searched for evidence or in order to make an arrest. Reasons must be provided for the searches and full and accurate written records of the conduct of the search and any seized property must be kept.
Arrest	PACE rationalised arrest powers. The basis for arrest is reasonable grounds for suspicion or where a summons is impractical. A summons is a formal call to appear in court.
Detention	Only permissible where necessary to secure or preserve evidence and usually involves more serious crimes or crimes where the person may be a threat to the victim or witnesses. For most offences, only 24 hours without charge is allowed. The custody officer who ensures the detainees welfare must be independent of the investigation.
Questioning and treatment of suspects	Detainees have a right to legal advice and to have someone informed of their detention. They should not be interviewed until after they have received legal advice if they have requested it. Accurate records must be kept. In addition, juveniles or individuals with a mental disorder must be interviewed in the presence of an appropriate adult.
Accountability and supervision	PACE stresses the need for accountability and supervision of the police. Full custody records must be kept for each detainee and the act created the Police Complaints Authority (PCA) which supervises investigations into allegations of police misconduct.

Figure 2.2 PACE policing practice

Traffic offences

There are a wide variety of traffic offences that the police must deal with. It is impossible to discuss them all, so only a selection of the most common are addressed here.

Failing to stop

If a person is involved in an accident in which anyone else is injured or any property is damaged they must supply their name, address and registration number of the vehicle if they are asked to do so.

Failing to report an accident

A person involved in an accident must report it to the police within 24 hours. Failure to do so is a criminal offence.

Exceeding the speed limit (non-motorway)

The seriousness of this offence depends upon the prescribed speed limit in question and by how much the speed limit was exceeded. For instance, a person who is 30mph over the speed limit is likely to face disqualification, whereas a person who was 10mph over the speed limit may only have a fine to pay.

Exceeding the speed limit (motorway)

The national speed limit for motorways is 70mph unless specific hazard warnings indicate otherwise. If this limit is exceeded you are liable to a fine or disqualification.

Drink driving

The police can request a breath test from any person who is driving, attempting to drive or is in charge of a motor vehicle in a public place. The acceptable amount of alcohol in breath is 35 micrograms per 100 millilitres of breath. The breath test can be requested by a uniformed officer if one of the following situations apply:

- the police officer has reasonable cause to suspect that a traffic offence has occurred.

- the police officer having stopped the vehicle has reasonable cause to suspect the person has consumed excess alcohol.

- the person in charge of a vehicle has been involved in an accident.

Offence	Penalty Points	Imprisonment	Fines (Levels 1–5)	Disqualification
Failing to stop	5–10	Up to 6 months	Up to level 5 (£5,000)	Possible
Failing to report	5–10	Up to 6 months	Up to level 3 (£1,000)	Possible
Speeding (non motorway)	3–6	/	Up to level 3 (£1,000)	Possible
Speeding (motorway)	3–6	/	Up to level 4 (£2,500)	Possible
Failing to provide a roadside breath test	4	/	Up to level 3 (£1,000)	Possible
Driving with excess alcohol	/	Up to 6 months	Up to level 5 (£5,000)	Compulsory
Being in charge of a vehicle with excess alcohol	10	Up to 3 months	Up to level 4 (£2,500)	Possible

Figure 2.3 Punishments for different traffic offences

Case study

You are a newly qualified magistrate – consider the following three cases and answer the questions below.

- A young mother is on her way to collect her children from school. She is in a hurry because she is late and they are due to leave for the airport shortly for a week's holiday in Mallorca. On her way she clips a stationary car causing damage to the wing mirror and drivers side door. It is her intention to notify the police on her return from holiday and she leaves a note on the damaged car telling the owner that she will be in touch in a week.

- A middle aged man is out for a night on the town to celebrate his daughter's eighteenth birthday. As the younger members of the party go on to a nightclub the man decides to go home as he has to be up for work in the morning. He knows he has had too much to drink to drive home safely, but his car is parked on a main street and he doesn't feel that it is secure enough to leave it overnight. He drives it 200 metres to a secure car park but is picked up and breath tested by the police who find him to be over the legal safe limit of alcohol.

- A doctor is on her way to conduct a home visit on an elderly patient. The patient sounded very distressed and the doctor is keen to be with her as soon as possible. Consequently she is caught travelling at 55 miles per hour in a residential district.

1 In each case what is the offence the person is guilty of?

2 What are the maximum penalties in each case?

3 Are there any mitigating circumstances in each case, which may reduce the penalties given by a court?

4 What do you think would be an appropriate penalty in each case?

Standards of conduct

The primary duties of a police officer are:

- the protection of life and property
- the preservation of the Queen's peace
- the prevention and detection of criminal activities.

In order to do this we have seen that there are many laws which grant the police powers which set them apart from the rest of the general public. As a consequence, the government and the public have the right to expect them to uphold the highest standards of conduct. This means that the police must also follow internal regulations regarding their behaviour, such as the Police (Conduct) Regulations 1999 set down rules with reference to the conduct of police officers in the following areas:

Honesty and integrity – Officers should be open and truthful in their dealings because it is vital that the public can have faith and trust in them.

Fairness and impartiality – Police officers must treat everyone with fairness and impartiality. This includes dealings with the public and with their own colleagues.

A police officer on duty

Politeness and tolerance – The police must treat the public with courtesy and respect and must not demonstrate abusive behaviour. They must avoid favouritism and all forms of harassment. As well as applying to the general public this particularly applies to the treatment of lower ranked officers.

Confidentiality – The police are exposed to a large amount of confidential data about members of the general public and the public need to be certain this information is held in confidence. Police officers must not use private information for personal gain. In addition they should not divulge confidential policy or operational information about the police force unless authorised to do so.

Following lawful orders – The police service can only operate effectively when it is a disciplined body. This means that unless there is good and sufficient cause they must obey all lawful orders given to them. They must support their colleagues in the execution of lawful orders and oppose improper behaviour, reporting it where appropriate.

Sobriety – Whilst on duty, officers must be sober and must not consume alcohol unless it becomes necessary for the proper discharge of their duties. For instance, if a police officer working undercover needed to drink in order to appear convincing.

Smart and professional appearance – Officers should always be well turned out and clean and tidy unless they are fulfilling duties which dictate otherwise.

Reasonable use of force – Officers should never knowingly use more force than is deemed reasonable, nor should they abuse their authority.

Conscientious performance of duties – Officers should attend work promptly when they are on duty and carry out their designated duties with diligence. In addition, whether on or off duty a police officer should not behave in a way which is likely to bring discredit to the police service.

Sanctions

A breach of the regulations may lead to the following sanctions depending on the severity of the misconduct:

- warning
- formal caution
- loss of pay
- loss of rank
- requirement to resign
- dismissal from service.

The regulations apply to all officers in all ranks while on duty. A breach of the regulations whilst an officer is off duty may still be punished if the offence is serious enough to indicate that an individual is not fit to be a police officer. For instance, if a police officer was found to be selling drugs in his or her off duty time then it would indicate he/she was not fit to be a police officer.

Case study – Police conduct

WPC Akhtar is a new recruit to the police service – she is on a temporary placement with the child protection unit. While there she sees a list of sex offenders in the local area and is horrified to find that one of the addresses on the list is the same street where she lives. WPC Akhtar shares this information with her husband in confidence. However, her husband then tells a neighbour and before long there is a mob outside the sex offenders home

1 Was WPC Akhtar right to share the information she came across with her husband?

2 Which parts of the police conduct regulations did WPC Akhtar breach?

3 What disciplinary procedures might be instigated against WPC Akhtar?

4 What effect has this breach of confidentiality had on the community?

5 What impact has it had on the sex offender and their family?

Theory into practice

Why is it important that police officers follow a code of conduct? What do you think would be the consequences if they didn't?

Key concepts

1 The government expects the highest standards of conduct from members of the public services.

2 Police officers must follow an internal code of conduct as well as obeying the same laws as everyone else.

3 Police officers who breach the code of conduct can be subject to discipline procedures.

4 The code of conduct can still apply to the behaviour of an officer even when they are off duty.

5 Police powers are balanced by safeguards against misuse.

Military law

As with the police force, the armed services is governed by stringent military rules, which have a direct impact on members of the armed forces both in their day-to-day operations and also the time they spend out of uniform.

People sometimes use the term 'military law' to apply to all of the armed services, but the term only applies to The Army. The Royal Navy is governed by Naval law and the Royal Air Force by Air Force law. There is no unified code of military justice in the UK as each of the three services has their own disciplinary code which enables the service authorities to try service offenders for offences committed both in the UK and abroad.

Troops on parade

Military offences

Desertion

Desertion is when a currently serving member of the armed services decides to leave the service without following the correct discharge procedure or notifying their commanding officer of their intention to leave. In times of war, this was an offence punishable by death. Today, a range of sanctions exist, such as loss of pay or loss of rank which can be used to deal with deserters who are tracked down and caught. Desertion is a major problem in today's armed services and tends to be caused by several main problems:

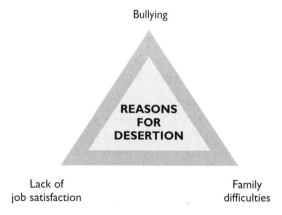

Figure 2.4 There are three main reasons for desertion from the Army

Family difficulties – Servicemen and women are often hundreds of miles away when a domestic crisis or family illness occurs and they may be denied permission to return home. The Army in particular is still considered to have a poor record of responding sympathetically to such incidents. Burke (2000) reporting for The Observer newspaper highlights several cases where court-martial proceedings were instigated for the following offences of desertion:

- a serviceman who wanted to save his marriage after a tour of duty in Germany was followed by his immediate posting to Northern Ireland

- a gunner in an artillery regiment deserted to help his girlfriend after she miscarried their child

- a soldier who deserted after being told that one of his parents had a fatal illness

Theory into practice

Why is the military often so inflexible about family issues? What are the advantages and disadvantages in being more flexible?

Bullying – This is also a major cause of desertion in the armed services, particularly amongst new recruits. Bullying can take many forms and can include physical beatings. The Army recognise the seriousness of this problem and is trying hard to change the entrenched military culture in which bullying was allowed to fester.

A Lack of job satisfaction – This can also lead to the desertion of military personnel. Recruits who sign up to be mechanics may end up as gunners or serving in an infantry regiment. It can be very difficult for junior servicemen and women to establish control over the way their career progresses. If attempts to transfer fail then some young recruits may run away.

You can see clearly how this aspect of military law sets servicemen and women apart from the rest of the population. A member of the general public may leave a job as and when they wish without fear of punishment, but a member of the armed services is tied to their service and does not enjoy the same freedom.

Absent Without Leave (AWOL)

This is another military offence that carries punitive sanctions attached to it. As with the offence of desertion, most AWOL cases occur in the junior ranks of infantry regiments who are often the lowest paid units in the army. Considering that the Army is several thousand servicemen and women under strength, AWOL cases cause severe manpower difficulties. The absences can range from 24 hours to several months. It is estimated that most infantry battalions have 2–3 soldiers AWOL at any one time. According to Burke (2000) this leaves two or three entire platoons of men unaccounted for.

Improper possession of military equipment

The Armed Forces has a large amount of weaponry and sensitive equipment worth millions of pounds. The services cannot afford to replace stolen or 'borrowed' equipment and some equipment may pose a danger to the general public or may be sought after by foreign powers, so access and possession of equipment needs to be strictly regulated.

Military discipline proceedings

These and other military and civil offences are punishable by military law in the same way a civilian would be subject to criminal law. Further examples of military offences are described in Figure 2.5.

Although the maximum sentences may seem excessive, remember that many incidents will be dealt with by the soldiers own commanding officer and a much lighter punishment may be received. Each offence is assessed on its own characteristics and only a few will merit the maximum sentence available.

The Army has jurisdiction to try a wide variety of cases, civil and criminal as well as military. Legal officers belonging to the Adjutant General Corps advise regimental officers on issues of evidence, drafting of charges, trial by court-martial and exercise of military jurisdiction overseas.

Military Offence	Maximum Sentence (upon conviction in court-martial
Misapplication and waste of public or service property	2 years
Failure to provide a sample for drugs testing	6 months
Obstruction of provost officers (Military Police)	2 years
Disobedience of standing orders	2 years
AWOL	2 years
Failure to report or apprehend deserters or absentee's	2 years
Malingering	2 years
Drunkeness	2 years
Fighting	2 years
Damage to and loss of public property	2 years

Figure 2.5 Military offences and their maximum sentences

Key concepts

1 There is no unified system of military justice in the UK. Each of the services has its own legal code.

2 These codes are updated every five years to ensure they are relevant.

3 Military offences are different from civilian offences.

4 Military personnel are subject to civilian and military law, so in effect they are doubly policed.

5 The codes are The Army Act 1955, The Air Force Act 1955 and The Naval Act 1957.

There are two ways in which military offences can be dealt with. Alleged offences may be tried summarily or by a court martial.

Summary trial

In a summary trial a soldier or a Non Commissioned Officer (NCO) will be dealt with by his or her commanding officer. The Commanding Officer (CO) has the power to restrict the liberty of a soldier for a period of up to 60 days. If the offender is a Lance Corporal the Commanding Officer may also reduce him/her to the rank of Private. The CO also has the power to levy a fine of up to 28 days pay. Military summary offences tend to be relatively minor and include occurrences such as short periods of absence or being late for parade. A military summary trial may also deal with some civilian criminal offences such as minor assaults.

The Armed Forces Discipline Act 2000 created the Summary Appeals Court in response to the Human Rights Act 1998. This court hears appeals against summary procedure and consists of a Judge Advocate and two officers who have had two or more years of service. The commanding officer of a naval base or the captain of a ship has wider powers than their RAF or Army counterpart. They may detain a naval rating for up to 90 days and can dismiss a person from the service. There is no provision for summary trials for officers in the Navy and there is only one kind of court martial which is equivalent to a general court martial in the Army.

Court-martial trial

Military and civilian offences, committed by a member of the Armed Forces, that are too serious to be dealt with by a summary trial are instead tried by court-martial. In the UK there are two kinds of court-martial trial.

District court-martial (DCM) consists of at least three independent officers including a Major or Lieutenant Colonel who acts as the presiding officer and a judge advocate who is a civilian appointed by the Lord Chancellor. This type of court-martial cannot try officers and is limited to a maximum sentence of two years imprisonment. Members of the DCM must not be junior to the accused in rank and have served for two years.

General court-martial (GCM) consists of at least five independent officers including the presiding Officer who is usually a Colonel or a Brigadier. These will be non-legally qualified Officers who decide on questions of fact, very much as a jury does in civilian cases. A judge advocate also sits in this court, but the difference is that this court can try officers for crimes and they can impose the maximum sentences for military and civilian offences if they choose to do so. The members of this court must have three years service in order to serve.

Operation of military trials

As with civilian courts there are a number of set procedures that must be followed if a case is to be conducted correctly. The Army Military Courts Guide Edition 1 (2002) outlines the following stages in a DCM or GCM trial:

1 Preliminaries and administrative briefings

2 Opening and assembly of court

3 Reading the convening order

4 Swearing in of court members

5 Formal warning by the judge advocate

6 Trial of the accused

7 Prosecution case

8 Defence case

9 Closing arguments by the prosecution and defence

10 Summing up by the judge advocate

11 Deliberation by the military members of the court

12 Announcement of finding (Verdict of guilt or innocence)

13 Defence mitigation if verdict is guilty

14 Consideration of defence by judge advocate and court members

15 Announcement of sentence

16 Dissolution of the court.

As with civilian trials, court-martials can vary in timescale from as little as an hour in the case of a straightforward guilty plea on a simple case to several weeks in a contested complex case.

Standing Civilian Court

Civilians can also be tried in military courts. These civilians are usually civil servants or support workers who fall under the command of an officer who commands a body of regular service personnel. The court they are tried in is called the *Standing Civilian Court*. It is presided over by a judge advocate sitting without a jury and it can try offences against English criminal law plus a small number of service offences.

Military Discipline and the Human Rights Act (HRA) 1998

The HRA has had a tremendous impact on military discipline and the operation of military trials. The Findlay case below outlines some of the problems that existed with the Convening Officer in court-martial trials. The HRA provided for the independence and impartiality of these trials and the abolition of the death penalty in the few military offences that retained it as punishment. It did this by forcing the government to amend some of the principles in the original armed forces acts by creating The Armed Forces Discipline Act 2000 (AFDA). The AFDA changed many things other than the abolition of the death penalty, such as:

- the right of the accused to select trial by court-martial rather than summary dealing

- the right of appeal against summary findings

- the creation of the Summary Appeals Court

- military custody over 48 hours must be authorised by a judicial officer.

Personal conduct under military and civilian law

The three armed services operate within a statutory framework of discipline that applies wherever they are based. Although wherever possible all three services follow the English legal system as closely as they can, in effect they have their own legal system. The laws which underpin these powers are as follows:

- The Army Act 1955
- The Airforce Act 1955
- The Naval Act 1957

These Acts are renewed every five years to ensure they are up to date and effective. Recent laws intended to change and update these original Acts are pieces of law such as:

- The Armed Forces Act 1996
- The Armed Forces Discipline Act 2000

These amendments are often needed because of the changing nature of society or because another law which has a major impact such as The Human Rights Act 1998 or even because of a landmark appeal case such as Findlay V United Kingdom 1997.

Discipline and good personal conduct is essential to the operational effectiveness of an armed service, which is why military personnel are subject to many more rules and regulations than their civilian counterparts. It is crucial for combat effectiveness that an armed force is alert and responsive, which is why the penalties for failing in this duty are so much more severe than with civilians. In essence, military personnel are doubly policed, firstly by the same criminal and civilian codes that all of the population should follow and secondly by an additional set of military rules.

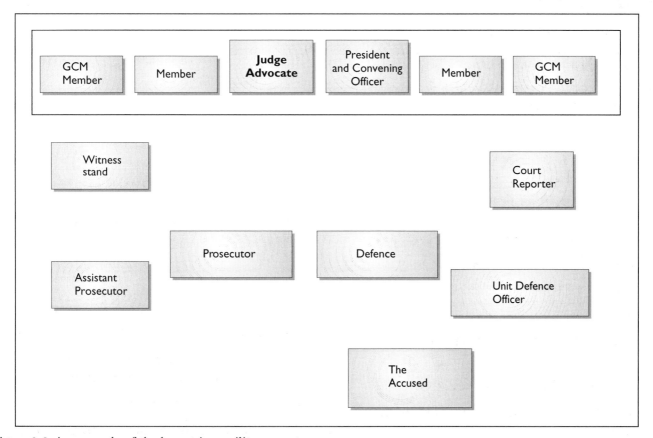

Figure 2.6 An example of the layout in a military court

Case study – Findlay v United Kingdom 1997

Before the case of Findlay, a court-martial was set up by an officer called the 'Convening Officer'. This officer would appoint junior officers to sit as officers of the court, he also appointed the prosecutor and had control over the prosecution procedure. He also had the power to dissolve the court, meaning that in theory he could disband a court-martial if it wasn't going the way he wanted it to. In addition, the findings and sentence of the court were subject to his approval. Clearly this situation did not mirror the impartiality of civilian trials and according to the European Court of Human Rights, the all powerful influence of the Convening Officer was not consistent with the aims of the UN Declaration of Human Rights or the Human Rights Act 1998 which states that a trial must be conducted by an independent and impartial tribunal

1 Why is it inappropriate to have a convening officer who is responsible for all of the duties described above?

2 Do you think a change in the way court-martial trials were run was necessary?

3 Why is it important that trials are impartial?

4 Should military trials be run on the same principles as civilian ones?

Key concepts

1 Military offences are punishable in two ways, either by summary dealing or court-martial.

2 Summary trial is dealt with by the Commanding Officer.

3 Appeals against summary trials are made to the Summary Appeals Court.

4 There are two types of court martial trial: District court-martial (DCM) and General court-martial (GCM).

5 The Armed Forces Discipline Act (2000) changed the way military offences were dealt with.

Legal institutions

English legal system

There are many different courts and legal institutions in England and Wales such as; magistrates court, crown court, court of appeal and the House of Lords. Each of them has a role to play in the larger system of justice. The courts fit together in a system which when simplified looks like Figure 2.7:

The magistrates court

The magistrates court is the most junior of all the courts in the English legal system. The country is divided up into 'commissions' which is then further divided up into petty sessional areas, or

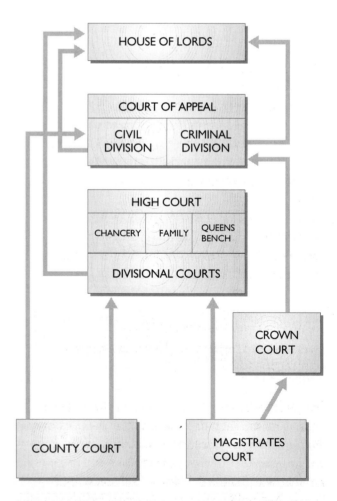

Figure 2.7 Structure of the courts in England and Wales

benches. Each bench has its own courthouse and clerk. Although this is the most junior court it is a vital part of the legal system due to its caseload. There are over 400 magistrates courts in England and Wales and each deals with local matters such as:

- 97% of all criminal cases
- civil family matters such as adoption, custody and maintenance
- granting of warrants, summonses and bail applications
- granting of licenses, for example for the sale of alcohol
- juvenile jurisdiction (offenders aged 10–17)
- summary jurisdiction (relatively minor offences)
- jurisdiction over some triable either way offences (mid-level offences)
- committal for trial for indictable offences (more serious offences).

The courts are staffed by magistrates whose job it is to decide guilt or innocence and provide appropriate punishments when needed. The maximum sentence that magistrates can levy for an offence is six months imprisonment and/or a £5,000 fine. If they feel an offence needs a stronger punishment than they are able to give they may send the case to a crown court, which has the power to deliver harsher sentences. Around 90% of people appearing before a magistrate's court plead guilty which simplifies and speeds up matters considerably.

Theory into practice

What are the advantages of pleading guilty in a magistrates court?

Magistrates have a long history in the English legal system. They date back to the Justices of the Peace Act 1361 which gave certain judicial powers to lay people. This meant that they had the ability to deal with criminal matters and some civil issues, but unlike magistrates today they were also entrusted with the running of local government. Today, there are two types of magistrates: Lay magistrates and District judges/Deputy district judges.

Lay magistrates

There are over 30,000 lay magistrates in England and Wales. They are also known as Justices of the Peace (JP). Lay magistrates are unpaid volunteers, they do not require any formal qualifications except that they are aged between 27–60 and of good character. They deal with the vast majority (about 97%) of all magistrates court work and are often described as the backbone of the criminal justice system. They are helped and guided by the clerk of the court who is legally trained (often a barrister) and they usually sit as a bench of three. This is to ensure fairness and avoid misuse of power. Magistrates are required to sit for a minimum of 26 sessions a year, but most sit for around 40 sessions.

Think about it

The backbone of the justice system is dependent on volunteers. What is your view on the use of volunteers in such an important service?

District judges/Deputy district judges

These judges were created by The Access To Justice Act 1999; they were previously called Stipendiary Magistrates. Prior to their appointment they have been fully qualified barristers or solicitors and are highly legally trained with a minimum of seven years experience of advocacy work. They are not volunteers and are paid a substantial salary. They may sit as sole judge in a court and do not need to sit with other magistrates in a bench.

Theory into practice

Why is there a need for District judges when Lay magistrates do the job for free?

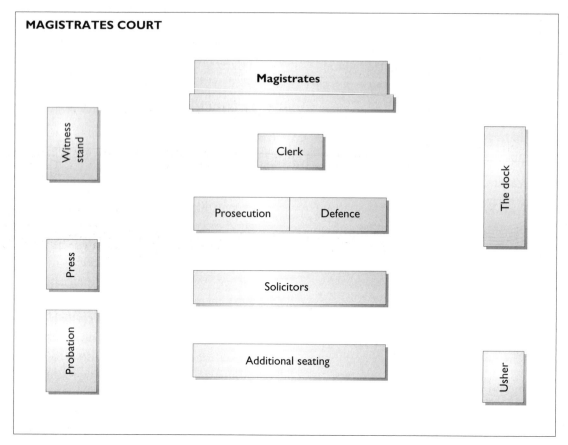

Figure 2.8 The layout inside a magistrates court

The clerk of the court

The clerk of the court advises the magistrates on issues of law and procedure. They do not take any part in the actual decision of the bench but are a crucial source of support for lay magistrates who may have no legal knowledge at all. They are generally legal professionals such as barristers or solicitors who are experts in law and have at least five years experience.

Theory into practice

Why would magistrates benefit from the presence of a court clerk?

What are the potential consequences of not having a court clerk?

Process of a magistrates court trial

The legal process followed in a magistrates court is as follows:

1 The magistrates hear a summary of the facts.

2 The defendant enters a plea of guilty or not guilty.

3 The prosecution puts forward their case.

4 The defence puts forward their case.

5 The magistrates give a verdict.

6 If the defendant is found not guilty they may leave the court.

7 If the defendant is found to be guilty the magistrates confer and seek guidance from the clerk on a suitable sentence.

8 The magistrates deliver a suitable sentence.

Theory into practice

Compare the procedure in a magistrates court trial with the military court procedure outlined earlier noting differences and similarities. What do you notice?

Case study – Magistrates court

Consider the following case:

● Jack is a 37 year old alcoholic who has a long history of violent alcohol related disorder. He is picked up in his local town centre under the influence of alcohol and behaving in a threatening manner to passers by. He is kept in police custody overnight to sober up and then taken to a magistrates court in the morning.

1 What powers do the magistrates have to sentence Jack?

2 What offence is he likely to be charged with?

3 What sentence do you think would be appropriate for Jacks behaviour?

4 What are the chances that Jack will plead guilty?

Theory into practice

List and describe five personal characteristics that you think would be useful if you were aiming to become a lay magistrate. How do these characteristics compare with the characteristics needed in other public service roles?

Key concepts

1 There are over 400 magistrates courts in England and Wales.

2 Magistrates courts deal with less serious criminal offences and some civil matters.

3 Magistrates courts deal with juveniles aged 10–17.

4 There are two types of magistrate: Lay justice and District judge.

5 Magistrates have maximum sentencing powers of 6 months imprisonment and a £5000 fine per offence.

Crown court

The crown court was established by The Courts Act 1971. It was created to replace the system of Assizes and Quarter Sessions which were outdated and unable to cope effectively with increasing numbers of criminal cases. There is only one crown court which is called The Central Criminal Court or the 'Old Bailey'. This one crown court has over 90 centres from which it operates throughout cities in England and Wales.

The crown court deals with four main areas of work:

● criminal trials of indictable and some triable either way offences

● appeals against the decisions of magistrates

● sentencing from magistrates court

● some High court civil matters.

Advantages	Disadvantages
Lay magistrates are a very cost effective and efficient way of administering justice.	Inconsistent decision making between benches.
Involvement of ordinary people makes the justice system appear fairer.	Magistrates tend to have a bias towards the police and are more likely to believe their evidence than the evidence of the defendant.
Groups of three are likely to give more balanced decisions.	Magistrates tend to be white, middle class and middle aged.
They have local knowledge and understanding.	Cases are not heard in much detail.

Figure 2.9 Advantages and disadvantages of the magistracy

The Old Bailey

Offences dealt with in crown court fall into four categories (See Figure 2.10).

The Crown court also operates a tier system for its external centres that dictates the kind of work they are allowed to do. There are three tiers of the crown court: the first tier deals with high court civil matters including any kind of triable either way or indictable criminal offence and hears appeals from magistrates court. The second tier deals with triable either way offences and indictable offences and hears appeals from the magistrates court. The third tier deals only with class four offences and appeals.

Process of a crown court trial

The legal process followed in a crown court is as follows:

1 Defendant pleads not guilty.

2 Jury are sworn in.

3 Opening speeches outlining the case for the prosecution and defence.

4 Prosecution witnesses called to give evidence and are cross-examined by the defence.

5 Prosecution case closes.

6 Defence witnesses called to give evidence and are cross-examined by the prosecution.

7 Defence case closes.

8 Closing speeches, which are summaries from the prosecution and the defence.

9 Judge sums up.

10 Jury retires to consider verdict.

11 Jury returns and a verdict is given.

12 If the defendant is found not guilty they are free to leave the court.

13 If the defendant is found to be guilty the defence will argue for a lenient sentence by providing the court with mitigating circumstances.

14 The judge gives a suitable sentence.

A jury is only used where a defendant pleads not guilty. Juries are found in only about 1% of all criminal cases.

The role of a judge

Judges have a very important role in the court system. They are legal experts on point of law if the prosecution and defence are in dispute. They manage and oversee the conduct of trials and sum up the jury when used in criminal cases. They also

Category	Offences
Class 1	Murder, treason, offences under The Official Secrets Act. Usually tried by a High Court Judge or Circuit judge.
Class 2	Manslaughter, rape etc. Again may be tried by a high court or a circuit judge.
Class 3	A wide variety of indictable and triable either way offences. May be tried by a high court, circuit or recorder judge.
Class 4	Robbery, assault, grievous bodily harm etc. Usually tried by a Circuit judge or a recorder.

Figure 2.10 Offence categories in a crown court

pronounce sentence if a defendant is found guilty. There are five kinds of judges in the court system and these are shown in order of seniority:

- High court judges are also called Puisne (pronounced 'puny') judges. They are the ones who hear the most serious cases in a crown court.

- Circuit judges travel around an area of the country called a circuit. There are 6 circuits in the country. They listen to middle range crown court cases and they also sit in the county court to hear civil matters. In some circumstances they might also be found in the court of appeal criminal division.

- District judges and Deputy district judges hear civil cases in the county court, usually this means dealing with small claims.

- Recorders and Assistant recorders are part-time judges who often still work as barristers and solicitors. They deal with some of the least serious crown court cases.

- District judges who work in magistrates courts and were previously called Stipendiary magistrates.

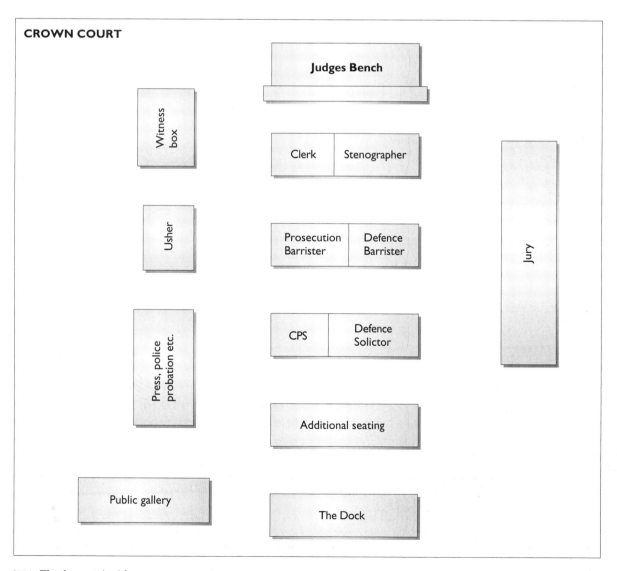

Figure 2.11 The layout inside a crown court

Judges roles are an important part of the legal system

Key concepts

1 There is only one crown court, but it has around 90 centres.

2 The centres are usually found in large towns and cities.

3 They deal with more serious criminal offences and some high court civil matters.

4 There are three tiers of the crown court.

5 A jury is used to decide guilt or innocence, but is only used in about 1% of criminal cases.

The House of Lords

Court of Appeal

The court of appeal consists of two divisions, criminal and civil and normally sits at the royal courts of justice in London. The appeals system has two main functions. Firstly, they put right any incorrect or unjust decisions made in the courts below them and secondly they help to promote consistent development of the law. The criminal division is presided over by the Lord Chancellor and hears appeals from the crown court, the civil division is presided over by the Master of the Rolls and hears appeals mainly from the high and county courts.

The House of Lords

This is the highest court of appeal in the UK. It hears civil and criminal appeals from England and Wales and may also hear certain cases from Scotland and Northern Ireland. The judgements of The House of Lords bind all courts below it. It hears about 70 cases per year and it operates on a majority judgement.

Case study – Diane Pretty

The case of 43 year old Diane Pretty was heard by the House of Lords in November 2001. Mrs Pretty had been paralysed by motor neurone disease that left her unable to end her suffering by committing suicide. She and her husband went to the courts in order to receive assurances that her husband would not be punished if he helped her end her own life, known as 'assisted suicide'. The piece of law she used to support her case was the Human Rights Act 1998. The five Law Lords who heard the case refused to give such an assurance on the grounds that the Human Rights Act 1998 was designed to protect lives, not end them.

1 What crime would Diane's husband have been guilty of if he'd helped her die?

2 Why couldn't Diane simply end her own life?

3 Do you agree with the decision of the Law Lords?

4 What are the implications of the judicial system approving assisted suicide?

5 Do you think that assisted suicide ought to be legal in this country? Explain your reasons.

Key practitioners in the legal system

We have already discussed lay magistrates and the role of the various types of judges but there are other important players in the legal system.

Solicitors

Solicitors may work alone or in a partnership with other solicitors. They deal directly with the public and offer a wide variety of legal services such as, all pre trial work, accident claims, conveyancing, contracts, wills, representation in court and divorce and family matters. There are around 80,000 solicitors in England and Wales and they are controlled by The Law Society, which has the power to discipline or strike off a solicitor for professional misconduct. The training of a solicitor usually starts with a law degree followed by a legal practice course that lasts one year and a training contract that lasts two years. There are other methods of becoming a solicitor if you have a non-law degree or indeed if you have no degree at all. Solicitors are able to act as advocates in the crown court if they have an additional qualification called an advocacy certificate.

Barristers

Barristers are considered to be self employed individuals and are not allowed to form partnerships with other barristers. However, in practice they usually share a set of offices which are called 'chambers' with other barristers in order to share costs and gain professional support and advice. They are generally associated with advocacy work, which is representing people in court, but they may also deal with matters such as drafting documents and offering expert advice on legal issues. Barristers are not allowed to deal directly with the public, they must instead take their instructions from a solicitor. There are over 9,500 barristers in England and Wales and they are governed by the General Council of the Bar, which acts in much the same way as other professional bodies such as The Law Society or the General Medical Council. Barristers must be a member of one of the four Inns of Court listed below which are based in London:

- Middle Temple
- Gray's Inn
- Inner Temple
- Lincolns Inn

Theory into practice
Why do barristers have to be a member of an Inn of Court?

There are two ranks of barrister:

Queens Counsel (QC) – these are more senior and experienced barristers who take on more complicated cases. A barrister must have at least ten years experience before becoming a QC. The majority of the judiciary are promoted from within the ranks of the Queens Counsel. Since very few QCs are women or from ethnic minority backgrounds this has significant implications for the composition of the judiciary.

A barrister in court

Juniors – these are less experienced barristers who deal with less complicated cases. Juniors also help QCs deal with cases in court.

Theory into practice
What are the implications in having a majority white male judiciary?

Key concepts

1 Solicitors have direct contact with clients.

2 Solicitors deal with a wide range of legal matters including crime, family and civil issues.

3 The general public cannot contract a barrister on their own, a solicitor must do it for them.

4 There are two kinds of barrister: QCs and Juniors.

5 Barristers deal with the majority of advocacy work in the crown court.

Theory into practice

● Once you have finished your National Diploma what steps would you have to take if you ultimately wanted to be a barrister?

● List the top six skills you think are important in a barrister.

Principles of the English legal system

The adversarial system

Ainsworth (1998) notes that it is a mark of a civilised society that punishment may be inflicted only after a finding of guilt by a court. This notion protects both society and the defendant. It protects society by ensuring that only the guilty (theoretically) are locked up giving them confidence in the state and its proceedings and it protects the individual by ensuring that they are not judged before the key facts are revealed which may exonerate them. It is not up to the defendant to prove his innocence, it is up to the prosecution to prove his guilt. This is called the 'burden of proof'. It is unethical to assume that someone is guilty without a fair and impartial examination of the facts by people unconnected with the case.

Theory into practice

What are the implications to society of people taking the law into their own hands?

The main feature of an adversarial system is that the preparation of the case is a matter for the prosecution and defence. The cases are prepared without court involvement and each party decides who will be a witness and what evidence they will use. The role of the judge is to act as an independent monitor who ensures that correct rules and procedures are followed. One side will present evidence and the other side will try and discredit it. This is a system favoured in common law countries such as the UK, Australia and the United States. It rests upon the assumption that each party is in an equal position and that the judge is an objective moderator in the process.

There are advantages and disadvantages to the adversarial system:

Advantages

● It appears to find the truth and protect legal rights.

● It is formal and clear rules exist.

● Less expensive to the government.

● Less delays.

● An impartial judge is crucial in delivering justice.

Disadvantages

● Parties are not equal. Defendants with more money can purchase high quality legal representation.

● The 'truth' is limited to the facts that are raised in the courtroom. Other information may be held back by either party.

● It is constrained by formal rules of evidence, which may make some important pieces of information inadmissible.

● The judge has no role other than as a decision maker. They cannot ask for further information or for further witnesses. They must be content with the information presented to them.

● The better presented case will win regardless of the truth.

The inquisitorial system

This is a system that is often viewed as an alternative to the adversarial system. It is primarily centred in European nations such as France and Germany. In broad terms it refers to a system in which the judge has primary responsibility for establishing the facts and moving the case forwards. In this model the judge is also the investigator and the prosecutor. The judge is not bound by the evidence presented to him by the parties involved, he may establish the truth using his own methods to gather relevant information.

There are advantages and disadvantages to the inquisitorial system:

Advantages

- The judge may establish the truth for himself, he is not reliant on evidence presented to him.

- The judge may call any witnesses he thinks are relevant.

- Appears fairer to all parties.

- Less battle, more discussion.

Disadvantages

- The system can be very expensive.

- The judge's investigations can be time consuming.

- The judge is not impartial and he may have a vested interest in the outcome.

Think about it

Consider the advantages and disadvantages of each system. Which system do you think is fairest and most impartial?

Trial by jury

The use of a jury has a long and distinguished history, but it has seen a decline in both civil and criminal cases over recent years. A jury is made up of twelve people in a criminal case and eight in a civil case. In a criminal case they appear in a crown court when a defendant pleads not guilty.

Juries are a fundamental principle of the legal system because the exercise of justice is by the people not the state. The guilt or innocence of a person is not decided by a judge who is in the employ of the state but by ordinary people in the community at large. Juries are not required to justify their verdict and there have been cases where juries have acquitted defendants despite strong evidence of guilt, to show disapproval of the law. To sit on a jury you must be aged over 18 and be registered on the electoral register. The main piece of law which currently governs jury trial is The Juries Act 1974.

There are advantages and disadvantages to trial by jury

Advantages:

- Ordinary people are represented in the justice system.

- Group decisions give fairer results.

- Public representation makes the system more open to scrutiny.

Disadvantages:

- Juries are untrained.

- Complex cases may be difficult to understand, particularly in civil cases.

- It is a compulsory system.

The jury system may be reformed in the near future. The Auld report published in October 2001 makes recommendations such as:

- smaller juries

- fewer people excused jury service

- perverse jury decisions can be challenged

- allowing juries to know about offenders previous convictions

- ensuring that juries are representative of the community.

Other national legal systems

Scotland

The development of a legal system in Scotland ran along different lines to that of England. Scottish Law was already well established by the thirteenth century although its roots can be traced back much earlier. During the early middle ages, Scottish lawyers were educated in Europe where Roman law still dominated and this had a major impact on the development of the Scottish legal system. In 1707 The United Kingdom was created due to the union of the Scottish and English parliaments and English law began to replace Roman law as the main source of foreign law. Today Scotland has a form of devolved government and its own parliament, which can create new Scottish laws again.

As you can see from Figure 2.12 there are many differences between the English and the Scottish systems, such as the types of court and judge, who has the responsibility for bringing a prosecution and who can create the law. Also, the jury system is slightly different in Scotland as a jury of fifteen is used in criminal cases and a simple majority verdict will suffice whereas in England we use a jury of twelve and usually require a unanimous verdict. However, there are many similarities between them, such as the fact they share use of the adversarial system and they are both subject to English and European Parliament legislation.

Scottish legal system	
Feature	**Detail**
Sources of law	• Legislation – law created by a parliamentary body • Court decisions – judicial precedent and common law • Roman law – historical origins • Cannon law – law of the Church • Udal law – Norse Law still applied in Orkney and Shetland
Legislature (who can create law?)	• English Parliament • Scottish Parliament • European Parliament
The courts	**Civil** • Sheriffs Court • Court of Session • House of Lords **Criminal** • District Court • Sheriffs Court • High Court of the Justiciary
Type of system	Adversarial
Process of a case	The Lord Advocate is responsible for bringing a prosecution on behalf of the crown. The process is then the same as English courts.
Judges	• High Court of the Justiciary – Commissioners of Justice • Court of Session – Senators of Justice • Sheriffs Court – Sheriff Principal or Deputy Sheriff Principal • District Court – Justice of the Peace

Figure 2.12 Features of the Scottish legal system

Theory into practice

List and describe the differences and similarities between the Scottish and English legal systems.

Key concepts

1   The Scottish system is very different from the English one.

2   The Scottish system had its roots in roman law, but English law became the major source of foreign law after 1707.

3   The Scottish parliament can make laws which affect only Scotland.

4   The Lord Advocate is responsible for bringing a prosecution.

5   Both the Scottish and the English system use the adversarial system.

Comparisons with European legal systems

The French legal system

The French legal system is strictly divided into two parts: the judicial order (*l'ordre judiciare*) which deals with both criminal and civil cases and the administrative order (*l'ordre administratif*) which deals with administrative disputes such as how government law affects other branches of the government or other countries. There is no crossover between these two orders and there is a court called *le tribuneau des conflits* that decides where a particular case should be tried.

As you can see from Figure 2.13 the French system is significantly different from either the English or the Scottish legal systems. Firstly, they use the inquisitorial system, secondly the system of judges and courts is different and thirdly the judiciary is chosen from the best legal students at the start of their legal career. There are some similarities such as the fact that the legislation made by the European Parliament is common across all three systems and although the courts

and judges are different they exist to perform similar tasks.

Theory into practice

Consider the tables on pages 22 and 24, describing the French and Scottish legal systems. Using a table with identical headings draw up the table for the English legal system based on the information you have been given throughout this chapter so far.

Key concepts

1   The French legal system is divided into two sections which have no crossover.

2   The French legal system uses the inquisitorial system.

3   Judiciary are appointed at the beginning of their career.

4   The French legal system is bound by the decisions of the European Parliament.

Legal process

Common law

Much of English law is unwritten. It has developed over the centuries by the decisions judges have made in important cases. The legal system that we know now began its development during the Norman conquest of 1066, but it really began to become an organised system during the reign of Henry II (1154 – 1189). When Henry came to the throne, justice was usually dealt with in local courts:

- *Feudal Courts* – local Lords dealing with issues arising from the peasantry or tenants on their land.

- *Courts of the Shires and Hundreds* – County sheriffs often sitting with a bishop or Earl to hear more serious cases.

According to most sources of information these early courts operated on local customs and as you would expect these customs often differed from

French legal system		
Feature	**Detail**	
Sources of law	• Legislation – law created by a parliamentary body • Court decisions – judicial precedent and common law • Roman law – historical origins	
Legislature (who can create law?)	• French Parliament • European Parliament	
The courts	**Civil** • **Tribuneau d'instance** – deals with small civil claims like our county court • **Tribuneau d'grande instance** – deals with larger or more complex civil cases like our High Court • **Court d'appel** – Court of Appeal • **Conseil d'etat** – Court of last resort for administrative matters	**Criminal** • **Tribueau pour enfants** – The equivalent of our Youth Court • **Tribuneau de police** – deals with low level criminal offences • **Tribuneau Correctionnels** – deals with medium level criminal offences • **Cour d'assizes** – deals with the most serious criminal cases and some criminal appeals referred to it by the court of appeal • **Cour d'appel** – Court of Appeal • **Cour de Cassation** – Court of last resort for judicial matters
Type of system	Inquisitorial	
Process of a case	• A case is referred to court • Public prosecutor orders an investigation and decides whether to close the file or bring the offender to justice • A trial is conducted before the appropriate tribunal	
Judges	Magistrates are appointed from the best and brightest lawyers at the beginning of their career and consist of • **Sitting Magistrates** who deliver verdicts • **Examining Magistrates** who defend • **Standing Magistrates** who prosecute	

Figure 2.13 Features of the French legal system

county to county. There was a lack of consistency in the law of the time which meant that courts in different areas might settle the same dispute in entirely different ways.

Henry II wanted a more standardised system of law in England and so he introduced the *'General Eyre'* which literally means 'a journey'. This General Eyre created a system whereby representatives of the King went out to the counties of England to check on their legal administration. They would sit in local courts and listen in to how the legal problems of the time were dealt with. Over time these representatives of the King came to be seen as judges themselves and were called 'Justices in Eyre'. The General Eyre disappeared around 200 years later and was replaced with a system of circuit judges from which our current High Court developed.

By selecting the best local laws from all over the country the judges gradually changed differing local laws into a system of law which was 'common' to the entire kingdom which is how common law originated. So in summary, common law is a judge made system of law originating in ancient customs which were brought together and extended by judges operating over many centuries.

Case study – Local customs

The right of the eldest son to inherit his fathers land, known as *'Primogeniture'* was almost universally applied across England. However, if you lived in Nottingham or Bristol the youngest son inherited the land. If you lived in Kent all of the landowners sons inherited the land in equal shares.

1   Why were customs different across the land?

2   Why would a standardised system of law be better than a fragmented system?

3   Why do you think sons inherited land but not daughters?

Common law was the sole source of law in England from the time of the Norman conquest until the fifteenth century. From the fifteenth century until the end of the nineteenth century, common law shared power with a new body of laws called equity. Equity is a group of laws which developed alongside common law as a result of dissatisfied common law plaintiffs who were unhappy with the way the law treated them. It developed because common law had many defects, particularly that the system was very rigid and sometimes not at all fair.

Equity and common law initially operated in conflict with one another and it wasn't until 1615 that this was resolved and a firm decision was taken by James I that when common law and equity were in conflict, equity should prevail.

Case study

Mistress Smith unduly influenced Master Jones into selling his 50 acre farm for £10,000 less than its true price. If Master Jones then decided not to hand over the land, Mistress Smith would be able to seek damages/compensation in common law even though she was the one who had behaved unfairly in the first place.

1   Which system of law provides a remedy for inequalities in common law.

2   Do you think it is fair that Mistress Smith can seek compensation from Master Jones?

3   Should Master Jones have to honour the agreement he made with Mistress Smith? Explain your reasons.

Law over time	
Prior to 1066	Local customs of the time. These varied from place to place.
1066 – 15th century	Common law developed from the General Eyre and became 'common' across the country.
15th century – end of 19th century	Common law and equity. Initially in conflict, these two bodies of law became mutually tolerant.
20th century – 1973	Primary source of law is statute law, also called legislation or Acts of Parliament.
1973 – current	UK statute law and sometimes law from the European Union. This change came about because the UK joined the European Economic Community in 1973.

Figure 2.14 How the law has changed over time

Why does the law need to change over time?

Key concepts

1 Common law began its development during the reign of Henry II.

2 It established a unified system of law which was common to the whole country.

3 Common law is based on judges decisions in important cases which are then used by other judges as a standard to follow in future cases.

4 Common law began to share power with equity in the fifteenth century.

5 From the nineteenth century common law began to be replaced by statute law.

Judicial precedent

Decisions made by a judge in a particular case are 'binding' on the decisions of future judges when the facts are the same. This procedure is known as 'Judicial Precedent' which is an important part of common law. It is based on the latin saying:

"Stare decisis et non quieta movere"

When interpreted, this means 'standby what has been decided and do not change the established'. The English legal system follows the rules of judicial precedent quite rigidly when compared with other countries. This means that courts in England and Wales must follow decisions already made in a higher or superior court and appeal courts are bound by their own past decisions. Figure 2.16 overleaf shows the hierarchy of the courts and explains which courts would be bound by which decisions.

Case study – Judicial precedent: R v R 1991

A married couple had separated, but the husband forced his way into his wife's home and forced her to have nonconsensual intercourse with him. Up until this time the common law rule was that a husband could not be criminally liable for raping his wife as the woman's marriage vows constituted ongoing consent for sexual relations. The judge in R v R 1991 recognised the changed attitudes of society towards the status of women and created judicial precedent which outlined that all non-consensual intercourse was rape regardless of marital status.

1 Why was rape within marriage not a crime until 1991?

2 Why did the judge create a new precedent in this case?

3 What were the implications on society of this new precedent?

4 Do you think the judge made the right decision in R v R?

How judicial precedent works

When a judge encounters a case where there may be a relevant previous decision made by the court they are currently in or another one in the hierarchy, they have four possible courses of action:

Advantages	Disadvantages
• **Consistency** – consistency in the law helps to provide a sense of equality and justice. • **Certainty** – because of the high number of recorded cases which have gone before, lawyers are able to advise their clients with confidence. • **Flexibility** – the options available to judges ensure that the law can develop and be applied fairly.	• **Rigidity** – judicial discretion can be limited. • **Bulk** – the sheer volume of prior cases can make understanding the law very time consuming. • **Illogical distinctions** – judges may look for justifications not to follow a precedent and create illogical distinctions to support them. • **Accident of litigation** – the court relies upon a suitable case appearing if it wishes to alter the law.

Figure 2.15 Advantages and disadvantages of judicial precedent

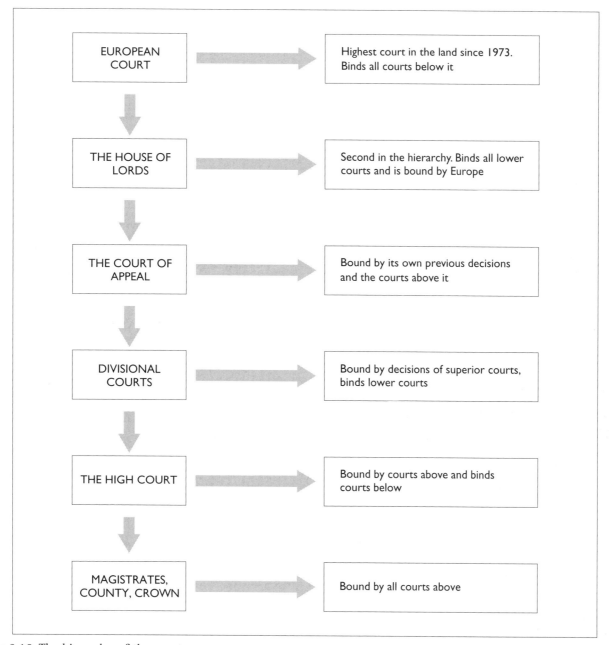

Figure 2.16 The hierarchy of the courts

- **Follow** – if the facts are very similar to the previous case then the judge will choose to follow the precedent which has already been set.

- **Distinguish** – if the facts are quite different from the previous case then the judge can distinguish between the two cases and doesn't need to follow the original precedent.

- **Overrule** – if the original precedent was set in a lower court the judge may overrule it if he/she disagrees with it. This means that

although the original case still stands the judge does not have to follow its precedent.

- **Reverse** – if the decision made by a lower court is appealed to a higher one the higher court may reverse the decision if they think the lower court has misinterpreted the law. They will then substitute their own decision for the previous one.

The last two courses of action can be problematic because if higher courts overrule or reverse the decisions of lower ones they can weaken the power of the lower courts. Judges think extremely carefully in these circumstances and it is relatively rare that these options are taken. Although most law these days is created through Acts of Parliament the law may still be made and refined through judicial decisions. Indeed, interpreting the Acts of Parliament themselves often calls for judges to give clarity to the law by interpreting complex legislation. In order to interpret the law, judges use one of several rules such as the 'literal rule' and the 'golden rule', which will be explained shortly.

Case study – Interpreting legislation

The Dangerous Dogs Act 1991 created all sorts of problems which courts had to resolve. For instance, the act specifically referred to 'dogs', which left the courts having to interpret the legislation regarding bitches. In addition, the law made reference to the control and destruction of various breeds of dog, but failed to give guidance on mixed breed dogs. This left the courts in a very difficult position.

1 What were the difficulties in implementing this act?

2 Do you think the act was designed to control bitches as well as dogs?

3 Do you think dog owners were right to challenge the government on the grounds that this act was flawed?

Think About it

Based on the advantages and disadvantages described, do you think the use of judicial precedent is a positive or negative feature of our legal system?

Statute law

Statute law is law which has been formally written down and recorded in an act of parliament. Statute law has become increasingly important

over the last 150 years or so and is made by parliament. Parliament comprises of three parts which each have a role to play in making the law.

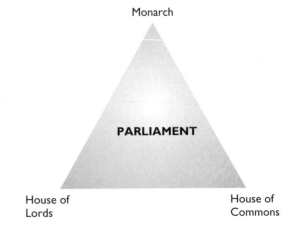

Figure 2.17 Tripartite legislation

Theory into practice

The 'tripartite' (three way) system was commented on as far back as 1713:

"every law being made in the first instance formally drawn up in writing, and made as it were a tripartite indenture, between, the lords and the commons and the monarch; for without the concurrent consent of all those three parts of the legislature no such law is, or can be made" Hale 1713 Pg 1

What do you understand by the above quote?

Key concepts

Statute law differs from common law in the following ways:

● created by Parliament, not by judges

● it is not bound by judicial precedent

● it can abolish and replace common law

● it is formally recorded in an act of law.

Bills

All potential statutes begin life as a 'bill'. A bill is a proposal for a piece of legislation. There are three kinds of bills.

- public bill
- private bill
- private members bill.

A **public bill** is usually a proposal for a large piece of legislation which will affect the whole country. They are created by the government currently in power and they are preceded by a 'green paper' which allows interested parties to consult and comment upon the ideas put forward. Examples of public bills are The Crime and Disorder Act 1998, Police and Criminal Evidence Act 1984 and The Theft Act 1968.

A **private bill** is usually proposed by a local authority or large corporation and will usually only affect the group of people who proposed it in the first place. For instance, if the building of a new motorway required a local authority to compulsory purchase land. An example of a private bill is The Henry Johnson, Sons and Co Limited Act 1996 which was an act which allowed the company of Henry Johnson, Sons and Co to transfer to the republic of France.

A **private members bill** is usually prepared by ordinary members of parliament who have to enter a ballot in order to be guaranteed the time in parliament that it takes to introduce a bill. This allocated time is very important because the reason private members bills often fail is lack of time for them to be debated. Sometimes private members bills are introduced as a way of drawing attention to a particular public concern, for instance the Wild Mammals (Hunting with Dogs) bill drew massive public attention even though it did not succeed in becoming law in that parliamentary session. Examples of private members bills are The Abortion Act 1967 and The Activity Centres (Young Persons Safety) Act 1995.

Bill procedures

There are seven stages that a bill must proceed through before it can become a statute or Act of parliament:

First reading – this is the notification to the house that a proposal is made. The title of the bill is read out and copies of it are made available. There is little or no debate at this stage.

Second reading – this is a crucial stage for the bill as it is the main debate on the proposals contained within it. The house must then decide whether to send it forward for the next stage. In practice, a government with a clear majority will almost always get its bill through this stage.

Committee stage – as you can see in Figure 2.18 this can be a complex part of the procedure. This is where the bill is examined in detail and the committee considers the changes it would recommend to the house. Most bills are dealt with in standing committees of about twenty M.Ps and this is the usual practice. However, if a bill is introduced late in the parliamentary session is may be sent to a select committee which can hear evidence from outside individuals or agencies. The members of the committees are chosen for their qualifications and personal or professional interests.

Figure 2.18 The stages of a bill before if becomes law

If a bill is controversial or very important this stage is examined in a committee of the whole house.

For private bills only the committee stage might be judicial. An example of a private bill is where anyone whose business or property may be affected can lodge a petition to amend a bill in order to protect their interests.

Report stage – the committee reports back to the house with suggested amendments, which are then debated and voted on by the house at large.

Third reading – the bill is represented to the House of Commons and a final vote is taken on whether to accept the proposed legislation, if the bill is accepted it is said to have 'passed the house' and is then sent on to the next stage.

House of Lords – the bill goes through a similar procedure in the House of Lords as it has already taken in the House of Commons and it must pass all of these stages in one session of parliament. The House of Lords cannot reject most legislation passed from the House of Commons although they do retain some powers such as the ability to reject a bill which attempts to extend the duration of a government for longer than five years. The House of Lords has less power than the Commons because they are not elected by the public.

Royal Assent – when a bill has successfully passed through both houses it must go to the monarch for approval and consent. It will then become law on a specified date. It is not usual for the monarch to give consent in person, it is normally done by a committee of three peers including the Lord Chancellor and this stage is just a formality. The last time a monarch refused a bill was Queen Anne in 1707 who declined to give consent to a Scottish Militia Bill.

There are advantages and disadvantages to law made by statute, some of which are outlined briefly in the table below.

Key concepts

1 Statute law is made by parliament.

2 It can abolish and replace common law.

3 A bill is a proposal for a piece of legislation.

4 There are three kinds of bills – public, private and private members bills.

5 Bills are approved by a seven stage procedure concluding with Royal Assent.

6 The Monarch has not refused to sign a statute law since 1707.

Delegated legislation

Parliament may create the legal framework of an act but leave it to others such as ministers and government departments to fill in the details. This is called delegated or subordinate legislation, but it is not inferior to ordinary statutes. There are three main reasons why delegated legislation is needed.

- there isn't time in parliament to debate all the small details of bills

- parliament may not be in session

- parliament may not have the technical knowledge or expertise to deal with the details.

Advantages	Disadvantages
Created by an elected body which represents the people.	Can be difficult to interpret.
Law can be made on any subject at any time, parliament does not have to wait for a suitable case to arrive in front of it.	Process can be time consuming and private members bills often fail.
Created by a formal procedure which includes checks and balances to ensure the law is appropriate.	The political party in power can control the legislative process.

Figure 2.19 Advantages and disadvantages to law made by statute

Figure 2.20 Advantages of delegated legislation

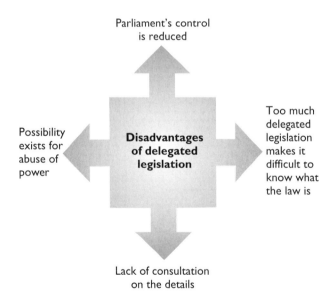

Figure 2.21 Disadvantages of delegated legislation

Problems arising in statute law

Statutes can be very complicated and very detailed and this can cause tremendous problems when they are applied in courts of law. Bennion (1990) identifies several problems which can arise in statute law:

- a word is left out

- a broad term is used

- an ambiguous word is used

- the events in a case were not foreseen when the statute was written

- printing errors.

It is up to the courts to settle disputes as to the meanings of words or clauses in a statute. It does this by using some generally recognised rules that the judge may choose to apply.

The literal rule

According to this rule, the workings of the act must be interpreted according to its literal and grammatical meaning. An example of the literal rule is the case of Whitely Vs Chappell (1868). The statute in this case was designed to prevent malpractice in elections and made it an offence to impersonate *anybody entitled to vote at an election*. The defendant was acquitted because he was impersonating a dead person and a dead person was not entitled to vote.

The golden rule

This is an extension of the literal rule which states that judges should interpret the law literally unless to do so would lead to an absurd or ridiculous result. For example, the case of re Sigsworth (1935). The court decided that a man who had murdered his mother was not entitled to inherit her estate even though the Administration of Estates Act 1925 said that where a will had not been made the persons estate should go to the next of kin. However in this case the next of kin was the person's murderer and this would have been a ridiculous result.

The mischief rule

This was established by a case called Heydon (1584). In this rule the courts try to discover what mischief the act of parliament was trying to remedy and then interpret the words accordingly. An example of this is Smith Vs Hughes (1960). A prostitute claimed that she was not soliciting for business even though she was attracting the attention of male passers by tapping on the window of a house. The Street Offences Act (1958) made it a criminal offence to solicit for business in a public place or a street. The prostitute argued that since she was not in a public place she was not guilty of an offence. The court found that the mischief that act had been created to remedy was to try and stop people being solicited in the street and since she was attracting the attention of people in the street she was guilty of an offence.

Theory into practice

Refer back to the case study on The Dangerous Dogs Act 1991 (page 27) and consider which rule the judge might use to help resolve the difficulties with this act.

Civil law

The purpose of the civil justice system is to resolve disputes which arise between individuals or companies rather than between individuals and the state. When there has been a breach of civil law one individual or company will sue another individual or company usually for money or compensation. The two parties involved are called:

Plaintiff vs Defendant

For instance if Ms Hassan was to sue Mr Johnson for breach of contract the case would be written like this:

Hassan vs Johnson

Hassan is the one making a complaint (plaintiff) and Johnson is trying to defend himself (defendant).

Figure 2.22 shows some of the main subdivisions of civil law; each deals with a specific set of rules which govern interaction between individuals and organisations. Although you do not need to explore these in any great detail the table gives you a brief summary of each so that you are aware of the kind of interaction they cover and what each involves.

The Woolf Report 1995 established several aims which it felt the civil justice procedure should try

Civil Law		
Subdivision	**Meaning**	**Example where law might be used**
Consumer law	Rules designed to protect consumers.	The return of goods that are faulty.
Property law	Rules governing property related matters.	The transfer of ownership of property.
Family law	Rules governing family matters.	A couple wishes to adopt a child.
Company law	Rules governing how companies operate.	A person wishes to set up their own company.
Law of tort	Rules governing duty to other individuals.	A person is injured by faulty machinery at work.
Law of contract	Rules governing agreements made between individuals or companies.	A person defaults on a hire purchase agreement.
Employment law	Rules governing work and employment.	A person feels they have been unfairly dismissed.

Figure 2.22 Subdivisions of Civil Law

to adhere to. Lord Woolf felt that civil justice should be

- fair in its decisions
- cost effective for plaintiffs
- time efficient
- understandable to the parties involved
- responsive to the needs of its users
- adequately organised and resourced.

Civil court structure

The civil court structure is complicated and depending on the nature of the case the following courts may be involved:

- Magistrates courts
- Crown courts
- County court
- High court – split into three divisions each with its own divisional court
- Court of Appeal
- House of Lords.

They fit together in a structure shown in Figure 2.23.

Claims will start in the court in which they are likely to be tried and this depends on two issues:

- the size and nature of the claim
- the complexity of the legal issues.

As a general distinction, smaller cases would be heard in the county court and larger ones in the high court. For instance, claims under £5,000 are automatically dealt with by the small claims court which resides within the county court. In addition, claims under £25,000 would normally begin in a county court and claims over £50,000 in a high court. For claims between £25,000 – £50,000 the complexity of the case would have to be examined in order to determine which court would be most suitable.

£5,000 or less	Small claims court
£5,000 – £25,000	Usually county court
£25,000 – £50,000	High or county depending on complexity
£50,000 and above	Usually high

Key concepts

1 Civil law exists to resolve disputes between companies or individuals.

2 Civil law has its own civil courts.

3 Civil law has many divisions each dealing with a specialised branch of the law.

4 The main purpose of civil law is financial redress (compensation).

5 The parties involved are called plaintiff and defendant.

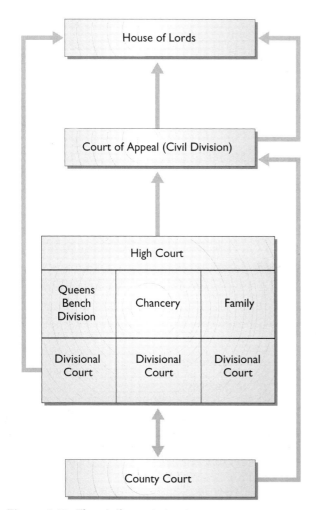

Figure 2.23 The civil court structure

Civil case procedures

The procedure of a civil case differs slightly between claims in the small claims court, the county court and the high court.

Small claims procedure

The small claims court is part of the county court, not a separate court in itself and is designed to deal with claims worth less that £5,000. The first step in the procedure is to take out a summons and pay a small fee based on the amount being claimed. The summons must contain written details of the claim, it does not need to be in great detail but it must be clear to the defendant and the court why the claim is being made and how much it is for. Once the summons is 'served', (the defendant has received it) they then have fourteen days in which to send back a defence.

At this point the defendant has several options:

- they may choose to pay the claim
- they may make an admission and agree arrangements to pay at a later date
- they may make a defence to the claim
- they may choose to do nothing.

If no response is received, the court may choose to rule in favour of the plaintiff automatically. If the defendant does defend himself, an informal trial follows. This trial or 'arbitration' is held in private and each party will have a fair and equal opportunity to state their side of the dispute to the presiding judge who may be a district or deputy district judge. This procedure can be quite quick and straightforward. Elliot & Quinn (1998) note that 60% of cases take less than thirty minutes. The judge will then make a decision whether to award compensation or not. It is difficult to appeal against small claims judgements unless one of the parties feels they were not given equal time or the judge is incorrect on a matter of law.

County Court procedure

There are around 230 county courts in England and Wales which deal with matters such as contract, tort, recovery of land, partnerships, trusts and inheritance. The county court has a fast track procedure which can be used to reduce the waiting time in county court procedure. This is used for cases between £5,000 and £15,000. County court procedure is the same as for small claims with the main difference being in the arbitration stage. Small claims are dealt with in an informal manner by a judge who undertakes the role of arbitrator whereas county court proceedings are heard in open court in a much more formal manner.

High Court procedure

The first stage in this procedure is to issue a writ which is drafted by a barrister or a solicitor and is then served on the defendant. A writ is a document similar to a county court summons and it is the most common way of starting an action in the Queens Bench division of the high court, which is the part of the high court which deals with such matters. The writ tells the defendant the person who is making the claim and why. If the defendant does not respond within fourteen days the judge may make a decision by default on behalf of the plaintiff. If the defendant intends to defend themselves against the claim they must

Advantages	Disadvantages
Quick, simple and cheap	May involve complex cases
Increases public confidence by seeing justice done	The paperwork could be simplified
Fully accessible to all members of the public	There are problems enforcing successful claims
	The financial limit needs regular updating to keep in line with Inflation

Figure 2.24 Advantages and disadvantages to the small claims procedure

complete and return an 'acknowledgement of service' form which states their intention to defend. The defendant must then submit a document called a 'defence', which must answer the claims made by the plaintiff and sets out any new facts which the plaintiff did not know or did not disclose. The plaintiff can then deny the defendants 'facts' or reply to them on a document called a 'reply'. This procedure will continue until both parties have exchanged every fact they think is relevant. At this point the pleadings are closed and the judge can see clearly the matter to which he or she must decide on. Following this a trial is conducted along adversarial lines with each side having its own witnesses. The judge then makes an appropriate decision regarding the case. The cost of a high court trial can be very expensive and is often prohibitive.

Case study – Civil law

Susan has had a disastrous haircut in a town centre salon. She complained at the time but the salon refused to put the problem right. Susan was left £90 out of pocket for the haircut and had to pay a further £100 to another salon to have her hair put right. She wants to sue the original hairdresser, but doesn't know how to go about it.

1 Which court would Susan use to sue her hairdresser?

2 Describe the steps she would have to go through to conduct a claim.

3 What amount should Susan claim in compensation?

Criminal law

Crime is a very difficult concept to define and what constitutes a crime can vary from time to time and place to place. The criminal justice process is one of the most important tools which society can use in controlling the behaviour of those considered to be criminal. A good criminal justice system should strike a balance between punishing the guilty and protecting the innocent. In England and Wales we use an adversarial system which creates a contest between two people. These two people are the monarch (on behalf of the state) and the accused.

A criminal case might be written as follows:

R vs Miller

- R = Rex or Regina (King or Queen)
- vs = Versus
- Miller = The accused

Criticism	Detail
Expense	The costs of the case can amount to more than the original claim was worth. This means people or companies can end up losing money in civil proceedings even if they win. The Woolf report found that this happened in 40% of cases where the original claim was worth £12,500 or less.
Delays	The civil justice procedure deals with a tremendous volume of cases and it is over-stretched. According to the Woolf report the current average waiting time in the county court is 79 weeks.
Injustice	If people cannot afford a lengthy trial they may have to accept an out of court settlement from the other party for a lower sum. This can create a sense of injustice.
Too complex	The procedure can be difficult to track and follow.
Enforcement	It can be difficult to enforce judgements and make sure that people who are successful in the civil courts can actually get their money from the other party.

Figure 2.25 Criticism of civil procedures

The criminal justice system

Progress through the criminal justice process can be a long and complicated procedure and at every stage criminal cases can be discontinued.

The majority of criminal cases begin with the defendant's first contact with the police. Although other agencies such as the Department of Social Security and the Inland Revenue may also initiate prosecutions, in the main prosecutions are instigated by the police. As the police have the responsibility for investigating crime, gathering evidence and the decision to charge a suspect their contribution to the English legal system is vital. The main piece of legislation which provides the police with their powers is the Police and Criminal Evidence Act 1984 (PACE) which regulates how the police conduct themselves in procedures such as:

● stop and search

● seizure of property

● powers of entry

● detention, treatment and questioning

● arrest

● interviewing.

Police officers may ask the general public questions at any time in order to detect and prevent crime, but the public do not have to answer them. Likewise, the public cannot be forced to go to the police station unless they are arrested. Powers of arrest allow people to be detained against their will and arrests may take place with or without a warrant.

Arrest with a warrant

The police apply to a magistrates court for a warrant to arrest a suspect. The warrant can be issued under the Magistrates Court Act 1980 and

Figure 2.26 Progression through the criminal justice system

must contain the name of the suspect and the offence they are alleged to have committed. The decision to issue a warrant or not rests solely with the magistrate. If the magistrate issues a warrant the police officer may then conduct the arrest, even if they have to use reasonable force to enter premises where they think the subject might be.

Arrest without a warrant

In reality many arrests are carried out without a warrant. Section 24 of PACE sets out general powers of arrest which may be exercised by the police as well as the public. A member of the public may arrest anyone who is in the process of committing or who has committed an 'arrestable' offence. They may also arrest anyone whom the public has reasonable grounds for suspecting is committing an arrestable offence.

The powers of the police officer are almost identical, except the police officer may also arrest an individual who might be about to commit an offence.

Arrestable offences are those which:

- the sentence is fixed by law, for example murder
- any crime for which an adult may be sentenced to imprisonment for a term of five years or more

- any offence which parliament has declared to be arrestable.

Offences which are not arrestable and for which an officer does not have a warrant for are dealt with under section 25 of PACE which states that if an officer has reasonable grounds to suspect that any non arrestable offences has been committed they may still arrest if any of the general arrest conditions are satisfied. (See Figure 2.27)

Caution

After arrest, the suspect will be taken to a police station for questioning and interview. Until 1994 a suspect could refuse to answer any questions without adverse consequences if their case later came to trial. However since the 1994 Criminal Justice and Public Order Act the right of a suspect to remain silent has been changed and the caution given to suspects is currently:

> "You do not have to say anything. But it may harm your defence if you do not mention when questioned something which you later rely on in court. Anything you do say may be given in evidence."

General arrest conditions section 25 of PACE	
Conditions	**Detail**
Identity	May arrest if – **1** The name of the person is unknown. **2** The officer doubts whether the name provided is accurate.
Address for service for a summons	May arrest if – **1** The person fails to provide an address. **2** The officer doubts whether the address is valid for a summons to be issued.
Preventative measures	May arrest if – **1** The person may cause injury to self or others. **2** The person is suffering from physical injury. **3** The person is causing damage to property. **4** The person is offending public decency. **5** The person is causing obstruction of the highway.
Protection	May arrest if – **1** The person is a threat to the vulnerable.

Figure 2.27 General arrest conditions under section 25 of PACE

The caution may be given at the following stages:

- At the stage where the officer suspects that a person who has not been arrested has committed an offence
- on the arrest of a person
- after the arrest prior to interview.

Charge

When an officer considers that there is sufficient evidence for a prosecution to succeed and that the suspect has said all that they are going to say the next step of the procedure is to charge the suspect with an offence. The custody officer may choose one of three options open to him or her:

1 charge

2 report – report the person for summons

3 bail – pending a charging decision.

Bail

It is important for the custody officer to decide whether the defendant should stay in custody or be released on bail after they have been charged (although people can be bailed before charge if the police wish to gather more evidence). Bail means that the person is free until the next stage in the process of their case. The laws relating to how bail is given and dealt with are laid out in the Bail Act 1976 and the Criminal Justice and Public Order Act 1994.

The police may also impose conditions on the bail that they give, such as:

- surrender of passport
- report to the police station at regular intervals.

A custody officer may refuse bail if they suspect the person:

- will not return to custody

- will commit further offences
- will interfere with witnesses or evidence
- needs custody for his/her own protection.

If the police refuse bail to a suspect they must present him/her at the magistrates court as soon as possible. If the magistrate cannot deal with the whole case at that time, then the magistrate makes a further decision on whether to grant bail or remand in custody until the matter can be resolved. In the UK money is not paid for bail.

Types of offences

All court cases proceed in the first instance to the magistrates court, but the offence may eventually be dealt with by another court. Which court an offence will ultimately be tried in depends on the type of offence. All criminal offences can be divided into three categories.

1 Summary offences

These are dealt with only in a magistrates court. Generally these offences are considered less serious and are punishable by a maximum of six months imprisonment and/or a £5,000 fine. Summary offences include:

- minor assaults
- driving without insurance
- indecent exposure
- assault on a police officer
- taking without owners consent (TWOC).

2 Indictable offences

These offences appear in magistrates court firstly, but are then committed automatically for trial in the Crown court. Generally these are the most serious offences and they are punishable by the penalty prescribed by law, which could be anything up to life imprisonment for certain offences:

- murder
- manslaughter
- rape
- blackmail
- aggravated burglary.

3 Triable either way

Either way offences can be tried in either the magistrates or the crown court depending on what the prosecution think is appropriate, what the defendant wishes and the nature of the case involved, for example the value of stolen property or the extent of injuries. These tend to be middle range crimes:

- indecent assault
- making off without payment
- obtaining services by deception
- going equipped for stealing
- handling stolen goods
- possession of a controlled drug.

Legal aid

Legal procedure is notoriously expensive and in some cases a person might have to pay their opponents costs as well as their own. We are all required to abide by the law equally and we should all have equal access to the law in times of need regardless of our financial circumstances.

The great inequalities in access to the law were addressed firstly by the post World War II labour government. The provision of legal assistance began in 1949 with the Legal Aid and Advice Act that provided state funding for legal advice and proceedings to those who otherwise could not afford to pay for it, but this only covered the costs involved in civil cases. It wasn't until the mid 1960's that criminal cases also qualified for aid.

The Access to Justice Act 1999 changed the rules for legal aid.

The system was reviewed by the government in the white paper 'Modernising Justice'. The review found that the system was problematic and the Access to Justice Act 1999 was devised with the intention of providing a system of legal aid which addressed the real legal needs of individuals in a manner which was efficient, of high quality and affordable. The new act created the Legal Services Commission (LSC) which exists to monitor the two new schemes which now exist for legal aid:

- Community legal service (civil matters)
- Criminal defence service (criminal matters)

Community legal service (CLS)

This service exists to provide assistance in matters of civil law such as providing advice on civil matters, resolving or settling disputes involving legal rights and help in enforcing legal decisions involving compensation. It does not cover some of the most commonly used areas of civil law such as:

- allegations of negligence
- conveyancing
- wills

- company/business laws
- boundary disputes.

The money for the CLS is provided by the Community legal service fund (CLSF). The main difference between this system and the old system is that the budget of the CLSF is capped, once it is gone it is gone and people may be refused assistance whereas in the other scheme there was no cap on the funding available.

Criminal defence service (CDS)

The CDS came into being in April 2001. Its job is to ensure that those involved in criminal proceedings have access to advice, assistance and representation. The CDS provides free duty solicitor access at police stations who are available on a 24 hour rota to assist those who are being charged, questioned or placed in police custody. Although this initial assistance is free it must be in the interests of justice for further representation to continue to be free. The level of funding in criminal cases is not capped and continues to be demand led. Only solicitors firms who have a contract with the LSC are able to offer state funded criminal defence. This defence falls into three categories:

1 **Advice and assistance** – this is the provision of advice and assistance from a solicitor. It covers aspects of criminal defence such as general advice, preparing a written legal case and getting legal opinions from barristers. It does not cover representation in court.

2 **Advocacy assistance** – this form of help covers the cost of preparing a case and the initial

representation in a magistrates court and crown court. This form of assistance is not means tested, but it is merit tested. This means the provision of defence must be in the interests of justice.

3 **Representation** – representation covers the cost of a solicitor to prepare the case and represent them in court. It may also cover the cost of a barrister in Crown court and the cost of appeals.

Theory into practice

Do you think the legal aid reforms made by the Access to Justice Act 1999 are more effective than the schemes that existed previously? Explain your reasons.

Key concepts

1 The system of legal aid was changed by the Access to Justice Act 1999.
2 Civil legal aid is now the responsibility of the Community Legal Service.
3 Civil legal aid has capped funding.
4 Criminal legal aid is the responsibility of the Criminal Defence Service.
5 Criminal legal aid is free in the initial stages and then is merit tested.

Advantages	Disadvantages
• The new system is intended to increase access to justice for those who need it most • There is increased control of the costs of legal aid • Better allocation of resources • Higher standards of work from legal professionals	• Budget capping may lead to some people being refused access to justice • Choice of legal representatives will be restricted due to limited legal service contracts being issued • Some of the most common civil cases are now ineligible for funding.

Figure 2.28 Advantages and disadvantages of legal aid

Role of public services in upholding and administering the law

Police

The police play a key role in the English legal system. They, along with other agencies and public services have responsibility for upholding and administering the law. However, the police no longer have responsibility for the prosecution of offenders. The Prosecution of Offenders Act 1985 took this power away from them and gave it to the Crown Prosecution Service. This was because it was seen as unfair and biased to have a public service which investigated and collected evidence also being responsible for prosecution.

Theory into practice

Why is it inappropriate to have a prosecuting agency that has also gathered evidence and investigated the crime?

The police still have a substantial role to play. They help to keep the Queens Peace by dealing with non-law tasks that help communities identify and solve local problems, such as youth nuisance or providing community forums. The police are also heavily involved in crime prevention initiatives, both working alone and as part of a multi-agency taskforce in accordance with the Crime and Disorder Act 1998. This may cover initiatives such as education on drugs in schools, neighbourhood watch and safer cities programmes.

The police also have a role to play in the detection of crime, although crimes are often reported to them by members of the public or other agencies. However, by detecting crime and intelligence gathering some crimes may be prevented and others solved much more quickly. This means suspects can be processed more efficiently and victimisation reduced.

Think about it

Discuss the pro's and con's of increasing the number of beat officers on patrol.

Case study – Intelligence gathering

A new scheme called the Intensive Supervision and Surveillance Programme is being established as a way of reducing the number of persistent young offenders who are repeatedly sent to prison. The £600,000 scheme which had its pilot in Rotherham, South Yorkshire relies on technology such as tagging, 24 hour surveillance cameras and voice verification technology to monitor offenders and gather intelligence about their movements. The pilot scheme found that persistent young offenders committed on average two thirds less crime while on the scheme. The scheme is eventually to be expanded to all 43 police force areas at an estimated cost of £45 million.

1 Why are persistent young offenders a particular problem in many urban areas?

2 What could be gained from reducing the number of persistent young offenders who end up in prison?

3 What might happen once the surveillance is withdrawn from the young offenders?

4 Are there any human rights issues in the constant surveillance of young people?

The police are also responsible for processing offenders. This includes activities such as warrants, arrests, stop and search, entry and seizure, charging, gathering evidence and preparing a case file to send to the Crown Prosecution Service. Without these functions being fulfilled a case could not lawfully progress to the criminal courts.

It is also a function of the police to uncover information in criminal cases which may help to establish the facts of the case. What constitutes lawful evidence is decided in conjunction with the CPS and this evidence must also be made available to the defence. Essentially the information the police uncover in the course of their investigation often forms the basis for legal arguments in a court of law. Officers must also be prepared to give evidence in court which will normally be factual in nature as generally police officers are considered professional witnesses not expert witnesses.

Fire service

The fire service have a limited role in the English legal system, but there are some areas of involvement such as the issuing of fire safety certificates for premises and arson investigation. Under the Fire Precautions Act 1971 it is the responsibility of each fire authority to enforce workplace fire precaution legislation in their area. It is an offence to fail to comply with these regulations which is punishable by fine in a magistrates court and up to two years imprisonment in a crown court. Clearly the fire service play a key role in the detection and processing of such offences. They may be the first people to spot a breach of regulations and will issue warnings and guidance on the breaches which may ultimately pave the way for legal action against the company or individual concerned.

The fire service also have a role to play in the investigation of non-accidental fires (arson). They perform this role in close liaison with the police as

Firefighters at work

the investigation into a non-accidental fire is entirely under police control and access to the scene of the fire after it has been extinguished is at the discretion of the senior police investigating officer.

Under The Fire Services Act 1947 the senior fire brigade officer has sole responsibility for extinguishing the fire and they may arrive on the scene prior to the police. It is very important that they recognise and record any evidence which may indicate that a fire is non-accidental and that this evidence is available to the police. Due to the specialised training of fire officers they may be able to provide the police with information and evidence about the origins, growth and decay of a fire and also assist the police in preservation of evidence at the scene which may be crucial to a later police investigation.

It would not normally be the job of a fire officer to provide expert witness testimony in a non-accidental fire case, this task is normally done by forensic scientists. As with the police, evidence from fire officers in court would normally be factual in nature as they are considered to be professional witnesses not expert ones.

Immigration service

Although not often considered when examining the public services, the immigration service has very strong links with the legal system and may enforce the law under a variety of statutes such as the Immigration Act 1971 and The Immigration and Asylum Act 1999.

The immigration service has access to wide ranging powers in order to uphold the immigration law. It can lay fines on haulage companies, airlines and individual carriers who carry undocumented passengers into the UK and can do the following:

● enter property

● take fingerprints without police assistance

● make arrests without police assistance

- detain asylum seekers without limit
- impose residence conditions and curfews
- impose forced dispersals
- forcibly remove people from the UK.

In essence, the immigration service has many of the powers exercised by the police and like the police could be considered to be a 'gatekeeper' for entry into the legal system.

Theory into practice

The immigration service does not have the equivalent of the Police Complaints Authority. Why is such regulation and monitoring important?

Ambulance service

The ambulance service does not play a substantial role in the upholding and administration of the law. As with the police and the fire service they may be called upon to give professional and factual witness testimony (medical evidence) in a court of law, but they cannot be considered to be expert witnesses.

Armed Forces

In peacetime the role of the armed services in the administration of justice is mainly limited to the prosecution of military personnel in criminal and military cases. However, in times of war they have a much larger part to play in ensuring the effectiveness and safety of our society. The Defence of the Realm Act (DORA) 1914 was passed in order that the government could suppress published criticism, imprison without trial and commandeer economic resources for the war effort. The agents the government used to fulfil these functions were the three armed services. DORA was also used to control civilian behaviour by limiting alcohol consumption and introducing food rationing.

In addition, in times of civil unrest the armed services may be called upon to act as support for the civilian services or if the civilian services decide to strike the armed forces may be called upon to fulfil their duties until the situation is resolved.

The armed services also have a military legal system which operates along parallel lines to the civilian criminal justice system.

Health and safety inspectorate

The key health and safety agency in the UK is the Health and Safety Executive (HSE). The HSE has several important roles in the administration of justice, particularly with regard to health and safety law such as The Health and Safety at Work Act etc 1974. These roles include:

- inspecting workplaces for hazards
- giving guidance on safety matters
- checking for compliance with the law
- enforcing the law by means of warnings and prosecutions.

Health and safety inspectors have the following powers:

- to enter and inspect premises at any time, if there is danger
- to ask for police escort if they feel they may be obstructed
- to take any personnel or equipment they feel is necessary for an effective investigation
- to take measurements, samples or photographs for evidence purposes
- to make safe or destroy any items with are dangerous
- to interview witnesses, under caution if necessary.

Company directors can be punished with fines and imprisonment if they compromise the health and safety of their employees or members of the general public. A company director was jailed for three months in 1996 for criminally exposing his employees and the public to dangerous levels of asbestos dust.

HM Customs and Excise

This public service organisation has a varied role to play in upholding and administering justice. First and foremost, customs and excise is a revenue gathering organisation. This revenue enables the government to pay for services such as the police and the courts and generally cater for the needs of society. Customs and Excise also play a large role in the government's war on drugs. Each year, officers seize cocaine, amphetamines, heroin and cannabis worth millions of pounds and prevent it reaching the streets. They also work very closely with the police service and immigration officers to deal with a variety of multi-agency issues such as asylum seekers.

Probation service

The probation service is an often forgotten member of the public service community. They have a key role in the administration of justice through the following roles:

● providing the courts with information and advice on how best to deal with offenders

● working with other agencies to reduce crime and disorder in local communities

● supervising the community sentences that the courts may impose

● running special programmes to combat persistent offending

● helping to prevent re-offending by offering support to offenders.

End of unit questions

1 What does PACE stand for?

2 What does DORA stand for?

3 What is the impact of the Terrorism Act 2000 on the public services?

4 Name the two kinds of court-martial trial.

5 What was the impact of the Human Rights Act on court-martial trials?

6 What is the purpose of the Summary Appeals Court?

7 What act of parliament changed the rules on legal aid?

8 Where would a summary offence be tried?

9 How did common law develop?

10 What is the process of a bill in becoming a statute?

11 What are the three kinds of bill that can become statutes?

12 Under whose reign did common law develop.

13 What is the name of the French court that deals with juvenile matters?

14 What is the current upper limit for the small claims court?

15 What is the role of the fire service in the English legal system?

16 What are the differences between civil law and criminal law?

17 What is meant by the term 'arrestable offence'?

18 What kind of business does the Crown court deal with?

19 When did European law become binding on the UK?

20 Describe the courtroom procedures of a court-martial trial.

Resources

Ashworth A: *The Criminal Process 2nd ed.*
Oxford University Press 1998

Denham P: *Law A Modern Introduction 4th ed.*
Hodder and Stoughton 1999

Elliot C & Quinn F: *English Legal System 4th ed.*
Longman 2002

Martin J: *The English Legal System 3rd ed.*
Hodder and Stoughton 2002

O'Riordan J: *AS Law for AQA* Heinemann 2002

Reed CP: *English Legal System* Old Bailey Press
1997

Roe D: *Criminal Law* Hodder and Stoughton 1999

Strickland C: *The English Legal System* Longman
1998

White R: *The English Legal System in Action*
3rd ed. Oxford University Press 1999

Assessment activities

This section describes what you must do to obtain a pass grade for this unit.

A merit or distinction grade may be awarded if your work demonstrates a deeper understanding of the topics and is of a higher quality. The highlighted sentences indicate the quality of work expected at merit and distinction level.

Assessment methods

Assessment for this unit could take a variety of forms such as presentations, projects, visual displays, reports and role-plays and you must be prepared to adapt your knowledge and information to suit all of these formats. It is important to pay close attention to the language used in each of the tasks as they signpost what is required of you. For example note the meanings of the following words used in your assessment activity:

Examine	To look at a subject closely in order to understand it and improve your knowledge
Consider	This means to think about and weigh up a subject
Explain	This means to make something clear and set out the arguments
Analyse	This means to look at a subject closely and interpret or evaluate your findings. Perhaps outlining the pro's and con's of a situation or suggesting changes and improvements
Describe	This means to say what something is like, it is a factual account of how something is or how it appears.
Compare	This means to look at the similarities between two or more objects or theories. In this case it means the similarities between court systems.

Assessment tasks

Using the materials within this unit and your own research, carry out the following tasks.

Task 1

Learning outcome 1 – Examine the key features of public service law

a) Using all of the acts outlined in this unit, explain how police activities are controlled by the law. Consider the implications of several pieces of legislation, which interest you most. You could consider PACE 1984 or other legislation such as The Human Rights Act 1998 or The Crime and Disorder Act 1998 all of which have a substantial effect on the activities of the police.

b) Explain, using appropriate examples, the effects of civilian and military law on armed forces personnel.

> To obtain a merit grade, you should explain, with *detailed* reference to appropriate legislation, how police activities are controlled by the law.

To obtain a distinction grade, you should *analyse*, with detailed reference to appropriate legislation, how police activities are controlled by the law.

Suggestions for outcome 1a

You could consider presenting this as a booklet which is aimed at new police recruits and is designed to educate them on how legislation impacts on their duties. It is important to remember that the police are subject to many restrictions on their conduct you must show how the relevant legislation places checks and balances on their actions and outline what the law permits them to do and what is forbids them to do.

Suggestions for outcome 1b

This task lends itself well to a presentation or a group discussion in which all members of the group participate. The task requires you to outline how both civilian and military law impacts on armed forces personnel. It is important to consider the different behaviour that is expected of armed forces personnel and the fact that military law forbids a great deal of behaviour which would not be considered out of the ordinary in civilian life.

Task 2

Learning outcome 2 – Examine English legal institutions and compare them with other national legal systems

a) Accurately describe the institutions and legal processes of the criminal courts in England and Wales.

b) Compare the features of the English legal system with those of other national legal systems.

To obtain a merit grade, you should *explain in detail* the institutions and legal processes of the criminal courts in England and Wales and you should *compare in detail* the features of the English legal system with other national legal systems.

To obtain a distinction grade, you should *analyse and compare* the features of the English legal system with those of other national legal systems.

Suggestions for outcome 2

This could be a very straightforward written piece, perhaps in the form of a short report which highlights the various types of courts and the processes they follow in order to fulfil their role. It could include a table as an appendix with supporting explanation which compares several different legal systems, such as England, Scotland, Ireland or an EU nation such as France.

Task 3

Learning outcome 3 – Examine the legal process in England in relation to the different types of law

a) Explain the differences between common and statute law, and criminal and civil law.

b) Explain now courts deal with three types of criminal offence

c) Explain how courts deal with civil matters

Suggestions for outcome 3

All of the tasks outlined in task 3 are pass criteria. This lends itself very well to the production of a 10 minute presentation which tackles each part of the task in turn. The use of powerpoint will enhance any presentation you deliver.

Task 4

Learning outcome 4 – Examine the role of the public services in the English legal system

a) Explain the role of the police in the English legal system

b) Explain the roles of at least two other public services in the English legal system

> To obtain a Merit grade, you should *compare the roles of the police and* at least two other public services in the English legal system

> To obtain a Distinction grade, you should *analyse the role of the police and the roles* of at least two other public services in the English legal system.

Suggestions for Task 4

You could use a role-play to achieve this task. Set up a mock courtroom using the court diagrams and information outlined earlier in this unit and bring into the witness box in turn a police officer, a firefighter and a Royal Military Police officer. Ask them to explain their role in the English legal system to the assembled courtroom.

To achieve a higher grade you could ask the mock judge or the barristers to make comparisons and analysis between the roles based on what they have heard in the mock courtroom.

LEADERSHIP

Introduction to Unit 3

This unit will help you identify and understand a whole range of essential qualities for successful leadership in a variety of public services such as the armed forces and emergency services. You will have the opportunity to develop and practice your own leadership skills and review your progress. In addition, you will explore both the practical and theoretical aspects of effective leadership and how these aspects vary in different situations. You will also have the opportunity to examine some case studies of famous successful leaders.

Assessment

Throughout the unit activities and tasks will help you to learn and remember information. Case studies are included to add industry relevance to the topics and learning objectives. At the end of each unit, end of unit questions test your knowledge and assessment tasks outline the evidence requirements required for assessment in order to obtain a Pass, Merit or Distinction as well as suggesting ways of providing assessment evidence. This unit is externally assessed so guidance on preparing for the IVA is also included. You are reminded that when you are completing activities and tasks, opportunities will be created to enhance your key skills evidence.

After completing this unit you should have an understanding of the following outcomes.

Outcomes

1 Examine **styles of leadership** and their effectiveness within the public services.

2 Evaluate **theories of motivation** and their relevance to the public services.

3 Identify and assess **qualities of leadership** and their relevance to the public services.

4 Investigate **personal leadership qualities**.

Styles of leadership

Definitions of leadership

There are many and varied definitions of leadership as leadership is not static and unchanging or a set of rules or a series of commands to follow. Leadership is a fluid and dynamic action, which listens and responds to the needs and demands of a 360-degree spectrum of individuals and organisations. The definition of leadership shown in Figure 3.1 is a relatively recent view. Throughout most of the last century leadership was seen as very much a one-way process between leaders and followers and the definitions of the time reflect this.

Think about it

Before you read about the definitions of leadership, take the time to construct your own definition, perhaps as a group of two or three. Once you have created your definition, read the statements and see how yours compared with the ones listed on the following pages.

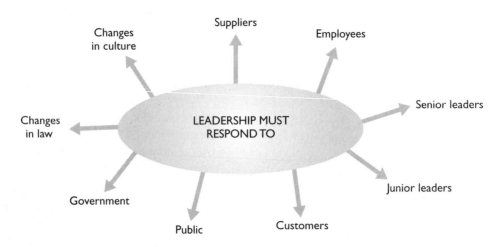

Figure 3.1 Responsive leadership

Steward

Steward (1927) defined leadership as:

> *"the ability to impress the will of the leader on those led and induce obedience, respect, loyalty and co-operation"*

This would seem like a commonsense definition of leadership to many and indeed it does have some merit as leaders may impose their decisions on others and equally they may inspire loyalty and respect. What Steward's definition doesn't account for is the participation of those who are being led. For many leaders, particularly in modern day organisations the support of a team of followers is essential and their viewpoint and expertise welcomed as a valuable resource in achieving common goals.

Steward's definition also does not account for the fact that even if a leader is successful in imposing their will on others this will not necessarily lead to an employee or follower feeling respectful, loyal or co-operative. In fact it may induce the opposite creating resentment, disloyalty and obstructiveness. The theory behind Steward's definition is authoritarian in nature and was very popular in a pre-war era when employees and followers were expected to know and accept their place in a hierarchy. This definition highlights a static and unchanging picture of leadership in which the flow of information is one way only – from the leader to the follower.

Copeland

Copeland (1942) defined leadership as:

> *"Leadership . . . is the art of influencing . . . people by persuasion or example to follow a line of action".*

This definition by Copeland is much more subtle and responsive than the one put forward by Steward. It moves away from a wholly authoritarian approach and acknowledges terms such as influence, persuasion and example, highlighting strategies such as negotiation and discussion as a means to an end. However, it is still an authoritarian view of leadership and the communication between leader and follower is still a one-way process. The difference between the definitions is that in Steward's definition you inform someone of the right course of action and for Copeland you persuade them that it's the right course of action – the end result is the same as the leader's chosen course of action will be followed. In essence this is authoritarianism with a friendly face.

Stodgill

Stodgill (1948) argued that leadership was:

> *"the process (act) of influencing the activities of an organised group in its efforts towards goal setting and goal achievement".*

This is a much more modern definition which was created in an atmosphere of burgeoning US capitalism in which large corporations were beginning to dominate. New forms of leadership were emerging that were much more people orientated rather than task focused.

This definition acknowledges that a group may have characteristics which are independent of the leader and that they may have a role to play in the goal setting agenda of an organisation. It acknowledges that a leader may not always need to be completely directive. It differs from Steward's definition in that the qualities of respect, loyalty and obedience are not mentioned.

How leadership is defined had moved away from the idea of 'command' of people or teams and moved towards management of progress towards goals. Stodgill's definition is much more democratic in nature than either Steward or Copeland, although an element of authoritarianism is still present in that the word 'influencing' is used which implies that the choices of the leader are still of more benefit than the choices of the group and the leader should therefore try and influence the group towards their way of thought.

Boles and Davenport

Boles and Davenport (1975) argued that leadership had become much more than influence or inspiring obedience. Instead leadership revolved around 'assisting' groups to move towards goals which were created for the common good.

Boles and Davenport also acknowledged that a central function of leadership was to help individual members of the group reach their potential and achieve individual goals as well as group goals. The changing definitions of the

1970s moved completely away from any hint of authoritarianism and fully into the field of participative and democratic leadership. The emphasis was on the role of the leader as 'facilitator'. A facilitator is someone who helps a group achieve its aims but may not have set those aims themselves.

A facilitator also ensures that members of the team are supported and encouraged to do their best. In this definition of leadership, communication between the leader and the team is a two way process which clearly contrasts with the earlier definitions of Steward (1927) and Copeland (1942). This trend continued throughout the 1980s with definitions of leadership becoming much more people centred, concentrating on concepts such as inspiring people rather than ordering them and reward for achievement rather than punishment for failure. Leaders became seen as 'enablers' – they enabled groups to move towards aims by ensuring that each member of the group was able to use their own initiative and experiences and develop a sense of responsibility for goal achievement.

These changing definitions of leadership encouraged innovation and delegation, for example leaders brought focus to a group rather than being the focus of the group. The 1990s built on this vision of inspiring groups but took on a much broader focus regarding strategy and communication.

Kotter

Kotter (1996) argued that leadership revolves around aligning individuals to be in the correct role, establishing a direction to move in and developing strategies to enable that movement. Leadership in Kotter's definition couples this with the ability to motivate and energise people to overcome political, bureaucratic and resource barriers in the achievement of the team's goals.

It is clear to see that throughout the twentieth century, definitions of leadership have become more complex and more involved. This mirrors how the role of leaders themselves have changed and become much more aware of the needs and requirements of multiple organisations and individuals rather than just giving orders.

Key concepts

1 The study of leadership has a long history.

2 An understanding of leadership is crucial to any public service employee.

3 Definitions of leadership can vary considerably.

4 Older definitions view leadership as a one way process with information moving from the leader to the follower.

5 More recent definitions view leadership as a two way process with information moving back and forth between leaders and followers.

6 The task of leadership has become more complex as organisations and public services have grown.

Think about it

Consider a current leader you are familiar with, such as a football coach, a teacher, a politician or a public service figure. Which definition of leadership outlined on pages 48–49 relates best to them?

Leadership theories

The *main* developments in the study of leadership that are relevant to the public services today have happened over the last century as shown in Figure 3.2.

Great Man Theories

Great man theories originated with the work of Thomas Carlyle in 1847 and its basic principle is that leaders are born, not made. This means that the ability and skill to lead are innate qualities found in individuals from birth and the skills needed to be a truly great leader cannot be learned – you either have them or you don't.

However, great man theory has largely been discredited as there is no scientific evidence to show a link between hereditary factors and leadership skills and no 'leadership' gene has been identified. Secondly, the theory supports the notion of a leadership elite who are in some way better than the rest of the population and are entitled to take control and lead us. This is a dangerous proposition – the ascription of positive or negative characteristics to individuals based on flawed assumptions about their genetic make up can lead to stereotyping prejudice and even genocide. The third reason that great man theories have largely been discredited is that it takes no account of situational or environmental factors. It assumes that a leader is always a leader regardless of the situation they find themselves in.

Trait Theory

Trait theory began its development in the early part of the twentieth century, but didn't really rise to prominence until the 1940s and the 1950s. Important researchers in Trait Theory are Bird (1940) who compiled a list of 79 traits of leaders, Jenkins (1947) who examined the traits of military leaders and Stogdill (1948) who offered a critical evaluation of early approaches to trait theory.

Traits are characteristics of individuals which make them who they are and the basis of this theory is that leaders have a different set of personal characteristics than followers. Traits which are thought to be central to leadership are the qualities listed on page 68. The idea is that if a person possesses these traits they have superior qualities which provide them with a natural ability to lead and that they are fundamentally different from their followers.

As with all theories there are many drawbacks to this approach. Firstly, researchers often argued that there was a definitive set of characteristics which could be applied to all leaders. This is a problem because it assumes that these traits will be applicable in all leadership situations from combat to classroom. It takes no account of situational factors, which may be very important

LEADERSHIP THEORY TIMELINE

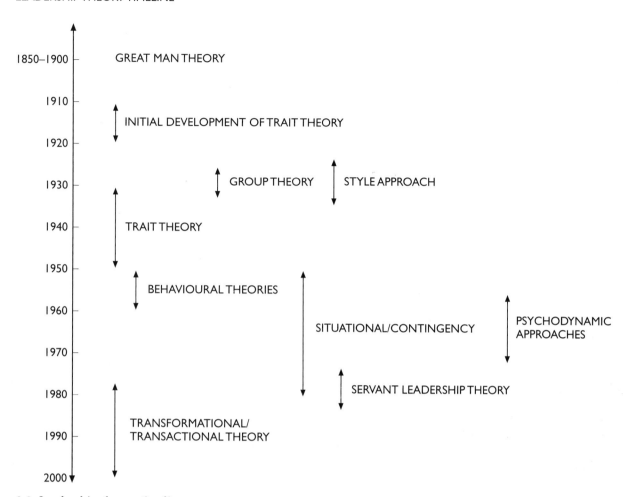

Figure 3.2 Leadership theory timeline

in how leaders emerge and take responsibility. In addition, it is very difficult to measure a person's traits – how do you measure flexibility or good judgement? Finally, another difficulty with trait theory is that leadership studies have not adequately linked these traits with leadership effectiveness.

Trait theory is still very popular but in a slightly modernised form. Currently, researchers have studied 'clusters' of traits and how they might suit particular situations rather than viewing traits as a whole. In addition, trait theory has become much more gender aware by recognising that effective leaders can arise in both sexes and that skills such as compassion, diplomacy and effective communication can make the difference between an effective leader and an ineffective one.

Behavioural Theories

Behavioural theories of leadership became very popular in the 1950s and 60s after the decline of trait theory. Rather than focusing on the qualities a leader does or doesn't have it examines how leaders behave with a particular emphasis on how they behave towards their followers. The patterns of behaviour that leaders use in achieving goals and motivating groups are grouped into 'styles':

- **people centred** – this type of leader focuses on the needs, problems and skills of their followers, seeing them as individuals with differing skills and abilities who might require differing levels of leadership support.

- **task centred** – this type of leader negotiates with followers on issues such as goals and deadlines. The decision making process is open for discussion and power is shared.

- **authoritarian** – this type of leader makes decisions about the way forward and expects others to obey.

In some instances, situational factors may influence the style of leadership used. For instance, a teacher may be authoritarian in a class of students but discursive in a team meeting with other teachers. A Police Inspector organising crowd control at a football match may use a task centred approach but back at the station when dealing with junior police officers, a people centred approach might be employed. Most leaders understand that just because a particular leadership style worked in one situation it doesn't mean it will work in all situations.

Theory into practice

Consider the description above of task and people oriented leadership approaches and address the following questions.

1 Which of the two leadership approaches described might be more suitable in a highly desciplined environment?

2 What situational factors might affect which leadership approach is taken?

3 Compare the two styles above with the ones listed on pages 57–62. How effective do you think they would be in comparison with the others described?

4 How could you develp your leadership skills in both a task oriented and people oriented way?

Situational/Contingency Theories

Situational theory emerged in the 1950s and developed throughout the 1960s, 70s and 80s. It was one of the first theories to consider the organisational and situational environment as a factor in leadership effectiveness. In this theory, the situation not only determines which style of leadership ought to be used but also which individual will emerge as leader. Clearly, in this approach the best leaders are those who can vary their style to suit the situation and be flexible and adaptable enough to work in a variety of situations. Contingency Theory is very similar which is why they are often grouped together. It focuses on the idea that leadership is dependent on a mix of factors being present in the situation.

This approach is of significant use in the pubic services where there are thousands of individuals, hundreds of groups and a wide range of situational contexts. For example, if a commanding officer has the skill to match an appropriate leadership style to a particular environment they will have a much better chance of achieving their goal and getting the best from their unit or shift.

There are some criticisms of the situational/contingency approach which it is important to consider. Firstly and in common with several other leadership theories, how leaders adapt to situations is not measurable. How is it possible to measure which leadership style is appropriate for which situation as many styles may be equally effective in an identical situation. Another criticism of situational approach is suggested by Doyle and Smith (2002) who argue that much of the research conducted in this area is based on US studies and may not apply to every culture. They suggest that cultural factors influence the way people carry out and respond to different leadership styles. For example, some cultures value courtesy and honour in leaders whereas other cultures might value morality and devout religious beliefs. Doyle and Smith also suggested that situational theories examine how leaders can adapt their style to suit a situation but they do not examine the wider political or organisational context in which the leaders operate.

Servant Leadership

Developed by Robert Greenleaf (1970) this theory of leadership argues that successful and effective leaders influence others as a result of dedicating their lives to the service of others. Therefore in this approach a leader exists to serve his or her followers and in doing so ensures the goals and aims of the group are achieved to the satisfaction of all. Servant leaders continually strive to understand and respond to the needs of their followers and in doing so create a more productive environment.

Transformational/Transactional Theory

These concepts were initially developed by Burns (1978) and Bass (1985). The transactional leader approaches his or her followers in the manner of a trade. For instance, an army officer participating in military simulations night offer his subordinates additional recreation time if they perform well. In the Fire Service strikes of 2002/3 the government lead the negotiations in a transactional manner by offering a pay rise in return for substantial reform in the service. Transactional leaders are very common in business life where they will deliver bonuses, training or time off if the performance of individuals is good enough. One of the major difficulties with transactional leadership is that it doesn't always work. What is demanded by either party may be unacceptable regardless of the reward offered, for example the fire-fighters strike.

Transformational leaders aim to make us better people by encouraging our self-awareness and helping us see the bigger picture of what we do. They don't try and bribe us with rewards for good performance. Instead they want us to overcome our self-interest and move towards achieving common goals and purposes which we share with the group. There are many examples of transformational leaders inspiring groups and individuals to achieve greatness. Examples are Mahatma Ghandi who led a peaceful and successful revolution to overthrow the British in India in the 1940s and Mother Theresa whose leadership of a religious order brought comfort to thousands of people in Calcutta and spread across the globe.

Key concepts

1 Theories of leadership have developed throughout the twentieth century.

2 Throughout the twentieth century theories have evolved away from examining the leader themselves to examining the process and purpose of leadership.

3 Older theories such as great man and trait approaches argue that only a select few are equipped to lead.

4 More recent theories such as situational theory argue that anyone can emerge as a leader given the right circumstances.

Roles of leaders

Leaders fulfil many roles:

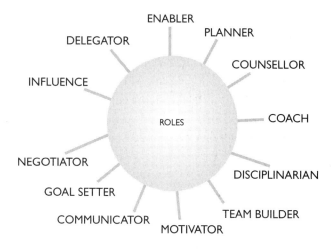

Figure 3.3 Roles of a leader

Theory into practice

Describe the roles and responsibilities of an army officer and compare them with the roles and responsibilities of a paramedic.

On many occasions the roles of a leader may come into conflict. For instance, if a team member's performance is so poor that it is compromising the achievement of team goals then the role of disciplinarian may have to come into force, but if the leader discovers that the poor performance is caused by personal difficulties they may have to juggle that role with that of counsellor.

The role of a leader is not easy and he or she may have to overcome personal difficulties and develop new interpersonal skills if they are to be effective. One of the most difficult balancing acts for a leader is the need to maintain a good working relationship with their team while having to make difficult decisions which may adversely affect some team members. It is important in such circumstances that a leader maintains a personal/professional divide; a personal friendship with a team member should not compromise the professional role they must fulfil. This is particularly difficult when a leader is promoted from within the ranks of the team itself.

Responsibilities of leaders

Leaders may be responsible for many different groups (see Figure 3.4), having to account for their actions with regard to personal conduct, dispersion of finances, strategic planning and the ultimate success or failure of a particular initiative. For example, a Chief Constable may

Case study

Jamila has been a police sergeant for five years working at a large city centre station. She has an excellent working relationship with the other sergeants based at the station and they work very closely together co-ordinating shifts of police officers to respond both to the needs of the community and the strategic direction of the constabulary. Although many of her fellow sergeants have more experience or more qualifications than her, she has been asked to 'act up' to the rank of Inspector to cover for a member of staff who is on long-term sick leave.

1 What difficulties might Jamila face from her team of sergeants if she accepts the temporary promotion?

2 What difficulties might Jamila face from other Inspectors?

3 What difficulties might Jamila encounter when the Inspector who is on sick leave returns and she returns to the rank of sergeant?

4 What strategies can Jamila employ to overcome the difficulties she might face in each situation?

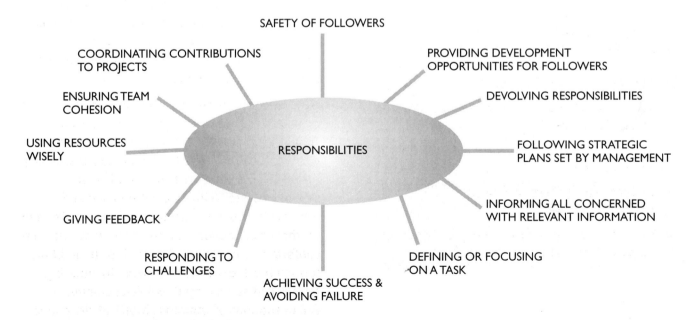

Figure 3.4 The responsibilities of a leader

have the responsibilities to any or all of the following groups:

- Government
- the general public
- local authorities
- multi-agency partnerships
- police officers at all ranks
- pressure groups
- individuals detained by the police
- victims of crime
- the Crown Prosecution Service
- the courts
- charities such as Victim Support
- local communities
- the local Police Authority
- Police Complaints Authority
- The Home Office
- the media

Case study

The BFU argued for a 40% pay increase taking average fire fighter salaries up to around £30,000. This figure was completely unacceptable to the government regardless of the points in its favour, such as increasing retention in the service and in return the government offered 11% if the service was reformed. The BFU rejected this out of hand.

1 Why does the BFU want an increase of 40% to fire fighters salaries?

2 Why do you think this amount was unacceptable to the government?

3 How have the principles of transactional leadership failed here?

4 How could transactional leadership be further adapted to help solve the situation?

Theory into practice

Consider how you could transform a team you are leading into a highly motivated, inspired team who think of others rather than themselves, when the job they have to do is routine, low paid and uninspiring? What difficulties would you encounter?

Leadership styles

There are a variety of 'styles', which individual leaders can choose to employ to lead in particular circumstances. A leadership style is the manner and approach of providing direction for a team, implementing plans and motivating people to complete a task. There are several different leadership styles each with its own set of advantages and disadvantages. Here we will describe and evaluate some of the more commonly known and used ones.

Authoritarian leadership

Sometimes this style is also called autocratic. It is often considered as a classic leadership style and is used when a leader wishes to retain as much power as possible and maintain control over the decision making process. It involves the leader telling the employees what they must do without any form of consultation and negotiation. Employees are expected to obey orders without receiving any explanation.

Generally this approach is not considered to be the most appropriate way to get the best response from a team in ordinary working life, but it has distinct advantages for the public services, such as the armed forces. It tends to work best in situations where there is great urgency and pressure to achieve as autocratic leaders often rely on threats or intimidation to ensure that followers conform to what the leader requires. In addition, this approach devalues employees by ignoring their expertise and input and discouraging demonstrations of initiative. Many of the public services encourage leaders to utilise this particular leadership style for very sound reasons:

- it maintains order and discipline
- it allows public services to be deployed quickly and efficiently
- it allows young and inexperienced recruits to know what to do and when to do it
- it allows large scale co-ordination with other shifts or units
- it ensures that decisions are made by those best equipped to make them
- it enables decisions to be made very quickly.

However although this style might be appropriate in public service life, it is not viable for other environments. Most non-uniformed public services, such as teaching and probation, have moved away from this approach over the last 30 years or so.

Some of the drawbacks of the autocratic/authoritarian approach are as follows:

- team members rely on the leader for instruction and do not develop initiative
- team members have less responsibility for their own actions
- team members may feel angry and resentful at being ordered to perform tasks without explanation
- it can lead to high staff turnover and absenteeism

An autocratic leadership approach is used in the Army

- staff may feel devalued and fearful of punishment
- staff morale may decline leading to poor job performance.

Theory into practice

After examining the autocratic style of leadership described above, consider how you would respond to this particular style if you were working under it?

Bureaucratic leadership

Bureaucracy is a system of leadership in which authority is diffused among a number of departments, offices and individuals and there is strict adherence to a set of operational rules. This is also often considered to be a classic leadership style and is often used in organisations that do not encourage innovation and change and by leaders who may be insecure and uncertain of their role. It involves following the rules of an organisation rigidly – 'doing things by the book'. People who favour using this style of leadership are often very familiar with the many policies, guidelines and working practices that an organisation may have.

If a particular situation arises that is not covered by known rules and guidelines then a bureaucratic leader may feel uncomfortable or out of their depth and will have little hesitation in referring difficulties to a leader higher up in the chain of command.

This approach is commonly found in many uniformed and non-uniformed public services. Often the public services are very large and bureaucratic and although it may seem unlikely, there are several situations where the bureaucratic leadership style may be the most appropriate one to use, for example:

- if a job is routine and unchanging
- if a job requires a definite set of safety rules and guidelines to keep employees and the public safe
- where large sums of money are handled.

However, if the bureaucratic style is used inappropriately it can have very negative consequences, leading to a lack of flexibility, an uninspired working environment and workers who only do what is required of them but no more.

The modern public services and the leaders within them have to deal with a constantly changing social and political environment and a rigid approach isn't always effective in view of this. However, the public services are the guardians of our safety and security and it is appropriate that they should have to follow bureaucratic procedures, which ensure the safety of the public and protect against the misuse of power. A balance must be found when using this leadership style in which rules and procedures are obeyed and understood without compromising flexibility, responsiveness and creativity.

Think about it

Consider an occasion when you have been subject to a bureaucratic style of leadership. Describe the situation to a colleague and then discuss how it made you feel.

Democratic (participative) leadership

In this approach the leader encourages the followers to become a part of the decision making process. The leader still maintains control of the group and ownership of the final decision but input from team members is encouraged and the leader informs team members about factors, which may have an impact on them and the project. This encourages a sense of responsibility in team members who feel that they have a vested interest in the success of a project or operation. This approach allows a leader to draw upon the expertise and experience of a team in order to achieve the best results for all. The democratic approach is viewed very positively by most leadership analysts as it can produce high quality work over long periods of time from highly motivated teams. However, its application in the field of public service work does have its drawbacks:

- democratic discussion takes time – a public service may have to respond very quickly so gathering the views of all members may not be a viable option

Style	Advantages	Disadvantages
Authoritarian	• Quick decisions • Clarity • Maintains discipline	• Does not trust employees • Employees have no input • Relies on threats
Laissez-faire	• Trusts employees • Leader can delegate • Employees feel empowered	• Goals may not be achieved • Roles and responsibilities poorly defined • Can be used as a cover for bad leaders
Bureaucratic	• Maintains order • Enforces routine • Policies are clear	• Employees may lose interest • Forms difficult to break habits • No negotiation
Democratic	• Employees are empowered • Recognises and encourages achievement • Promotes team building	• Lengthly decision making process • May not be cost effective • Discipline may be compromised

Figure 3.5 Advantages and disadvantages of leadership styles

- a participative approach may not be the most cost effective way of organising a service – the time of police officers is expensive and it may be more worthwhile doing the job that they are paid for rather than talking about how to do the job they are paid for

- this approach is not really appropriate if the safety of team members is paramount – safety is not open for negotiation and a public service must endeavour to protect its members from harm wherever operationally possible. Equally, when members must risk their personal safety in the defence of others, it is not open to discussion

Although this style wouldn't necessarily be appropriate for use among the lower ranks of the public services it certainly has application in meetings or projects involving senior officers who will expect to be consulted with and listened to.

Case study

Tom is the lead social worker on a local authority initiative to reduce the amount of youth crime occurring in the centre of a large city. He has called a meeting to discuss what the current problems are, how effective current preventative action is and to create a plan to move forward in achieving the local authorities goals. Many organisations are involved in this initiative such as the police, drug awareness groups, victim support and local business owners, all of whom have sent a senior representative to this important meeting. After reviewing his preparation notes for the meeting, Tom decides to take a participative approach to the meeting, rather than using another style.

1 Why do you think Tom chose to employ a participative style for the meeting?

2 What are the advantages to Tom in using this style?

3 What are the advantages to the project as a whole in using this style?

Laissez-faire leadership

The laissez-faire approach can also be called the 'hands off' approach, free reign approach or the delegative approach. This style differs from the others in that the leader exercises very little control over the group and leaves them to establish their own roles and responsibilities. Followers are given very little direction but a great deal of power and freedom. They must use this power to establish goals, make decisions and resolve difficulties should they arise. This style is difficult to master as many leaders have great difficulty delegating power and authority to others and allowing them the freedom to work free from interference. It is also a difficult approach to use on all groups of followers as some people experience great difficulty working without a leader's direction and projects or goals may fall behind schedule or be poorly organised.

In general, a laissez-faire approach is most effective when a group of followers are highly motivated, experienced and well educated. It is important that the leader can have trust in their followers to complete tasks without supervision and this is more likely to happen with a highly qualified team.

It is also a good approach to use when dealing with expert staff that may know more about a subject than the leader themselves. For example, in a murder enquiry the supervising officer would employ a laissez faire approach to a scenes of crime officer or a forensic investigator. The experts know what they are there to do and can be safely left to get on with it leaving the supervising officer to attend to other tasks.

However there are situations where a laissez faire style may not be the most effective style, for example when a leader lacks the knowledge and the skills to do the job and employs this style so that the employees work covers the leader's weaknesses. In addition, it would be inappropriate to use this style with new or inexperienced staff that may feel uncomfortable if the direction of a manager wasn't readily available. For instance, a commanding officer would not approach the training of new recruits with a laissez faire manner but as an individual progresses through a rank structure they will become more skilled, experienced and trustworthy and they may encounter this style more often.

Key concepts

1 All styles of leadership have advantages and disadvantages.

2 The key is to use the appropriate leadership style in the appropriate situation.

3 The authoritarian style of leadership is when the leader tells others what to do and how to do it.

4 The bureaucratic style of leadership has clearly outlined procedures which must be followed if you are to know what to do and how to do it.

5 The democratic or participative approach encourages discussion between employees and the leader when making decisions.

6 The laissez-faire approach lets followers establish their own roles and responsibilities.

Styles used in public service

The public services are constantly changing due to changes in public expectations, changes in law and the current political environment. As a result, the styles of leadership used are changing and evolving too.

The public services receive their strategic plans either directly from the Home Office or must draw up their own plans under the prevailing political will of the time, meaning that even very senior officers often have no input into the goal setting of the organisation which is then imposed on its employees. This would seem to indicate that an authoritarian style would be the most effective in public service work, but a public service leader must be ready to respond to many challenges, with a whole range of leadership techniques either singly or all at once. As a result, public service leaders must be highly adaptable and comfortable using all styles of leadership. An example of a public service officer using multiple styles of leadership in an arson case is shown below in Figure 3.6:

Case study

Jack has been a leading fire fighter with Green Watch for the last 2 years. While attending a warehouse fire at night, his sub officer is injured and rendered unconscious leaving Jack in command of 15 other fire fighters. Green Watch is a close-knit group who work together extremely well and are experienced and competent. There is no immediate risk to the public as the warehouse is empty and the surrounding area is deserted due to the late hour. However, there is substantial threat to neighbouring property if the fire cannot be contained.

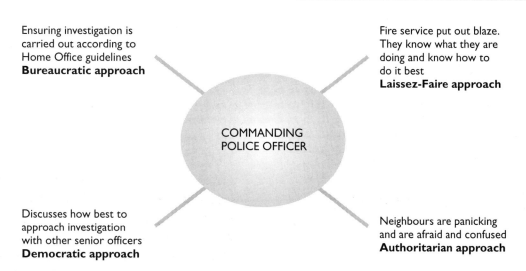

Figure 3.6 Multiple styles of leadership for a senior police officer in an arson case

1 Assess how effective a democratic approach would be?

2 Assess how effective a laissez-faire approach would be?

3 Which style do you think is the most appropriate for Jack to employ?

Case study

A small infantry unit of 6 men are trapped behind enemy lines in desert conditions. They must maintain radio silence in order that they are not detected by the enemy. They have enough water and rations for 72 hours but the journey they must make to return to safety is approximately 6 days long. 2 of the men are experienced in desert conditions but 3 are relatively new recruits. The Commanding officer must lead them to safety.

1 Assess the effectiveness of an authoritarian approach in this case.

2 Assess the effectiveness of a bureaucratic approach in this case.

3 How effective do you think a combined approach would be and which styles would you combine?

Employing the right approach

Employing the right approach in the right situation is crucial if a leader is to successfully achieve their aims. The costs to a team or organisation of bad leadership can be high in terms of finance, goodwill and motivation and the benefits of effective leadership cannot be bought with any amount of money. This is particularly true in the public services: see Figure 3.7.

Motivation

A simple meaning of motivation is the will to act. It is a factor or factors, which encourage you to perform a particular task or duty. Motivation also governs how well a task will be performed and it applies equally to individuals and groups. The public service sector is becoming highly competitive with increasing private sector involvement in traditional public services. This means that the police, fire service, customs and many other uniformed services must have a highly motivated workforce if they are to compete effectively against private security companies, private prisons and private healthcare. The public services are becoming increasingly concerned with low levels of motivation amongst workers which

Leadership in the public services	
Benefits of effective leaders	**Costs of bad leaders**
<ul><li>Organisations will retain good quality staff</li><li>Staff will go that extra mile in order to do a good job</li><li>Efficiency and cost effectiveness</li><li>Staff feel valued</li><li>Tasks are completed successfully</li><li>Discipline is maintained</li><li>Teamwork is encouraged and team members support each other</li><li>Teams will work towards common objectives</li><li>Teams will perform better in highly pressurised or dangerous situations</li></ul>	<ul><li>Staff will leave</li><li>Staff will not be motivated to do a good job</li><li>Resources such as time and money will be wasted</li><li>Tasks may not be done properly or left incomplete</li><li>Staff may disobey or be mutinous</li><li>Social order may decline</li><li>Lives may be lost</li><li>Territory and valuable assets may be lost</li><li>Equipment may be faulty or unfit for purpose</li><li>Teams may collapse under difficult circumstances</li><li>Staff will be more concerned with their own self interest rather than achieving a common goal</li></ul>

Figure 3.7 Benefits of effective leaders and costs of bad leaders in the public services

may be caused by under funding from the government and overwork which can lead to:

- strikes/industrial disputes
- high absenteeism
- low productivity
- poor quality performance.

Motivated workforce

A motivated workforce will have the following characteristics:

- higher productivity
- a greater sense of urgency
- better quality work with less waste.

Think about it

1 Discuss and make notes in small groups why you think people are motivated to join the services in the first place. Compare your notes with the findings of other groups.

2 Now perform the same activity to explain why some public service employees may want to leave their chosen public service.

A motivated workforce is also necessary if obstacles to performance such as under funding, under staffing and bureaucracy are to be effectively overcome. There are many mechanisms which can be employed to ensure a motivated workforce who are motivated to work harder, be more efficient and cost effective. (See Figure 3.8)

Motivating mechanisms can be good (positive motivation), such as job satisfaction and financial reward or bad (negative motivation) such as fear of punishment. Although both are effective it is generally accepted that positive mechanisms are a much better approach over a long term period and create additional benefits for a public service such as happy, healthy employees who are prepared to give goodwill and support the organisation in achieving its goals. A negatively motivated employee will feel resentful, stressed and may actively seek employment elsewhere. It is not an effective long-term strategy.

Think about it

Think about a situation you have been in when you have been subject to negative motivation and a situation where you were faced with positive motivation. How did you feel in each situation? Which strategy was most effective in motivating you and why?

Some of the motivating mechanisms are internal or intrinsic such as beliefs, needs and personal interests and some are external such as family pressure or danger. How these factors affect

Figure 3.8 Motivating mechanisms

individuals is difficult to predict. Each individual is unique and will not be influenced in the same way by the same stimuli.

For example, some individuals thrive on danger whereas others avoid it. Each individual will respond to a unique set of motivational factors and a leader must try and accommodate these factors if they are to gain the best performance from their team.

Motivation theories

One of the best ways for a leader to understand how to motivate teams and individuals is to have an understanding of motivational theories.

Maslow's hierarchy of needs

Abraham Maslow developed his theory of motivation throughout the 1950s and 60s. His theory argues that human motivation is based around a set of needs, which operate in a hierarchy. The hierarchy can be shown as follows:

Figure 3.9 Maslow's hierarchy of needs

According to Maslow each level of the hierarchy must be satisfied before an individual can progress towards the next.

Physical needs – These are the most basic motivating factors for humans: they consist of the need for food, water, shelter, clothing and warmth.

Without these, people will not be concerned with achieving their full potential. A leader must ensure that his or her followers have these needs fulfilled if organisational goals are to be achieved. Leaders and employers can provide for these needs in many ways but the most usual is to provide employees with money in exchange for their service. This money will then be used to provide for these needs.

Safety needs – Once our most basic needs are satisfied we can progress upwards towards the next level. Safety needs include a stable environment, personal security and an absence of fear. In short, the individual seeks a safe and secure environment, which acts as a foundation for the development of further needs.

Social/relationship needs – Individuals need to have social interaction with a range of people if they are to become fulfilled. This can include socialising with friends and colleagues, love and affection from family and partners. These needs are fulfilled through social clubs and interest based activities.

Esteem needs – Individuals need to feel appreciated and respected. They need to know that they are adequate and competent in the things they strive to achieve and receive recognition for their efforts.

Self-actualisation – This is a very difficult need to define. It revolves around reaching an individual's full potential and winning and striving to achieve further wealth or satisfaction. It is about the pursuit of happiness and each individual has different requirements for happiness.

Firstly as you move through the divisions of the hierarchy there is a distinct move from extrinsic (external) factors, which must be satisfied by the environment such as food and safety, towards intrinsic (internal) factors such as fulfilling ones potential which can only be satisfied from within. As a result, the higher a person progresses up the pyramid, the more difficult it becomes to influence a person's motivation because internal factors have more weight. Maslow's hierarchy has a significant impact in all workplace environments including those of the public services because it provides a blueprint for what a leader needs to provide to motivate followers.

However, there are some potential weaknesses in Maslow's theory. Firstly human behaviour is very complex and may respond to several needs at a time, not just one. In addition, there are examples of individual's who do not progress up the pyramid in linear fashion. For instance, representatives of some religious orders may forego food, water and shelter in the search for spiritual self-actualisation. It has also been argued that there is very little evidence to support Maslow's hierarchy and what little evidence there is only relates to Western nations such as UK and USA.

Theory into practice

How could a senior naval officer use Maslow's theory to motivate his or her personnel?

Douglas McGregor – Theory X and Theory Y

McGregor's book 'The Human Side of Enterprise' (1960) built on the work begun by Maslow. In it he proposes two theories, which explain employee or follower motivation, he calls, these theories **Theory X** and **Theory Y**.

These two theories are direct opposites of each other, viewing employees in very different ways. They describe how individuals behave in their working lives and discuss how best an X person or a Y person could be motivated to achieve more.

Theory X

Generally this theory assumes that the average employee or follower:

- dislikes work and will avoid it if possible
- lacks ambition
- dislikes responsibility
- prefers to follow rather than lead

- does not care about organisational goals
- seeks security above all else
- resists change.

This is a traditional theory that has often been used in business settings which assumes that individuals are only motivated by money, benefits and a fear of punishment. The suitable leadership strategy is therefore to closely supervise employees and followers and ensure that they work within a controlling structure, which offers incentives such as financial rewards in return for better performance. However, McGregor acknowledged that Theory X has several potential flaws. Firstly, it relies on lower needs as motivating factors but in a modern society most lower needs are no longer primary motivating factors. Secondly, there is no acknowledgement that financial reward may not be the best way to motivate all employees. As a result of these weaknesses McGregor developed the opposing Theory Y.

Theory Y

Theory Y assumes that individuals are best motivated by their higher needs such as esteem and self actualisation. These needs in contrast with the lower needs are not easily satisfied and require continual development. A typical Theory Y employee is as follows:

- self directed
- may enjoy work and see it as a source of satisfaction
- will work towards organisational goals
- accepts and seeks responsibility
- is creative and innovative
- has potential to develop further.

In this theory it is essential that organisations create an environment where individuals have the chance to display this behaviour. Theory Y individuals do not respond well to threats and co-ercive leadership styles. Neither do they always require financial reward for motivated behaviour. The chief motivating factor here is the employees own search for professional fulfilment. There are several implications of theory Y that will help organisations build a motivated and committed workforce.

- Delegate responsibility throughout an organisation rather than hold power and responsibility centrally.

- Introduce appraisal systems which encourage employees to set professional goals and take responsibility for ensuring that they are met.

- Utilise a participative and democratic management style. This will encourage self worth and esteem in employees leading to increased motivation.

Think about it

Imagine you have recently joined a public service of your choice. Discuss in small groups whether you would be a theory X or a theory Y recruit.

Frederick Herzberg – two factor hygiene and motivational theory

Hertzberg's hygiene and motivational theory is based largely on the work of Maslow but Herzberg focuses much more on the work environment than Maslow's principles. The theory is based on two factors.

Hygiene factors (dissatisfiers)

These are basic human needs at work. Their presence does not increase motivation in individuals or groups but their absence will cause dissatisfaction and unrest. Examples of hygiene factors are shown in Figure 3.10.

Individuals cannot be motivated until hygiene factors are fulfilled. In effect, Herzberg has translated Maslow's lower level needs, which apply to a person's existence and translated them into the basic needs required in a productive workplace. Herzberg has therefore much more practical application to the public services than Maslow. Once hygiene factors are met, leaders and employers can begin to deploy motivators.

Motivating factors (satisfiers)

These are the factors which actually drive individuals to achieve goals. They enrich the job of an employee or follower encouraging them to work harder and more productively. Motivators can be described by the terms shown in Figure 3.11:

In order to achieve a motivated employee, the presence of hygiene factors must be combined with the presence of motivating factors creating what Herzberg termed 'job enrichment' – see Figure 3.12. Management should focus in rearranging work so that motivating factors can impact the

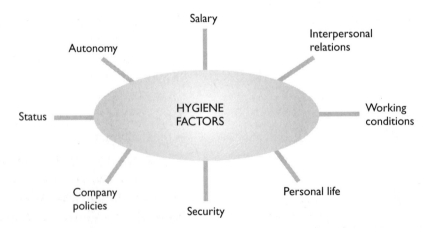

Figure 3.10 Herzberg's hygiene factors (dissatisfiers)

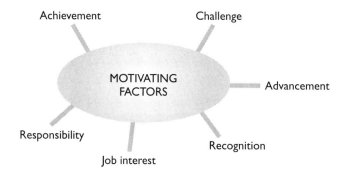

Figure 3.11 Herzberg's movitating factors (satisfiers)

individual by enlarging job roles, ensuring there is sufficient job rotation to maintain employee interest and sufficient recognition and advancement to cater to an individual's ego and esteem needs.

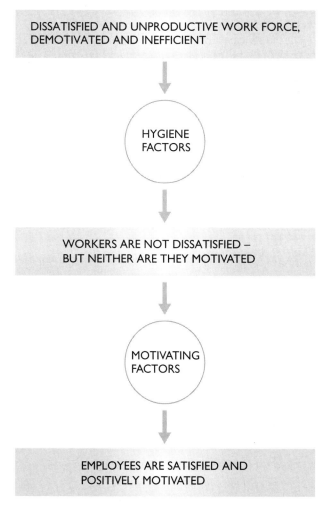

Figure 3.12 Flow diagram of Herzberg's Theory

> ### Theory into practice
>
> In Herzberg's model, what factors might provide evidence of poor motivation in an organisation?

Alderfer's ERG theory

Clayton Alderfer developed the ERG theory of needs (1972) based again on initial work by Maslow in the 1950s. Alderfer developed a hierarchy of needs similar to Maslow but consisting of three groups needs rather than five.

Existence needs

These are the basic requirements for physiological existence. They are satisfied by material conditions and physical substances. It relates closely to Maslow's physiological and safety needs and includes food, clothing, shelter and safe working conditions.

Relatedness needs

This is built upon the natural desire of humans to build and maintain interpersonal relationships with others. It revolves around giving and receiving feedback, acceptance, confirmation and understanding. This function must be met in large part by an individual's co-workers.

Growth needs

These needs are met by the personal development of an individual. It is satisfied by meeting and overcoming challenges, using skills and abilities and advancing and being recognised within a workplace.

Alderfer also recognised that more than one need may be influential at any one time and that there may be different levels of motivational achievement in different parts of our lives. For example, an individual who has a very successful personal life may not have progressed through the hierarchy in a professional capacity.

Key concepts

1 Maslow's motivation is based around a hierarchy of needs of which lower needs must be fulfilled before higher needs can be attained.

2 McGregor argues that there are two types of employees, ones who have to be closely supervised and controlled (X) and ones who are self directed and motivated (Y).

3 Herzberg argues that the absence of basic needs at work causes dissatisfaction. Only when these needs are met at work can leaders begin motivating employees.

4 Alderfer argues that we may be motivated differently in different parts of our lives.

5 Many of the theories shown above are based on the initial work of Maslow.

Case study

You are the senior Customs officer at a small local airport that deals mainly with national flights and low cost airline flights to Europe. You have a small team of five officers to help you of whom three are new recruits to the service in the process of gaining experience and expertise. The remaining two are approaching retirement age. Difficulties are arising in the team and it is having a negative effect on the effectiveness of the unit. The difficulties are as follows:

- the new recruits are becoming disillusioned with the service, as the slow pace of work at the airport isn't what attracted them to join Customs and Excise

- the older officers resist change and like what they know

- the younger officers feel resentful towards the older officers resistant attitude

- the older officers feel resentful to the younger ones for wanting to change established practices.

As the senior officer you must balance all of these differing needs and expectations to come up with a workable solution which suits all parties.

1 Describe how you could apply Maslow's theory to this situation.

2 How might Alderfer's approach be of help?

3 What might Herzberg's theory have to offer in resolving the situation?

Case study

As the Commanding Officer (CO) of a Royal Air Force base you must oversee the preparations to mobilise a squadron of fighter aircraft, pilots and ground support personnel to a volatile situation in the Middle East.

The base is very poorly motivated to perform the tasks required of them as there has already been two cancelled mobilisations in which the preparation work was done and then the orders were cancelled. In addition, the personnel are leaving behind families and loved ones to enter a situation which may put their lives at risk. It is your job to ensure that the tasks are completed on time and everyone is fully prepared to go.

1 What contribution could McGregor's theory X and theory Y make to the motivation of the base?

2 How could an understanding of Maslow help the CO?

3 Which theory of motivation would you use if you were the CO of the base?

Motivating factors

Aside from organised theories of motivation such as those proposed by Alderfer and Maslow there are also motivating factors which can increase productivity that are particularly influential in public service life (see Figure 3.13).

Motivating factor	Explanation
Promotion	The tall hierarchical structure of most public services offers excellent prospects for promotion. Each promotion brings with it new responsibilities, financial rewards and recognition of achievement. The use of promotion can be a very effective motivational tool in public service life.
Salary	This is a very good motivating factor in the public services but since pay increases are at the discretion of the government it is seldom-used. If one public service is given a substantial raise there are then implications across the public sector because the government cannot raise all public salaries.
Group behaviour	This is a very effective public service motivational tool. Generally Police officers, fire fighters and Armed Forces personnel can be extremely motivated in supporting colleagues and will often expose themselves to extreme danger in order to help fellow service members and achieve organisation goals.
Job satisfaction	One of the great virtues of a public service career is the ability to help people and contribute to the well being of society. Seeing a job well done or lives saved due to your actions can compensate in large part for mediocre pay or an anti-social shift system. Most public service employees decide to join a service through a genuine desire to help others.
Equality with other groups of workers	Nothing demoralises a group of workers more quickly than not being appreciated or given the same sense of worth that other groups have for doing similar jobs. So a good way of motivating a group is to ensure that they are seen as equal with other groups. For example, a typical army soldier earns approximately £12,000 a year. This ranks as one of the lowest public service salaries and the consequences of this are poor recruitment and retention and high levels of desertion and AWOL. If they were given equality with services such as the Police who have a basic salary of around £21,000 they might become more motivated and energised solving problems of dissatisfaction and absenteeism.
Accountability	Knowing that you are under scrutiny from independent agencies and the general public can be a great motivator to achieve organisation goals such as: ● value for money ● performance success ● response times.
Fast track schemes	The Police and the Prison service have graduate fast track schemes which encourage highly educated individuals to join and progress rapidly through the ranks. This can also motivate existing public service employees to improve their educational level in order to progress faster themselves. A better-educated workforce will be more competitive.
Job rotation	Some public services such as the Police have a policy of ensuring that employees have the option to move through many different departments and experience a variety of work. For example, a typical retiring Police officer may have spent time in: ● traffic ● CID ● community policing. This keeps job interest throughout a lengthy career therefore helping to sustain motivation.

Figure 3.13 Motivating factors which can increase productivity

Theory into practice

Using newspapers and the Internet examine how three of the motivating factors shown in the table on page 67 relate to the following issues:

- the fire service strike
- low recruitment into infantry regiments in the army
- the anti-social nature of shift patterns in some services.

Case study

Inspector Singh is the leader of the British Transport Police's (BTP) recruiting division. The team consists of three full time civilians, three full time BTP Constables and seven other Officers who assist in interviewing and assessment but are not primarily attached to the recruiting section.

The BTP needs to recruit on average 12 people a month from a total pool of 180 applications per month. Currently the team has a 6-month backlog of applications to deal with and is only managing 6 new recruits each month. This is having a knock on effect on force strength and may shortly begin to compromise operational effectiveness and transport safety. Inspector Singh must resolve these problems but he is unsure of how to proceed.

1 Suggest and explain 3 appropriate methods of maximising productivity which Inspector Singh may find useful in his recruitment team.

2 Describe how the following motivational theories could explain why Inspector Singh's team is not meeting its goals and how using the theories could help him re-energise his team:

- Alderfer's ERG theory
- Herzberg's hygiene and motivational theory
- McGregor's theory X and theory Y

3 Other than a lack of productivity and a backlog, what other signs could Inspector Singh look for in assessing whether his team is demotivated?

4 What factors should Inspector Singh look for as signs that his motivational strategies are working?

Qualities of leadership

The following kinds of leadership qualities are likely to be found in successful leaders and in particular public service leaders.

Characteristics of successful leaders

Leadership qualities vary from leader to leader and situation to situation. The qualities that would make a good military leader may not be appropriate in the caring sectors and vice versa. Many people have naturally developed leadership qualities which can assist them in achieving goals and others have the capacity to learn how to be a leader through experience and instruction. There are very few people who cannot acquire at least some leadership qualities which would serve them in their daily lives and careers.

Adaptability

All good leaders should be able to adapt and incorporate new information and new challenges. This is particularly important in public services where the political climate or operational conditions can change with very little or no warning.

Charisma

Charisma lies in the personality of a leader. It is the energy, vision and charm of a person which when communicated to others inspires loyalty, enthusiasm and a willingness to go that extra mile. Charismatic leaders can often get followers to perform tasks they wouldn't otherwise do simply by virtue of their personality.

Communicator

An effective leader must communicate with a variety of organisations and individuals ensuring that they actively listen to what they are told and they are clear and unambiguous in their response. This is crucial for public service leadership who must often rely on a range of communications equipment to transmit directives and orders. For instance, radio communications can be difficult to interpret and it is vital that a public service leader is skilled at both face to face interaction and communication across distances in difficult conditions otherwise lives may be put at risk and national security compromised.

Embraces responsibility

There can be no leadership without a willingness to take responsibility for the success and completion of a task or goal. Good leaders understand the weight of their duties and do not shirk them or transfer blame for failure elsewhere. As leaders rise through the ranks of organisations their responsibilities become greater and so do the penalties for failure. In rigidly hierarchical organisations such as the public services this is of particular importance. Leaders who shirk responsibility or blame others do not gain the respect and loyalty of those serving under them which may compromise operational effectiveness.

Altruistic

Altruism means putting the needs of others before your own needs. A good leader must consider the well being of their team even if it causes inconvenience. The position of leader means that in many circumstances you may be well placed to give yourself easy jobs and easy rewards while giving the less interesting or less popular jobs to others. This is not an appropriate way to behave; leaders must be seen as fair and even handed. If you misuse your power to favour yourself you will not have power for long.

Organised

Organisation is a key factor in all public service organisations. Leaders often have a tremendous amount of information to collect, interpret and utilise. They cannot do this without being highly organised and structured in the way in which they approach their job. This means attending meetings, storing data, monitoring the progress of large teams, small teams and individuals. If police duty rotas were not organised in a timely fashion, officers would not know when to attend work. If the security services failed to file intelligence reports correctly, crucial details of potential terrorist threats could be missed. If armed forces equipment is not regularly checked and repaired, combat effectiveness will be compromised.

Enthusiastic

Enthusiasm is contagious. If a leader is excited about a project and feels the thrill of a challenge then that can be communicated to all of the followers who can help him/her achieve that goal. An employee who has enthusiasm transmitted to them by an effective leader will work harder, longer and more creatively than one who has not. This has clear manpower and resource implications for the public services: an enthusiastic and dynamic team will be more efficient and have a better chance of achieving deadlines than those for whom work is boring or routine.

Knowledgable

Leaders are not expected to be experts in a chosen field as often they will have people in their team who fulfil that role. However, a leader should have a sound working knowledge of the principles which apply in achieving a goal. For instance, a Police Inspector is not expected to have a law degree but they must understand the major sections of the law that apply to the police such as The Police and Criminal Evidence Act (1984) or The Human Rights Act (1998). Equally a Customs and Excise Officer does not require a pharmaceutical qualification but they should understand what drugs look like, how they can be detected and the likely routes for entry into the UK. Being knowledgeable and up-to-date means a leader can guide and advise others and understand the obstacles and challenges faced by their team.

Assertive

Many people confuse being assertive with being aggressive. Aggression is never to be encouraged in a leader: it implies emotional immaturity and a loss of control and will quickly lose a leader respect and create a climate of fear and blame. Assertiveness is when a leader is clear about their authority and is not afraid to speak out to reinforce their rights as and when necessary. A timid leader will give a team little focus or direction and will be easily intimidated or forced to back down by more dominant members of the team. In public service organisations, discussions do have their place as a management tool but sometimes tasks simply need to be done without argument or questioning and an assertive leader is vital for this.

Consistent

A good leader is consistent in their approach to tasks and their manner with staff. Leaders should not display favouritism or show dislike openly and should avoid swings of mood, which can leave staff uncertain or wary. A good leader is a solid and stable rock which staff can revolve around and refer to while working towards goals. This does not preclude them being innovative or dynamic but it does mean they should remain level headed and professional at all times.

Case study – Inconsistent leadership

Adam is a 28-year-old Prison officer. He has been in the service for 5 years and has an exemplary service record. Recently he was transferred to a new prison and is becoming increasingly unhappy to the point at which he is considering leaving the service. The problem lies with his team leader, a female officer who has been recently promoted. Adam's concerns centre round the fact that she swings between being rude, sarcastic and uncooperative to being friendly and helpful. When a member of the team approaches her they never know what response they are likely to get and the team is falling into disarray and is in danger of failing to meet its objectives of keeping the prison safe and secure. Adam has noticed that the unprofessional side of the officer is never on display in the presence of senior officers. However the prisoners have begun to pick up on the internal tensions in the team and this has the potential to become a very volatile situation.

1 Why might the female prison officer be behaving in such an inconsistent manner?
2 How do you think the team members feel about such inconsistent leadership?
3 Why is consistency so important in public service leadership?
4 Describe and explain the methods by which Adam and his colleagues could respond to the situation?
5 If you were in Adam's position what would you do?

Sense of humour

The pressures and responsibilities of leadership are such that the ability to find humour in a situation can be a great stress relief technique. In addition, shared humour can bond a team and encourage co-operative and supportive relationships between colleagues on all levels of an organisational hierarchy.

Diplomacy

The job of a leader is not an easy one and there will be times when you have to communicate information or feedback that you would rather avoid or that you know would make someone unhappy. However, leadership is not a popularity contest, it is about doing what needs to be done whether it is a pleasant duty or not. Diplomacy and tact can go a long way in building supportive relationships and developing your team members through constructive criticism and appraisal.

Conflict resolution

Leaders must be skilled in the art of resolving conflict between all levels within an organisation and also between the organisation and external contacts. Leadership is often about balancing the needs of one group against the needs of another and keeping both groups happy.

Role model

In many circumstances a leader must also be a role model for followers or employees and this is particularly true in the public services. An army officer cannot discipline soldiers for uniform infractions if they don't wear a uniform correctly themselves. Equally a police inspector cannot discipline the lower ranks for failing to complete paperwork if they are in the same position themselves. A leader cannot ask followers to do something they are not prepared to do themselves. They must uphold the highest personal and professional standards if they expect their employee's to do the same.

Experience

In most cases, the more leadership experience a leader has, the more effective their skills will be. A paramedic with 15 years experience may lead a team at a multiple victim road traffic accident with more direction and knowledge than a paramedic with 6 months experience of leadership. This will be to the benefit of the victims, other attending public services and the paramedics themselves. However, experience alone is insufficient to make a good leader as individuals with many years experience can be slower and less responsive to change than more inexperienced leaders who are not influenced by views and methods which may be outdated.

Age

This quality of leadership is arguable. It is often said that as you mature you gather more experience and command more respect from followers. Alternatively, the dynamism and idealism of youth is infectious and can motivate entire armies, for instance Joan of Arc was only 19 when French troops under her leadership routed English Forces from France. The age of

leaders tends to be culturally specific. This means that in some societies age is valued and appreciated and in some cultures the same is true of youth.

Think about it

In groups select two leaders from any walk of life and debate their qualities in relation to the categories described above. Remember, you and your colleagues may not agree!

Theory into practice

You have to give feedback to a junior member of your team on their performance which has been far short of what is expected in your service. How would you approach and conduct this difficult task? What leadership qualities would you need to demonstrate?

Leaders of the 20th century

When considering leadership characteristics it is important to consider that even if an individual has all of the desired characteristics, he or she will not necessarily become a leader. They may not choose to or there may be others who are more suited to the role. It is also important to remember that individuals who do not have many of these skills can still emerge as powerful and effective leaders in certain circumstances. Times of personal, professional or national crises can generate leadership qualities in individuals which had previously lay dormant. We will now examine the profiles of the following successful and effective leaders:

- Winston Churchill
- Nelson Mandela
- Mahatma Ghandi
- Dr Martin Luther King
- Mother Theresa

Winston Churchill (1874–1965)

> *"It was the nation, that had the lion's heart. I had the luck to be called upon to give the roar"*
>
> Winston Churchill (1954)

Winston Churchill was born into a well-recognised military and political family on November 30th 1874. After serving as a military officer in three campaigns and also as a war correspondent he developed skills which set him on the road to greatness and many of the qualities which would help save Britain from Nazi invasion 40 years later were already emerging. These qualities included intense patriotism, an unshakeable belief in the greatness of Britain and her empire, inexhaustible energy, a strong physical constitution, a willingness to speak out on issues despite the fact that to do so would prove unpopular, meticulous organisational skills and an indomitable spirit which inspired and motivated others.

When the First World War broke out in 1914, Churchill was Lord of the Admiralty and as a consequence had a crucial role to play in the events of 1914–1918. The experiences that Winston had during the First World War achieved two things; firstly it educated him about political office and large-scale battle tactics and it helped him come to terms with his leadership failings.

Not all of Winston's military campaigns in World War I were successful. In 1915 he was instrumental in sending a naval and army force to Gallipoli in the Mediterranean. Gallipoli was a disaster and cost thousands of allied solders and sailors their lives. Admitting responsibility, Churchill resigned both political and military office; he would not regain his pre-war political status for over 25 years. Followers who make mistakes are often forgiven but for leaders the situation is much more serious. Failures by leaders last much longer in the minds of the public than successes.

It seemed that his troubled political years helped developed his leadership skills and mental faculties to such an extent that in the hour of

Britain's crisis at the beginning of World War II his skills and abilities matched the requirements of the situation better than his political contemporaries. During the 1930s Churchill was not a political bystander; he spoke out vigorously on the rise of totalitarian regimes such as the Nazi party which was developing across Europe at the time. This ensured that when confrontation between Britain and Germany inevitably arose, Churchill stood out as a statesman who had fought against the threat of Nazism for many years while other politicians had tried to appease Adolf Hitler.

Winston Churchill

The nation felt they had found a politician who understood the situation and whom they could trust. Churchill was again appointed to head up the admiralty office on the same day that war officially broke out on September 3rd 1939.

Norway fell to the Germans in April 1940 and was quickly followed by the fall of Belgium and The Netherlands in May. Neville Chamberlain, the Prime Minister at that time lost the confidence of parliament and resigned. It was clear at that point that Churchill had the skills and spirit to unite and lead the nation. He was installed as Prime Minister to a coalition government headed by a war cabinet of 5 leading statesmen. The situation Churchill inherited from Chamberlain was desperate. After the fall of France, Britain stood without substantial allies and faced most of 1940 under German air bombardment and the constant threat of Nazi invasion. Churchill used his personal skills and patriotism to motivate and inspire the British public to endure the hardships they faced with fortitude and resourcefulness. Churchill also used extensive diplomacy and communication to forge alliances between nations with differing political and social philosophies. Churchill was instrumental in holding together the communist Soviet Union and capitalist US in a firm and dynamic alliance, which eventually prevailed over the axis powers.

Churchill's leadership qualities were present from the early days of his military and political career but it is fair to say that some of the decisions he made in his early career did not enhance his status as a leader. He only achieved real greatness under a particular set of circumstances. His obituary written upon his death in January 1965 notes the following:

> "His career was divided by the year 1940. If he had died a little before that he would've been remembered as an eloquent, formidable, erratic Statesman. An outstanding personage, but one who was not to be put in the class of such contemporaries as Lloyd George or even Arthur Balfour. Yet all the qualities with which he was to fascinate the world were already formed and matured. They awaited their hour for use"

The hour came with the declaration of war and Churchill rose to the occasion with the nation alongside him. Despite his many and varied leadership skills it is unlikely that he would have risen to greatness without World War II. In this brief profile of a leader it is clear to see that the circumstances Churchill found himself in allowed his best abilities to dominate in a way they might not otherwise have done.

> ### Theory into practice
> Describe the leadership qualities that Winston Churchill had.

Mohandas Karamchand Ghandi (1869–1948)

Mohandas Ghandi was born into a devout Hindu family in Gurjerat, Western India on October 2nd 1859. He studied law at University College, London where many of the leadership qualities he would later demonstrate began to be developed. After qualifying as a lawyer he returned to India where he worked hard to establish a legal practice of his own.

Ghandi's legal practice was not a great success and in 1893 he was employed as a legal advisor to an Indian company, which had interests and investments in South Africa. This change in employment necessitated Ghandi's move to South Africa where he represented the Indian community against the system of racial discrimination called 'apartheid' which denied rights to non-white individuals. He was shocked and appalled at the widespread denial of civil rights to Indians living in South Africa and spent the next 21 years fighting oppression.

During his work in South Africa he coined the term 'satyagraha' which in Sanskrit means truth and firmness, to describe his technique of non-violent civil disobedience, which proved so effective. His leadership and vision encouraged the South African government to make several concessions to his demands and by 1914 they had done so, including recognising Indian marriages and the abolition of poll tax. Ghandi returned to India in 1914 but the time he spent in South Africa was an effective apprenticeship for the leadership challenges he would face at home. During his time in South Africa Ghandi demonstrated a variety of leadership skills.

- Commitment – he served the Indian community for a period of 21 years, only returning home when substantial changes had been won.

● Action – Ghandi did not simply speak out against injustice. Using the principle of 'Satyagraha' he motivated and organised collective action and led these actions from the front. Although he was imprisoned and beaten on many occasions, the actions he took as leader did not waver despite such difficulties.

● Service – Ghandi's time in South Africa was a textbook example of Greenleafs (1977) principle of servant leadership. Ghandi did not lead for any other reason than to serve the needs of the oppressed Indian population.

Mohandas Ghandi

However notable and remarkable Ghandi's achievements in South Africa were, it is for his leadership in India that he is most revered. Returning home in 1914 Ghandi became involved in the campaign for Indian independence and home rule. The British colonisation of India was exploitative and often brutal and the living standards of millions of ordinary Indian citizens were very poor. Using the experience he had gained from South Africa he began campaigning for Indian freedom. The British government was not pleased at the thought of losing such a rich and productive colony and in 1919 the British

Parliament passed the Rowlatt Acts, which gave the Indian colonial authorities emergency powers to deal with the growing revolutionary threat.

Indians reacted against the Rowlatt Acts and Ghandi's principle of non-violent resistance spread to millions across India. After the massacre of thousands of Indians in various atrocities by the British, Ghandi became increasingly instrumental in the organisation of non-violent civil disobedience campaigns such as mass resignations of Indian officials and symbolic marches against corrupt laws. Other techniques he advocated in his philosophy of non-violence were 'sit ins', which blocked streets and disrupted the running of the colony by the British.

In a predominantly Hindu nation he was seen as a spiritual symbol and the name 'Mahatma' meaning 'Great Soul' was conferred on him. Ghandi was often in and out of prison during the 1930s and 40s but he never lost sight of his aims and he never lost compassion for those he served.

Ghandi's ultimate triumph came in 1947 when India was finally granted independence from British rule. This profile shows a leader with great compassion, strength of will, wisdom, experience and spirituality. His ideology of non-violent resistance became a blueprint for many resistance groups worldwide and he was an exemplary role model not only for his own followers but also for many other leaders who had their own battles with oppression to fight and win.

Nelson Rolihlahla Mandela (1918–)

"I have fought against white domination and I have fought against black domination. I have cherished the ideal of a democratic and free society in which all persons live together in harmony and with equal opportunities. It is an ideal which I hope to live for and to achieve, but if needs be, it is an ideal for which I am prepared to die"

Nelson Mandela (1964)

Mandela was born in the Transkei region of South Africa on July 18th 1918. He was the son of the principle councillor to a ruling African Chief and upon his father's death his guardianship fell to the Chief who intended to groom the young Mandela to assume a position of respect and influence. Deciding upon a career as a lawyer he went to university where he became active in political issues and was elected onto the student's representative council. This interest in political issues was to last a lifetime eventually costing Mandela a 27-year prison term.

After qualifying as a lawyer, Mandela set up a legal practice in Johannesburg where he tried to deal with the appalling consequences of the system of apartheid which existed in South Africa. For many decades an oppressive system of laws and regulations had limited the involvement of the majority of black South Africans in the politics and governance of their country and concentrated wealth and resources in the hands of a white minority. The cases Mandela saw there made him become increasingly active in the anti apartheid movement as every case he dealt with reminded him forcibly of the humiliation and suffering of black South Africans. In 1942 Mandela joined the African National Congress (ANC) and along with other young Africans he began to change the movement

Nelson Mandela

into a more responsive and dynamic organisation. At first the tactics of the organisation were peaceful and non violent and revolved around boycotts, strikes and civil disobedience and this is reflected in the leadership qualities that Mandela demonstrated at the time. He showed respect to people and was given respect in return which demonstrates elements of both charismatic and transformational leadership. At this time he was also developing skills such as self confidence, communication, organisation, and very clearly led by example.

Mandela's legal practice began to become a problem for the government and they tried to block its work by attempting to have Mandela disbarred from the legal profession and by trying to relocate his Johannesburg offices to a more rural setting where his clients would not be able to see him during working hours. Mandela resisted these moves and became more militant as a result.

It was during the 1950s that Mandela began to move from a non-violent stance to a more radical approach. Seeing that passive resistance was not achieving political goals, Mandela and the ANC began a more aggressive campaign of disorder using techniques such as sabotage against economic and government installations to try and achieve their aims of a democratic and free society. After the ANC was declared illegal in 1960 he became a rebel against government authority and the military leader of armed resistance movements.

One of Mandela's greatest leadership qualities was the ability to adapt his style of leadership according to circumstances and at no point was this more important than the 27 years he spent in prison after being given a life sentence for sabotage in 1964. During his imprisonment he became a symbol of the struggle against apartheid and became an inspiration to millions of people throughout the world. Mandela continued his fight against prejudice and discrimination whilst in prison. He refused several offers of freedom made to him by the South African government in return for a commitment of peace and non involvement arguing that only free men can negotiate. He took upon himself a cloak of moral dignity and did not turn his back on his vision despite tremendous temptation to do so. Mandela was released from prison on February 11th 1990 and immediately resumed working towards the goals of a free and democratic society.

In 1991 he was elected leader of the ANC and suspended its armed struggle in an attempt to win public support and reassure the fears of white South Africans. He was awarded the Noble Peace Prize in 1993 and became the first democratically elected President of South Africa in 1994. Although many racial difficulties and inequalities still exist in South Africa, apartheid is now gone and the rebuilding of inter-racial relations is already underway which is in large part due to the visionary and unwavering leadership of Nelson Mandela.

Mother Theresa (1910–1997)

Mother Theresa was born in Skopje in present day Macedonia to parents of Albanian descent on August 27th 1910 and her real name was Gonxhe Agnes Bojaxhiu. At the age of eighteen she became a nun, joining the Irish Catholic order of the Sisters of Loreto, which operated missions that gave service to the poorest sections of India. She was posted to Calcutta in India where she initially worked as a teacher, educating children in geography and history in a Catholic school. She learned Hindu and Bengali to help her perform her duties and aid those she taught. This demonstrates an understanding of the need to appreciate and value the culture of others and demonstrates an aspect of her spiritual and compassionate leadership. She understood that every individual can make a difference in the lives of another and she inspired many others to follow this principle of giving of themselves in order to aid others.

In 1930 when Gonxhe was 20 she was given the name Theresa to signify that she had left her own identity behind and had begun a new life of service to God. Eventually she became principal of the school where she had taught. However admirable her life had been so far it wasn't until 1946 that her real calling came to the fore and the

inspirational leadership skills that she became so admired for began to appear.

While being treated for tuberculosis, Theresa received a calling to help the poorest of the poor. Consequently she left her position as school principal and began to work in the slums of Calcutta with dying and desperate individuals who held little hope for a change in their circumstances. In 1950 she established her own religious order called the Missionaries of Charity whose role it was to help all individuals in the slums. This included the establishment of hospitals for the sick, hospices for the dying and orphanages for children to provide care for those who had been abandoned or had lost their parents.

In the years that followed she inspired others to join her order and work with her to provide services such as mobile health clinics, food kitchens, leper hospitals, addiction assistance and health services to prostitutes. One of Mother Theresa's greatest achievements was to inspire others to help groups in society which had largely been ignored or abused.

Many of the slums inhabitants saw Mother Theresa as a living saint because of her work and in 1979 she received the Nobel Piece Prize for her services to the poor. Her order had grown immensely by then and had spread throughout India and across the world having almost 2,000 nuns and 120,000 volunteers working in almost 200 different locations. There are many examples of her bravery and compassion for societies

Mother Theresa

forgotten members. For instance, in 1982 she negotiated a temporary ceasefire in war torn Beirut in the Middle East so that over 35 mentally ill children could be rescued from the conflict.

She died on September 5th 1997. Theresa was a quiet leader who did not become heavily involved in political struggle and certainly never advocated violence. She dedicated herself to a task and never wavered in her devotion to it. She made sacrifices and encouraged others to join her in fulfilling her duties. Not all leaders are high profile individuals; often much can be achieved through continuous peaceful, non-threatening work which does not undermine the work of governments.

Theory into practice

Which theory of leadership does this profile of Mother Theresa most exemplify? Can you think of any other leaders who demonstrate similar qualities?

Dr Martin Luther King (1929–1968)

"I have a dream that my four children will one day live in a nation where they will not be judged on the colour of their skin but by the content of their character".

Martin Luther King (1963)

Martin Luther King Jnr was born on January 15th 1929 in Atlanta, Georgia to a strongly religious family. After attending university he gained a doctorate in theology by the age of 26. During his university studies he became familiar with the struggles and works of Mahatma Ghandi whose non-violent activism had proved so successful in achieving Indian liberation from the British. Martin Luther King was to adhere to these principles throughout his long civil rights crusade.

Upon completion of his doctorate King returned to his home city of Atlanta to begin work as a baptist minister like his father before him. It was at this time that he became involved in the fight

to end segregation and bring equal rights to all citizens of the US regardless of creed or colour. One of the most notable examples of King's leadership are the bus boycotts in 1955 and 1956. On December 11th 1965 Rosa Parks refused to give up her seat on a bus to a white passenger. The bus driver ordered her to move, but she remained seated. She was then arrested and taken to court where she was convicted of disobeying the cities segregation rules and fined $10 plus court costs. The same afternoon Dr King was elected President of the Montgomery Improvement Association. As leader he urged all the black citizens of Montgomery to boycott the bus system and not to use them again until the bus companies halted the practice of discriminatory seating. It took eleven months but finally the non-violent protests were successful and the bus companies backed down.

Dr Martin Luther King

Dr King was unafraid to speak out against injustice even at great personal cost and he along with other civil rights leaders galvanised America into change. The Nobel Piece Prize was awarded to him in 1964 due to his unwavering belief in the power of change without bloodshed. However on April 4th 1968 he was assassinated on the balcony of his hotel room. He was thirty-nine years old and left a widow and four children.

After news of Dr King's death spread, the African-American community manifested their grief at his passing with violence. There were spontaneous riots in over 130 cities across the US where 20,000 arrests were made and 45 people lost their lives. The Civil Rights Bill that King had fought so long and hard for was passed only a few days later changing the context of race relations in America for generations of African Americans to come.

Theory into practice

What personal qualities did Martin Luther King have which helped him emerge a national civil rights leader and how did he motivate his followers?

Why did Dr King's assassination cause such widespread anger and grief?

Theory into practice

Think of a leader you have admired in your own life. List the qualities that they brought to their role and describe how they made that person a better leader.

The emergence and selection of leaders

Leaders can emerge in many different ways:

Birth

Ruling Monarchs are selected on the basis of the birth order of the male heirs. The eldest son of a monarch will inherit the throne and become King automatically. If there are no male heirs then the birth order of the female heirs will be used. In addition to the monarchy, many tribal societies have used heredity as a basis for leadership selection with tribal leadership passing from generation to generation within the same family.

The advantage of a system of leadership by birth is that a society or group has consistency over a period of time and the next leader is groomed to perform the leadership role from birth. The disadvantages are that no matter how qualified and able you are to lead, you will never have the opportunity unless you are born into it. In addition, this system of selection takes no account of the fact that a very unsuitable individual may one day hold immense influence.

Queen Elizabeth II's Coronation

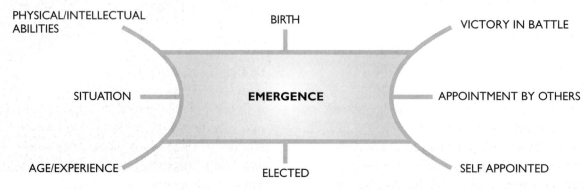

Figure 3.14 How leaders emerge

Appointed by others

It may be that an individual is appointed to a position of leadership due to their exceptional personal skills and abilities. Alternatively, it may be that no one else is willing to do the job and it is given to an individual by default or it may be that an individual is appointed as leader because they have used fear and intimidation against those with the power to appoint them.

Being appointed by others is a traditional technique used in the public services where appointment by others is generally on the basis of merit and experience. In theory, this ensures that the best people to lead will eventually be given the chance to do so. The problem with this technique is that often 'who' a person knows rather than 'what' they know can influence whether they are chosen for a position of responsibility.

Self-appointed

These are individuals who see a need for their skills and step in to fulfil a leadership role. These leaders tend to be very forceful and dominant in their dealings with others or in how they approach a situation. Sometimes self appointed leaders can be a definite advantage in getting previously stagnant tasks completed or in shaking up a complacent set of employees to encourage them to be competitive and motivated. However, self appointed leaders have been through no selection procedure and have no checks or balances on their behaviour which means they can do just about anything they like. This is often most clearly seem in dictatorships where a single individual or regime maintains the balance of power through fear and intimidation.

Elected

Elected leaders are chosen in a vote conducted by the people they will serve. Generally those wanting to be leader will put forward a manifesto which describes the things they will do if they are elected and the voters read it and decide who they think would best serve their interests. This is a system used widely to elect individuals to power in government and international organisations and when it is run fairly and democratically, the will of the people should prevail. The public are more likely to respect and accede to the wishes of a leader that they themselves have chosen.

However, this method of selection has many flaws. In some countries, elections are not conducted in the democratic manner that we know in the UK. For example, certain people are not allowed to vote or votes are 'lost' before being counted. Equally, unscrupulous candidates may intimidate voters into choosing them with threats of violence or punishment or frighten them so much that they decide not to vote at all. This can happen even in so-called secret ballots where no one is supposed to know how an individual voted. The fact of the matter is that if an unscrupulous candidate or

Voting on polling day

government wishes to influence an election they can, such as organising the transport of the ballot boxes to be counted or counting the votes themselves.

One of the major difficulties with elections is that often the most popular candidate will win regardless of how suitable they are for the job. Since candidates are made popular or unpopular primarily by media coverage of their actions it may be that the candidate who has the support of the media will win. In some instances this is because the controlling politician owns elements of the media. For example, Silvio Berlusconi the Prime Minister of Italy has a controlling interest of 98% of the nations mass media.

Situation

Sometimes a leader will emerge due to a unique set of factors which suit their skills and abilities at a particular time in their lives. It may be that an individual has expert knowledge or prior experience which sets them apart from other people or it may be an issue which they feel passionately about.

These leaders tend to perform extremely well in the situation they were created leader for, but may lack leadership abilities when the situation changes. They are not all round leaders and are often replaced once they have performed the duty they were created leader for.

Victory in battle

Historically, this was a very common way of selecting a leader. Warriors were brave and fearless and organised the destruction of those harming a community. This made them a natural choice to lead but prowess in battle does not necessarily translate to organising a community of men, women and children or a large organisation with many levels. However, victory is seen as a test of innate abilities such as strength of character and the will to motivate others, all of which are desirable in a leader.

It may surprise you to know that a modified version of this leadership selection technique is still prominent in today's corporate and business organisations and also in many of our public services. If an army officer runs a particularly successful military campaign they are likely to receive commendations and promotions. Similarly, in the police service an officer who heads up a particularly successful anti-crime operation substantially improves his or her chances of progressing up the leadership ladder.

Age/experience

In some societies and organisations, leadership is decided on the basis of age and length of service. This means that as you age you automatically become more senior to those who are younger than you. This system has the advantage of placing people in leadership positions who are experienced and mature and for whom the whole community can respect. This type of leadership selection may be culturally specific and found in societies which value the knowledge of elders such as Japan.

However it could be argued that wisdom does not necessarily come with age, it comes primarily from experience and it is possible that many younger members of a community can have vast amounts of life experience which may equal or even surpass the older generation. In addition, circumstances constantly change and it is often younger people who are quicker to adapt and respond to change.

Physical/intellectual abilities

Some leaders are selected due to a series of physical and intellectual challenges which they must demonstrate they can overcome. This ensures that individuals with physical prowess and intelligence have the opportunity to develop their leadership skills. This system of selection is very popular in the public services where at many levels of advancement from recruitment to promotion you may be required to complete a series of tests evaluating your literacy, memory, expert knowledge and communication skills. One example of this kind of test is The Police Initial Recruitment Test.

However, the ability to pass tests does not necessarily make a good leader as the strongest and most intelligent person in the world may lack the motivational and leadership skills which are essential in running a large organisation.

Key concepts

1 Leaders may emerge in many ways.

2 All methods of selection have advantages and disadvantages.

3 The most popular public service selection method is appointment by others.

4 The media can have significant influence on the selection of public leaders.

5 Some methods of selection such as age are culturally specific and may occur more in some societies than others.

Personal leadership qualities

The public services are hierarchical organisations built firmly on rank structures and promotion opportunities and it is likely that at some point in your future career you will be looking for an opportunity to move into a leadership role. In order to be ready for the challenges that leadership responsibility brings, you must be aware of your own leadership and motivational strengths and be prepared to overcome your weaknesses.

Complete the following questionnaire by ticking the appropriate box 1–5

1 = I do not have this skill at the moment

2 = I am trying to develop this skill

3 = I am ok at this skill

4 = I am good at this skill

5 = I am very good at this skill

Personal leadership questionnaire					
Adaptability	**1**	**2**	**3**	**4**	**5**
I can respond well to timetable changes at college					
I can respond well to last minute shift changes at work					
I cope well in new and unfamiliar situations					
When new information is given to me I incorporate it immediately into what I already know					
If I am given a new role I do not complain I simply do the job to the best of my ability					

Communication	1	2	3	4	5
I perform well in presentations					
I am good at role plays					
I say what I mean and mean what I say					
I can communicate to a range of people from a variety of backgrounds					
I always listen to what others say to me					
I have a good attention span					
I am familiar with and use electronic communication methods					
I can give effective briefings to groups					
I can provide constructive feedback to individuals					
If I don't understand something I will ask questions					
If I know that I am struggling I seek help					

Responsibility	1	2	3	4	5
When something is my fault I admit it					
I volunteer for tasks that I don't have to do					
I understand that when I say I'll do something it means I have to do it					
I do not shirk my duties by making excuses as to why things aren't done					
I keep a firm hold on tasks that I am jointly responsible for with others					
In group tasks I understand that the responsibility I have is for the whole task; not just my bit of it					
I do not let other things distract me from my responsibilities					

Organisation	1	2	3	4	5
I always take to college or work everything that I need					
I arrive on time at college or work					
I plan time to complete work I am given to do at home					
I sort and file all of the information I receive as soon as I receive it					
If I am asked for a piece of information I usually know where to find it					
I always meet set deadlines					

Enthusiam	1	2	3	4	5
I try to be enthusiastic about a task even when I do not want to do it					
I do not moan or complain about tasks I am given					
I encourage others to be enthusiastic					
I give the same time and attention to tasks I don't like as I would with tasks I do like					

Assertiveness	1	2	3	4	5
I feel able to say no if I don't want to do something					
If I am in a leadership role I feel comfortable expressing my authority					
I am not easily intimidated by others					
I speak up if I disagree with something					
I will intervene if I see someone being bullied or abused					

Conflict resolution	1	2	3	4	5
I am able to avoid conflict by being professional and not personal					
When two of my colleagues disagree I am able to help them reach a compromise					
I do not take sides in the conflict of others					
I do not cause conflict by being rude or aggressive					
I do not bring my emotions into conflicts					

Consistency	1	2	3	4	5
I am not 'moody' with colleagues					
I do not let my personal problems interfere with how I treat people					
I am always professional and approachable					
I do not treat some people differently than others					

Figure 3.15 Personal leadership questionnaire

Assessing your results

Section	Max score	Your score
Adaptability	25	
Communication	55	
Responsibility	35	
Organisation	30	
Enthusiasm	20	
Assertiveness	25	
Conflict resolution	25	
Consistency	20	
Total score	**235**	

Calculate your results for each section by adding together the numbers 1–5 that you ticked for each question and entering the results in the table opposite. The last step is to add up all of your section scores to make a grand total.

Making sense of your results

Score 47–84   Your leadership skills are undeveloped at present. There are many areas for you to begin to improve and work on if you hope to lead groups of individuals.

Score 85–122   Your leadership skills are beginning to develop but there are still many areas for you to work on if you want to be effective as a leader.

Score 123–138 Your leadership skills are beginning to establish and your weaknesses are fairly evenly balanced by your strengths. This is a good foundation to build upon and improve.

Score 159–196 Your leadership skills are developed and your strengths outbalance your weaknesses. You have the makings of a sound leader if you continue to develop these skills.

Score 197–235 Your existing leadership skills are of a very good standard and although you may have a couple of weak areas you are well suited to a leadership role. However, you need to build on these skills with practical experience, which will enable you to identify your weaknesses and overcome them.

In addition, if you look at each area of leadership assessed you will see clearly that there are some areas in which your skills are less developed than others. These are the areas which you need to consider improving if you are to be a well balanced and effective leader.

Application of leadership

Case study 1

You and 3 colleagues have been asked to prepare a 15-minute presentation on theories of motivation in your leadership unit. You are keen to get a distinction grade for this piece of work but you are not sure that your colleagues have the same commitment to the project that you do. The deadline is tight and you only have a few days to get organised.

1 How will you decide who leads the group?

2 How will you divide the work up?

3 How will you record and monitor the progress of each individual and the project as a whole?

4 Who has responsibility to ensure the project is completed on time?

5 What techniques could you use to motivate your fellow group members?

6 What style of leadership would be the most effective with this group?

Case study 2

You and 4 friends are driving to the cinema on a rural road at night. As you come round a bend you see that a car has overturned in the middle of the road and 2 of the occupants are unconscious inside. A further occupant is conscious but hysterical. You and one of your friends are qualified first aiders and another friend has a mobile phone.

1 How do ensure your own safety and the safety of your group as you deal with the incident?

2 How would you summon help?

3 How would you motivate your friends to help when they are scared and upset?

4 How would you deal with the people in the overturned car?

5 What style of leadership would be most effective in this situation?

Case study 3

You attend a gym class with a friend and while you are getting changed you see that your friend's back is covered in bruises, welts and small burns. You are shocked and surprised but when you ask your friend about it she tells you its nothing to be concerned about.

1 Would you choose to pursue the matter further or be reassured by your friend's comments?

2 Do you have a responsibility for your friend's safety?

3 Would you discuss the situation with anyone else in order to seek advice and guidance?

4 How would you encourage and motivate your friend to confide in you and seek help?

5 How would you avoid conflict with your friend during this process?

Improving leadership

Action plan

Once you have identified the areas of your leadership qualities which require development the next step is to plan how the changes can be made and to monitor your progress towards these changes. One of the most effective ways of achieving this is by using an action plan.

An action plan is a method used to help you turn areas of weaknesses into areas of strength and to help you monitor the process so that you know how far you have progressed towards your goals. For example, if your area of weakness was a failure to brief fellow team members effectively, then your objective would be to become effective in that skill by using methods such as briefing notes and providing written information.

There are several things, which ought to be present in a personal action plan:

- identify the problem
- set an objective to achieve
- detail how you intend to meet your objectives
- describe the support you need from others
- list any resources you might need access to
- dates for review or completion.

You should make a point of reviewing and revising your action plan regularly in order to monitor your progress in achieving your aim to become a more effective leader.

Appraisal

Another similar method of personal development is a process called appraisal which is widely used among the public services. It is an organisational version of a personal action plan which is usually conducted by your immediate line manager.

During the appraisal process you will be given constructive feedback on your performance and encouraged to discuss your career aspirations. Conducted effectively, appraisal gives you the opportunity to identify your strengths and weaknesses, to set performance targets and to identify training needs and career development.

Identifies strengths and weaknesses

↓

Ensures that the role you fulfil makes use of your identified strengths

↓

Identifies how your weaknesses could be overcome by training

Figure 3.16 Structure of an appraisal

Case study – Appraisal

Hazel Chang is a new recruit to the probation service and in the 6 months she has served so far she doesn't feel she has made a major impact to the role. She is concerned that her supervisor thinks very little of her and this is causing Hazel to lose confidence in her abilities and make mistakes. The issue of paperwork in particular is causing Hazel a great deal of distress and she is falling further and further behind. Hazel's six monthly appraisal is due shortly and she wants to make the most of it to improve her performance and rebuild her confidence.

1 How should Hazel prepare for her appraisal?
2 What questions should she ask when she is in her appraisal?
3 What support should she ask for from her supervisor?
4 How should she take the constructive criticism given to her by her supervisor on aspects of her job performance?
5 What should she do to improve her performance after the appraisal?

Theory into practice

Get a colleague or tutor to give you a mock appraisal. Then draw up an action plan based on their comments with a view to improving your leadership skills. This may be particularly useful as often others see us very differently from how we see ourselves.

Theory into practice

Evaluate the personal action plan example below. Do you think that the proposed action shown will help to achieve the set targets? Would your action points have been the same if you were in a similar situation?

Personal action plan

Area/s for development:

I'm not meeting set deadlines for my college work and when I do meet them the work is often being returned to me because it is incomplete. I am also late most days for college so I am missing some of my lessons which means I don't understand some of the things I am asked to do.

Targets to achieve:

1 To meet deadlines for my coursework.

2 To make sure my work is complete before I hand it in.

3 Get to college on time.

Actions required by you:

- Speak to my tutor and explain that I work for 20 hours a week at a local call centre and this is affecting my performance.
- Speak to my work supervisor and see if my hours can be reduced from 20 to 12 hours per week.
- Discuss money with my parents and see if they would be willing to pay for my bus fares and lunches so that I can reduce my hours at work.
- Spend additional free time on assignment work and create an assignment timetable so that I know which pieces of work are due in at what time.
- Speak to my tutor about getting additional notes if I am late.

Actions required by others:

- Tutor to be supportive while I am trying to sort out my working hours by providing me with information that I miss in class.
- Work supervisor to be sympathetic to the fact that college has to come first and help me reduce my hours.
- Parents to understand that I need some money for college and that I would be prepared to do chores at home to earn it if necessary.

Resources

MONEY!!!!

Regular tutorials with my tutor.

Dates for review/completion

I will review the situation every two weeks to see the progress I have made and change the action plan if needed. Dates: 30th Jan, 15th Feb, 1st Mar, 15th Mar

By the 15th March I should have achieved my targets completely.

Figure 3.17 An example of a personal action plan

End of unit questions

1   What are the principles of 'great man theory'?

2   When did situational theories of leadership begin to emerge?

3   Who developed the concept of servant leadership?

4   List five benefits of effective leadership.

5   List five costs of ineffective leadership.

6   What is a leadership style?

7   List and describe four commonly used leadership styles.

8   What is motivation?

9   List five factors which may encourage motivation.

10 Who developed the 'hierarchy of needs?'

11 Describe the principles of McGregor's theory X and theory Y.

12 What are hygiene factors?

13 What does ERG stand for in Aldefer's theory of motivation?

14 What might be signs of dissatisfaction in a workforce?

15 List and describe five qualities of leadership.

16 What were Winston Churchill's primary leadership qualities?

17 Why did the US civil rights movement require leaders like Dr King?

18 Why was Mohandas Ghandi given the name 'Mahatma'?

19 List five ways in which leaders emerge.

20 What is an appraisal?

Resources

Adair, J. *Effective Teambuilding,* London: Gower 1986

Adair, J. *Great Leaders,* Guildford: Talbot Adair Press 1989

Adair, J. *Effective Leadership,* London: Gower 1993

Adair, J. *Effective Motivation,* London: Macmillan 1996

Alderfer, C. *Existence, Relatedness and Growth: Human Needs in an Organisational Setting,* Free Press 1972

Bass, B. *Leadership and Performance Beyond Expectations,* London: Free Press 1985

Bird, C. *Social Psychology,* New York: Appleton Century 1940

Boles, H. and Davenport, J. *Introduction to Educational Leadership,* Harper and Row 1975

Burns, J.M. *Leadership,* New York: Harper and Row 1978

Copeland, N. *Psychology and the Soldier,* Pennsylvania: Military Service Publishing 1942

Fiedler, F.E. *A Theory of Leadership Effectiveness,* New York: McGraw-Hill 1967

Gardner, J.W. *On Leadership,* New York: Free Press 1993

Goleman, D. *What Makes A Leader,* Harvard Business Review, Nov-Dec 1998

Greenleaf, R.K. *The Servant as Leader,* Indianapolis: Robert Greenleaf Centre 1970

Heller, R. *Motivating People,* London: Dorling-Kindersley 1998

Hersey, P. et al (8th Ed) *Management of Organisational Behaviour,* Englewood Cliffs: Prentice Hall 2000

Herzberg, F. et al *The Motivation to Work,* New York: Wiley 1959

Jenkins, W. *A Review of Leadership Studies With Particular Reference To Military Problems,* Psychology Bulletin, 44, 54–79 1947

Kotter, J. *Leading Change,* Harvard Business School Press 1996

Machiavelli, N. *The Prince,* London: Penguin 1961

Maslow, A. *Motivation and Personality,* New York: Harper and Row 1954

Maslow, A. *Maslow on Management',* New York: Wiley 1998

McGregor, D. *The Human Side of Enterprise,* New York; McGraw-Hill 1960

Pegg, M. *Positive Leadership,* Gloucester: Management 2000 1997

Plato (Introduction by Lee, D.) *The Republic* London: Penguin 2003

Roebuck, C. *Effective Leadership,* London: Marshall Publishing 1999

Rost, J. *Leadership For the Twenty-First Century,* New York: Praeger 1991

Seeman, M. *On the Meaning of Alienation,* American Sociology Review 24, 783–791 1959

Spears, L. *Insights on Leadership,* London: John Wiley 1997

Stodgill, R.M. *Personal Factors Associated With Leadership: A Survey of the Literature,* Journal of Psychology, 25, 35–71 1948

Stodgill, R.M. *Handbook of Leadership: A Survey of Theory and Research,* New York: Free Press 1977

Sun Tzu (Translated by Sawyer, R.) *The Art of War,* London: Harper Collins 1994

Assessment activities

This section describes what you must do to obtain a pass grade for this unit.

A merit or distinction grate may be awarded if your work demonstrates a deeper understanding of the topics and is of a higher quality. The highlighted sentences indicate the quality of work expected at Merit and distinction level.

Assessment methods

A number of assessment strategies may be used in order to achieve the learning outcomes, such as oral presentations, group discussions, written assignments, research projects and role-plays, or a combination of these. It would be a good idea, though it is not essential, to use a variety of methods in order to develop different skills. What is important, however, is that you understand and comply with the key words that may be specified in the grading criteria. For example, if you are asked to 'analyse' something, then make sure that you do not merely describe it. Similarly, if you are asked to 'evaluate' something, then make sure you do not merely summarise it.

Key words

Here are some key words that are often used for grading criteria – make sure you understand the differences between them.

Examine	To look at a subject closely in order to understand it and improve your knowledge
Consider	This means to think about and weigh up a subject
Explain	This means to make something clear and set out the arguments
Analyse	This means to look at a subject closely and interpret or evaluate your findings. Perhaps outlining the pro's and con's of a situation or suggesting changes and improvements
Describe	This means to say what something is like, it is a factual account of how something is or how it appears.
Compare	This means to look at the similarities between two or more objects or theories.

Assessment tasks

Using the materials within this unit and your own research, carry out the following tasks.

Task 1

Learning outcome 1 – Examine styles of leadership and their effectiveness within the public services

Outline the different styles of leadership and describe the use of at least two different styles in two of the public services.

To obtain a merit grade, you should compare and contrast at least two different styles of leadership and their use in at least two of the public services.

To obtain a distinction grade, you should assess the effectiveness of at least two different styles of leadership and justify their use in two of the public services.

Suggestion for Task 1

This could be conducted very effectively as a group role-play. Create a situation whereby you are on a talk show which is examining styles of leadership. Each member of the audience represents a different service and has a different leadership style. Members of the audience discuss their style and how it is useful in the public services. To obtain a higher grade, you could follow this up with a written piece which details the similarities and differences between each style and assesses the effectiveness of each style.

Task 2

Learning outcome 2 – Evaluate theories of motivation and their relevance to the public services.

Describe three theories of motivation and relate their relevance to at least two public services.

To obtain a merit grade, you should *analyse* and contrast different motivation theories as applied to at least two of the public services.

To obtain a distinction grade, you should draw conclusions relating to the different applications of motivation theories in at least two of the public services.

Suggest and explain three appropriate methods of maximising the productivity of groups in the public services.

Suggestion for Task 2: Small-group presentation

Describe the following three theories of motivation and decide how relevant they would be if they were used in the police services and the army.

- Maslow's Hierarchy of Needs
- McGregor's Theory X and Theory Y
- Herzbergs's Hygiene Factors.

Using the same two public services (police and army) suggest and explain three methods of maximising productivity within groups in these public services.

To obtain a higher grade, ensure that your presentation also analyses and contrasts the three theories described above and draws conclusions as to how each theory could be applied to the two public services that have been specified.

Task 3

Learning outcome 3 – Identify and assess qualities of leadership and their relevance to the public services

Identify qualities of leaders in public services explaining how these are applied in at least four different situations.

> To obtain a merit grade, you should establish and analyse different ways in which leaders are selected or emerge.

> To obtain a distinction, you should critically evaluate the selection process of a public service leader.

Suggestion for Task 3: Report

Using the information contained within this unit, write a report which identifies at least ten different qualities which are useful for leaders to possess and consider how they would be used in the following situations:

- a major incident
- an appraisal of a junior member of staff
- organising a shift system which accommodates the needs of individuals
- reporting to senior ranks about an ongoing problem.

To obtain a higher grade you should also analyse the various ways that leaders are selected or emerge and critically evaluate the selection procedure of a senior public service officer such as a police inspector or army officer.

Task 4

Learning outcome 4 – Investigate personal leadership qualities

Undertake a review of personal leadership qualities.

> To obtain a merit grade, you should analyse personal leadership qualities and identify needs for personal development.

> To obtain a distinction grade you should *monitor and evaluate* personal leadership developments in relation to specified targets and objectives.

Suggestion for Task 4: individual project work

Using the questionnaire in this chapter assess your personal leadership qualities.

To achieve a higher grade you should analyse the results of your leadership questionnaire highlighting your strengths and weaknesses and create an action plan which sets targets and objectives for you to achieve in order to improve your leadership skills. You need to monitor this action plan regularly.

THE UNIFORMED SERVICES

Introduction to Unit 8

This unit looks at the work of the uniformed public services and the career opportunities that exist within these services. The conditions of service for some of the services are outlined as well as opportunities for career development, either by promotion or specialisation. You will also learn about the range of skills required when applying for a career in the public services as well as the selection process.

Assessment

Throughout the unit activities and tasks will help you to learn and remember information. Case studies are included to add industry relevance to the topics and learning objectives. This unit is internally assessed. At the end of each unit, end of unit questions test your knowledge and assessment tasks outline the evidence requirements required for assessment in order to obtain a Pass, Merit or Distinction as well as suggesting ways of providing assessment evidence. You are reminded that when you are completing activities and tasks, opportunities will be created to enhance your key skills evidence.

After completing this unit you should have an understanding of the following outcomes.

Outcomes

1 Examine the **roles, purpose and responsibilities** of a range of uniformed services

2 Examine a range of **jobs and conditions of service** within the uniformed services

3 Investigate the **application and selection process** for a given uniformed service

4 Explore the **entry requirements and opportunities** for career development within a given uniformed service.

Roles and responsibilities of the uniformed services

The uniformed services cover a wide range of activities, from anti-terrorist work to humanitarian aid to working with local communities. Some services cover many roles while others are concerned with quite a narrow, though no less important, purpose. The police, for instance deal with accidents and emergencies as well as keeping public order and maintaining the law, whereas the role of the ambulance service includes the transport of patients to and from hospitals. In all of the services, however, there are a range of roles that an operative can fulfil and opportunities for specialisation and promotion. Some parts of the job are going to be routine but at other times few jobs can offer the excitement and reward of working in the uniformed services.

There are many uniformed services as shown below.

1 The Armed Forces
   - the Army
   - the Royal Navy
   - the Royal Marines
   - the Royal Air Force

2 Emergency services

- police

- fire

- ambulance

3 Other uniformed services

- Her Majesty's Coast Guard

- prison service

- Her Majesty's Customs and Excise

- private security services

This book will focus on the role and responsibilities of The Armed Forces and the police service in particular with opportunities to research the other services through case studies.

An Army officer

The role of the Armed Forces

The Armed Forces are those services which operate and maintain weapons as part of their role. These weapons could be warships and submarines (Royal Navy), fighter and bomber aircraft (Royal Air Force), or tanks, assault rifles and grenades (the Army). All of the services also have a huge number of support staff, from cooks to doctors to administrators, to ensure that everyone can do their job to the best of their ability.

The Army

The Army is mainly responsible for land warfare. This includes infantry and cavalry (tanks and other fighting vehicles) attacking and holding ground or defending land from attack. The soldiers are supported in their role by the Army Air Corps (AAC) and the Royal Artillery (RA). The Army Air Corps uses attack helicopters to target the enemy and can also provide reconnaissance. The RA fire the big guns at enemy installations and forces.

Specialist support comes in the form of communications expertise from the Royal Signals, maintenance of vehicles and equipment from the Royal Electrical and Mechanical Engineers (REME)

and combat engineering (building bridges, clearing minefields, etc) from the Royal Engineers. In order to keep the combat arms and technical units running, the Army has a vast range of other specialists including doctors, dentists, vets, instructors, chaplains, band members, lawyers, cooks, clerks and intelligence personnel.

The Royal Navy

A Royal Marine soldier

The Royal Navy, also known as the Senior Service, is responsible for carrying out the Defence Mission at sea and can carry out a vast range of tasks throughout the world. It carries the UK's nuclear deterrent (carried on submarines), can provide humanitarian relief, undertakes peacekeeping, creates hydrographic charts (effectively maps), patrols maritime resources (oil fields and fisheries), undertakes anti-drugs patrolling, search and rescue and military action. In order to carry out all of these roles the Navy has just over 120 ships and even its own soldiers called the Royal Marines.

The Royal Marines are a highly trained amphibious force, trained to fight in all environments, from deserts to mountains to jungles. The Royal Navy also has an air force, the Fleet Air Arm that operates from aircraft carriers. In addition to its combat ships, the Navy also needs a huge support network, just as the Army does. The ships of the Royal Fleet Auxiliary provide logistic support in the form of food, ammunition, fuel, etc. Again, like the Army, there are a vast number of trades in the Navy, ranging from Commando to chef, mechanic to medic and surveyor to steward. Although most of the Navy's work is done at sea, there are large Naval bases that require staff on dry land, but most, if not all, Navy personnel will get the opportunity to travel the high seas.

The Royal Air Force (RAF)

This force is the youngest, but most technical of the forces. Its task is to deliver aerial power, whether in the form of bombers or fighters, surveillance aircraft, transport and support aircraft and re-fuelling aircraft. The RAF's aircraft all operate out of airbases which are defended by the RAF's own soldiers, the RAF Regiment. Like any other military base, they are effectively self-sufficient towns with their own mechanics, doctors, police, chefs, administration staff, etc. in addition to the large number of people who work with the aircraft, both on the ground and in the air. The RAF carries out humanitarian and peacekeeping duties as well as defence tasks. For example, the RAF has specialised teams of

An RAF Regiment soldier

mountain rescue personnel with helicopters who are on standby to offer humanitarian aid throughout the UK.

Armed forces working together

The forces have historically worked together throughout history as army soldiers and tanks have to use either ships to cross the sea or aircraft to fly. At several times in the past the UK's military has had to work as one to complete its objectives. The D-Day landings in the Second World War and the Falklands conflict in 1982 are two examples.

The concept of Joint Forces is very strong in today's military and most operations and exercises will emphasise "jointness" in the future. It is usual to find an Army soldier working on a Navy ship alongside sailors or RAF airmen sharing an airbase with Army personnel. Harrier aircraft, once split between the RAF and the Navy, are now combined into Joint Force Harrier. Helicopter training now takes place at Joint Helicopter Command which makes use of expertise from all three services. There are also Joint Rapid Reaction Forces ready to be deployed to hot spots worldwide in a very short space of time.

Key concepts

1 The Armed Forces use weapons as part of their role.

2 The Army is responsible for land warfare but are supported by artillary and attack helicopters.

3 The Royal Navy is responsible for carrying out the Defence Mission at sea.

4 The Royal Marines are soldiers from the Royal Navy.

5 The Royal Air Force delivers aerial power.

6 The RAF Regiment are soldiers from The Royal Air Force.

Armed Forces responsibilities

The Armed Forces are under the command of the **Ministry of Defence (MOD)**. This is the Government department concerned with the safety of the United Kingdom and its interests, mostly, but not exclusively, from external threats. Like any other organisation, the MOD has a mission statement, which outlines what its actual purpose is. The Defence Mission (quoted from the MOD's website) is to:

● Defend the United Kingdom, and Overseas Territories, our people and interests;

● Act as a force for good by strengthening international peace and security.

Theory into practice

The Armed Forces have a highly defined mission statement from the MOD containing 8 missions and 27 tasks. Search the Internet to find them all and make notes on each of the tasks.

Protecting the nation

As part of the defence mission, the Armed Forces are charged with the responsibility of **protecting the nation**. An example of this was in February 2003 when soldiers and light tanks were moved in to provide additional security at Heathrow airport in response to intelligence reports of terrorists plotting to shoot down commercial aircraft. Squadrons from the RAF's Tornado F3 air defence fighter are always ready to defend our airspace and the forces also aid the emergency services where necessary, for example Military Aid to the Civil Power (MACP). This allows a Chief Officer of the Police to request military aid either for specialist equipment and personnel, for example bomb disposal squads or for troops as at Heathrow. Military personnel are also brought in to aid with other national emergencies, for example covering for the fire fighters' strikes in 2003, helping build emergency flood defences and destroying the carcasses of cattle killed in the foot and mouth crisis of 2002.

Defence of our overseas territories

The forces are also charged with the **defence of our overseas territories**. These are areas that are classed as British but are not part of the British Isles. During the height of the British Empire this would have included large parts of North America, Africa and India where the British had colonies and a strong military presence. By the end of the Second World War, however, many of these colonies had been returned to native power and Britain now has relatively few overseas lands under its control. Most of these are islands, some of which are uninhabited. Many, however, are not and some are even desired by other countries, for example:

● **The Falkland Isles in the South Atlantic** – These islands are inhabited by British citizens but are relatively close to the shores of Argentina, who has made many arguments to own the islands. In 1982 Argentinean forces landed on the islands to claim them for their country but the UK was quick to retaliate, with a joint forces task force which set sail and reclaimed the islands by force.

- **Gibraltar** is an isthmus on the southern tip of Spain, but is British territory. Its position in the Mediterranean has made it an important strategic site. During the Second World War all civilians were moved off the isthmus and replaced by British soldiers, sailors and airmen. The civilians are back now but a military force is still present. Every so often the Spanish make suggestions that Gibraltar should be returned to Spain, but have not tried to take it by force for hundreds of years.

Defending the UK's people and interests

In addition to defending land, the forces are tasked with defending the **UK's people and interests,** for example the oil platforms in the North Sea which is an important resource for the United Kingdom. These resources are defended by the Royal Navy's Castle Class ships, which can accommodate a 25-man platoon of Royal Marines. Should any terrorists seize control of an oil platform, an anti-terrorist squad from the Special Boat Squadron would be sent in if a peaceful outcome could not be made.

Think about it

On the surface, the Armed Forces seem to be mostly concerned with warfare. Why then do they operate under the Ministry of *Defence*? Why is the word defence so important?

Acting as a force for good

The second part of the Defence Mission is not so easy to define. Claiming to **act as a force for good** requires a definition of the word *good* but what is good for one side is not necessarily good for another. For the Armed Forces, we can assume that their definition of good ties into the first part of the mission: the good of the nation and its interests. This includes international relations and what is good for the UK's allies. An example of this is the Second Gulf War in 2003, where British forces supported the American services in the war to attack the Iraqi leadership. In this conflict the Americans and the British went against the wishes of several of the major players in the United Nations, especially France and Germany, by using military force.

Strengthening international peace and security

The Ministry of Defence would no doubt argue that in attacking Iraq they were **strengthening international peace and security** by eliminating a link in the international terrorist network and neutralising a regime which may have had weapons of mass destruction. In this way, the British forces could be seen as **acting as a force for good.**

Similar operations were undertaken in Afghanistan against the people believed to be responsible for the terrorist destruction of New York's Twin Towers. British Royal Marines patrolled large areas of arid mountainous terrain searching for Al Qaeda terrorists and their bases, while other units secured Bagram airport while it was repaired. The RAF provided aerial reconnaissance and aerial refuelling during the operation.

Peace-keeping troops in Kosovo

Nowadays, the British forces go overseas on operational duties not just as combatants. In Kosovo, for instance, British soldiers were deployed as part of NATO's peacekeeping force. This involved patrolling and ensuring that opposing sides did not attack each other, as well as policing the country's elections, ensuring fairness. Other units were responsible for other humanitarian work such as repairing the water supply and making it available. This humanitarian aid is becoming more and more the type of work carried out by the Armed Forces. This can range from medical support from services medics, logistic support, for example delivering food, medical supplies, etc where needed to disaster relief in cases of floods, famine, etc.

The RAF carries out search and rescue operations by specially trained personal in the UK, working closely with the emergency services and local Mountain Rescue teams. This is humanitarian aid carried out on home soil. The Royal Navy carries out a similar role on the sea.

The forces work not only "jointly", but also with forces of other nations. British forces often train in other countries (many are stationed abroad) and take part in exercises with the forces of friendly nations. It is rare nowadays for UK forces to go into operations alone. Most conflicts and missions are part of coalition task forces working alongside other NATO or UN countries. Even in the case of the Second Gulf War, where the UK acted without UN sanction and the approval of the whole of the European Union, British forces were not acting alone but in close co-operation with the forces of the United States and other nations.

Case study – Operation Telic 19th–20th March 2003

Operation Telic was the military operation involved in Iraq during the Second Gulf War. It featured a joint task force of Royal Navy (RN) ships and Marines, Royal Air Force (RAF) aircraft and crew (both air and ground) and Army units capable of mounting a sustained deployment in Iraq, including support personnel.

British forces were engaged in a number of tasks throughout the war, many of which were in support of, or working with, other Coalition units (mostly US forces). On the 48 hours of the 19th and 20th of March 2003. RN Submarines lying in the Gulf launched tomahawk missiles against command and control centres in Baghdad in order to disrupt the military power structure. In addition, the Royal Marines mounted an assault by boat and helicopter on the southern coast of Iraq to secure several oil wells. During the First Gulf War, Iraqi forces caused great environmental damage by sabotaging their own oil wells in order to cause disruption to Coalition forces. This time, the Marines were successful and secured the oil wells.

In support of the Marines, Navy ships provided artillery support from their guns. Guns from Army artillery (on detachment to the Marines) also provided support. The Marines were aided from the air by RAF Tornado fighter bombers who neutralised Iraqi artillery positions. Naval ships were also busy in the Gulf clearing mines from the area around the port of Umm Qasr in order that Royal Fleet Auxiliary ships could deliver humanitarian aid.

Meanwhile, Royal Engineers from the Army were disabling any bombs or other problems encountered by US troops as they secured yet more oil wells elsewhere in Iraq. Army combat units were also moving towards Iraq's second largest city, Basra, along with US soldiers. RAF Harrier aircraft were involved in providing aerial support during the operations. Other RAF aircraft were undertaking surveillance, reconnaissance and aerial refuelling throughout this time.

As can be seen, the Armed Forces can carry out a vast range of missions in a conflict, often working together and with other forces, even in such a short period of time. They do not stop once the fighting is over, either. Land taken by ground forces needs to be secured to prevent it falling into enemy hands or damaged by sabotage. Many of the Iraqi cities and towns were also without food, water and power and it was vital that British forces could give them humanitarian aid in order to rebuild the country once the ruling regime had been ousted.

Armed Forces work

Life in the Armed Forces is extremely varied, depending upon the service and the particular job or rank held. However, there are a number of similarities between the forces:

- **Uniform** – one of the most noticeable aspects of life in the services is the wearing of a uniform to a set standard – it must be clean, neat and tidy. Uniforms are worn for a number of reasons: identification of service, unit and rank, fostering a feeling of belonging and pride and practical work, for example camouflage combats.

- **Rank structure** – this is the chain of command which defines responsibilities and who is in charge of who. Except for very rare circumstances, everyone has someone of a senior rank who is responsible for them and oversees their work. Of course, the more experience you have the more you are expected to be capable of doing your job without being told. Opportunities for promotion are available to most people, depending upon suitability.

- **Training** – all of the services have very good training opportunities for personnel. This includes training for particular roles, for example aircraft technician, dog handler, diver and promotion opportunities as well as more conventional qualifications like NVQs. It is even possible to go to university and obtain a degree through the forces. Like many of today's businesses, the forces recognise the importance of developing their personnel and lifelong learning.

Armed Forces marching in formation

Case study – The SA80 assault rifle

This is the weapon used by most of the UK's Armed Forces. It was born after the Falkland Campaign, where British soldiers were outgunned by Argentinean conscripts with fully automatic rifles. The British soldiers at the time were armed with single shot SLRs, powerful but not able to put a lot of lead in the air. After the war the forces demanded better weapons and the British company Enfield who made very efficient military weapons in both World War I and World War II came up with a bullpup design (where the magazine is behind the pistol grip) for an assault rifle able to keep up with armies worldwide.

At this point in time, the Soviet forces had been using Kalashnikov assault rifles (inspired by German weapons made near the end of WWII) for almost forty years and the Americans had been using their M16 assault rifle since the 1960s. British forces were overjoyed at having a fully automatic assault rifle until it started falling to pieces. Various parts used to fall off, for instance the bayonet, when the weapon was firing. There were also problems with stoppages and it needed to be kept very clean. Soldiers named it the Palitoy Gun after the toy company that used to make Action Men in the 1970s. Some Special Forces have refused to use the weapon, preferring the American M16. German company Heckler and Koch have now taken over manufacture of the weapon and have tried to fix the faults by making the SA80A2.

- **Discipline** – the forces require a certain standard of dress (uniform) and behaviour to be followed. This includes following orders from superiors, performing your job to the best of your ability and keeping yourself and your equipment clean and tidy. There are also drill sessions where recruits learn how to march in formation which builds teamwork as well as reinforcing discipline and learning to follow orders.

- **Risk and danger** – due to the nature of the Armed Forces there is always a risk of danger and even death. The main purpose of the forces is the defence of the nation and as such all personnel are required to do what is necessary. As a result clerks, medics, cooks, etc are all trained to use their rifles if they need to.

Wearing a uniform also makes military personnel stand out as targets. When travelling off duty, forces personnel are required to travel in "civvies" (civilian uniform) to avoid being targeted by terrorists (mostly the IRA for the last few decades) and other threats.

Military training can also be dangerous. Although health and safety is very important, accidents can happen and training has to be as realistic as possible to be effective. This means training in dangerous environments including the jungle, desert, as well as mountains, at night and in harsh weather using live weapons and ammunition.

- **Routine** – much of the day to day work will involve routine tasks such as maintenance, paperwork and administration. Many military personnel work from 9.00 to 5.00, 5 days a week although they may be working on a ship or in an exotic foreign location.

Life isn't always routine, however. All of the forces have training exercises where they practice being at war or under attack, and have annual fitness tests to complete.

- **Military law** – whilst in the Armed Forces, personnel are subject to two types of law: civil law, which applies to all people in the country and military law (see page 7). Military law is concerned with offences likely to be encountered in the forces such as desertion, going absent without leave (AWOL) and unofficial use or possession of weapons and ammunition. Infringement of military law can have extremely serious consequences, including incarceration, fines and being expelled from the service.

Case study – Ambulance service

Being an ambulance driver, Asha is responsible for getting patients to and from hospital. This involves being at the correct address or hospital entrance at the right time and driving carefully. Many of the patients she deals with are elderly, ill or disabled, which means that Asha has had lots of training involving lifting wheelchairs, customer care and first aid. She also has a good knowledge of the local area and enjoys helping people.

Although she enjoys her job, Asha wants to progress from the Patient Transfer Service to being a Medical Technician or Paramedic, responding to 999 calls. This involves several weeks of training including medical training and further driving tests. During training there are lots of examinations and assessments to ensure competence. If she does make it to paramedic she will be able to give emergency medical treatment and communicate her diagnosis to hospital staff. As a paramedic she would have do annual re-assessments and re-qualify every three years to ensure that she is up to scratch.

Theory into practice

Find out what the Fire Service Act 1947 and the Fire Precautions Act 1971 contain and what they mean to the firefighters working within these Acts.

Organisation of the police force

The police service is not a national organisation; instead it is divided into 43 separate police forces, each with their own budget, officers and run by a Chief Constable. Each force is divided up into divisions, which have a number of police stations. To join the police you must apply to a particular police force.

A police force has a tripartite structure governing its roles and responsibilities:

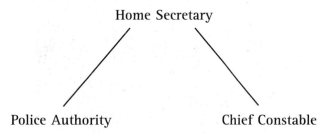

The Home Office is the government department responsible for the police forces as well as some of the other emergency services. The minister responsible for Home Office is the **Home Secretary** who works closely with the Prime Minister and the purpose of the Home Office is to ensure that the society of England and Wales is safe and tolerant. Safety can be linked with the police, fire and prison service.

At a regional level, the police are accountable to the **Police Authority**. This is made up of local councillors (two thirds) and magistrates (one third) to ensure that the local people have a say in the how their police force runs.

The final part of a police force's top structure is the **chief constable** which is the highest rank in the force.

In this structure the police are controlled by Government, the local people and by their own internal mechanisms. Remember that the police are a powerful organisation and in all tyrannical regimes the police are used to enforce the tyranny and usually deal harshly with dissidents. England and Wales' tripartite structure ensures that no one group has overall control and can use the police for its own ends.

However, the Home Office does hold the balance of power over the other two elements in that it controls 51% of the force's finances and it appoints the Inspectors of Constabulary who examine how a force works to ensure its efficiency. If a force fails its inspection then some of the Government funds will be withheld.

Purpose of the police service

The police service's statement of common purpose and values reads as follows:

1 The purpose of the police service is to uphold the law fairly and firmly

2 To prevent crime

3 To pursue and bring to justice those who break the law

4 To keep the Queen's Peace

5 To protect, help and reassure the community

6 To be seen doing all this with integrity, common sense and sound judgement

7 We must be compassionate, courteous and patient, acting without fear of favour or prejudice to the rights of others

8 We need to be professional, calm and restrained in the face of violence and apply only that force which is necessary to accomplish our lawful duty

9 We must strive to reduce the fears of the public and, so far as we can, reflect their priorities in the action we take

10 We must respond to well founded criticism with a willingness to change.

1 Upholding the law

The prime objective of the police is **to uphold the law**. This means, that police officers need to have a fairly good grasp of British law. Considering the high salaries and training given to lawyers to interpret the law and make it work for their purpose, this is quite a tall order. Much of police training is dedicated to studying law, but one of the main pieces of legislation they need to be aware of is PACE, the Police and Criminal Evidence Act 1984, which sets out how the Police can operate (see page 3). This first statement also dictates that they must uphold the law "fairly and firmly", intending to show determination and a lack of bias.

2 Preventing crime

Prevention of crime is what we expect from the Police and the keyword here is *prevent*, to stop it before it happens. Much police work is done on this issue, from television adverts to visiting homes and businesses to offer security advice. It can also be the simple presence of police officers on patrol in a community or area. Prevention of crime is a much more efficient use of time, money and resources for the police than chasing offenders.

3 Bringing to justice

Again, you would expect the police service to pursue and bring to justice those who break the law. A lot of time and effort is spent trying to catch offenders, whether it be on foot or through investigation and this can be a highly visible, exciting and therefore media-grabbing form of police work.

4 Keeping the Queen's Peace

Keeping the **Queen's Peace** is an old concept: that while the lords and people of the country remained true to the monarchy, the King or Queen would provide the nation with peace, security and stability. Therefore, the Police are simply required to keep the Peace. This explains how someone can be arrested for disturbing the Peace.

5 Protecting and helping the community

Community constables play a large part **to protect, help and reassure the community** partly through their presence, but also in working closely with the community. For example, getting to know the local head teachers, businesspeople and religious leaders as well as neighbourhood watch groups, youth workers, schoolchildren and community workers. Your local police force may send out a newsletter every few months to remind people that they are working for the community's benefit and to inform them of the good work that has been done.

A police officer on duty

6 Integrity, common sense and sound judgement

When carrying out their role, the police force must have **integrity, common sense and sound judgement**. Without these attributes it would be difficult for society to have any trust in the police and what they do. It is extremely important to the service that they are seen to act in accordance with these attributes, both as a force and as individuals.

Prejudice

Police duties should be carried out politely and without any bias, whether favourable or otherwise.

Reacting to violence

Police officers sometimes come under attack and have to defend themselves or others, or they may have to use violent actions to restrain and arrest people. All officers undergo rigorous training to prepare themselves for this, including re-training if they are to be redeployed on patrol after doing other jobs.

Not only are they trained in restraint techniques and self defence but also how to respond to threatening behaviour. In this instance, they are only allowed to use reasonable force which means only using force as a last resort when other forms of communication have failed, for example talking people out of a fight. Use of weapons such as batons and pepper spray are for well trained officers and firearms may only be used by specialists when somebody is in grave risk of physical danger. The police have very strict guidelines on the use of physical force, with a reaction scale that they must adhere to and force should only be used 'to accomplish our lawful duty' and for no other purpose.

Reducing public fears

Ultimately, the police work for the public (through their representatives in the government and the Police Authorities) and should share their priorities. Of course, there are times when this can be at odds with police work, especially when it is in direct opposition to the other statements of purpose. Examples of this sort of opposition could be the police use of personal and sensitive information in the fight against organised crime or terrorism.

Accepting criticism

The police have to be ready to accept justified criticism and to act upon it. There are many bodies which examine the police's actions, some official, such as the Police Complaints Authority others less so, such as newspapers and other media journalism and the public at large. Police forces are regularly inspected by Her Majesty's Inspectorate of Constabulary who decide whether the Force is working efficiently and deserves the full amount of funding from the Home Office.

Theory into practice

What does the Police and Criminal Evidence Act 1984 (PACE) contain and what does it mean to the officers who have to work with it?

The role of the police service

The police forces in the United Kingdom are responsible for law and order in their region. The roles and responsibilities of the police are wide ranging and varied, for example minor traffic offences, dealing with major accidents, anti-terrorist operations and liasing with local communities. For this reason, each regional police force has specialist units to tackle tasks which the average patrol officer is not trained for, for example mounted police, firearms unit and underwater search unit. The roles of the police forces include the following areas.

Dealing with accidents

Whenever an accident occurs, the police are always quick to attend and help in any way they can. All police officers are trained in first aid and will do what they can to help injured people before medical assistance can arrive. Sometimes the easiest way of doing this is to isolate the area to prevent the public from coming to harm, for example at the sites of road traffic accidents. These areas also need to be kept clear because there may be forensic evidence which may be useful later on. For example, the length and direction of skid marks may be vital in determining how an accident occurred. Similarly, any objects scattered around the accident (wreckage, debris, personal effects, etc) can provide more evidence.

Dealing with emergencies

Emergencies can take many forms and can be natural due to flooding, severe weather or land slides or man-made, either intentional such as bombs or hijackings or accidental rail crashes or chemical accidents. The police are an important and accessible resource to use in such situations as each region has a police force with local police stations. This means that most of the country is covered by a group of well trained and disciplined officers who can help at any accident or emergency without having to travel vast distances. In this role, the police can operate in a number of ways while working closely with the other emergency services such as paramedics and doctors or fire fighters. One example is the Selby rail disaster in 2001.

Local community work

Working with local communities is high on the police services' priorities. The community police officer works with the community on a day-to-day level as well as actually living in and being a part of the community. This officer gets to know many of the people who live and work in the area, helping them where possible and providing a reassuring presence. This involves building relationships and dealing with on-going problems in the community. Local crime prevention is high on their agenda and their knowledge of the community and its environment is invaluable in that respect. They liase very closely with local schools, informing young people of the many temptations and dangers that they may encounter such as drugs, joy riding, accidents and theft. Much of this work is preventative, but it also creates a link between the young people and the police.

Local police stations are also valuable assets to the community as the local officers are the ones who will deal with crime in the area, arrest offenders, take statements and appear in court.

Anti-terrorist work

Mostly a force's Special Branch carries out anti-terrorist work, although other officers may become involved in certain cases, such as the Firearms Unit or local police officers. Investigations are carried out in much the same way as the police investigate any crime, arrests are made and the process goes through the court system. In fact since the Anti Terrorism Crime and Security (ATCS) Act 2001 came into being 12 foreign nationals have been arrested on charges of terrorism. However, the threat of terror to the United Kingdom is not a new thing, regardless of how 9/11 changed the world. Due to the situation in Northern Ireland, security services have had to be very diligent about terrorist bombs and mortar attacks. Subsequently, there is a strong infrastructure in place to deal with such measures.

The Special Branch works in liaison with several other services including the military and the Secret Services, MI5 (responsible for national security) and MI6 (who have an international espionage role). However, the security services are not the only ones involved. The government can create legislation (such as ATCS 2001) and the Chancellor of the Exchequer can freeze the financial assets of known terror groups, meaning that they cannot spend any of their money and hopefully cannot acquire weapons to create terror. Also, in relation to international terrorism, the UK Intelligence and Security Committee has strong links with similar agencies overseas, such as the CIA, FBI and NSA in the USA.

Responsibilities

As they are a public service, the police have many responsibilities. Firstly, they are responsible for carrying out the 10 purposes listed on page 98 which shows that the Police have some responsibility for the law, the community and the Queen's Peace.

The police are also responsible for doing their job properly and are inspected to ensure their efficiency. This is the government's responsibility who must ensure that the finances are being well spent and are deserved. All forces are accountable for their budget which must pay for everything including staff, vehicles, equipment, property, utilities (water, electricity, etc), promotional information (including newsletters, job ads, etc) and anything else the force requires.

The police, like most organisations, must provide an indication of how well they are doing. Areas for concern are identified, such as percentage of 999 calls answered within the required target time, number of public disorder incidents and percentage of reported racist incidents are used as **performance indicators**. Using performance indicators, you can compare one force with another to see which one performs best at certain things.

Think about it

How do you think performance indicators affect police officers? Are they helpful or do they just create more work and bureaucracy? Who do you think they are of use to?

Police service life

Life in the police service is in some ways very similar to life in the military: uniform, rank structure, discipline, etc with the obvious differences (military law). There can be risk and danger, but to a large extent police officers can avoid dangerous work a lot easier than forces personnel. However, police work can be more routine and there is lots of paperwork to be done. Even patrol officers who are not desk-bound must fill out large numbers of forms whenever they apprehend a suspect or arrest someone. As we shall see later in this chapter, literacy skills are very important to the police.

Theory into practice

During your course you should have the opportunity to meet police officers. If you get an opportunity, ask them what their daily routine consists of.

Theory into practice

Find out about the roles of these other alternative uniformed services:

- Prison officers in private prisons
- British Rail Transport Police
- Private security officers
- United Kingdom Atomic Energy Authority Constabulary

Key concepts

1 The uniformed services all have distinct roles covered by their mission statements and the government department responsible for them. The armed forces can act as an emergency service to cover for the other services or to assist them.

2 The emergency services work within the UK and the armed forces can work throughout the world.

3 All of the services have legislation which defines what they do, for example PACE 1984 for the Police, Fire Service Act 1947 and Fire Precautions Act 1971 for the Fire Service.

4 The uniformed services are all accountable to the government and the community they serve. This includes spending their budget wisely and being able to justify the spending as well as being responsible for their actions.

5 Most uniformed service work can be a division between routine work and excitement and danger, although some specific jobs will be safer/more dangerous than others.

Jobs and conditions of service

The uniformed services offer an enormous variety of jobs at operational level. For example, in the Navy you could be a chef, a writer, a marine engineering mechanic, a meteorologist, medical assistant or musician. In the police force you could train to be a dog handler, a member of the firearms unit or a mounted officer.

Operational jobs

Firefighter

The main role of a firefighter in the fire service is to respond to emergencies, whether they involve fires, rail crashes, chemical spills or road traffic accidents. As a result, they have to be trained to deal with all different types of emergency they may encounter and training, whether it be to learn new skills or to practice existing ones, is a very important part of the firefighter's job. Firefighters must also ensure that all the equipment they use is in good working order which can include testing and maintenance of the equipment and even repairs.

Fire prevention and developing community links are also important parts of the job. While police officers are responsible for preventing crime, fire fighters have a similar responsibility to reduce fires. This includes visits to schools to do fire safety talks and demonstrations or visits to businesses or community buildings to assess risks.

Operator mechanic in the Royal Navy

Communications operators work as part of the Navy's Warfare Branch and are responsible for allowing the ship to keep in contact with aircraft, shore bases, other ships and any other relevant allied forces. Working on the ship's bridge, the operator receives and sends messages using a wide range of equipment including satellite communications, modems and radio. Once information has been received it must then be directed to the Officer of the Watch. Information is one of the most vital components of warfare, so long as it is up to date and used by the right people and it is up to the communications operator to ensure that this happens. Communication operators are also responsible for the ship's on-board communications network.

Firefighters visit schools to give fire safety talks

Being part of the ship's crew, the communications operator must also be responsible for safety duties, just as every other member of the crew is. This includes extensive fire fighting training, with plenty of drills as all personnel need to know how to combat fires on board the ship.

Not all posts are at sea and the Navy has land bases that must be staffed by communications operators. An operator's career can include tours on ships along with periods of work on land.

Aircraft technician in the RAF

Aircraft technicians are the engineers who work on the RAF's aircraft. Their job is to keep the aircraft in safe working order to enable the aircrew to complete their mission, whether transporting troops or equipment in a Hercules, a search and rescue operation in a Sea King helicopter or to deny enemy forces the use of their runways by blowing them up in a Tornado. Aircraft technicians specialise in one of five areas: airframes, propulsion, avionics, aircraft electrical and weapons. Technicians work on operational bases and usually follow their squadron if it goes on a tour. In times of war, aircraft may have to move out to be closer to the front line or on the front line and their technicians need to move out to be with them.

Theory into practice

Research the service you wish to join and the responsibilities undertaken at operational level.

Tank crewman in the Army

Tank crewmen start their career by driving tanks in either the Household Cavalry or the Royal Armoured Corps. The Household Cavalry drive Scimitar reconnaissance tanks to gain battlefield intelligence, while the RAC has Challenger main battle tanks that can engage enemy tanks and forces. The Challenger is a 60-ton behemoth with

reactive armour and a 120mm gun and is the equal of any tank in the world. With this amount of power comes quite a bit of responsibility. The tank driver needs to be able to get the tank where it needs to go while avoiding obstacles in the terrain, both natural and man-made as well as enemy fire. The main objective in using a tank is to get it to where its gun can be most effective. Tank crews therefore must work as a very efficient team in cramped conditions.

Like all Army personnel, the tank crewman is primarily a soldier. He needs to keep his rifle with him at all times and should he be separated from his vehicle has to fight back to his own lines where he can be redeployed to another vehicle.

Conditions of service

Conditions of service are the areas you really need to know before you even consider joining a uniformed service. For instance, did you know that standard length of service in the Royal Navy is 22 years or that in the Army you're paid 24 hours a day? Look at Figure 8.1 which gives the conditions of service in the Army and the fire service. A few other examples are listed below:

- whilst on duty firefighters should not wear make up or hair products (hairspray, gel, etc), nor should they wear rings, earrings, watches or bracelets

- police officers must follow a strict code of conduct, which involves, among many other things, not taking part in politics and prompt payment of any debts.

- all personnel in the Army have to pass an annual personal weapons test and an annual combat fitness test to stay in the force. Failure to pass the tests results in remedial training and a repeat test. Failure of the test at this stage could lead to expulsion from the Army.

Conditions of service		
	Army	**Fire service**
Basic starting pay	£30.47 per day.	£16, 941 per annum.
Retirement age	Eligible at 55, if served long enough.	50, with 25 years of service.
Shift patterns	Varies with job and operational conditions. In times of war it can be 24 hours a day, 7 days a week.	42 hour week, 2 day shifts and 2 night shifts followed by 4 days off.
Starting holiday entitlement	30 working days plus public holidays.	28 days plus public holidays.
Benefits	Forces travel cards; inexpensive accommodation, docked at source; inexpensive food, docked at source; free medical and dental care; access to sport and fitness opportunities.	Access to fitness equipment at station.
Training opportunities	Ongoing; opportunities for technical and educational training; opportunities for specialisation and promotion, both requiring further training and development.	Ongoing; opportunities for technical training; opportunities for specialisation and promotion, both requiring further training and development.

Figure 8.1 Conditions of service in the Army and the fire service

Theory into practice

Investigate the conditions of service in your chosen uniformed service to see if there is any other useful information on terms and conditions of service before joining.

Alternative uniformed job opportunities

In addition to the traditional uniformed services that we have looked at, there are some alternatives. Many are part-time and some can earn you an extra income. However, many of the operational requirements of the regular services undertaken on a part-time basis also apply. For example, part-time soldiers in the Territorial Army still have to pass annual tests and could be sent on operational duties if there is a war.

Most uniformed services have part-time/voluntary opportunities that you may want to try to see if you like the job and the culture. They serve a valuable purpose by supporting the regular services and sometimes get to do things that the regulars don't.

Retained firefighters

These are part-time firefighters, ready to drop everything whenever there is an emergency they are needed for. Often they are in rural areas and provide a low cost alternative to full-time firefighters. However, being required for emergencies at short notice requires that they live or work very close to the station, usually about a mile away. Clearly, retained firefighters need to have considerate employers if they have an additional full-time job.

Part-time firefighters use the same equipment and engines as regular firefighters so therefore require similar training. Ongoing training usually takes place one evening a week. Retained firefighters are paid a small retaining wage plus payment for each incident that they attend.

Special Constables

Special Constables work alongside full-time Police officers, but are volunteers who either want to learn more about police work (usually with a view to joining the service) or want to help their community. Their work is usually locally based, such as foot patrols, community link initiatives and assisting at accidents and incidents.

In general, Specials support regular officers in their job, although Specials have the same powers and similar uniforms. However, as volunteers they are unpaid. Specials undergo a similar application process to that of full-time officers and have an ongoing training timetable. Their conditions state that they must work at least 4 hours per week in addition to training sessions, although these hours are flexible. Some Police Forces have a rank system for their Specials, with promotion working as it does for regular officers.

The Territorial Army

The Territorial Army (TA) are a substantial part of the Army (about one quarter) and are a part-time workforce of paid volunteers. They support regular units of the Army and can also help the local community in emergencies, for example floods. At one time the TA was very much a domestic force with its main purpose being defence of UK soil, like the Home Guard in the Second World War. During the Cold War this was seen as a high priority as NATO was constantly expecting communist forces (the Warsaw Pact) to invade the West. Now the TA work alongside regular units, sometimes providing a role not covered in the regular Army, for example TA SAS units.

The TA's structure is the same as the regular Army, with regiments, corps, etc. The TA has 2 different types of units. The *Independent Unit* is a locally based unit and tends to have either a combat, logistics, engineering, medical or communications role. They recruit locally and their personnel train primarily to be soldiers. *Specialist Units* recruit locally and their soldiers are more specially trained (either due to their civilian occupations or previous regular service). Specialisation can include medicine, engineering and telecommunications.

Soldiers in the TA are paid and those in independent units are required to attend regularly on a weekday evening for training and routine work. Weekend work is also necessary, with a minimum of 27 days to be completed each year and a two week annual camp is also mandatory. This is the minimum, however, and many TA soldiers attend much more. Tax free bounties are given to soldiers who complete all of their minimum attendance requirements. Specialist units require a minimum of 19 days per year to be completed.

Conditions of service are otherwise very similar to those of the regular Army. One of the most important things to bear in mind with the TA is that it is an active part of the Army and TA soldiers can be placed on active duty alongside regulars, even in wartime. During the first Gulf War many TA medics and doctors were called up to serve in the Gulf much to their surprise and horror.

The Army Cadet Force (ACF) and the University Officer Training Corps (UOTC) also come under the TA umbrella. Adult staff in both are members of the TA, with their officers holding full TA commissions. The ACF is the Army's youth organisation which encourages young people with an interest in the Army. The UOTC is much the same but for university students. All students in the UOTC are automatic officer cadets and can apply for a full commission. Many of the staff in both the ACF and UOTC have experience of being in the regular Army but it is not a requirement and it is possible to rise through the ranks.

Non-uniformed job opportunities

Not all members of the uniformed services are uniformed. Each of the services have a huge support team responsible for a range of services. For example, the fire service, has non-firefighters for catering, vehicle maintenance, information technology, clerical and administration.

Her Majesty's Customs and Excise officers are both uniformed and non-uniformed. Those visible officers working Customs at sea and airports clearly wear uniforms, but most work in offices and wear suitable civilian clothing. Their rank scheme is similar to that of many other civil service organisations and there are several grades available at entry: Administrative assistant (AA), Administrative Officer (AO) and Executive Officer (EO). Much of the work done by AAs is office based and clerical while AOs have to use a little more initiative and may get to do jobs outside the office. EOs have much more autonomy and may be in charge of other officers; they may also work out of the office. Customs and Excise work can be quite varied, from working with and enforcing VAT laws to investigating smugglers to scrutinising financial documents to uncover fraud.

Application and selection process

This section looks at the application and selection process of obtaining a job in the uniformed services providing you with essential information for entry into this field.

Application

Entry requirements

Entry requirements are what you need to be able to do the job and it stands to reason that the more specialised and responsible the job is the more requirements will be asked for.

Requirements can mean anything from academic qualifications to how good your eyesight is to what your nationality is. For jobs in the uniformed services these requirements should be quite easy to find either from careers leaflets, the Internet or at careers offices. Figure 8.2, overleaf gives you examples of the entry requirements in the police service, Armed forces and fire service.

Different jobs will have different requirements, even in the same service.' For example, you could join the Navy at basic level with no formal qualifications but you will only be considered for mechanic level at the technical trades and you still have to pass the entrance exam. Technical entry requires GCSE equivalent qualifications but start at technician level and you also need to pass the exam. Officer level requires A Level equivalents (many applicants have degrees) but the work is at a managerial level. Qualifications are important, especially if you want to rise through the ranks. Some services, for example the police, have an accelerated fast-track scheme for graduates to move them up the ranks quicker than normal.

Qualifications

Officers in the Armed Forces need much higher levels of qualifications than those in the emergency services because forces officers are going straight into a managerial role or have greater amounts of responsibilities, for example pilots and navigators in the RAF. Some specialisms are only open to graduates, as it would cost the forces too much money to train all their candidates for these posts. It also ensures that there is a broader range of experience and training as the graduates come from various universities nationwide. Specialisms requiring degrees include veterinarian officers in the Royal Army Veterinarian Corps and medical and dental doctors in any of the services. It is also common for graduates to be promoted quicker.

There is no equivalent of officer entry into the emergency services, although graduates may be eligible for fast track promotion. However, everyone starts at the same level, regardless of

Entry requirements for officers

	Height	Age	Health	Eyesight	Nationality	Academic	Finances	Convictions
Police officer	No height requirements	Minimum of 18½ years, can apply at 18	In good mental, physical and dental health. Medical examination	No eye defects, able to distinguish primary colours, unaided. Vision of not less than 6/36 in each eye, may be considered with laser surgery (12 months after surgery)	United Kingdom, Commonwealth or European Union citizen with no residency restrictions	Good command of English (tested)	Financially sound	All convictions and cautions to be declared; judged on an individual basis
RAF officer	No restrictions	17½ to 29 although some specialisms may have different maximum age limits	In good mental and physical health. Medical examination	Chronic eye conditions, detached retinas, corneal transplant and incisional Keratectomy not acceptable. Some surgery acceptable	Citizen of and born in Britain, the Commonwealth, Dependant Territory or the Republic of Ireland. Lived in the UK for last 5 years	5 GCSEs A–C including Maths and English; 2 A levels. Some specialists require degrees. Graduates may get better starting pay and promotions	Not applicable	All convictions and cautions to be declared; judged on an individual basis

	Height	Age	Health	Eyesight	Nationality	Academic	Finances	Convictions
Army officer	Within normal limits for age and weight in proportion to body	Must be over 17 and 9 months, and under 29, can appy at 17	In good mental and physical health. Medical examination	Right eye no less than 6/9, left eye no less than 6/36, some types of surgery are unacceptable	Citizen of the British Isles, Ireland or the Commonwealth or born in these countries	5 GCSEs A-C including Maths, English and Science or a language; equivalent to 2 A levels. Some Corps require specialist qualifications	Not applicable	All convictions and cautions to be declared; judged on an individual basis
Navy officer	Minimum height 157cms, 163cms for Marines	17 to 32, although some specialisms may have different maximum age limits	In good mental and physical health. Medical examination	Detached retinas, corneal transplant and surgery to improve vision not acceptable	Citizen of and born in Britain, the Commonwealth, Dependant Territory or the Republic of Ireland. Lived in the UK for last 5 years	3 "acceptable" GCSE passes including English and Maths; 2 A levels. Some specialists require degrees	Not applicable	All convictions and cautions to be declared; judged on an individual basis
Firefighter	No restrictions	Over 18	In good mental and physical health. Medical examination	Good uncorrected vision, 6/6 in each eye, and good colour vision	No restrictions so long as applicant can legally work in the UK	No formal qualifications literacy and numeracy skills tested	Not applicable	All convictions and cautions to be declared; judged on an individual basis

Figure 8.2 Entry requirements for Officers in the uniformed services

qualifications, going through the same training and probationary periods.

Although the police and fire services do not require qualifications, they do need a good level of literacy and numeracy as officers are required to accurately complete a lot of paperwork in both jobs. The selection procedures for both services contain exams to test these skills.

Age

Most forces want their officers to be a minimum of 18 which is when potential officers will have finished college or sixth form and gained the minimum required qualifications.

The emergency services prefer to have people with "life experience" which enables them to communicate effectively with all types of people and be able to cope with incidents and accidents. Some people acquire these qualities early in life, others need a bit more experience. If the selection officers don't think you are up to the required level they will tell you what to do in order to improve your skills.

Health

All the services expect their personnel to be in good health, physically and mentally and many conditions are stipulated as undesirable, for example many of the services do not allow people with asthma to join, because of the physical nature of the job. All of the services also require a certain level of fitness, both in terms of endurance and strength and many have fitness tests with specified pass rates to ensure that all recruits are starting with a minimum standard of fitness.

The use of recreational drugs is not permitted and many of the services have random drug tests for their personnel. Anyone showing positive will be dismissed.

Eyesight

Eyesight is often treated as a separate category for the services and most have strict requirements. The numbers quoted on some of the requirements

are for the Snellens test (your optician should be able to give you the test). The Police obviously need to have good vision, as much of the job is observation related. The same can be said of the fire service who work in dangerous situations and environments. The Army are very prescriptive about the standards they expect for vision, with the main emphasis on the right eye. The reason for this is that the SA80 assault rifle which is the standard weapon for all of the armed forces, cannot be fired left handed because the spent cartridges are ejected to the right.

Good eyesight is important in the uniformed services

Height

Most services now have no minimum height requirement, with the exception of the Navy and the Royal Marines. However, the Army set out requirements for applicants size and weight to be proportionate to body and age.

Nationality

The Police now accept any EU applicants so long as they can legally work in the UK.

Finance

If you want to join the Police, you need to have stable finances. The Police do not allow applications from those with money problems.

Serving officers also have to inform their superiors if they encounter financial difficulties.

Think about it

Why do you think it is so important for members of the police to have stable finances?

Criminal record

All of the services want to know if you have a criminal record and will check on applicants to find out if this information has been omitted from their application. Previous offences are not necessarily a bar on joining the uniformed services, but lying about them is.

Additional requirements

There are also some additional criteria that some services specify. For example, South Yorkshire police state that all applicants must have a full driving licence.

Equal opportunities

All services have an equal opportunity policy regarding recruitment including gender, race, sexuality and culture. All of the services are open to women, though there may be some jobs that they are not allowed to do:

- Army – Infantry and Cavalry units (the Combat Arms)
- RAF Regiment – the Air Force's soldiers who guard the air bases do not allow women into their ranks
- Royal Navy – does not allow women to become divers
- Royal Marines – women are excluded from all parts of this service.

It is only since the 1980s that the forces have started opening up many of its posts to women, for example:

- **1989:** female RAF pilots allowed to fly combat aircraft

- **1990:** women allowed to serve on Navy fighting ships
- **1998:** female soldiers allowed to join 70% of Army units, almost doubled from 40%. The Army also changed physical training procedures, allowing women to train at the same standard as the men and the All Arms Commando Course was opened to women.

Think about it

Why are women barred from combat roles? Can you think of reasons why women should be allowed in combat units?

Desired qualities

In addition to the specified requirements, there are also certain qualities that uniformed services personnel need to display. One of the most important is teamwork. The uniformed services can only work if everyone is working together and great emphasis is centred on creating teamwork, for example through sport. You will need to show that you are able to work in a team, whether by quoting examples of group work or team sports experience.

Communication is another quality highly rated by the services. Teamwork is no good without communication with other people. Communication is tested in literacy tests and application forms, as well as in interviews. The services also expect their members to be reliable. What is your attendance like at college? Are you always on time? Do you have the proper equipment with you? All of these things are what they will ask for in references.

Adaptability is also essential in the services. You will need to be able to cope with a range of different conditions and environments and do your job efficiently. Each day may bring a different challenge and you must be able to adapt your way of working to deal with it.

The application process

Once you have chosen the service you want to join and you meet all the requirements you need to complete an application form. The process to follow is shown below:

1 Contact the service and ask for an application form

In the case of the Armed forces this could be as simple as going to the Armed Forces Career Office and telling them what you are interested in.

For the emergency services you need to find out where the recruiting office is (usually at the headquarters building) so that you can write to them requesting an application form and information. Make sure that your letter is well written and clean.

2 Complete the application form

Completing the application form is an important part of the selection process as the application will not be considered if it has been filled in incorrectly:

- **Photocopy the form** – fill in the photocopy first so that you make all your mistakes on the photocopy. Also get someone to check your draft copy as other people can spot mistakes you may not see.

- **Read the instructions** – if it says use black ink, then use black ink and complete the form neatly.

- **Find out all the information you will need** – you may need to know the address and telephone number of your referees (make sure they know you've put their names down) or

what grades you got in your GCSEs. Gather the information together and keep it to hand when you fill the form out.

- **Character and experience** – some forms may ask you to write about situations you have been in to see if you have the proper character and experience for the service. They may ask for an example of how you handled conflict or to write about a time when you used teamwork to complete a task. Think about these sections very carefully. Try to remember examples from work, school, sports clubs, cadets or just life in general. This is where you can show that you have "life experience".

- **Personal statement** – most forms will ask you to write about additional information that you think would be relevant to your application. Make sure that it's relevant, well written and easy to read. Tailor it to the job specification that you'll get with the form.

- **Check the form** – make sure it's easy to read and nothing is missing.

- **Get someone else to check it** – ask a teacher, a careers officer or even a responsible friend. If you can get one of your referees to check it, so much the better; they'll have a much clearer understanding of what's needed for the reference.

3 Send a curriculum vitae if specified

As well as an application form or instead of an application form, you may be asked to send your curriculum vitae (CV). CVs include your address, qualifications and work experience and any other relevant information (sporting achievements, leisure activities, etc). It's also a good idea to ask two professionals you know if you could put them down as referees, such as teachers or people you've worked for before. If you are unsure how to write a CV, there is plenty of help available at careers offices.

Keep your CV handy when you're filling out the application form as it has got all the same information on it.

Once you have a general CV, try creating a job-specific CV which is tailored to the requirements of the job. For example, you may want to emphasise your sporting achievements for one job and highlight your commitment and teamwork skills for another. For another job it may be more relevant to concentrate on academic qualifications or last year's summer job.

The selection process

The next stage of the application process is the selection process which varies from service to service.

Police selection

Once you have successfully completed the application form you should be invited to an assessment centre. You will receive full information on where the centre is and what will be expected of you and should take plenty of time to practice for the tests.

Police Initial Recruitment Test (PIRT)

The PIRT is the first test you will undertake and consists of the following:

- 2 short written tests to see how good your communication skills are, then a verbal logical reasoning test to test the same

- a numeracy test

- 4 role plays – you are placed in a corridor with 4 doors off it. Each door has a role play task written on it. The tasks will be something similar to a customer service problem rather than a police-related task, such as deal with an irate customer while pretending to be a store manager. You have a certain amount of time to prepare and then you have to go in and interact with an actor in the room. Also in the room will be a selection officer who will mark you.

- an interview with a selection officer.

During the tests and the interview the selection officers will be looking for the following competences that are deemed to be important for all Police officers:

1   community and customer focus

2   personal responsibility

3   resilience

4   respect for diversity

5   problem solving

6   teamwork

7   effective communication.

Medical and fitness test

If you have been successful in the first test you will be sent information about the next step which is a medical and fitness test. You will be told about the fitness test beforehand so that you can begin training for it. Unit 9 will give you plenty of advice about fitness tests and how to prepare for them.

The Police work related fitness test consists of the following elements:

- **Speed and agility test:** run along a short 13 metre course around 4 cones in 27 seconds or less

- **Grip strength test:** using a grip dynamometer, squeeze as hard as you can. Pass rate is 32kg

- **Dynamic strength test:** using a machine called a dyno you test your back strength by pulling the bar towards you; you need a score of 35kg to pass. To test your chest strength you get on the other side of the machine and push the bar away from you; you need to exert 34kg to pass.

- **Bleep test:** (also called the multi stage fitness test) this involves running between shuttles placed 15 metres apart while a series of bleeps is played. You need to be at the shuttle line each time the bleep plays. Unfortunately, the time between the bleeps decreases so you have

It is important to train in preparation for a fitness test in the uniformed services

to run faster with each level. Pass rate is level 8 and 1 additional shuttle.

Once you have passed the fitness test and the medical test, all of your references are checked and a security vetting check is taken. As long as everything is acceptable you will be offered a place as a police trainee.

If at any point you fail in the selection process you will be informed what you did wrong and given feedback on how to improve. Take notice of this and work hard at it as you can re-apply. You are allowed 3 attempts at the fitness test, after which you need to wait 6 months before re-applying to the Force.

Selection tests in other services

Other services have different selection procedures, but there are some elements common to all:

- **Eligibility test** to ensure that you meet the requirements. Usually a form/questionnaire to fill in.

- **Psychometric tests** that test your standard of literacy, numeracy and mechanical understanding. These tests can include comprehension questions, arithmetic and numerical problem solving, memory tests and spatial reasoning tests. They are usually multiple choice and often there is a time limit. The Army test (BARB) is done on a touch sensitive monitor and a computer. The computer then prints out which jobs you are suitable for based on your score. Few people are good at all the different types of questions and you usually find one or two will be very difficult to answer. Your local library may have books on how to pass psychometric tests and opportunities to practice the tests.

- **Medical test** to make sure that you are healthy.

- **Presentations** are sometimes used to gauge how you perform in uncomfortable situations and to test your communication and planning skills. The key is to prepare well, practice your presentation and ask for questions at the end.

Think about what questions could be asked and prepare answers for them.

- **Interview** to see what kind of person you are, what your motivation is and what qualities you have. The forces use interviews to decide which branch/unit you ought to join. Preparation and planning will ensure the interview process runs smoothly:

  1 Know where you're going and how long it will take to get there. Take a practice run if you need to, but make sure it's at the same time of day as the interview as traffic conditions vary. Organise your transport before hand.

  2 Think about what kind of questions you may be asked and have answers prepared. Find books on interview techniques which will give you an idea of the kind of questions to expect.

  3 Learn as much as you can about the service and the jobs it does. Knowledge of local work is good as this will show the interviewer how keen you are.

  4 Think about questions that you can ask. Look at the conditions of service on pages 104–105 and think about what things you'd like to know about the job, the training and the selection process.

  5 Dress appropriately and smartly. Iron your clothes, polish your shoes and make sure your hair is tidy. When applying for a post in the uniformed services you need to show you can present yourself in the proper manner.

  6 Turn up early and inform the receptionist or a member of staff who you are and what you're there for. Make a good impression by being polite and smile because you're assessed from the moment you walk in the door.

  7 Try to relax. The more relaxed you are the better you'll perform.

- **Physical test** is undertaken by most services to see if you have the fitness needed and the motivation to get fit in the first place. Many

services use the bleep test for endurance purposes so practice it as much as you can. Other tests used include press ups, sit ups, timed mile and a half runs, pull ups and so on. The fitter you are before the test the easier it will be.

The forces usually require you to go away on a selection weekend to test aspects such as teamwork, communication and how you cope being away from home and in a disciplined environment. The Royal Marines selection course is the Potential Royal Marines Course run over three days at the Commando Training Centre in Devon. There you undertake lots of fitness training but also see what military life is like and talk to Commandos in training.

One important thing to remember is that the selection process is a two-way thing. You get to look at the service as well as them looking at you. You can ask them questions and raise any concerns so that you know whether it is the right decision for you.

Key concepts

1 Different services have different requirements for different jobs.

2 Requirements can be academic, physical or concerned with your nationality and past.

3 All require a good standard of health and fitness and a good command of English and numeracy.

4 Certain qualities are important to all the services, for example teamwork and communication.

5 Some of the qualities and requirements may need work such as improving your fitness, practicing your communication skills, doing written tests.

6 You need an up to date CV to help you with application forms.

7 Always photocopy application forms, fill them out in rough and get someone to check them.

8 Be tidy, smart and professional at selection courses. Remember what you're there to demonstrate.

Entry requirements and opportunities

Preparation prior to basic training

All services provide different roles and therefore need to have different elements in their basic training which you need to prepare for. However, there are some training aspects that are common to all services.

Before your training begins you will be given comprehensive information about the course: where you'll be, what you'll be doing, what you need to bring with you, etc. Study this carefully and ensure that you know what everything means. There will also be a contact number or email in case you have any questions about the training course.

Before basic training begins it is advisable to do the following:

- Do as much physical training as possible to increase your fitness. Basic training is very tough: long days, early mornings, lots of new people and experiences. It will be very tiring physically and mentally so the fitter you are before you go the easier it will be. Look at Unit 9 to see the kind of training you should be doing. Don't just go to the gym and work on strength because it will only slow you down, do lots of running and aerobic work. If you already play a sport or do an activity, then keep it up. Sport is a good way of keeping fit and a good stress release. Many services include swimming in their training programmes so it's a good skill to have before you go.

- Practice some of the skills you'll be learning in training. For example, in the forces you will have to cover navigation and first aid, so if you can already use a map and compass then get out onto the hills and practice. Try to learn as much as possible about the service and the

job you are going to be doing as any preparation will make life easier.

- Make sure that you have all the required items before you go (appropriate clothing, personal documents, wash kit, etc). Again if you have any queries, then ask. Don't turn up on the day with the wrong kit or without something essential.

- Most uniformed services expect you to take care of your personal belongings which means cleaning and ironing your uniform and polishing your footwear. If you can't do these things now, it's a good time to learn.

Basic training in the police force

Training for the police lasts 2 years, although this includes a long period of probation where trainees are on the beat and doing the job of a police officer. The training has 6 stages:

1 Introduction to policing

This takes place within the Force you have applied to and lasts up to 2 weeks. During the first week, trainees receive their uniform and are sworn in as police officers before a magistrate. They now have all the powers and responsibilities of all police constables.

2 Core skills

This section of training takes place at the National Police Training Centre and concentrates on the main skills and knowledge required of police officers. Core skills include training for self defence and restraint techniques as well as the situations in which these techniques are allowed. Police officers need to have knowledge of relevant laws and these are also covered as well as legislation that affects the police such as PACE 1984. Assessment will be by tests and simulations (role plays) which will be observed and marked. This stage lasts for 15 weeks and following completion of this stage, trainees receive a week's leave.

3 Local procedures

The next stage takes place back within the force you have applied for at their training centre for 2 weeks to learn about the District and the local procedures and community. Preparation will also be made for the next stage.

4 Tutor patrol

This stage is based at the District the trainee is expected to work at and lasts 10 weeks. During this time the trainee will be putting what they have learnt into practice on patrol accompanied by a Tutor Constable.

5 Review and preparation for independent patrol

This is a 2 week course at the Force training centre to review the tutor patrol phase. Further training is available if necessary and trainees are prepared for independent patrol.

6 Independent patrol

Carried out at Division level, this will make up the remainder of the probationary period. This involves patrolling as a Police officer without the aid of a tutor. Performance will be monitored to ensure that probationers work to the required level and more training will take place, for a minimum of 30 days throughout this stage.

Training for prospective Metropolitan officers is slightly different with only 3 phases and a focus on policing in London.

At numerous points throughout basic training, probationers must repeat and pass the fitness test to continue training. Stage 2 includes fitness to a higher standard than the fitness test so potential recruits should work to improve their fitness in preparation. It is important to continue with physical training throughout the probationary period to pass all the tests. Currently there is no annual fitness test for Police officers but some believe that there soon will be.

Due to the large amount of information that needs to be learnt at the start of training, much of the work is in classrooms. The later stages involve little classroom work, however, as the probationers are out on patrol practicing their skills.

Training at Force level is concerned with local procedures and special needs of the community that may be unique. For example, a rural force will have different demands upon the officers than a force with many towns and cities. The same is true of divisional training.

Basic training in the Army

Basic training in the Army for non-commissioned ranks consists of 12 weeks of soldier training which is called Phase I training as follows:

- Week 1

  This week is an introduction to training where recruits look at aspects such as basic drill and marching, map and compass and weapon familiarisation. Fitness tests are taken to assess recruits fitness levels and there are talks on equal opportunitities and how to behave. Army protocol is also taught: who to salute, who to call Sir and whose orders to take.

- Week 2

  This week is based around fieldcraft skills such as camouflage, using ration packs, building bashas (shelters) and movement at night.

- Week 3

  In week 3, recruits get to fire weapons, but only on a computer shooting range. Recruits are offered plenty of practice of this important skill over the week.

- Week 4

  Graduating from the computer simulations, graduates now to get to fire live rounds on a 25m course.

- Week 5

  Week 5 is a week of tests as fitness is assessed once more and fitness levels should be higher than week 1. Drills are also tested with recruits expected to be "Passing off the Square" by the end of the week. After this recruits can wear the headdress of the unit they will join after basic training.

- **Week 6**

  At this point in the training, recruits are usually given a break and allowed some leave to go home.

- **Week 7**

  Week 7 is based around assault courses and night firing. As fitness levels are expected to be quite high by now, recruits have to complete the assault courses in full kit with webbing and weapons.

- **Week 8**

  This week usually includes a 3 day exercise practicing what has been learnt so far including section combat. The Annual Personal Weapons Test is also included in this week.

- **Week 9**

  Week 9 includes further training and another fitness assessment.

- **Week 10**

  Week 10 consists of adventure training in a National Park such as Snowdonia, the Lakes or the Peak District involving canoeing, climbing, hill walking, caving, orienteering, etc. All these areas are important for building self-confidence and teamwork skills.

- **Week 11**

  Everything recruits have learnt so far will be examined this week, such as final fitness assessment and night exercise, usually in practical situations.

- **Week 12**

  Preparation for Passing Out, where recruits finally become soldiers as witnessed by parents and family.

Following Phase I soldiers are allowed some leave before moving on to Phase II training where they learn how to do the job they joined for. For some units, for example Infantry this may take a few weeks. For more technical trade-based jobs it could take 2 years. Following Phase II soldiers are posted on active duty.

Passing Out ceremony in the Army

Basic training for officers

Basic training for officers is different. They are the managers of the Army and need to learn how to lead their soldiers in addition to all of the above. Their training is done at Sandhurst and lasts for 44 weeks, split into 3 terms. After completing term 3, recruits become a Second Lieutenant or Lieutenant (if they have a degree) and start Phase II training. Upon finishing Phase II they are posted to command their own platoon or troop of up to 20 soldiers.

Theory into practice

Investigate the basic training for another service. How long does it last? Where does the training take place and what do recruits study?

Non-completion of basic training

Not all recruits make it through basic training. This can be for a number of reasons, some of which are listed below:

- **Injury** can be common during intense physical activity. Basic training usually starts recruits off gradually to avoid problems, but accidents can always happen. In the case of the Army, some injuries may lead to back–squadding where the recruit has to wait to recuperate before joining another group of recruits. If the injury is too serious it may end the recruit's military career as they may not be capable of doing the job adequately.

- **Personal problems** can cause recruits to leave, such as problems with relationships at home or problems with other recruits. Some people join the services too early and just get homesick. Training staff always try to counsel recruits to do what is best for the recruit. Sometimes recruits are advised to leave in order to mature a little or sort their problems out and apply again.

- **Fitness** factors can lead to recruits leaving. Sometimes the training is too physical for some people, no matter how hard they try. Jobs in the uniformed services can be very physical and it can be better to leave in training if recruits are not capable of doing the job.

- **Wrong perception of service** – Everyone has ideas about what it's like to be in the uniformed services. Careers information tries to give a realistic view of service work and life, but it is always different to live the life than to read or watch about it. Sometimes the reality does not match up with the picture people may have in their head. It may be too physical, too disciplined, too easy or just not suitable. Again,

it's better to leave during training than to have to do a job you do not like.

Think about it

Discuss other reasons why recruits may leave the services and how these reasons could be avoided? What are the drop out rates for particular services? Do you think training programmes should be changed in light of the drop out rates?

Skills developed during basic training

There are a range of skills developed during basic training including:

- technical
- teamwork
- communication.

Technical skills

Technical skills are the specific skills required by the service. For example, the Armed Forces require their recruits to learn how to fire and operate assault rifles, Navy recruits learn how to fight fires on ships, Police recruits learn about the law and how it affects their job and Prison officers have to know how to interact with the inmates and how to deal with riots.

Teamwork skills

Teamwork skills are essential in all of the uniformed services and recruits are encouraged right from the start to consider themselves as part of a team and to work together. This can range from playing team sports together, helping fellow recruits with problems with their studies or cooking together on exercise. This is a skill that selection officers look for in potential recruits but is certainly developed during training in all the services. Often this is emphasised through adventure training where recruits have to depend on each other for their lives, for example when rock climbing. Throughout the training programme recruits will be given problems that they cannot solve on their own to make them see the benefits of teamwork. Towards the end of their training recruits should be working as a team without conscious thought.

Communication skills

Sometimes linked with teamwork, communication is essential to all the uniformed services. In the Army, for example communication is important to ensure that everyone knows what the situation is on the battlefield, where friendly troops are and how many enemy forces there are. The Police need to be able to communicate with all kinds of people, for example when taking statements from witnesses, liasing with other services personnel at an accident or defusing potentially violent situations. Paramedics need to be able to communicate with their patients or witnesses in order to determine their best course of action and to communicate symptoms and injuries effectively to doctors and other specialists.

Theory into practice
What other qualities and skills are developed during basic training?

Career development

This final section looks at the prospects that are available to people serving in the uniformed services. This includes promotion but also opportunities for changing roles, specialising in different jobs and further education and training. Career development is a big part of life in the services with all personnel encouraged to make plans for their career and develop themselves, both professionally and personally.

Rank structure

All of the uniformed services use a rank structure to show seniority. The higher you climb on the rank ladder, the more responsibility you have, either for other people or for more important jobs or equipment. Personnel in some jobs are required to have a minimum rank in order that they can perform their job properly. An example of this is the Army Military Police who are promoted to Lance Corporal upon finishing phase II training.

The Armed Forces have 2 rank structures: enlisted personnel and commissioned ranks (officers). The 2 different rankings represent an important division in the forces between officers and the other ranks. Both have different messes (bars or common rooms) and rarely mix outside of doing their jobs.

Officers are responsible for managing the service and making all the big decisions. An Infantry Lieutenant, for example, will decide how the platoon will assault an objective (where the assault group will move from, where the machine gun will be set up, etc). The non-commissioned ranks are the ones who do the job (that's not to say that the Lieutenant won't be part of the fire fight, of course).

The Lieutenant's second in command (2IC) is a Sergeant, a non-commissioned officer who oversees the other soldiers doing the job. Sergeants have years of experience behind them while Lieutenants are only starting their military career. The Sergeant is therefore invaluable to the officer as he knows the platoon and how to motivate them and his military skills are well practiced. It is not unusual for lieutenants to ask sergeants for advice. The same is true of all the forces with junior officers being assisted by non-coms. Later in their careers, officers tend to have an idea of how the Army works but they usually have command of more men and are assisted by higher ranking sergeants (or Warrant Officers). It is possible for non-commissioned ranks to become officers but they have to go through the a selection process and, if successful, go through officer training.

The tables below show how the ranks correspond between the Forces. As you can see the Army has more non-commissioned ranks than the RAF and Navy. However, the tables are a simplified version of the rank structure as different regiments and trades can have different ranks or different names for ranks. In the Army, for example, a Private can be called Trooper, Gunner, Sapper or Signalman depending upon his/her regiment. In the RAF, there are additional ranks for different trades, for example Chief Technician and Master Aircrew.

In both rank structures, the higher up you go, the fewer people are present and at the top of the officer range, the posts are usually held by one person (so far only men). For example, there is only one Marshal of the RAF and only one Admiral of the Fleet. Although Field Marshal is the highest attainable rank in the Army, generals are the highest ranking Army officers we currently have.

Non-commissioned ranks of the Armed Forces		
Army	**RAF**	**Navy**
Warrant Officer Class 1	Warrant Officer	Warrant Officer
Warrant Officer Class 2		
Staff Sergeant	Flight Sergeant	Chief Petty Officer
Sergeant	Sergeant	Petty Officer
Corporal	Corporal	Leading Rate
Lance Corporal		
Private	Able Rate	Junior Technician
Private	Able Rate	Senior Aircraftman/woman
Private	Able Rate	Leading Aircraftman/woman

Commissioned ranks of the Armed Forces		
Army	**RAF**	**Navy**
Field Marshal	Marshal of the Royal Air Force	Admiral of the Fleet
General	Air Chief-Marshal	Admiral
Lieutenant General	Air Marshal	Vice-Admiral
Major General	Air Vice-Marshal	Rear admiral
Brigadier	Air Commodore	Commodore
Colonel	Group Captain	Captain
Lieutenant Colonel	Wing Commander	Commander
Major	Squadron Leader	Lieutenant-Commander
Captain	Flight Lieutenant	Lieutenant
Lieutenant	Flying Officer	Sub-Lieutenant
Second Lieutenant	Pilot Officer	Midshipman

Figure 8.3 Non-commissioned and commissioned ranks of the Armed Forces

Promotion

In the uniformed services, you have to show your commitment to the service by serving for a minimum amount of time before you can apply for promotion. For example, in the Police and Fire service, officers can only apply for promotion once they have finished their 2 year probationary period. In the Army you can expect to serve 5 years before promotion to Corporal. In many ways, going for promotion is the same as applying for a job: you need to show the required qualities and experience and there must be a vacancy.

There are many reasons why members of the uniformed service want to climb up the ranks and gain promotion in their chosen careers, for example, as you rise up the promotion ladder you get more pay and promotions can present challenges and, in turn rewards.

Promotion in the Armed Forces

In the Army, for a Private to be eligible for promotion he must have:

- **Experience** – usually about 5 years of being a Private, to prove that you can do the job.

- **Military training** – having a wide range of training and specialisation, for example sniper will prove adaptability and interest in the service. The forces have many courses that you can apply for to test and teach leadership, for example The Junior NCO (JNCO) Course is a pre-requisite for Lance Corporals.

- **Technical training** – again the forces provide courses that are more technical such as driving qualifications, IT qualifications, etc. For some trades these qualifications may be essential, for others just desirable.

- **Education** – formal qualifications such as GCSEs, A levels, BTECs and NVQs are all useful and show ability. If you join the forces without some of these qualifications, you can take them while you are serving. The forces offer excellent opportunities to improve your qualifications.

- **Recommendation in annual report** – all soldiers have an annual report from their Commanding Officer, a bit like a school report, showing how well they are doing. If they are showing leadership qualities and progressing well it will be noted in their report and a recommendation for promotion made.

If you meet all of the above criteria you could be put on a list with all the others who deserve promotion. This list is graded in merit order and if you are near the top and there is an opening for the Lance Corporal post then you may be promoted. The higher you progress up the ranks, the harder it is to get to the next level, both in terms of competition and of the qualities you have to prove. To rise through the ranks you have to pass several courses, usually 1 or 2 per level. For example, to gain a Corporal's stripe in the Infantry, you need to complete the Section Commander's Battle Course. For Sergeant you must pass the Platoon Sergeant's Battle Course and Education for Promotion I (EFP I) course and be recommended in your annual report.

Promotion in the fire service

The fire service have a slightly different procedure. After the 2 year probation period, Firefighters can apply for promotion. A firefighter must be able to prove that they are suitable and eligible for the next rank and this can be shown through experience of doing the basic job and experience of specialisation and different jobs. If accepted, the Firefighter must complete a number

A firefighter in action

of written and practical exams. The examinations for leading firefighter are as follows:

- **Written exams**
  1. Operations
  2. Fire safety education and enforcement
  3. Human resource management
  4. Business administration
- **Practical exams**
  1. Standard drill
  2. Fireground procedure drill
  3. Equipment test

The written papers must be taken over 3 consecutive years; the practicals must be passed within 3 years of passing the written exams. This means that even while they are working toward promotion, Fire fighters are still gaining practical experience.

Theory into practice
Investigate the promotion requirements for the police service.

Key concepts
Promotion depends upon a number of things:

1. Experience/years served.
2. Qualifications.
3. Training.
4. Leadership qualities.
5. Recognition of the above, such as recommendations.

Specialisation

In all of the services there are a range of specialist jobs that become available only after you have completed your full training. These jobs are so specialised that only trained operatives can be considered to do them. For some people, specialisation can be a more rewarding reward than promotion: you don't have the responsibility of looking after others, but you get to do a more specialised job and there are lots of new things to learn. Many Police Constables stay at the same rank throughout their career but move around from department to department, changing specialisms.

In order to qualify for a specialisation you have to fulfil the required criteria. It's just like applying for a job all over again. Just because you can do the basic job doesn't mean that you can do a specialist role. In the Police, for example if you want to be a traffic motorcycle officer you need to know how to ride a motorcycle and in the case of mounted Police, how to ride a horse. Firearms Police need to have good, cool nerves and high hand-eye co-ordination in addition to higher than average fitness.

Once you can prove you meet the criteria for the post you need to know if there is a vacancy in that unit. If the SAS Regiment you want to join is full then you have to wait for someone to leave before you are considered, no matter how good you are. If there are vacancies then you may be considered. This may take the form of an application form and interview or another selection course. In the case of the SAS, they require potential members to show very high levels of fitness and military skill and competition for places is extremely high. If you are lucky enough to pass the selection process then you are in training again for your new job. The length of training varies with the specialisation.

Specialisms available in the Royal Marines

In a relatively small force like the Marines the following specialised jobs may be applied for if there is a vacancy:

- Armourer
- Chef
- Drill Instructor
- Mountain Leader
- Stores
- Vehicle Mechanic
- Heavy Weapons
- Landing Craft Crew
- Royal Marines Police
- Driver
- Physical Training Instructor

These jobs can only be applied for once recruits have passed the 30 weeks training, the Endurance Course, Tarzan Assault Course, speed marches and 30 mile march to obtain the green Commando beret.

Specialisms available in the police

These are some of the specialised jobs that may be available in some Police Forces, once the 2 year probation period has been successfully completed.

- Dog Handler
- Traffic
- Special Branch
- Firearms Unit
- Underwater Recovery Unit
- Air Support
- Mounted Police

Theory into practice

Choose another uniformed service and research the specialised jobs available to operatives.

End of unit questions

1 Give an example of humanitarian aid carried out by the Armed Forces.

2 Where have British forces fought a war to defend overseas territories?

3 Find the Mission Statement for the Coastguard Service.

4 What is the name of the UK's assault rifle?

5 List the roles of the fire service

6 List the roles of the police service.

7 Make a list of positive points of being in the services.

8 What are *performance indicators*?

9 What are "conditions of service"?

10 What do Special Constables do?

11 What percentage of the Army does the TA make up?

12 List the entry requirements for the service of your choice.

13 What are *psychometric tests*?

14 Describe the selection process for the service of your choice.

15 Make a list of interview dos and don'ts.

16 Describe the basic training for a service of your choice.

17 List the personal qualities required by the service of your choice.

18 Why do some people drop out of basic training?

19 List the rank structure of a service of your choice.

20 What is the difference between commissioned and non-commissioned ranks? What does *commissioned* mean?

Assessment activities

This section describes what you must do to obtain a pass grade for this unit.

A merit or dstinction grate may be awarded if your work demonstrates a deeper understanding of the topics and is of a higher quality. The highlighted sentences indicate the quality of work expected at merit and distinction level.

Assessment methods

A number of assessment strategies may be used in order to achieve the learning outcomes, such as oral presentations, group discussions, written assignments, research projects and role-plays or a combination of these. It is a good idea, though it is not essential, to use a variety of methods in order to develop different skills.

It is important that you understand and comply with the key words specified in the grading criteria. For example, if you are asked to 'analyse' something, then make sure that you do not merely describe it. Similarly, if you are asked to 'evaluate' something, then make sure you do not merely summarise it.

Key words

Here are some key words that are often used for grading criteria – make sure you understand the differences between them.

Examine	To look at a subject closely in order to understand it and improve your knowledge
Consider	This means to think about and weigh up a subject
Explain	This means to make something clear and set out the arguments
Analyse	This means to look at a subject closely and interpret or evaluate your findings. Perhaps outlining the pro's and con's of a situation or suggesting changes and improvements
Describe	This means to say what something is like, it is a factual account of how something is or how it appears.
Compare	This means to look at the similarities between two or more objects or theories.

Assessment tasks

Using the materials within this unit and your own research, carry out the following tasks.

Task 1

Learning outcome 1 – Examine the role, purpose and responsibilities of a range of uniformed services

Outline the roles, purpose and responsibilities of two named uniformed public service organisations

Describe the implications and positive and negative aspects of working in the uniformed services on a personal level

To obtain a merit grade, you should *analyse* the positive and negative aspects of working in the uniformed services

Suggestion for outcome 1: small group presentation, followed by a discussion.

Firstly, in groups of three, research two named services and describe why those services exist and what they do, including examples of recent work. You could choose to cover local services, such as your regional police force or fire brigade, or nearest Army/TA regiment. Allow 15 minutes to cover all the information and ensure that all members of the group are fully involved (everybody should do an equal share of presentation and research). Using visual aids would be advantageous.

Secondly, in a larger group, discuss the implications of being in a public service. Remember, this is where you can pick up a merit – you must analyse, not just describe.

Both of these tasks should be recorded and an assessor's testimony would also be useful.

Task 2

Learning outcome 2 – Examine a range of jobs and conditions of service within the uniformed services

Explain the range of jobs that are available in the uniformed services at operative level

Suggestion for outcome 2: piece of personal written work

Write an assignment explaining which jobs are available to operatives in one uniformed service, including an investigation into the conditions of service for that uniformed service.

Obviously, this would be most useful to you if you look at the service you wish to join; you'll then know what's available to do and what's required of you in that service.

If your choosen career is the Armed Forces there is a lot of information available on the Internet and careers offices are also very useful. For other services, you should make contact with your local station to see what information they can offer.

Task 3

Learning outcome 3 – Investigate the application and selection process for a given uniformed service

Compare the entry requirements for an officer in two different public services

Outline the selection process for a job in one of the uniformed services

Suggestion for outcome 3: individual written work and role plays

First part: draw up a table comparing the entry requirements for an officer in at least two public services. Following this, look at the requirements to see if you would be acceptable for that service. If you are not up to standard, explain why and outline what you can do to improve and get to the required standard?

Second part: obtain application forms for the service you would like to join (most service websites tell you how you can do this) and fill it in completely and accurately. Once this is done, in groups of four you can then role play the application and selection process:

- Look through each other's application forms to ensure that they have been filled out properly.

- Interview one another. This involves a bit of research into what kind of questions are asked in an interview. Don't forget to research good answers to the questions as well.

- Carry out any written tests that are used by that service. Your tutors should be able to help with this or you could contact your nearest station or careers office to see if they have any sample tests for prospective applicants.

- Carry out any other tests, for example fitness, role plays, etc

Again, recording your role play will be good practice as well as proving that you've done it.

Task 4

Learning outcome 4 – Explore the entry requirements and opportunities for career development within a given uniformed service

Describe the entry requirements and opportunities for career development in one of the uniformed services

> To obtain a merit grade, you should *analyse* the entry requirements and opportunities for career development in one of the uniformed services

> To obtain a distinction grade, you should *evaluate and justify* the entry requirements for career development in one of the uniformed services

Suggestion for outcome 4: individual report

Produce a report detailing the opportunities for career development in one of the services and then look at the entry requirements for these opportunities. Remember that career development is not only about promotion: there are plenty of things to do in all the services that do not involve gaining rank.

This is another area where you can work for a higher grade. To get a Merit grade you need to show *analysis* of this information. For a distinction, you must *evaluate and justify* the things you have written about. This will mean comparing the requirements with the opportunities (evaluating) and explaining why they exist (justifying).

PHYSICAL PREPARATION FOR THE UNIFORMED SERVICES

Introduction to Unit 9

This unit looks at the physical preparation required for entry into the public services and the range of training methods provided to develop fitness for the uniformed services. It also provides the opportunity to undertake fitness testing procedures and tests for the uniformed services in a 'safe' environment. In addition, you will design and implement your own training programme to prepare for a uniformed service of your choice.

Assessment

Throughout the unit, activities and tasks will help you to learn and remember information. Case studies are also included to add industry relevance to the topics and learning objectives. At the end of the unit there are assessment activities to help you provide evidence which meets the learning outcomes for the unit. You are reminded that when you are completing activities and tasks, opportunities will be created to enhance your key skills evidence.

After completing this unit you should have an understanding of the following outcomes.

Outcomes

1 Investigate and demonstrate the need for **safe practice** in the physical training environment

2 Explore the range of **uniformed service fitness tests**

3 Research, conduct and analyse the range of **fitness training** types and techniques

4 Undertake a **training programme** to prepare for a uniformed service of your choice.

Note: the information in this unit is meant as a guide and does not replace the need for professionally qualified experts to oversee your tests and training. Specialists such as these can offer even further advice on safety and training.

Safe practice in the physical training environment

When carrying out your physical training session:

- ensure you know what your aims are and that the type of training fits your aims, for example a strength session that involves huge amounts of running doesn't suit the aim

- check the participants are wearing appropriate clothing and footwear and are safe to perform the activities

- check the appropriate equipment is available, you know how to use it properly and that it's safe to use

- remember to start with a warm up and ensure you use appropriate stretches for the body parts you will be using

- always plan to finish with a cool down, stretching the muscles you used

- keep a copy of your plan with you and write some prompts on it so that you don't forget certain things

- ensure the venue has a completed risk assessment – try to look at the venue to see what the risks are and what the suggested controls are that you should take.

Health and safety

When a fitness session of any kind (training or testing) is about to begin, the whole area and equipment to be used must be prepared, made safe and ready. Following the health and safety points below will eliminate most potential problems and lead to a safe and effective session.

Area checks

The place you are going to use for your training should be suitable for that purpose and must be safe. The following factors must be taken into account for any training area:

- the indoor floor area should be dry and clear of equipment and other obstacles

- fire exits should be clearly marked and free of obstructions

- you must know what the emergency procedures are in the case of a fire, including the position of the fire alarm, fire exits and meeting points

- you must know the location of first aid equipment and qualified first aiders

- you must know the location of the nearest telephone

- no glass containers (or other shatterable material) must be taken into the training area

- the outdoor floor must be suitable for the activity, for example clear of debris, stones, glass and not too wet or muddy for the activity

- in cold weather, well used fields can have ridges that freeze leaving hard, sharp edges

- you must ensure you have ample daylight if training outdoors

- check the weather forecast and arrange alternatives if necessary.

Theory into practice

Carry out a health and safety check of your sports hall or fitness suite including the location of telephones, first aid equipment, etc. Are there any health and safety problems?

Equipment checks

The equipment being used for your training should be:

- inspected regularly to ensure that it is in good condition and safe to use – if in doubt *do not use it!*

- used in the correct manner, for the correct purpose. For heavy weights you may need a spotter (a friend to support the weights if you are struggling and to replace the weights safely if you cannot complete the repetition)

All training equipment should be checked before use

- properly replaced when no longer needed

- checked before use, for example collars are properly fitted to bar/dumbbells, suitable resistance (weight) is used, no frayed cables or loose parts and bar/dumbbells are equally weighted

- understood before it is used – ask for an induction or read the instructions.

Participant checks

After ensuring that the area and equipment are safe and suitable to use, it is important to check that you and any other participants involved are ready for exercise. Ensure the following:

- suitable footwear is worn, for example running shoes for running and climbing shoes for climbing

- tie all laces

- wear comfortable and non-restrictive clothing, taking account of the weather when outdoors

- remove any jewellery (it can injure you or others and can easily be damaged)

- do not chew gum as you could accidentally swallow it and choke

- avoid eating for at least 2 hours before training to allow the food to settle

- do not take part if you are ill or injured or too tired

- complete a proper warm up before the main session

- end the session with a cool down

- drink plenty of fluids (preferably water or specific sports drinks) before, during and after training as you need hydration long before you feel thirsty – especially important in hot conditions

- don't forget sun screen and/or a hat in hot weather if you are outside

- ensure that everyone is in the right state of mind and ready to perform the activities in the proper manner

- try not to train alone, both for safety reasons and motivation.

It is important to ensure you are properly dressed for exercise

Principles of standing-in

Standing-in applies to following exact guidelines with reference to safety whether you are running a fitness training programme or on the front-line in action. For example, if a trainer is training recruits and has to leave in the middle of the programme and someone takes the trainer's place, there should not be any change of instruction from one trainer to another as they should be following the exact same guidelines. Likewise, in the line of action, if a senior member of personnel is injured, the next person in authority must 'stand-in' and follow the same military guidelines.

Warm ups

One of the most important, but often under-appreciated, components of the fitness session is the warm up. It prepares the body and mind for exercise and helps to prevent injuries. Once you have checked the venue and all participants, it is essential to complete a warm up. This should be done progressively, starting gently and slowly increasing the work load.

There are 2 parts to a warm up:

1 **Aerobic phase**
   This is used to raise the heart beat. By stimulating the heart and the lungs, blood circulates around the body and literally *warms* the body up. This is important as muscles which are cold can be easily damaged. Any rhythmical activity that can be kept up for the required time is acceptable, for example running, cycling, rowing, stepping and skipping. This part of the warm up should last about 5–10 minutes, but obviously varies on the individual and the environment. If you start sweating, you're ready for the next phase.

2 **Stretching**
   This follows the aerobic phase and uses the muscles that are going to be used in the session's activities. For example, if you are climbing you would stretch the arms, fingers,

back and legs. Practicing the actual skill you will be doing later can also be included in the warm up as long as it is done gently and not at full speed. This part of the warm up can prevent strain in the muscles that are going to be used in the session. The stretches should be held for about 10 seconds, with this phase lasting 5–10 minutes.

Once the warm up is completed, your body will be ready to start working harder. You will also be more ready psychologically to take part in the session as you've had 10 minutes getting used to working your body. This can be important if you haven't been particularly active prior to the session.

Theory into practice

Pick a sport or activity and create a warm up specifically for it, including detailed stretches.

Cool downs

A cooling down period is just as important as the warm up and should follow on at the end of the session. The cool down does the opposite of the warm up by bringing the heart rate down to normal levels and preparing you for leaving the fitness environment. It is also very important in preventing injury and muscle ache. Again, there are 2 parts to a cool down routine:

1 **Light aerobic work**
   This is essential in slowing the heart rate down. If you stop training abruptly, your heart rate will actually continue to increase, which is not healthy. By doing some moderate work the heart starts to calm down and blood flow returns to normal, preventing it from pooling in the muscles used. This has 2 advantages. Firstly, without a regular supply of oxygenated blood the brain ceases to function and shuts down leading to fainting. Secondly, the blood in the muscles will contain poisons created in

Warm up and cool down exercises are important parts of a fitness session

the anaerobic energy process and oxygen breaks down these poisons.

Any rhythmic activity like light jogging, walking, light cycling or rowing can be used to cool down. Aim for 5–10 minutes to give the heart time to get used to the change in work rate.

2 **Stretching**
Stretching can help the muscles recover from the session and prevent aching. By stretching the muscles used, blood flow is stimulated and fresh oxygen is delivered. Flexibility training is also best done at the end of a session, when the muscles have been worked hard and can be stretched further resulting in an increased range of movement. Stretches during the cool down should be performed for a minimum of 15 seconds. This part of the training session can also be turned into suppleness training, adding another fitness factor into your session.

Figure 9.1 Upper body stretches

Figure 9.2 Lower body stretches

Cool downs are also important psychologically as they allow your mind to calm down and remove any stress, aggression, competitiveness, etc that may have built up during the session or test.

Theory into practice
Using the same sport or activity chosen on page 135, create a cool down routine specifically for it, including stretches.

Pulse ups

Pulse ups are a training technique used to get the heart working and to develop cardio-vascular stamina. It's a good way of working the heart and can be used as a warm up, starting slowly and increasing the pace. Stretching should still be included in the warm up. It can also be used after a warm up to develop stamina.

Pulse ups involve changing the intensity of the activity to make the heart work harder and easier in sequence. For example, pulse ups could be practiced in a sports hall by walking the length of the hall, then sprinting, jogging twice, sprinting, walking, sprinting, jogging, etc. The change in pace ensures that the heart experiences overload and the body is pushing the anaerobic threshold. In this way it is similar to *interval* and *fartlek* training (see page 151). Clearly this is not recommended for unfit people or those with heart problems.

Flexibility and stretches

At one time, weight lifters concentrated on building strength and simply lifted weights. Consequently, their bodies became heavily muscle bound and they had very limited movement around their joints. This is because they did no flexibility or suppleness training (stretching). It is now accepted that all of the 'S' factors (strength, stamina, suppleness, speed, skill, sleep and psychology) are important to general fitness.

Unfortunately, some activities can inhibit flexibility which means that you will need to do stretches to maintain suppleness. These activities tend to be those that do not allow the muscles to use their full range of motion, for example boxing, football, running and hockey. For such activities the cool down should include plenty of stretching of the muscles used.

Flexibility training has a number of advantages:

- stretching increases the range of movement around a joint thereby reducing the chance of injury to muscles, tendons and ligaments

- it decreases the tightening of muscles after exercise and reduces muscle soreness

- greater speed and power can result from actions using a wider range of movement

- muscle shortening due to muscle bulking (leading to being muscle bound) is prevented

- coordination between muscle groups is enhanced allowing for better skill acquisition

- muscles can be more easily relaxed, which can lead to psychological relaxation

- some sports/activities require a high degree of flexibility for proper performance, for example martial arts, dance, gymnastics and climbing.

Types of stretching

There are many ways to stretch muscles, some of which are outlined below.

Dynamic stretching

As *dynamic* means moving, this type of stretching involves controlled movements of the arms and legs to the limits of their range of movement. You must ensure the movement is controlled, not jerky. Martial artists use dynamic stretching to increase flexibility for high kicks. The action must be started gently and the range is increased gradually; to about 10–12 repetitions only. This can be used as part of a warm up as the movement also increases heart rate and blood flow.

Active stretching

This form of stretching is the most difficult to do but the most effective and also gives the best indication of an individual's flexibility. Active stretches are put into the position and held there without support, only using the strength of the muscles to hold it there. One example of this is a martial artist demonstrating a high kick and leaving his leg in the kick position. Fifteen seconds in one stretch is the maximum time an active stretch should be held for.

Active stretching can be very effective

Passive stretching

With this form of stretching, the stretch position is made and held where the muscle feels stretched (but not painfully so) for 10–15 seconds. The stretch does not move and is sometimes called *static stretching.* A partner can help you to maintain the stretch.

Isometric stretching

This type of stretch appears to be static but actually involves using resistance in the muscle. This builds strength in the stretched muscle and is much more effective than using passive stretching alone. Isometric stretching needs something to resist, to force against. This can be the floor, a wall or a partner. An example is the calf stretch, where you stand with your hands on the wall as if you were trying to push the wall.

Proprioceptive neuromuscular facilitation (PNF) stretching

This involves a combination of passive and isometric stretching. First the stretch is held statically then resistance is applied isometrically, followed by a final passive stretch. For best results PNF stretching should be done with a partner. When researched, this form of stretching has shown the best results.

Purposes of stretching

Stretches can be done for a number of purposes:

Preparatory stretching is what you do in a warm up: gently stretching to prepare the muscle for activity and to prevent injury. Remember that in a warm up you are not trying to improve your flexibility, you are just warming the muscles.

Maintenance stretching is done to ensure no loss of suppleness. If you don't need to increase your flexibility you will practice maintenance stretching. By repeating the warm up stretches for a slightly longer time in your cool down you will maintain your level of flexibility.

Developmental stretching is done to increase suppleness. As discussed earlier, this is best done after exercise (perfect for cool downs) while the muscles are warm. PNF stretches are good for improving flexibility and you should aim to increase your range of movement with each stretch. Hold developmental stretches for longer than the others, usually more than 15 seconds is necessary to show improvement.

Good practice for stretching

You must be aware of the following points when stretching muscles to avoid injury:

- do all stretches properly as incorrect stretches can put excessive stress on joints and lead to injury
- do not bounce when stretching to increase the range of movement – it is dangerous, ineffective and can result in injury.
- start stretches gently and increase the range of movement gradually
- stop if you feel pain
- stretch regularly to avoid decreasing your flexibility
- stretch before and after activity (stretching during an activity will not be detrimental)
- do not bend the head back as the neck is very delicate and easily damaged – head rotations are good for preventing injury to the neck but avoid rolling the head to the back, just go side to side.

Theory into practice

Research a range of stretches that can be performed in a warm up/cool down period.

Uniformed service fitness tests

Most uniformed services have a fitness test as part of their selection process. They are used to ensure that:

- all new recruits start training at a minimum standard level of fitness

- applicants have the necessary motivation to perform in the services

- applicants understand that fitness is important to the job

- applicants will be able to physically do the job they are applying for.

The fitness tests are chosen to best represent the needs of the service and are often reviewed. Reviews can lead to changes so it is beneficial to keep up to date with the service you wish to join.

Police fitness tests

The police service work-related fitness test is a standard test used nationally by all forces as part of their selection process. If accepted, recruits will have to repeat the test at various times in their training/probationary period, so maintaining fitness is important. At the National Training Centre recruits will undergo more rigorous physical training and tests, but the work related fitness test is the entry selection test.

There are 4 areas:

1 **Speed and agility test**

Home Office reviews have suggested that this test be taken out of the police fitness test but some services, such as South Yorkshire still use it to test applicants.

This test involves running a slalom course through cones marked out over a 13 m course. The 4 cones are laid out along the course and there are 3 lines: start line, finish line and end

line. The course is to be run as follows and must be completed within 27 seconds to achieve a pass:

- sprint from the start line to the end line going around the end cone and back to the start (see Figure 9.3 overleaf)

- without stopping you must then negotiate the slalom course sprinting around the cones there and back

- after running around the start cone, you again sprint to the end line, around the end cone, back to the start, around the start cone and to the finish line.

2 **Grip strength test**

Grip strength is measured using a grip dynamometer which measures strength in the forearm. The dynamometer is held in the hand and the arm raised until it is straight and the hand is above the head. From this position squeeze the dynamometer as hard as possible while lowering the arm to the side. Stop squeezing when your arm is at your side and the readout will tell you the score. You have 2 attempts and your best score is used. The pass rate is 32 kgs.

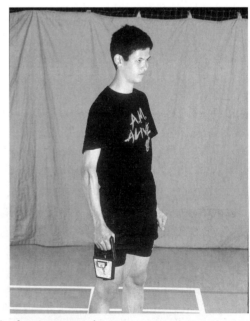

A grip dynamometer in use

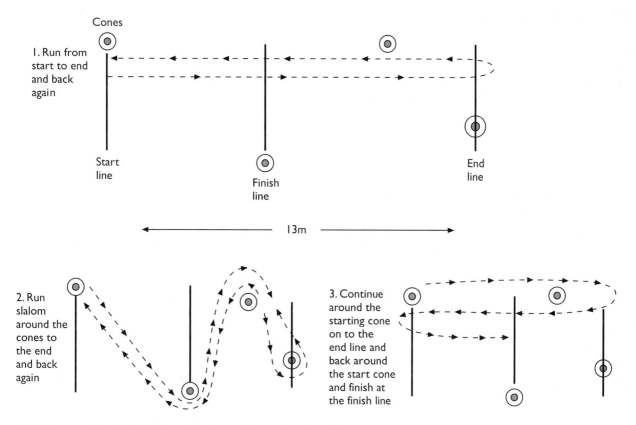

Figure 9.3 The speed and ability test for the police work-related fitness test

3 Dynamic strength test

This tests your upper body strength in your back and your chest. The equipment used is called a dyno and is similar to a rowing machine but both sides are used. To test the back, sit with your chest against the padding, grasp the handles and pull until your hands are level with your sternum. You then have 3 warm up attempts followed by 5 full strength pulls. The average of the 5 scores is recorded and the pass rate is 35 kgs.

To do the chest test, go around to the other side of the machine, sit down with your back to the padding, grasp the handles and push. Again, after 3 warm ups you get 5 full strength attempts. Your average score is shown on the monitor and the pass rate is 34 kgs.

4 Multi-stage fitness test

This test is used to measure aerobic fitness (stamina/cardio-vascular) by using the 'bleep

test'. Cones are set up 15 m apart which you have to run between. You have to keep time to a series of bleeps played on a cassette. The time between the bleeps is the amount of time you have to run between the cones. As the test goes up in levels, the time between bleeps decreases, meaning you have to run faster. The pass rate is level s.4. This means that you must get to level 5 and then continue to run for 4 bleeps at that level. This is the level that the Home Office has suggested, but some services require a higher pass rate. The pass rate used be level 8.1, but has been lowered by most police services. Check with the service you wish to join what level they require for a pass.

Theory into practice

Evaluate the police work-related fitness test. What relevance do the tests have to police work?

The prison service fitness tests

In many ways the prison service is similar to the police service as they both fall under the responsibility of the Home Office; they both deal with offenders and they share a near-identical work related fitness test.

The prison service fitness test is identical to the police test except that it has 1 additional element which is the **shield technique test**: you must hold a 6 kg shield during control and restraint techniques.

Think about it

Is the police work-related fitness test relevant to the prison service? How similar are the job roles? Does the prison service deserve its own fitness test?

The Royal Navy fitness tests

Pre-joining

The Navy will soon be implementing a new fitness test called the pre-joining fitness test. This is an aerobic test performed on a treadmill at a fitness centre and consists of running 2.4 km (1½ miles) in as fast a time as possible. The following table shows the times required to pass the pre-joining fitness test by age and gender.

Age	Male	Female
16 – 24	12 mins 20 secs	14 mins 35 secs
25 – 29	12 mins 48 secs	15 mins 13 secs
30 – 34	13 mins 18 secs	15 mins 55 secs
35 – 39	13 mins 49 secs	16 mins 40 secs

The purpose of this test is to ensure that recruits pass their Phase I training and to give them some confidence prior to carrying on training.

Phase 1

During Phase I training, recruits will have to pass a more involved fitness test before they can move onto trade training.

For Ratings, the test consists of:

- **Aerobic fitness test** as detailed for the pre-joining fitness test with the same pass times.

- **Swimming test**: swim 40 m, then tread water for 3 minutes, then exit unaided.

- **Strength test**:

Men	Time
23–26 press ups	2 mins
39–53 sit ups	2 mins
5 × 60 m shuttle run	53–59 secs

Women	Time
17–19 press ups	2 mins
29–43 sit ups	2 mins
5 × 60 m shuttle run	66–72 secs

For Officers, the test consists of:

- **Aerobic fitness test** as detailed for the pre-joining fitness test but with different pass times as follows.

Age	Male	Female
16 – 24	11 mins 13 secs	13 mins 15 secs
25 – 29	11 mins 38 secs	13 mins 50 secs
30 – 34	12 mins 05 secs	14 mins 28 secs
35 – 39	12 mins 34 secs	15 mins 09 secs
Over 40	Special regulations apply	Special regulations apply

- **Swimming** and **strength** test as Ratings.

Theory into practice

Explain the relevance the tests have to jobs in the Royal Navy?

The Royal Marines fitness tests

Applicants for the Marines complete the Potential Royal Marines course (PRMC), which is a 3-day course held in Devon and includes assault courses, fitness tests, shooting, interviews and drill. The fitness elements are split between days 1 and 2:

Day 1

- Gym test:
  - Bleep test (20 m course)
  - Press ups: 20–60 in 2 mins
  - Sit ups: 30–80 in 2 mins
  - Pull ups (overgrasp: palms away from you): 3–6.
- Swimming test: swim 1 length of breastroke.
- Assault course: complete the high obstacle course and assault course in teams to show teamwork.

Day 2

- Aerobic test: 3 mile run in a squad in 22½ mins.
- Gym test: individual and team tasks to show teamwork and determination.

Theory into practice

What do the tests in the PRMC show? Which of the S factors (strength, stamina, speed, skill, suppleness, sleep and psychology) are represented? (see pages 138)

Theory into practice

Fitness tests in the uniformed services are subject to change. Research the fitness tests currently used in the Army, RAF and Fire Brigade to see if there has been any recent alterations to their tests. The website addresses on page 154 can be used as a starting point for your research.

Running in a squad can be used to test aerobic fitness

The PRMC is one of the most physically demanding selection courses, but is good preparation for the Commando Training Course (CTCRM). At all times during the PRMC recruits are being observed to see if they have the qualities required to be a Royal Marine Commando.

Fitness training

This section looks at ways to improve your fitness including circuit trainings, running, weight lifting and stretching. You will find out about lots of different types of training so you can tailor your very own fitness programme.

Note: if you have any concerns about your health before starting a training programme then consult your doctor before trying any exercises. The practice of any of the following activities is at the participant's own risk.

Remember: warm ups should be completed prior to using any of these training programmes and cool downs should be used at the end of any session. If you are just starting a fitness programme then start gradually to avoid injuries.

Glossary

The following words are used throughout this section. Please read the meanings of those words which are unfamiliar:

Barbell is the long bar that weights are put on either end. It is used 2 handed.

Circuits are an alternative to sets. Once you have done the required number of reps, instead of moving onto the next set you move to another exercise. Going through all the exercises in sequence is 1 circuit; 4 circuits means going round and doing each exercise in sequence 4 times.

Dumbbells are the shorter 1 handed free weights.

Failure means not being able to do the exercise any more. Some strength programmes suggest doing a set until failure: this just means keep going until you can't do any more.

Free weights are weights such as dumbbells and barbells which are not part of a machine (something with cables, etc for doing specific exercises). Free weights are more versatile and there are almost countless exercises you can do with them.

Hypertrophy is what happens to muscles as a result of weight training. The muscle fibres are torn during training and during the rest period they knit back together, making muscles stronger and bigger. The opposite of hypertrophy is *atrophy*, which can occur if muscles are not used adequately.

Maximum lift is the heaviest weight you can lift in 1 rep for a given activity. For a maximum you will not be able to lift a heavier weight and if you can only do the maximum once it is called 1 repetition maximum (1RM). If you can do an exercise twice before failure it would be 2RM (2 repetitions maximum), etc.

Reps short for *repetitions* means doing the exercise. 1 rep is doing the exercise once, so 10 press ups is 10 reps.

Resistance is the weight lifted. High resistance is heavy weight, low resistance is a light weight.

Rest is what you do in between sets or circuits and means what it says. Resting allows the muscles to recover so that you can continue training.

Sets are collections of reps. For example, 10 reps may be 1 set after which you would rest before starting the next set of 10 reps. Sets are done one after the other. For example, you may do 4 sets of 10 reps.

Circuit training

Circuit training is a method of training rather than a specific programme. It is most suitable for stamina training and can be done in the gym or in any big area which is safe enough. A bank of 10–15 exercises are completed in a sequence which is then repeated in order.

Circuits can either be timed, where you do the exercise for 30–60 seconds before moving to the next or have a set number of reps (usually 10–20). Rests should be made after each exercise (10–60 seconds), and after each circuit (20–60 seconds). Exercises should be done in rotation which should avoid using the same body parts in sequence. For example, sit ups followed by squat thrusts followed by press ups ensures all muscles are used and none are over fatigued. This form of continuous exercise is good for aerobic fitness and it helps to build some strength and muscle stamina.

When preparing a circuit training programme you must remember the following:

- everyone should know how to carry out the activities and what the format is

- there should be adequate space between stations and participants

- exercises should be properly executed as rushing the exercise will not have the full benefits and could be dangerous

- rest times depend upon the fitness of participants: lengthen rest time if appropriate

- the number of circuits depends on participant's fitness levels

- get a proper induction to any equipment used

- don't forget warm up and cool down exercises

- follow all health and safety guidelines.

Gym circuit

A gym circuit can include several exercises (10–15) using free weights, aerobic machines and multi-gym.

1	Bicep curls
2	Exercise bike
3	Shoulder press
4	Skipping
5	Abdominal crunch
6	Bench press
7	Lat pull down
8	Exercise bike
9	Squats
10	Upright row

Reps: (15–20) with low resistance

Time: 30 secs each activity

Rest: 10 secs after each activity and each circuit

Circuits: 3

Frequency: 3 times per week

Figure 9.4 An example of a gym circuit

Floor circuit

This is the more traditional concept of circuit training which is usually done in a sports hall and consists of a number of activities scattered evenly throughout the area. The aim is to run between the stations, performing the exercises in sequence. Equipment which may be useful for floor-type circuits includes: benches, pull up bars and dip bars.

1	Running on the spot
2	Press ups
3	Abdominal crunches
4	Squats
5	Dips
6	Pull ups
7	Step ups
8	Abdominal crunches
9	Squat thrusts
10	Press ups

Time: 30 secs each activity

Rest: 10 secs after each activity and each circuit

Circuits: 3

Frequency: 3 times per week

Figure 9.5 An example of a floor circuit

Theory into practice

Find 6 additional exercises that can be done in a floor circuit training session and learn how to do them properly.

Strength training

The main purpose of this type of training is to build strength in the muscles used and the best way to build strength is by following a programme using free weights or machines. This is also known as **resistance training**, as it uses resistance (weights) to train against.

If you are strength training with weights equipment you must always know how to use the equipment properly and safely and how to do the exercise properly. There are many different types of machines available, all of which need to be used in a specific manner and many different exercises that can be performed using machines and free weights. The best way to learn how to use the equipment available is to ask a qualified fitness instructor.

In order to build strength you need to understand some of the principles of fitness:

- **Overload** is when you make the muscles do more work than they are used to by either increasing how often you train, increasing the resistance or reducing the rest time between sets or increasing the number of reps or sets.

- **Reversibility** is what happens if you stop training. Once you start training you can't afford to stop as the muscles will revert back to their original strength and any gains will be lost.

- **Progression** applies to all training programmes. After 6–12 weeks you should re-evaluate your programme and make changes otherwise you will not progress. As you get fitter, stronger or more flexible you need to adjust your training to make it harder.

Using free weights helps to build strength in the muscles used

Strength programmes

There are numerous different types of programmes for developing strength. Many are advanced programmes for experienced weight lifters and body builders and may cause injury if your body is not used to lifting heavy weights.

General training programme

Before beginning a strength training programme you should first carry out a general training programme using weights to allow your muscles, tendons and ligaments to gain some strength before subjecting them to heavy stress.

Number of activities: 8–10

Resistance: 30–50% maximum

Reps: 8–12

Sets: 2–4

Rest: after each set, 30–60 seconds

Frequency: 3–4 times per week

Duration: 12 weeks

Figure 9.6 Format for general training strength programme

Strength training programmes

After 12 weeks either modify your general training programme or move to a different programme, for example strength or stamina. You may find that you need to increase the intensity as you progress through the programme. Don't add too much weight and progress gradually as it takes tendons and ligaments longer than muscles to get conditioned.

Number of activities: 5–10

Resistance: 80–100% maximum (use a spotter)

Reps: 3–6

Sets: 3

Rest: 3 minutes after each set and 3 minutes after each exercise

Frequency: 3 times per week

Duration: 6 weeks

Figure 9.7 Format for strength training programme

Repetitions should be done slowly and controlled in order to gain strength.

This kind of training will obviously put a lot of strain on the muscles, so it is vital that you rest for 48 hours before training the same muscles. To get round this problem some people train different parts of the body on different days.

Pyramid training is an alternative strength programme using a sequence of gradually increasing weight while decreasing reps up to 1RM and failure.

Resistance: 55 kg	**Reps:** 1
Resistance: 50 kg	**Reps:** 2
Resistance: 45 kg	**Reps:** 4
Resistance: 40 kg	**Reps:** 6
Resistance: 35 kg	**Reps:** 8
Resistance: 30 kg	**Reps:** 10

Figure 9.8 An example of a pyramid training programme

When undertaking strength training, you must remember the following:

- when picking weights up always bend the knees, keeping the back straight
- ensure you know how to correctly use the equipment
- ensure you know how to correctly and safely do the exercise
- load and unload weights evenly
- check equipment before use and report any damages/problems
- always ensure that trained staff are present
- if using heavy weights get a friend to spot you
- create a programme and stick to it
- don't overtrain: your body needs rest days
- exhale while lifting and inhale while lowering the weight
- complete a general programme before starting a specific programme

- start with a warm up, end with a cool down
- wipe equipment down after use and replace weights on their racks.

Case study: example training programmes

Judith is hoping to enter the police force when she finishes her course. During the first year of the course she took up running and is now quite a competent runner. She has recently completed a general training programme on weights and is about to begin a strength programme in order to help her pass the standards of the job related fitness test.

General training programme:

Monday	Circuit training 30 mins, flexibility 30 mins
Tuesday	Weights: strength
Wednesday	Running: 4 miles, flexibility 30 mins
Thursday	Weights: strength
Friday	Running: 4 miles, flexibility 30 mins
Saturday	Weights: strength
Sunday	Rest or flexibility 30 mins

Strength programme:

Warm up –	5 mins on jogger, stretch upper and lower body 5 mins
Chest press –	5 reps at 5 kg warm up 3 sets: 4 reps at 25 kg
Leg press –	5 reps at 10 kg warm up 3 sets: 4 reps at 45 kg
Bicep curls –	5 reps at 5 kg warm up 3 sets: 4 reps at 15 kg
Shoulder press –	5 reps at 5 kg warm up 3 sets: 4 reps at 30 kg
Lat pull down –	5 reps at 5 kg warm up 3 sets: 4 reps at 20 kg
Cool down –	5 mins walking on jogger, stretch upper and lower body 10 mins

Speed training

Speed is the ability to move a part of the body quickly which is developed by first practicing the technique slowly to enable the neurons in the muscle to adjust. When practiced at speed the neurons then improve their speed at moving the muscles. Speed depends on the following factors:

- mobility/flexibility
- strength
- muscular endurance
- skill.

To train for speed you therefore need to train for strength, stamina and suppleness. Specific speed training should also be carried out, but only when the body is rested, not tired from a previous training session.

The speed training activity you choose will depend upon your goals and can usually be combined with skill training. For example, if you need speed for martial arts, then practice kicks and punches at speed in your martial art sessions. The bleep test is a good way of building speed as it is also used in many tests for the services. This test builds stamina while also increasing speed at the later levels. Other training for improving running speed can include timed runs (like the 2.4 km runs used by the Army and Navy) and shuttle runs (as used by the Navy).

The whole of the nervous system is involved in movement and to allow actions at speed, the mind and the nervous system need to be able to remember how to operate the muscles efficiently. This means that speed training must be practiced regularly.

Speed training must be practiced regularly to maintain fitness levels

Stamina training

There are 2 types of stamina:

- cardio-vascular endurance: the ability to run, walk, swim, etc for long periods of time. The work is done by the heart and can be kept up for an extended period of time. We will examine this type of training in detail later.

- muscular endurance: the ability of a muscle to repeat an action several times. This is what we will be examining in this section.

Muscular stamina is one of the main types of fitness desired by the uniformed services as can be seen in their fitness tests. Exercises that emphasise muscular stamina include:

- press ups
- sit ups
- pull ups
- burpees
- squat thrusts
- dips
- squats.

One of the best ways of training for local muscle endurance is circuit training which can also aid areobic conditioning. When practiced in the gym, it will not aid aerobic fitness, but it will improve strength.

> **Number of activities:** 10–15
>
> **Resistance:** 30%
>
> **Reps:** 15–20 (or timed)
>
> **Circuits:** 2–4
>
> **Rest:** 10 seconds after each activity and each circuit
>
> **Frequency:** 3 times per week
>
> **Duration:** 6 weeks

Figure 9.9 Format for stamina training programme in the gym

In stamina training repetitions are high and weights are low. Repetitions should also be done quickly (but carefully). After 6 weeks you should review the programme and alter it accordingly. Your strength will probably have increased during this period so you may need to increase resistance or repetitions.

Safety notes for stamina are the same as those listed for circuit training and strength training.

Suppleness training

Suppleness training is an important part of your fitness regime and can be improved by including stretching activities as part of your programme. Flexibility and stretching has been covered extensively on pages 137–139 and different types of stretching are also outlined on these pages.

Think it over

Discuss stretches which used to be popular but are no longer used as they are considered unsafe.

Skill training

All activities involve skill which can be learnt from demonstrations and videos and improved by practicing the activity. Fitness training also helps to develop your skill as strength, suppleness, speed and stamina allow you to perform more efficiently.

However, if the skill is imperfect then practicing it will only make it harder to improve. To prevent this athletes use drills and circuits to practice specific skills or parts of skills to make them more effective such as footballers practicing tackling, shooting and movement skills rather than playing football all the time.

If you already do a sport or activity, then keep it up. You will be learning skills and keeping yourself fit in preparation for any fitness tests.

Agility training

Agility means quick moving and nimble and is a combination of the following:

- coordination
- speed
- balance
- strength.

As a result, speed and strength training are important when developing agility and flexibility training can develop coordination and balance. Dynamic sports such as: martial arts, football and basketball will also aid agility.

Both the police (see pages 139–140) and the prison services use an agility test for potential recruits. Agility is also useful for firemen when they are inside burning buildings trying to fight fires and rescue people and soldiers use agility to move on the battlefield safely and when boarding and exiting combat vehicles.

One of the best ways to improve your score on an agility test is to practice it. It is a simple test to carry out: all you need is some cones, a flat area and a stopwatch.

Case study: agility training in the military using battle drills

Lance Corporal Eric's infantry section have been sent out on patrol when they come under enemy fire. As soon as the shots are heard all 8 soldiers drop to the ground and crawl away to try to find cover (if the enemy see where the soldiers are they could shoot them, so by crawling away they stand better chance of not being shot). Eric calls out to see who's injured and if anyone saw where the shots came from. Everyone is fine and someone saw muzzle fire from the woods to the west.

The section breaks into two fire teams who take it in turns to practice fire and movement: when Eric's team zig zags towards the enemy position, the other team provides cover by firing at the woods. Eric's teams dashes right to left to avoid being shot for a few feet then they dive to the floor and crawl to the side to provide covering fire as the other team get up and zig zag toward the enemy.

The teams continue in this fashion until they reach the enemy and Eric destroys their position with a grenade.

Cardiovascular training

Cardiovascular (CV) training uses the muscles of the heart and encompasses aerobic, stamina and endurance fitness. CV fitness includes the ability to walk, run, swim, row, etc for long periods of time and is important to the services as it is one of the main indicators of all-round fitness.

The energy for CV work comes from oxygen, which is why it is also called aerobic fitness (with oxygen). Unlike weight training which uses anaerobic work for energy, aerobic work leaves no poisons in the muscles as long as your muscles are conditioned for the exercise. The by products are water and carbon dioxide (exhaled and sweated out) and it is the only form of training that burns off fat which can be useful in weight control (under

proper guidance). However, aerobic work does not start as quickly as anaerobic does and requires a minimum of 15 minutes to get any benefit.

Running, walking, swimming, cycling, etc at a steady continuous pace can be used to develop aerobic fitness. For best results, the training should be performed for at least 20–30 minutes and at least 3 times per week. This type of training is called long slow distance (LSD) training. Due to the nature of the muscles involved (primarily the heart) CV training can be performed more regularly than anaerobic training and 4–6 times per week is acceptable.

Running is seen as the most effective way of developing this kind of fitness, but does have a higher incidence of injuries than swimming or walking. Good running shoes are essential and they should be replaced every 6 months if used frequently.

Other activities which are often very good for LSD training are:

- canoeing
- hill walking/mountaineering
- vigorous dance
- skiing.

Running for a minimum of 15 minutes can develop cardiosvascular fitness

Heart rate training

To do CV training effectively you must be working in your training zone which means that your heart must be beating hard enough to get some benefit but not too hard to be dangerous. This is shown as a percentage of your maximum heart rate (MHR). To work out your training heart rate you firstly have to work out your MHR which is 220 minus your age. Then you need to find out your resting heart rate (RHR). Find somewhere nice and quiet to lie down for 20 minutes. After this time find your pulse and count it for 6 seconds. Multiply this by 10 to find your pulse beats per minute (BPM) and this is also your RHR.

MHR − RHR = Working Heart Rate (WHR)

WHR × 60% + RHR = upper end of training zone

WHR × 70% + RHR = lower end of training zone

Case study: example of training heart rate

Jamil is 23 so his maximum heart rate (MHR) is 197 (220 − age).
His resting heart rate (RHR) is 52
He can now calculate his working heart rate (WHR) which is MHR − RHR:
197 − 52 = 145 (WHR)
Jamil should aim to train within the lower and upper end of his training zone:
Lower end is WHR × 70% + RHR:
145 × 70% + 52 = 139
Upper end is WHR × 60% + RHR:
145 × 60% + 52 = 147

When taking part in aerobic activities, he should ensure that his pulse is somewhere between these numbers; any less and the training will not be effective and no benefit will occur. Any higher and he risks working his heart too hard and damaging himself.

The very maximum he should do is 197 (MHR) and this should not be kept up for extended periods.

You should aim to keep within the lower and upper end of your training zone when doing aerobic work; any less and you won't be working efficiently, any more and you're getting into heart rates you won't be able to keep up safely for long.

Theory into practice

Work out your working heart rate and your lower and upper heart rate training zones.

Techniques of running

Interval training

This is a technique used by athletes to improve the heart's ability to deliver blood and oxygen. It involves training at a very high level followed by a period of light work. This cycle is then repeated. Interval training is usually associated with running but can be used in cycling and other activities.

During the intense period, work is done anaerobically and the heart works hard to pump oxygen around the body leading to an oxygen debt. In the recovery stage the heart is not working as hard, the oxygen debt is repaid and any poisons created are destroyed. This type of training improves the cardiovascular system, making better use of oxygen and more efficient removal of poisons.

This technique is dangerous for those who are unfit or who have heart problems and it is best to start with LSD training before moving on to interval training.

Fartlek training

Fartlek is Swedish for "speed play" and is a combination of both long slow distance and interval training. Again this form of training involves changing speed, but at varying levels including walking, jogging and sprinting. This uses both the anaerobic and aerobic energy pathways and is very good for developing fitness. An additional factor in Fartlek training is the use of hills. Steep terrain obviously increases the intensity of the work, especially if you sprint uphill, then jogging downhill will repay the oxygen debt.

Fartlek can also be used while cycling. One of the best places to practice Fartlek is in the National Parks and other hilly areas as the view is usually better and it makes a pleasant change from training in the gym or running on the road. Just remember to be more prepared for bad weather and remember that mobile 'phones don't often work in hilly areas.

Theory into practice

Take part in a range of fitness training programmes and monitor your performance over time. Which programme do you feel is most suitable for your needs? Explain why.

Key concepts

1   All uniformed services jobs have periods of physical activity and therefore have fitness tests.

2   Physical training is potentially dangerous if not carried out safely.

3   Health and safety checks on the venue, equipment and participants should be carried out every session.

4   Warm ups are essential before starting physical activity. They consist of 2 phases: cardiovascular warm up and stretching.

5   Always finish with a cool down: light cardiovascular work and longer stretching.

6   Flexibility is important for all physical activities, but must be carried out properly to be effective and safe.

Training programme

In the previous section we looked at various types of training programmes. Now you can put into

practice what you have learnt to create your own personalised fitness regime. Read the following guidelines to help you:

● Take a fitness test, preferably for the service of your choice

● Identify areas that need development. Even if you passed, there are probably some things you would like to improve.

● Look at the different training types and see which one corresponds most with your areas for development. For example if you performed well on the strength tests but failed the bleep test, create a cardiovascular programme featuring LSD running and a circuit training set. This will increase your aerobic fitness as well as maintaining strength and local muscular endurance.

● If you haven't trained before, start with an easy programme, either general fitness or circuit training and work up from there. Learn to do the exercises properly and you will start to see improvements in a couple of weeks.

● Get your programme checked by a qualified trainer to ensure that it is relevant and set to the right standard. A trainer may be able to offer improvements or alternatives that may suit you better.

● Every month or so, redo the fitness test and record your scores. Hopefully, you should see an improvement.

When you create your programme, write it down and stick to it. Remember to use the FITT system:

Frequency: how often you train

Intensity: how hard you train

Time: how long you train for

Type: of training done

Using this system will ensure that your training is at the right level and enable you to increase your fitness without too much discomfort and modify the programme as required.

Remember that your training programme is designed specifically for you. Your objectives are personal ones and not intended to lead to competition with anyone else. Friendly competition can be helpful when taking part in fitness testing but when training you should stick to your own regime as everyone will have different training needs due to age, sex, fitness history, health, body type, muscle fibre make up, etc.

Sample fitness programme

Aim: to improve aerobic fitness and strength in the upper body and legs in anticipation of joining the Army.

Monday:	run 2 miles, flexibility training as part of cool down
Tuesday:	general weights programme:

2 sets:		
	Bicep curls: 10 kg	10 reps
	Leg press: 40 kg	15 reps
	Chest press: 30 kg	10 reps
	Sit ups	20 reps
	Lat pull down: 30 kg	10 reps
	Shoulder press: 20 kg	10 reps
	Triceps press: 20 kg	10 reps
	Upright row: 20 kg	10 reps

Wednesday:	as Monday
Thursday:	as Tuesday
Friday:	as Monday
Saturday:	rest
Sunday:	rest

Rationale: this programme is designed to improve cardiovascular fitness, flexibility and muscular strength and endurance.

Note: Your rationale should state the aim/objective of your programme and should justify your choice of training type and techniques. This will show that you understand your fitness needs and the different types of fitness and training.

Development plan: fitness testing will take place after 4 weeks on the programme.

The programme will be reviewed after 6 weeks taking the following into account:

- performance in fitness test
- body's adaptation to running
- body's adaptation to weights.

If the body has adapted well and the running and weights are now completed relatively easily, the programme will be changed using the FITT system to ensure overload for the muscles and to prevent boredom.

Fitness testing will continue on a 4 week basis, programme reviews on a 6 week basis.

Note: During the review stage of your development plan you should try to evaluate your training plan and your sessions. Does the programme match the objectives? Is it at the right level, or is it too hard or too easy? Are your sessions effective or do you need to be more motivated? Make suggestions for improvement of any problems.

Health and safety and induction to equipment

When starting a training programme you should be aware of the health and safety issues highlighted on pages 133–134. If you have any concerns about your health, however slight, then consult your doctor for a thorough assessment.

Ensure that you have a full induction for any equipment you will use. Fitness equipment can be dangerous if not used properly and any techniques performed incorrectly will have limited benefits and can be damaging.

Theory into practice

Take part in an induction at your local gym/fitness centre to get experience of the types of fitness equipment available and how to use it. If possible, visit other gyms to find out about other types of equipment.

Fitness techniques

In order to complete a fitness programme you need to compile a bank of techniques suitable for the type of programme. For example, in weight training you need to know which exercises work the muscles you want to develop and how to do the exercises properly. When stretching, you need to know how to perform the exercises using the correct techniques otherwise you can cause serious damage to your body.

End of unit questions

1 List the S factors and explain them.

2 How many parts are there to a warm up?

3 How long should a warm up take?

4 Describe an effective cool down.

5 What are pulse ups?

6 What should you check before starting a fitness session?

7 What is passive stretching?

8 What is active stretching?

9 What is PNF stretching?

10 Describe the police work related fitness test.

11 How many types of circuit training are there?

12 Sketch a plan of a circuit training session for use in a sports hall.

13 What is pyramid training?

14 What is agility?

15 Explain interval training.

16 In terms of running, what is LSD?

17 What does Fartlek mean?

18 What is gym agility?

19 What does FITT stand for?

20 Describe the following principles of fitness:

- overload
- progression
- specificity
- reversibility.

Resources

Websites

Sports Coach:
http://www.brianmac.demon.co.uk/scnpopup.htm

Police recruitment:
http://www.policecouldyou.co.uk/home/

HM Prison Service:
http://www.hmprisonservice.gov.uk/

Royal Navy: http://www.royal-navy.mod.uk/

Territorial Army: www.ta.mod.uk/

Recruitment in fire service:
http://www.fireservice.co.uk/recruitment/physical.php

Army units and physical training:
http://www.army.mod.uk/atr_pirbright/student_info/training_program/index.htm

Army recruitment selection centre:
http://www.army.mod.uk/royalsignals/careers/rsc.html

Police service fitness guide:
http://www.policecouldyou.co.uk/default.asp?action=article&ID=26

Prison service basic fitness and fitness training:
http://www.hmprisonservice.gov.uk/filestore/656_722.pdf

Royal navy fitness standards:
http://www.royal-navy.mod.uk/static/pages/5112.html

Military fitness and training:
http://www.mfat.co.uk/rm.php?page=rm1

Assessment activities

This section describes what you must do to obtain a pass grade for this unit.

A merit or distinction grade may be awarded if your work demonstrates a deeper understanding of the topics and is of a higher quality. The highlighted sentences indicate the quality of work expected at merit and distinction level.

Assessment methods

A number of assessment strategies may be used in order to achieve the learning outcomes, such as oral presentations, group discussions, written assignments, research projects and role-plays or a combination of these. It is a good idea, though it is not essential, to use a variety of methods in order to develop different skills.

It is important that you understand and comply with the key words specified in the grading criteria. For example, if you are asked to 'analyse' something, then make sure that you do not merely describe it. Similarly, if you are asked to 'evaluate' something, then make sure you do not merely summarise it.

Key words

Here are some key words that are often used for grading criteria – make sure you understand the differences between them.

Examine	To look at a subject closely in order to understand it and improve your knowledge
Consider	This means to think about and weigh up a subject
Explain	This means to make something clear and set out the arguments
Analyse	This means to look at a subject closely and interpret or evaluate your findings. This can include an outline of the pro's and con's of a situation or suggestions for changes and improvements
Describe	This means to say what something is like – it is a factual account of how something is or how it appears
Compare	This means to look at the similarities between two or more objects or theories.

Assessment tasks

Using the materials within this unit and your own research, carry out the following tasks.

Task 1

Learning outcome 1 – Investigate and demonstrate the need for safe practice in the physical training environment

Demostrate the principles of standing-in

Plan and take part in a warm up and cool down using the correct components in a safe environment

Organise and carry out a physical training session in a safe environment demonstrating health and safety awareness.

> To obtain a merit grade you should *explain the use* of the components in a warm up and cool down and you should *analyse and evaluate* the physical training session.

Suggestions for Task 1: practical session and written evaluation

1 Plan a full training session in detail: outline what you intend to do in the warm up phase, main session and cool down. Mention any health and safety issues and how you intend to ensure safety. You should also explain the components of the warm up and cool down activities and why you chose the activities you did.

2 Carry out the session safely, not forgetting all of your safety checks.

3 Complete an analysis and evaluation of your session including whether it went to plan and whether it fulfilled your objectives.

Try to record your practical session and get a witness statement from your assessor.

Task 2

Learning outcome 2 – Explore the range of uniformed service fitness tests

Research, explain and undertake the range of uniformed service fitness tests

Suggestion for Task 2: presentation

1 Find out what the fitness tests for each of the services consist of, including pass rates.

2 Undertake each of the tests and record how you did in each activity of each test.

3 Present your research and records to your peers, explaining which of the fitness tests you passed.

Record your presentation and again get a witness statement from your assessor. Don't forget that many of these assessments can also be used for key skills.

Task 3

Learning outcome 3 – Research, conduct and analyse the range of fitness training types and techniques

Explain the different types and methods of circuit training and techniques of running training.

Explain the reasons for gym agility.

> To obtain a merit grade, you should *analyse* the different types and methods of circuit training and the techniques used when running training.

Suggestion for Task 3: written report

Write a report explaining why members of the public services require gym agility and how this can be achieved. You must explain and analyse the range of fitness training types that are available.

Task 4

Learning outcome 4 – Undertake a training programme to prepare for a uniformed service of your choice

Design, plan and complete a training programme in preparation for an entry test to a uniformed service incorporating the fitness types and techniques.

To obtain a distinction grade you should *evaluate* and *justify own performance* and the training programme

---

Suggestions for Task 4: practical session and written evaluation

1   Plan a full training programme of 12 weeks duration to prepare for one of the public service fitness tests. Outline what the test is and which areas you struggle at. What activities do you need to do to get you to the required standard? By now you should have undertaken each of the fitness tests and know what you need to work on. Include your scores from the first test.

2   Carry out your training programme. Follow this with another fitness test and record your scores.

3   Evaluate and justify both the training programme and your own performance in both the programme and the test. Did the programme better your performance in the test? Why did you choose the activities in the programme? Did you make any mistakes and how can you learn from them?

EXPEDITION SKILLS

Introduction to Unit 11

This unit looks at the skills needed to take part in a walking and camping expedition in open country. These skills include navigating with map and compass, choosing the correct equipment for an expedition, campcraft, etc. Competence in these skills is necessary for many uniformed services. For example, in the Armed Forces maps are used to identify where the enemy is located. The Forces also use expeditions as part of their basic training. This type of activity is encouraged by other uniformed services, too. Police officers may have to search remote areas for evidence or when aiding Mountain Rescue teams. Paramedics could also be called to assist in such situations.

As well as learning how to live safely in the countryside, this unit also covers environmental good practice and looks at the bodies responsible for looking after the outdoors areas.

The final part of this unit reflects the purpose of outdoor activities in education, the world of business and the uniformed services by looking at skills such as teamwork, communication and leadership as well as confidence building, self-reliance and a sense of adventure and discovery.

Assessment

Throughout the unit, activities and tasks will help you to learn and remember information. Case studies are also included to add industry relevance to the topics and learning objectives. At the end of the unit there are assessment activities to help you provide evidence which meets the learning outcomes for the unit. You are reminded that when you are completing activities and tasks, opportunities will be created to enhance your key skills evidence.

After completing this unit you should have an understanding of the following outcomes.

Outcomes

1   Demonstrate effective **navigation skills** in open country

2   Describe the **equipment** used in walking and camping and demonstrate an understanding of its uses, properties and care

3   **Plan and carry out** an expedition involving an overnight camp

4   Take part in two other **outdoor pursuits**.

Navigation skills

Navigation is simply the process of getting from one place to another. This includes:

● choosing a suitable route

● following the route accurately

● dealing with hazards along the way.

In order to carry out the above, certain items of equipment are required. The most essential piece of equipment is the **map**.

Maps

Maps can come in many forms, from street maps to geological maps and many scales, from world maps to maps of school or college grounds. Essentially, a map is a two dimensional representation of the ground viewed from above and can be used to enable travel between destinations.

The UK National Grid is a metric system and therefore all measurements are in kilometres. If you are unsure, make a note of how to convert between centimetres, meters and kilometres:

1 mile = 1.6 kilometres

1 kilometre = 1000 metres or 100,000 centimetres

1 metre = 100 centimetres or 0.001 kilometres

Most maps will have conversion charts along the bottom for converting distances but it's still useful to know how to convert without having to unfold the map and measure it.

Maps can show various types of information:

Topographic maps show the physical features of the ground such as rivers and buildings.

Contour maps have lines that connect things of the same value, such as height above sea level. Weather maps showing isobars are also contour maps.

Choropleth maps show some other form of data such as population, health, crime, education, agriculture, etc.

Map scales

One of the most important features of a map is **scale**. This is how distance is represented on a map and is shown by means of a ratio. The ratio 1:50,000 means that 1 cm on the map equals 50,000 cm (500 m or 0.5 km) on the ground (1×50,000). For example, 16 cm on the map would be 800,000 cm on the ground. You could use anything to measure the distance on the map (inches, metres, thumb nail, etc) just as long as you multiply it by the ratio scale to determine what the distance is on the ground.

This ratio is quite a common map scale for expedition use. It gives enough detail to plan and follow a route without having too much information to confuse you. Being quite a large scale it also allows large coverage on one map sheet rather than having to carry several maps for one journey (though for long expeditions this is unavoidable).

Another common scale is 1:25,000 when 1 cm on the map is 25,000 cm on the ground (250 m or

0.25 km). With this scale you can show much greater detail and have more information on the map, which can be useful if you are trying to find a precise location. Twice the scale also takes up twice the space, which means that you will need twice the number of maps for the same expedition.

Map manufacturers

For walking in the United Kingdom there are two manufacturers of suitable maps:

1 **The Ordnance Survey (OS)** is a government agency responsible for mapping the country. The OS began in the eighteenth century when the Scottish Highlands were mapped in order to allow troops to be effective in putting down the Scottish rebellions. The rest of the UK was eventually mapped and the OS went on to create the National Grid system and placed triangulation pillars on hills throughout the country. The OS provides a wealth of mapping information for the government, business and leisure purposes. For expeditions the most useful maps are the 1:50,000 scale Landranger maps and the 1:25,000 scale Explorer maps.

2 **Harvey Maps** produce maps solely for outdoor activities such as walking, cycling and horse riding. As a result, they only produce maps of popular outdoors areas, rather than full coverage of the country. The signs and conventions used are different to those used by the Ordnance Survey so care must be used when transferring between maps. Harvey produce Superwalker maps at 1:25,000 scale, Walker's maps at 1:40,000 scale and cycling and horse riding maps in a variety of scales.

Theory into practice

Using the table overleaf and by looking at the range of maps, decide who the target audience is for each of the maps shown on the table.

OS Landranger 1:50,000	OS Explorer 1:25,000	Harvey Superwalker 1:25,000	Harvey Walker's 1:40,000
40 × 40 km area: large scale for long expeditions. Coverage of whole country.	Smaller area with greater detail, sometimes 2 sided to show coverage of whole area, for example Peak District: Dark Peak. Whole country coverage.	Popular mountain areas in great detail; detail relevant to walkers/cyclists etc.	Large scale but still showing lots of detail. Covers large area for expeditions. Smaller sheets than Landranger: more convenient to use.
Negatives: sometimes does not give enough information, for example walls and fences.	*Negatives:* possibly not enough coverage of expedition area so may need to carry several maps for long journeys.	*Negatives:* not available for all areas; no connecting sheets for longer journeys.	*Negatives:* not available for many areas.

Figure 11.1 A comparison of a range of maps

Theory into practice

Compare the conventional signs for different maps and scales. How are they different? Which do you think are easier to use, OS or Harvey?

The National Grid

The Ordnance Survey created the National Grid to be able to easily plot the location of places in the UK. The National Grid comprises 100 kilometre grid squares, each one with 2 letters to identify it. These grid squares are broken down into smaller grids which are the ones you see on maps (both OS and Harvey maps). On maps the grids have numbers running up the side and along the top and bottom. Using the National Grid letters and the numbers from the map can give a unique code to the grid square.

The numbers along the horizontal axis are Eastings, the vertical ones are Northings. To give a grid reference start with the Eastings, reading the

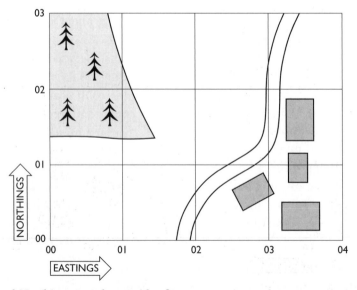

Figure 11.2 Using Eastings and Northings to take a grid reference

numbers to the left of the column that the square is in. Then use the Northings in a similar way, reading the numbers on the line below the row containing the square. Put both sets of numbers together (Eastings followed by Northings) and you have a 4 figure grid reference. For example, in Figure 11.2 the corner of the forest is located in 01 (Eastings) and 01 (Northings) which gives a grid reference of 0101.

If you can't remember whether to take the reading for Eastings or Nothings first, try to remember the following saying: 'Along the corridor then up the stairs.'

As mentioned previously all maps have a 2 letter code that identifies where it is located in the National Grid. When put before the 4 figure reference this gives a 1 Kilometre square reference that is unique to the whole country.

A 4 figure reference isolates an area of 1 square kilometre. Looking at a map you can see that a lot of information can be found in 1 grid square, so a 4 figure grid reference isn't very specific if you're trying to pinpoint a specific place or organising a meeting place. For a more accurate location, a 6 figure grid reference is used. To do this you have to imagine the grid square divided up into yet more squares, a 10 × 10 grid. Starting at the left hand corner of the square, count the tenths along the Eastings to give a number between 0 and 9

which you then add to the Easting number for the grid square. Do the same for the Northings and you have a 6 figure grid reference.

A 6 figure grid reference gives an area of 100 square metres. This is a much smaller area than the full grid square but can contain several features, so you must be specific about the description.

Theory into practice

Using the smaller grid shown in Figure 11.3, give a six figure grid reference for the corner of the forest.

Can you find out the grid references for your home and your college?

To get a more accurate location you can split the square up even more into 8 figure grid references or 16 figure grid references. These references are used for artillery bombardment in the Army using computers and satellite information.

To get 6 figure grid references easily, try using a roamer. These are sometimes found on compasses or on clear plastic sheets. They consist of 2 sides of a square with each side divided into tenths and numbered and usually appear for 1:50,000 and 1:25,000 scales. Placed over the map they allow you to accurately determine the 6 figure grid

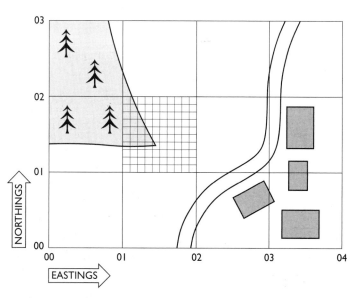

Figure 11.3 Map showing one grid square divided up into a 10 × 10 grid

reference. Roamers are also useful for measuring distance on maps as they represent 1 kilometre divided into 100 metres.

Height and contours

When on an expedition, knowing what the land looks like is important. Is there a steep uphill slog ahead or is it an airy ridge with exposure on either side? Does the route go downhill or is it worth contouring to prevent having to come uphill again? Much of this relies on the height of the ground. On maps for expeditions, height is shown in a number of ways:

Hachures

Hachures represent cuttings or embankments, such as those you would expect to find on a railway line. They usually represent steep but low changes in height on man-made banks and ditches (archaeologists use them to record earthworks on their survey plans). They consist of a line of triangles: the flat axis represents uphill and the point always points downhill.

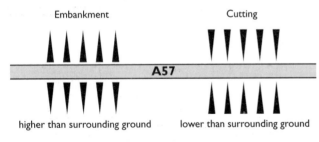

Figure 11.4 A simple map showing hachures

Shading

Shading is used as an artistic way of showing relative height. It is especially effective in mountainous areas to show the general shape of the hills/mountains and is used by the OS on some 1:25,000 maps as it makes the shape of the land easier to visualise.

Spot heights

Spot heights are points of known height determined by survey. They appear on the map as a dot (full stop) followed by a height in metres. They are useful for telling you the height but also for surveyors as a place of known height.

Trianulation pillars

Trianulation pillars (trig points) are concrete posts placed at convenient locations (often at or near the summits of hills or mountains) to enable surveying. Like spot heights they have a known height. They are no longer used for OS map surveys but are useful for other map/plan makers. Find out which symbol denotes a trig point on maps.

Contours

Contours are used extensively to show the lay of the land. They quite simply link up areas of the same height, thereby showing the shape and steepness of the land. Contours are the map reader's greatest source of information and most advanced techniques make use of them. There are several features of contour lines:

- every fifth contour line is thicker than the others to make counting easier

- in mountain/hilly areas there is a 10 metre gap between contours. In areas with less height difference the gap is 5 metres

- long contour lines will have numbers on them (in multiples of 5 or 10 metres) to make it possible to work out height

- when contours are close together a magnifying glass is useful to count them all

- contours close together mean steep ground

- contours further apart mean a gradual incline

- no contours indicates flat(ish) land

- higher numbers on a contour line indicates uphill whereas numbers decreasing indicates downhill

- when you can't find numbers on the contours and you don't know if there is an increase or decrease in height, look for streams and rivers: water always flows downhill and forms valleys.

Theory into practice

Can you find out what height your college is?

Some specific features may be shown by contours such as:

1 **Convex hill**: the bottom of the hill can't be seen from the top and could hide dangers, for example a steep fall.

2 **Concave hill**: (see Figure 11.5) the base of hill is visible from top.

3 **Ridge**: a long thin area (see Figure 11.6), which can be the summit of a mountain, for example Crib Goch which lies next to Snowdon or may lead off from the summit or a low lying similar feature. Ridges separate rivers (the high ground in-between) and are usually easier to travel along than valleys or re-entrants.

4 **Spur**: a similar feature to a ridge but smaller and not as elongated (not as finger-like).

5 **Valley**: these are channels created by rivers which can look like ridges unless you read the contour numbers accurately. Compare the contour heights in Figure 11.7 to those of the ridge.

6 **Re-entrant**: a small valley, created by a stream. It can easily be mistaken for a spur.

7 **Plateau**: a flatish area found on the top of some hills/mountains, for example Kinder Scout in the Peak District. A plateau may make for easy travelling, but not always. Kinder's plateau, for example is a maze of groughs, re-entrants and spurs making travel and navigation difficult.

To help you use contours, draw a cross-section of a route as follows:

● Take a piece of blank paper and follow your route on the map, marking off each contour (with its height) along the edge of the sheet.

● Using graph paper draw a line the length of the route. Then draw vertical lines up from either end of the horizontal. Mark these lines with the contour heights encountered on the route, for example 100, 110, 120, 130, etc.

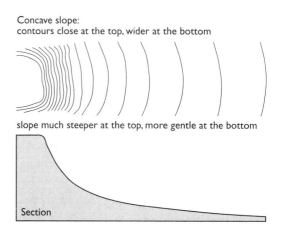

Concave slope:
contours close at the top, wider at the bottom

slope much steeper at the top, more gentle at the bottom

Section

Figure 11.5 Contours showing a concave hill

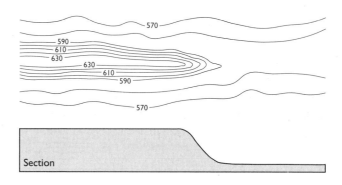

Section

Figure 11.6 Contours showing a ridge

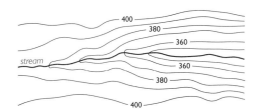

stream

Figure 11.7 Contours showing a valley

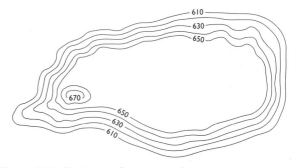

Figure 11.8 Contours showing a plateau

● Using the first piece of paper mark on the contour heights at the correct height and distance with small crosses, then join the crosses up. This will show you a cross-section of the route, where you can see how steep it will be.

Theory into practice

Draw a 3 dimensional drawing of an area shown on a map with all the features such as rivers, hills, mountains, buildings and roads. Don't try an area too big but make sure it uses a range of contour features.

Distance

We've seen that the scale of the map affects how much is shown and what size it is. Using a map, distances can be accurately worked out by using:

● **String:** using a length of non-stretchy string follow the route exactly. Now you can place the measured length of string against the scale at the bottom of the map to read off the distance.

● **Roamer:** some compasses have roamers on them which can be used to measure the distance. Using this method only allows you to measure sections as long as 1 kilometre at most so you need to be able to add all the sections together as you go. This can be tricky on routes with few straight sections.

● **Paper:** using a similar principle to the string method. Starting at one corner of a piece of paper use the edge to mark off the route, turning the sheet of paper to follow the route. Eventually you end up with several marks on the edge of the paper which can be measured against the scale on the map.

● **Map measurers:** these can come in a variety of shapes but most contain a small wheel which enables you to run it over the route. When finished there will be a readout or dial to read off the distance. Be sure to read off the correct scale.

Theory into practice

Work out the distance of your route to college in the morning?

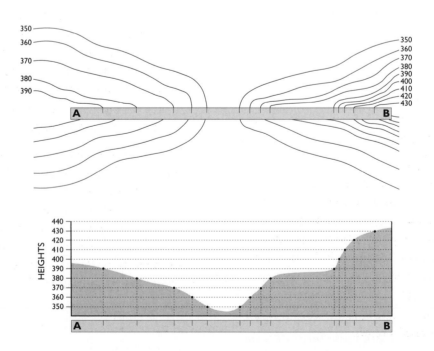

Figure 11.9 How to create a contour cross section

Using the map with the ground

So far we've looked at how you can use the map for route planning. However, when you are outside you need to be able to relate the map to the ground and vice versa. Firstly you need to **set the map**: the most important thing to remember is that the map is never upside down and that it doesn't matter which way up the writing is. To set the map:

- fold the map up as small as you can so that you have only got a small area on view

- identify features on the map which should be visible: hills, buildings, walls, blocks of forests, lakes, masts, etc

- look around you and locate the same features in the distance

- orient the map so that the features are all aligned both on the map and on the ground.

Once you've set the map you need to keep it that way. This means that if you take a footpath to the left you need to move the map round so that what you're facing on the ground is lined up with the map. This way you have a much better idea of where you are on the map. One technique that orienteers use is thumbing. This means always having the thumb of the hand holding the map on your position pointing in the same direction you are going.

Distance

We've looked at measuring distance on the map. To transfer that knowledge to the ground there are 2 techniques you can use:

1   **Pacing:** measure 100 metres and count how many steps you take to walk there. This is your pacing for 100 metres. Try it again, this time only counting the steps of either your right or left foot (the number should be half, or close to half, the full pacing number). Remember this number as it can aid you in navigating on featureless terrain or at night. However, pacing is affected by several factors:

- terrain: soft snow, bog, cloughs can cause you to take shorter steps

- gradient: going up or down steep slopes

- load: carrying a heavy rucksack will again shorten your steps.

Try pacing 100 metres in all of the above situations. Your pacing will be different for each one. Make a note of the number for each factor on a small piece of paper and laminate it. Keep this laminate with your compass and then when you need to navigate in difficult situations you have your pacing details to hand.

2   **Timing:** you will find that you have a natural speed at which you walk. This again will be influenced by certain factors:

- fitness

- terrain

- gradient

- load.

Once you know how fast you travel in an hour, you have a useful navigation aid. By checking the time at certain points on your journey you can have an indication of how far you have travelled. If you are looking for a meeting point, measure the distance and work out how long it will take you to get there. If you're walking past that time then you've probably missed your meeting point and should search again. Use the table on page 166 to help you work out your timings.

The top row shows speed in kilometres per hour and the left hand column is distance in metres. To find out how long it will take to walk a certain distance, find the distance in the left hand column and then read along the row until you reach the column of the speed you're travelling at, for example to walk 500 metres at a speed of 3 kph would take 10 minutes.

Distance/metres	Speed/km per hour				
	2	3	4	5	6
1000	30	20	15	12	10
900	27	18	13.5	10.8	9
800	24	16	12	9.6	8
700	21	14	10.5	8.4	7
600	18	12	9	7.2	6
500	15	10	7.5	6	5
400	12	8	6	4.8	4
300	9	6	4.5	3.6	3
200	6	4	3	2.4	2
100	3	2	1.5	1.2	1
Remember: +1 min for 10 metres climbed					

Figure 11.10 Measurement of distance covered by timing

Theory into practice

Using the above table, how long would it take to walk 300 metres at 6 kph and 800 metres at 5 kph?

The bottom line of the table contains a useful correction to any timings. Travelling uphill is harder and takes longer: accepted practice is to add 1 additional minute for every 10 metres climbed. This is only for ascending; going downhill generally does not affect your speed.

Copy this table onto the back of the card detailing your pacings to make a very useful navigation aid.

The compass

Along with a map the most important navigation tool is the compass. This is a magnetised tool which points to magnetic north which means you will always know the location of north if you have a compass. Once this is known, you can work out other directions relative to north and relative to your own position.

Types of compass

There are various different kinds of compass, each for different purposes:

- **Base-plate compass:** this is the type you need for map–reading and expeditions. The base-plate should be long enough to take bearings with on the map and should be transparent so you can read the map whilst using the compass. It's also useful to have rubber tabs on the underneath to help it stay in place on laminated or covered maps.

  The compass housing contains the magnetised needle, which should have an indicator to tell you which end points north – usually coloured red. The housing should be able to turn fully through 360 degrees, though with some resistance – the magnetised needle is surrounded by liquid to ensure the needle doesn't move around as much and settles quicker. Around the housing the compass should be graduated into degrees (360) or both degrees and mils (6400) for military models. Mils are another method of measuring angles. To convert degrees to mils, times the degrees by 17.78.

- **Prismatic compass:** these are circular "tins" that open to reveal a compass housing and a hinged sighting lid. Prismatic compasses are used for sighting by looking at the objective through the sight on the lid and reading off the bearing. They can be quite sophisticated and professional ones can be very expensive. Traditionally used by the military, they are not very suitable for map-reading as they have no base-plate.

- **Hybrid compass:** base-plate compasses with sighting features which offer the best of both of the above. They can come in various forms, including those with a hinged cover over the compass housing; inside the cover is a mirror to allow you to read bearings while sighting your objective.

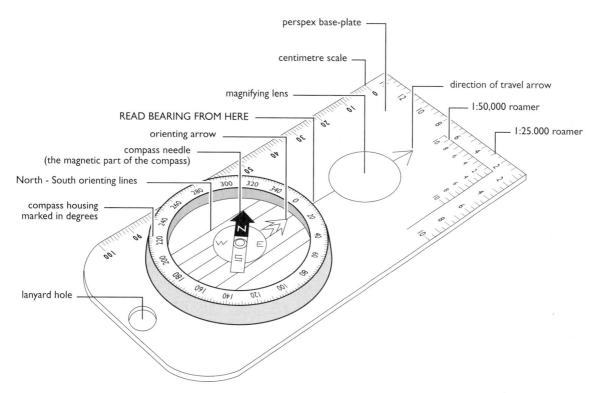

Figure 11.11 An example of a base-plate compass

- **Thumb compass:** a compass housing with a strap for your thumb. This type of compass is used in orienteering for the hand holding the map and to be used with the thumbing technique. It is not useful for expeditions.

- **Wrist compass:** a compass housing worn on the wrist. This type of compass is not very useful for expeditions, but can show you quickly and easily which direction is north.

- **Card compass:** often a simple round casing with a floating card inside it. The card is marked with the cardinal points and the part of the card which is magnetised is also coloured to represent north: it therefore turns to the north.

- **Gyrocompass:** sophisticated electric devices that do not use the Earth's magnetic fields. This type of compass is used on aircraft and large sea vessels and is highly unsuitable for expeditions.

There are various other devices that mimic compasses or share their attributes, but in this unit we are mostly concerned with base-plate compasses.

Compass uses

Base-plate compasses have several useful features which allow you to use the compass for a range of uses:

1 Roamers can be used for measuring distance as they're already divided into 100s of metres for the relevant scale (make sure you use the right scale). Base-plates also have measured rulers which can be used for the same purpose, though you may need to do some simple maths in conversion.

2 As they are to scale with grid squares and are divided into tenths, roamers are also useful for taking grid references more accurately than using the eye.

3 The compass can also be used to **set** the map. To do this simply place the compass on the map and move them both around until you have the magnetic needle aligned to the north

on the map. Now both the map and compass are pointing north and you have a better idea of directions. As there is a difference between magnetic north and grid north you should adjust the compass dial by adding in the magnetic variation. Now the map is set with north.

4   The main purpose of a base-plate is for taking bearings, both from the map and from the ground. Before looking at taking bearings we need to explore the concept of the cardinal points and to see how many north points there are.

The cardinal points

The cardinal points are the 4 main points of direction: North, East, South and West and are used to identify differences in direction between places. For example, Scotland is north of England, but south of the Arctic Circle. The cardinal points can be split up to give further accuracy, for example north-west, north-east and directions such as north-north-east (which is slightly more to the north than north-east). North-north-west by north is even closer to north. There are a total of 32 compass points.

> ### Theory into practice
> Draw a diagram showing the cardinal points and all their smaller divisions (the compass points).

North points

There are several different types of north. When using a map and compass you use 2 of them and must know how to change between them.

1   **True north:** this is the geographic North Pole, which is the top bit of the axis the Earth moves around. Clearly this is the North Pole and can be identified at night by the Pole star.

2   **Grid north:** the north that the maps make. Maps are a flat, 2 dimensional representation of the Earth. However, the Earth is round and has 3

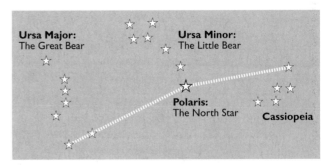

Figure 11.12 How to locate the North Star

dimensions which means maps can't have the same north. In order to make maps, the curve of the Earth is "flattened" out which skews the north. On maps, grid north is to the top.

3   **Magnetic north:** the Earth has a magnetic field which is what the magnetised part of the compass works with. Unfortunately, the magnetic north is not at the same place as the true North Pole. At the moment it is in Canada, just north of Hudson Bay, which is west of true north for us in the UK.

In addition, the magnetic pole moves slightly, requiring a correction to be made to any compass bearings. This is called **magnetic variation** and is marked on maps, along with where it will move in the future.

Taking bearings

As we have seen, compasses are usually graduated into degrees. There are 360 degrees in a circle which enables you to give a degree bearing for any point around you. Using the base-plate allows you to use that bearing with the map to either find out where to go or where you are.

To find out which way to go you need the map. Locate your position and the position of your destination. To be effective, bearings shouldn't be very long distance: it's better to do a series of short legs accurately than one long leg that goes off course. As a general rule, bearings should be the length of a compass base-plate at the most. Once you have these points all you need to do is:

1 Put the base-plate on the map so that your position and your destination are lined up with the compass. The line of direction arrow on the compass must be pointing in the direction you need to go.

2 Turn the compass housing so that the orienting arrow on the compass housing lines up with the north-south grid lines on the map. When they do you can read off the number where the direction of travel arrow meets the compass housing. This number is your grid bearing.

3 Take the compass from the map. Before you can travel on your bearing you need to change it to a magnetic bearing. The bearing we just took was based on the map, using grid north. In order to use the magnetic needle on the compass it needs to be adjusted. The map will tell you what the magnetic variation is for the area and how it will change with time. It is usually entitled 'North Points'. This number should be **added** to the grid bearing. Now hold the compass to your solar plexus with the direction of travel arrow pointing out in front of you and turn around until the magnetic needle aligns with the orienting arrow on the housing. You are now facing the way you need to go.

Theory into practice

What is the bearing from your college to your home?

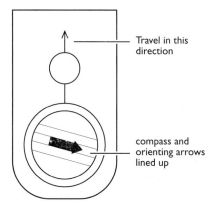

Travel in this direction

compass and orienting arrows lined up

Figure 11.13 Compass fully aligned to travel on a bearing

The following points should be noted when taking and following a bearing:

- Never take bearings over long distances; 500 metres should be the maximum. If you have any slight deviation this will be magnified the further you walk.

- Always ensure the compass is straight and level when you are holding it in front of you.

- Remember that compasses are magnetic: avoid metal fences, pylons, ice axes and other iron items when taking bearings.

- Pick a point in the distance that is on the line you intend to follow and walk towards that; it's less likely that you'll deviate if you have something to aim for. Even better is to have an alignment of two static objects/features.

- If necessary, measure the distance and use pacing to guide you to your destination.

- To ensure that you're still following the route you can take a back bearing. To do this turn around to face the direction you came from. Hold your compass in front of you and check the bearing back to the point you started from. This should be 180 degrees less than the bearing you are walking on.

- In poor visibility you may need to use other members of your party to help. For example, have someone at the back of the group to check the bearing and who can inform the leader if they go off the line of the route. Two people could also count the pacing to ensure it's right or leap-frogging is another useful skill. This is when one person walks out on a bearing from the group and when the group start to lose sight of the walker they call to stop him and then walk out to him. The second person then does the same, watched by the first walker and so on. The benefit of leap-frogging is that corrections can be made by the group and there is always a reference point to walk to.

Compass to map bearings

If you want to identify on the map a feature that you can see on the ground, the process for this is similar to taking a map bearing just in reverse:

1 Point the compass at the feature, ensuring that the direction of travel arrow is pointing straight at it.

2 Turn the compass housing until the orienting arrow lines up with the north part of the magnetic needle and read off the bearing. This bearing is magnetic and needs to be changed to a grid bearing. In order to do this you must **subtract** the magnetic variation from the bearing.

3 Now place the compass on the map with the base-plate lined up with where you think your position is. Turn the whole compass round until the orienting lines on the housing match up with the north-south gridlines on the map. The feature you're looking for should be on the line your base-plate makes.

Think it over

It can be difficult to remember what to do with the magnetic variation, so think of a rhyme to help you such as

Grid to mag: add;

mag to grid: get rid

Try to find other rhymes to aid you in remembering how to use magnetic variation.

Walking techniques

When walking a route there are a number of techniques that can aid you in reaching your destination:

- **Hand rails:** linear features that you can follow along, for example rivers, walls and fences, footpaths, power lines and hedges. Ensure you remember to leave them at a certain point as it can be very easy to carry on following a footpath when you should have turned off 3 kilometres ago.

- **Attack points:** recognisable features that you can use to take a bearing from. It's always better and easier to take a bearing from an easily identifiable point, for example the corner of a forest, a track junction or a building.

- **Collecting features:** these are features that you "collect" on your route and can also be called tick off features. For instance, you may have to cross a road, pass a footpath junction and ford a stream before turning off. All of these features an be used as collecting features as you collect them before changing direction. Obviously you have to study the route carefully before you set off.

- **Aiming off:** if the feature you are aiming to reach is something like a wall junction or stream junction it is unlikely that heading straight for that point will get you there. You are more likely to end up either side of it and not know which way to go. To prevent this, you can deliberately aim off to the side; that way you know which direction to go in once you reach the wall or stream. This technique is sometimes used in conjunction with attack points.

- **Contouring:** at some points in your route you may have to descend a little and then have to walk up again to get to the same height. To avoid this you can walk round on the same contour

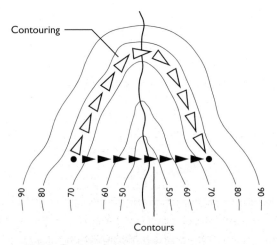

Figure 11.14 Contouring on a map

line. The distance will be further but not as difficult as going up which always takes longer.

- **Searches:** one type of search that can be used solo as well as with a group is the spiral search. Reset your bearing to magnetic north and walk on that bearing for a predetermined distance, for example 100 metres or the limit of visibility; turn 90 degrees to the right, east, and walk twice the first distance; from there turn another 90 degrees right, south and walk three times the first distance. Continue in this manner turning 90 degrees to the right and extending the distance walked. This method covers a relatively good amount of ground and allows you to see the ground from various directions. It is also useful in that it is straightforward to return to your starting point.

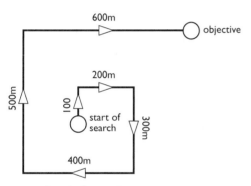

Figure 11.15 A spiral search on a map

Case study – navigation skills

Alan and Ayesha are walking in the Peak District. They intend to do a quick visit to Bleaklow Stones but as they are having lunch at the stones a thick mist descends, reducing visibility to about 5 metres. Looking at the map, they realise that they must use their compasses otherwise they could be wandering the cloughs and bogs for days. Alan wants to head in the general direction of Bleaklow Head, saying that they'll easily pick up the Pennine Way path there. Ayesha isn't so sure as she's been on Bleaklow before in poor weather and knows that the paths aren't always clear and that you can easily miss one of the cairns or guide posts. She suggests heading in an easterly direction, crossing three streams before meeting Black Clough and its footpath which leads to Bleaklow Head.

Alan looks at the map and measures that the footpath is 700 metres away which is a bit too far to walk on a bearing but he thinks that Black Clough is a big enough feature for them not to miss, even if the path is indistinct. The first stream they need to cross is 300 metres from their position and the next two are each about 100 metres apart, so they decide to *pace* out these distances to ensure that they're on the right track, using the streams as *tick off features* and Black Clough as a *hand rail feature*. Ayesha estimates that they should reach Black Clough in about 8 or 9 minutes, at a pace of about 5 km per hour (the terrain isn't easy, but they are fit and not carrying much equipment). If they haven't reached the clough in 10 minutes then they know they will have missed it.

Satisfied with their calculations, the two set off in an easterly direction, using their compasses to guide them and pacing the distances to the streams. The going is tougher than they expected, but in just under 10 minutes they arrive at a notable stream cut into the plateau that must be Black Clough. Luckily, they pick up the footpath which leads them to Bleaklow Head, but there all paths peter out and there is no obvious route out. Ayesha takes a *bearing* to the Hern Stones: 180 degrees, due south. Remembering the *magnetic variation*, she adds 4 degrees to get a magnetic bearing of 184. Alan does the same and gets 182 degrees. They are out by 2 degrees but this isn't too bad as they will only be walking about 600 metres and hope to spot guideposts along the way. As the visibility is so poor they decide to *leapfrog* the route, with Alan walking off ahead and Ayesha guiding him left or right, telling him when she can no longer see him.

At Hern Stones they see the footpath that will lead them to the Pennine Way. Not trusting that it will be distinct all the way they take a bearing and measure the distance to ensure that they always know where they are. Luckily the path leads straight to the Pennine Way and runs along a stream bed which is easily followed all the way to the road where they get picked up by their lift.

Route cards

Route cards are very useful aids when carrying out any expedition. They include all the destinations, distances, timings, descriptions of the route and escape routes all on one sheet that can be checked at a glance. It is also useful to leave a copy at home with a responsible person who can contact the emergency services in the event of the group not reaching their destination or not calling in on time.

The following information should be included on a route card:

- the **destination** which shows the day's objective.

- the date as you will have several route cards for a long expedition.

- the **speed** you expect to travel at; if you are backpacking across uneven terrain this speed will be slower than usual. A note of timing adjustment for height climbed is also shown.

- **emergency contact number** showing who to contact if there is a serious problem which will affect the expedition. This person should also have access to a copy of the route card.

- the place and the 6 figure grid reference that you are setting off **from**.

- the place you're heading **to**.

- the **distance** which is measured between the 2 points, either in metres or kilometres.

- **rest** periods showing any time out for lunch stops, drink breaks, etc

- **time taken (a)** – how long it takes to walk the distance including rests.

- **time taken (b)** – a record of how much additional time it will take to go up the height climbed.

  Every single contour that goes up must be counted to determine total **height gained**. Contours going down are not counted but if you cross the same contour several times it does count (going up hill still takes time even if you're going back down again).

- **time (a+b)** is the total time that the journey will take, accounting for distance, breaks/rests and height climbed.

- **height lost** does not affect the timing but is valuable information. Again, you must count every contour that you go down.

- **direction** can be recorded as a **magnetic** bearing if you are going to set off on a straight line to your objective. Otherwise it's more useful just to mention the general compass point direction of the next objective, especially if the route meanders.

- **description** is brief and has pertinent information that may be useful to help you when you leave for the next objective.

- **escape routes** showing nearest routes off the mountain and to civilisation where help can be summoned which can be useful for emergences and foul weather.

Navigation toys

These are (usually) expensive accessories that can be useful when undertaking expeditions. They are by no means essential for walking but can provide a check on navigation skills or give additional information.

Altimeter

This device uses atmospheric pressure to tell you what height above sea level you are at. This can be helpful in mountains as you can count the contours on the map to aid positioning. They are affected by weather systems, of course and need to be reset every now and then, but you need to know your exact height to be able to do this.

Global Positioning Systems (GPS)

These are electronic navigation devices about the size of a mobile phone that rely on information from satellites to identify their position. Once

Destination: Bleaklow Stones   **Date:** 21/6/03

Party members: I M Lost, H Elp, May day, O Ops

Speed: 4 km/hr, +1 min/10 m climbed   **Emergency contact number:** 0114 2659 098

From	To	Distance	Rests	Time taken (a)	Height climbed	Time taken (b)	Height lost	Direction	Time (a+b)	Description	Escape routes
Cairn, Nether Moor 147873	Druid's Stone 134874	1300m	0	19.5	140m	14	0	278	33.5	From flat head uphill to stone on 2nd footpath	Lady Booth Brook to YHA
Druid's Stone 134874	Spot height, Hartshorn 115877	2400m	0	36	60m	6	30m	W	42	Carry on along footpath, at Upper Tor head up to high ground	Ollerbrook Clough to Vale of Edale
Spot height, Hartshorn 115877	Ford, Blackden Rind 115883	650m	0	9.75	10m	1	30m	012	10.75	Follow bearing across plateau to footpath	Golden Clough to Grindsbook Booth

Figure 11.16 An example of a route card for part of a 1-day journey (represents 3 checkpoints)

switched on they need time to locate available satellites to get a fix. They also need open access to the sky and valleys. Built up areas, under bridges and inside buildings can block access to satellites. When you have a fix you are told your location, often in terms of longitude and latitude which must be converted to grid references.

GPS systems can be programmed with a route which can tell you which way to go for each objective, even if you are going astray. In this way they act as an electronic route card, but you should still leave a copy of the route with someone responsible.

Many people look upon GPS as a way to avoid navigating with a map and compass but GPS systems are an aid to navigation, not a replacement as they are not always 100% correct, they don't work in valleys, they require batteries which can run out (especially in cold weather) and they are not totally waterproof.

Equipment

Walking is one of the county's favourite activities. With this in mind it isn't too surprising that there is an overwhelming amount of clothing and equipment to choose from when you are preparing for an expedition. It's important to ensure that you've got suitable equipment for the expedition to avoid discomfort or a call out for the Mountain Rescue. This section, looks at the kind of equipment that you will need to take on an expedition including clothing, walking gear, camping gear and safety equipment.

Season usage

Most of the equipment outlined in this section such as boots, tents and sleeping bags is categorised as to season use. This tells you what conditions the equipment is suitable for. The season ratings are as follows:

- **One season:** suitable for use in the warmest conditions in Britain – summer. Generally this kit is going to be lightweight but not very warm and often not very robust. As conditions tend to get worse the higher you go, one season gear is really only suitable for low-lying environments.

- **Two season:** slightly warmer and more robust, suitable for warm springtime and low hills.

- **Three season:** kit in this category will be suitable for most conditions in Britain outside of winter which means sleeping bags will give protection below 0 degrees centigrade and boots will be suitable for mountain paths and harsh weather.

- **Four season:** this is winter kit and can sometimes be unsuitable for use in other conditions as it may be too warm, heavy, bulky or less comfortable. Four season can also refer to boots and tents for high mountains.

- **Five season:** suitable for expeditions in very cold areas and at altitude. This kit is often very expensive due to the fabrics used and owing to the small market. It can be lighter than equivalents in lower ratings because of advanced fabrics and manufacturing methods.

Season rating is only a guide and many other things need to be taken into consideration, such as how much you feel the cold and the weather. It can be cold, stormy and wet even in summer and one season equipment can be inadequate.

Personal equipment

Clothing

Clothing for walking in the outdoors needs to be:

- lightweight as you may be wearing or carrying them for a long time

- quick drying as Britain is renowned for its changeable climate and rain

- durable

- comfortable, both for you and for the climate.

As a rule, it is best to choose synthetic fabrics (nylon or polyester and their derivatives) rather than natural fabrics as wool is heavy (and soaks up water) and not very compressible and cotton takes a long time to dry and steals your body heat to do so. Polycotton isn't too bad so long as there's less than 50% cotton.

Clothing layers

For maximum protection and warmth, clothes should be worn in layers as follows:

- **Base layer** worn next to the skin. This layer provides a small amount of warmth, but its main function is to prevent the body from getting too sweaty. To do this it "wicks" moisture (sweat) from the body to the outer layers, preventing you from getting too damp and uncomfortable.

  Wicking is the process that modern outdoor fabrics use to absorb moisture (including sweat) and transport it to the outside of the fabric where the moisture will evaporate and flow through the next layers of clothing. Cotton does not wick as a cotton T-shirt will absorb moisture and stay wet.

- **Thermal layer** worn over the base layer to provide warmth. A fleece is usually used in this layer as it's good at trapping heat and is highly breathable. Also called the **mid layer** it includes trousers and shirts. Parts of this layer may not be necessary in good weather.

- **Outer layer** also known as the **shell** acts as a protection from the wind and the rain such as waterproofs. Most waterproofs nowadays are breathable, allowing the sweat wicked by the base layer to pass through the outer fabrics, not leaving you sweaty and damp underneath your clothes.

Waterproofs

Waterproofs need to be windproof and waterproof. A jacket needs to fit comfortably over the top of your other layers and overtrousers comfortably over trousers. All waterproofs need taped seams to prevent water entering through the seams and nowadays are breathable (although different fabrics have different rates of breathability and even waterproofing).

Waterproof fabrics simply stop water from getting through them. They are impermeable to water droplets, rain, puddles, splashes of water, water pistols but are not always breathable as old-style waterproofs can get very wet from the inside due to sweat.

Water-resistant means the fabric will repel some water, but after a while, or under intense rain/water it will start to let water in and you'll get wet. Water-resistant clothes will be breathable, possibly more breathable than waterproof items, but they don't offer the same protection as waterproofs and should never be used in place of a waterproof.

The easiest way to check to see if a garment is waterproof is to check the seams. In heavy rain, water can force itself through stitched seams, so waterproof fabrics need to have some tape to cover them. In some clothes you can see the tape on the inside, covering the seams. If you can't actually see the inside of the face fabric (if there's a lining or some insulation) just squeeze the seams between your finger and thumb. If you can feel some stiffness around the seam then it's taped and waterproof, If not, then it's not fully waterproof whatever fabric it's made from.

Generally waterproofs consist of a durable face fabric (this is the fabric that you see and touch) and a waterproofing layer that keeps water droplets out and allows water vapour to escape. It can come in two forms: a laminate or a coating. Laminates (such as Gore Tex) are thin layers of waterproof, breathable fabric bonded to the outer fabric (which offers durability and windproofing). Coatings are applied to the inside of the face fabric and will allow water vapour through, but

keep rain out. In general, laminates are usually more waterproof and breathable than coatings and coatings can wear off the fabrics. Laminates, however can be punctured, so they do require some care. Finally, the outer fabrics are given a water-resistant coating to allow rain to run off the jacket. This prevents the fabric from getting soaked, which would interfere with breathability.

Features to look for in a waterproof jacket are:

- breathable fabric
- hood with wired or stiffened peak and drawcord to keep the hood in place and stop it flopping about in the wind
- Velcro fastening at the cuffs to allow for ventilation and ease of taking on/off
- hem drawcord to keep all the warmth you've created inside your clothing system
- pockets for putting equipment in (not necessarily waterproof)
- map pocket/Napoleon pocket which is a water-resistant horizontal pocket under the zip flap able to take a folded OS map.
- zip flap with Velcro and/or press-stud fastening to stop water from getting in through the zip
- pit zips to allow ventilation under the arms.

Theory into practice

Compare the difference between the features and prices of a waterproof fabric jacket and a water-resistant jacket.

Features to look for in waterproof trousers are:

- breathable fabric
- zips up the side, either full or part so that you can get trousers on over your boots when the rain comes. Make sure there's a gusset or flap behind the zip to stop water getting in. Full zips are essential for winter mountaineering when you could have spikes on your feet
- some form of waist fastening. Most waterproof trousers have elasticated waists, but they can

fall down slowly if you're wearing a rucksack and walking at a decent pace. Those with drawcords as well at the waist make life a lot easier.

Like anything else, using your waterproofs incorrectly can lead to damage. The more lightweight they are, the easier they are to hurt. In general:

- avoid using your waterproofs for sitting on as this can puncture laminates and damage coatings

- use the clothes for their specified purpose. Using lightweight running waterproofs for scrambling on the Glydders is asking for trouble and will negate any guarantees

- try not to get your waterproofs too dirty. Caking the outer in mud will prevent any breathability

- don't store your waterproofs rolled up. This will only create weaknesses along creases and damage the fabrics. Hang them up as you would any other coat

- wash coated and laminated waterproofs in dedicated washing formulae as normal washing liquids/powders strip garments of any waterproofing. If in doubt check the garment's own instructions or call the manufacturer

- reproof waterproofs after washing. This can be done with sprays or with wash in liquids (pop it in the washing machine with your waterproof). Proofing fluids need to be activated by heat, so hang them out on a hot day or tumble dry/low iron. Always read the label first to see if the fabric will melt in tumble dryers or under irons

- keep synthetics away from fires as they melt. Always be careful when cooking.

Case study

Soldiers in the Falklands discovered that synthetic fabrics melted into gunshot wounds due to the heat generated by the rounds. This made it much more difficult for medics to treat them.

Thermal layer tops

The thermal layer keeps you warm and is usually your top layer, if it isn't raining. This layer can have several layers to it depending on the weather. If it's really cold you might want a light fleece top under another fleece jacket, especially if you feel the cold easily. In summer you may be able to do without a thermal layer altogether when you're walking. You'll probably still need one at night however, and sometimes it can be colder than you think up on the mountains.

Fleece is the fabric commonly used for warmth. It has many benefits:

- high warmth to low weight ratio

- retains warmth when wet

- available in a variety of weights and is therefore versatile in creating garments for different climates

- highly breathable

- can be bonded to other fabrics to create windproof warm layers, making them more versatile.

Fibre pile is also used in conjunction with Pertex to create windproof, showerproof, warm layers that are used in winter. This style of garment has been pioneered by Bufallo and is very popular with outdoor professionals as it can replace all of the layering systems.

Alternatively, in cold weather, insulated garments (sometimes called duvets, just like the cover found on beds) can be used. These are either filled with down or synthetic fabrics very much like sleeping bags. Figure 11.17 compares the performance of down (natural, animal product) versus synthetic filling.

The outers of these garments are usually lightweight synthetics that are windproof and quick drying with water-resistant coatings. Occasionally they are made with waterproof outers but this tends to result in a bulky garment best used in very cold, wet conditions that is too warm for walking in. Duvets are often used in winter as spare emergency clothing when standing around or eating.

Down	Synthetic
High warmth to weight ratio	Good warmth to weight ratio; more advanced fabrics are approaching the performance of down
Long lasting; keeps its loft for years	Compresses after time and use; loses some loft
Clumps together when wet: needs care when washing and in British climate	Retains warmth when wet
Feathers tend to "migrate" out of outer fabric	

Figure 11.17 Comparison of down versus synthetic filling in duvet clothing

Thermal layer trousers

Mid layer bottoms are usually in the form of trousers. Often these are not insulated, as the legs do not lose much heat, but they need to be windproof, durable quick drying and comfortable for walking in. Most are made from polyester or polycotton although some more technical and robust fabrics are available (and tend to be more expensive). British Army lightweight trousers have been popular with walkers for a long time as they fulfil all the above criteria as well as being inexpensive. However, their pockets are limited and it's easy to lose equipment from them. Tracksuit bottoms are usually suitable as long as they are quick drying. Lined trousers are usually too hot for summer, but can be fine in cooler weather.

In extremes of weather, lightweight trousers are not necessarily suitable. For the height of summer shorts are good as they can avoid overheating but they do leave the legs bare and vulnerable to nettles, thorns and sunburn.

For winter, light or mid weight fleece trousers are available. Stretch fleece tights are still acceptable in these conditions although they are expensive. Fleece salopettes are also available and have the benefit of adding warmth to the upper body and don't have the tendency to slip down that some trousers have when walking.

Think about it

Discuss the type of thermal layer (mid layer) trousers you find most comfortable to wear in cool weather for an expedition.

Care of mid-layers

Some items in this layer are just like normal clothes and require the same amount of care. They're usually not as expensive as waterproofs and aren't as delicate. However, you should ensure the following:

- keep away from fire/heat as synthetics melt easily

- wash fleece inside out as it doesn't pill (make bobbles on the surface) as much if you do this.

- don't use fabric softener as it inhibits windproofing

- don't use biological washing powders/liquids

- always read the manufacturer's care and washing labels.

Base layers

In warm weather this is underwear and a T-shirt, in cold weather it can be thermals and long johns. Base layers, just like all the other layers, need to be synthetic as natural fabrics hold too much water (sweat) and can be uncomfortable when wet. Silk base layers are available but tend not to work as well as well as synthetics. Sports t-shirts are popular (especially football shirts) and acceptable so long as they aren't cotton.

Tops can be long or short sleeved depending on preference. Zip necks are useful in winter for ventilation when ascending and keeping warm when still. They shouldn't be too baggy or they won't work efficiently and you may need to fit other layers over them. Bottoms need to be comfortable and quick drying. Long johns are good for winter as they can add some warmth and help wick the legs when covered in several layers.

The purpose of this layer is to transport sweat away from the body to the outside environment where it can be dispersed, leaving you drier. In doing this, the moisture disappears but the sweat chemicals are left in the fabric which can make them smell unpleasant. The very technical base layers in gear shops often have anti-bacterial treatments but they are expensive.

When taking care of base layers, follow the guidelines for thermal layers.

Theory into practice

Draw a flow diagram of the layering system showing how it all works.

Clothing accessories

Some accessories such as hats, gloves and gaiters are essential for expeditions whereas others may depend on personal taste.

Hats

Hats are essential, whatever the weather:

- on hot days you need a hat to keep the sun off (either a baseball cap or sun hat)

- in colder weather (and at night) you'll need something warmer as you can lose up to 60% of your heat through your head

- balaclavas can be useful as they also cover the neck, ears and part of the face

- hats are also useful in rain, especially those with peaks to stop the rain going in your face.

If you're expecting sunny weather (regardless of the season) then don't forget sunscreen and sunglasses.

Gloves

Gloves are an important part of your personal equipment:

- if you're expecting rain or snow take more than one pair as wet gloves are not pleasant

- waterproof gloves are good but tend to be bulky and can be expensive

- mittens are good for keeping your hands warm but restrict finger movement

- grip palmed gloves can be useful, especially if you're expecting to use your hands a lot, for example ropework and in winter conditions for poles and ice axes.

Gaiters

Not everyone likes to use gaiters but they are essential in winter conditions as they:

- cover the lower part of the leg and go over the tops of boots

- keep stones, mud, snow, etc out of your boots

- stop the bottom of your trousers getting dirty and wet

Front fastening are much easier to use. If they have a cord (or bootlace) that goes under the sole of the boot then put a cord-lock device on them to prevent having to tie knots in them.

Think it over

Discuss in groups the type of hat, gloves and gaiters that you would take on a summer expedition and then for a winter expedition. What about if you were expecting a range of weather conditions?

Footwear

Socks

When choosing walking socks, be aware of the following:

- avoid nylon football socks as they will rub and cause blisters

- most walking socks are woollen or use a blend which is good as it makes them warm if they get wet

- thick socks are needed to soak up the sweat and provide some padding and protection at potential rub points

- modern technical socks are worn on their own, but are expensive. They have different thicknesses and blends of fabric at the heel, toes, etc

- waterproof over socks are good if you expect to get your feet wet. Don't wear them as slippers as this can damage them. Care for them as you would waterproofs as they are made of the same fabric.

Boots

Footwear for outdoor activities comes in a wide range of types and styles depending on their purpose, from sandals to plastic mountaineering boots. For low level trails on easy ground, trainers are acceptable. Walking trainers and approach shoes are made for this kind of activity and will give better support and be more comfortable. In summer you can wear sandals to keep your feet cool. They are good for wearing after a day's walking to allow the feet to breathe and allow air to tender parts, increasing healing time.

Some multi-activity trainers are suitable for more than trail walking, running and biking. They are available with stiffer soles and sticky rubber on the front to allow them to be used for light climbing and scrambling.

For hillier ground and rougher tracks and trails you'll need boots as they are more robust and offer more protection, especially at the ankle. Choose boots with a flexible sole that will flex when you walk and be comfortable. In addition you shouldn't be able to feel stones through the soles of these boots. Boots can be made of leather or fabric and many have waterproof linings to keep your feet dry.

On more serious ground, such as rocky mountain paths and scrambling, you need a stiffer sole for more support. The uppers will be more robust although it can still be leather or fabric. These boots are called 3 or 3–4 season boots.

Winter walking requires fully stiffened boots to take crampons. These are called 4 season boots which are heavy and bulky, suitable for mountain walking throughout the world. Generally these type of boots are made of leather though more serious mountaineering boots can be made of flexible plastic.

	Sole	Fabric	Comfort	Terrain
Approach trainers	Flexible or semi-stiff	Usually fabric	Generally good	Varies, depending on purpose
2–3 season hill boots	Flexible	Leather or fabric, often waterproof	Good	Low trails to easy hill paths
3 season mountain boots	Semi-stiff	Leather or fabric, often waterproof	Good to moderate	Spring to autumn mountain use
4 season mountaineering boots	Stiff	Leather, plastic or both	Moderate to poor (worst case)	Can cope with all, best in mountains. Plastic and hybrids for winter only

Figure 11.18 Recommended shoes and boots for different terrains

When choosing boots, be aware of the following guidelines:

- when you know what type of boot you need, try lots on to get the most comfortable.

- try boots on in the afternoon as your feet will have swelled after walking around all day. Wear the socks you will use for expeditions.

- walk around as much as possible in the shop, preferably up and down stairs and on inclines and uneven surfaces to check if there are any rub points.

- wear new boots as much as possible at home on carpeted surfaces. If they hurt you can take them back and exchange them.

- clean boots after wearing them by rinsing and scrubbing if necessary. Use polish lightly on leather boots as polish can cause stitching to rot and leather to crack. If you can scrape the polish off with your finger, there's too much on.

- don't polish suede/nubuck/fabric boots. Rinse and/or scrub them, then apply a waterproofing spray if necessary.

- leather tends to be more durable but fabric is usually lighter and more breathable.

- waterproof liners won't last forever. They use similar fabrics to other waterproofs and are therefore susceptible to damage.

Other personal equipment

Having the right clothing is half way ready to being kitted out for an expedition but there are other bits of kit that you need to be able to cope competently and comfortably.

Rucksacks

There are many different rucksacks available from lightweight mountain rucksacks to enormous expedition rucksacks. Like boots, you must decide whether you are going to be doing day walks between spring and autumn, backpacking for days, winter mountaineering or climbing.

Rucksacks are measured in litres but different manufacturers have different ways of measuring the litreage of their rucksacks, so one 65 litre backpack may be a different size to another 65 litre backpack. One way of measuring is by using beans. Dried beans are shovelled into rucksacks using scoops of a known size; the number of scoops is counted and the litreage worked out from that.

Deciding how many litres you need depends on how much you have to carry:

- if you're going for a day's walking in fair weather you may only need 15–25 litres for lunch, drinks and a jacket

- the worse the weather, the more clothing and emergency kit you'll need. You may also need specialist equipment such as climbing gear. In these situations you will need between 30–50 litres depending on the amount of equipment you need. Rucksacks this size can also be used for lightweight, fair weather backpacking.

- for multi-day trips when you will be expected to carry everything you will need while away such as tent, clothes, food, stove, fuel and sleeping bag, a rucksack of 50 litres and above is suitable

- on extended trips or trips to remote areas and high mountains or military operations where you may need to carry lots of ammunition and food, you will need a rucksack of 80+ litres.

Back system

The back system on a rucksack is the bit that touches your back and can be very important, especially on heavy rucksacks:

- Some very small rucksacks have no back system which means there is no support or padding on the back of the rucksack, just the same fabric as on the front and sides. This type of rucksack is lighter than other types but you have to be careful how you pack it or you could have flasks or cameras poking you in your back. It can also be sweaty in hot weather or if you're being very active.

- Adjustable back systems are found on bigger expedition rucksacks. They allow you to get a personalised fit by adjusting the length between the hip belt and the shoulder straps, along with other minor adjustments. This is particularly useful if different people are going to use the bag. Adjustable back systems aid comfort but add quite a lot of weight. These rucksacks always have some kind of padding for comfort as well.

- Most other rucksacks use padded back systems. The back length is a standard length (though some come in a range of sizes, such as medium and large). Bags with this type of back can be of any size from little cycling rucksacks to huge military bergans. The padding is for comfort and to give the rucksack some shape so it doesn't just flop about. Some bags have removable padding down the back that can be taken out and used as a sit mat. Others may have channels without padding to allow some air to circulate and lessen sweatiness.

- Venting back systems feature a piece of mesh, which sits against the back and has a gap between it and the fabric back of the rucksack. This type allows lots of air circulation and doesn't stop breathable fabrics working. Usually found on smaller bags (10 to 40 litres) as this system tends to be less robust and can't take heavy loads.

Except for the first category, nearly all rucksacks will have a frame to provide support. Frames are internal, lightweight metal staves that can be bent to the shape of your back, although they are pre-formed so it's best not to adjust them too much.

All rucksacks will fit differently, even those by the same manufacturer. When choosing a bag try on many different types and walk around with them on. Fill them with the type of weight you expect to carry to see if the shoulder straps dig in painfully. If the back is adjustable get advice on how to use it. You may be carrying everything for weeks so the fit is important. For larger bags that will be carrying heavy loads, the waist belt is the most important thing to fit as you want all the weight to be transferred to the hips rather than the shoulders.

There are special rucksacks available for women which have different shaped shoulder straps and hip belts to suit the female form. In addition, litreage tends to be slightly less than their male counterparts. In some cases they may be suitable for males with slighter build and some women may find "standard" bags more comfortable.

Fabrics

Fabrics on rucksacks vary and are measured in denier with the higher numbers being tougher (and heavier). Small day-walking bags may have a denier of 200 whereas military, climbing and expedition bags can have a denier of 1000.

Most rucksacks are made of some form of nylon, which is relatively lightweight but degrades in sunlight (over a long period of time). Some use polyester, which is a bit heavier. In order to lose weight, some lighter fabrics have a grid pattern of stitching on them that prevents tears and rips from spreading (hence its name: ripstop). Canvas is used by some manufacturers because of its durability.

Some rucksacks can use a mixture of fabrics to maximise durability and lightweight. Areas that are prone to abrasion, such as the base, could be 1000 denier, whereas the sides may be ripstop. Back fabrics are likely to be of lighter fabrics, too. Some have wicking foam on the contact areas to remove sweat and aid breathability.

Most rucksacks are not waterproof. They will have showerproof coatings but generally the stitching is not seamed so water can get in through the seams. In order to prevent all your clothes and sleeping gear getting sodden, it's worth investing in some form of rucksack liner or cover (or both if you're expecting to get very wet). Liners can be as simple as bin bags, although they tend to tear a bit easily. Tougher plastic bags are available at gear stores for lining the rucksack as well as neoprene liners with waterproof closures at the top and sealed seams.

Rucksack covers are a cover for rucksacks to protect them from rain and damage. Some rucksacks even come with fold away rain covers secreted in the base or lid. Soldiers tend to use rucksack covers for protection but also because they can break up the bag's shape, aiding camouflaging.

There are some waterproof rucksacks available which have sealed seams and special roll-away openings to prevent water getting inside. However, it is still worth putting everything inside plastic bags just in case.

Compartments and pockets

Most rucksacks have just one compartment to put equipment in and some may have 2 compartments that can convert to just one large compartment. This can be useful if you want to separate some items of your kit, such as sleeping bag and stoves or fuel and food. Remember that the bottom compartment will also need a lining to keep the contents dry.

Most rucksacks have pockets for storing things that you may need easy access to such as hats, gloves and torch or that you don't want near other things such as fuel for your stove. Lid pockets are popular on most rucksacks and don't interfere with anything, although the contents are likely to get wet in rain. Side pockets can be found on many rucksacks and are often useful but they can get in the way, especially if you are climbing or scrambling. Climbing and mountaineering bags have smooth sides for this reason.

Closure systems

In general, rucksacks can have 2 forms of closing at the top:

1 **Lid and buckle(s)** is most common on walking rucksacks as the lid offers more weather protection and is less likely to break than a zip. They can be fiddly sometimes and take longer to open.

A standard rucksack

2 **Zip access** is used on some bags, though generally these are for cycling, ski-ing or urban uses. They make it a lot easier to get in the bag but zips can break quite easily if you overload the bag's capacity and they are not as water-resistant as full lids.

Specialised features

There are all sorts of other features that rucksacks can have. Remember, although some specialised features may be useful, they do add weight which you will need to carry.

- Ice axe carriers for attaching ice axes to the front of the rucksack. Alternatively, these carriers can be used for trekking poles.

- Side compression straps to squeeze the bag together when it's not full packed to prevent the weight from being too low and therefore uncomfortable. However, they are also useful for strapping sleeping mats, tents, trekking poles, ice axes and other linear things to the side of the rucksack.

- Rope straps under the lid for strapping a rope. These straps are useful for climbing rucksacks.

- Gear loops which can be found on hip belts and are for attaching climbing gear to when climbing with the rucksack. These are only useful for multi-pitch and winter climbing.

- Little pockets for hydration packs and little holes to allow the tube out of.

Theory into practice
Draw up a table showing the main features and uses of a variety of types of rucksacks.

Map and compass

Protecting maps from rain is very important. Wet maps can simply disintegrate when used in the wet, rendering them totally useless. To avoid this, there are a couple of things you can use:

1 **Map cases** usually have some sort of zip-like fastening to allow the open map inside. There are a variety of types and sizes, just remember to have enough of the map visible for your route.

2 **Laminated maps** are maps that have been covered in thin, see-through plastic sheets. This makes them waterproof and much more durable than paper maps.

Don't forget your route card either. Like your map it needs to be close to hand and it's preferable to keep both together. If you're following a route in a guide book, then keep that handy also. Remember to protect anything paper from water; plastic wallets are good for route cards.

Compasses are simple yet important devices and it is essential to look after them properly:

- don't store them near other compasses or iron objects as this can demagnetise or polarise them

- avoid any types of magnets

- when taking bearings beware of electricity pylons, iron fences, ice axes, etc as these will affect the magnetism of the compass and therefore the bearing.

Knife

A small pocket knife rather than a huge survival knife is fine for camping in the UK. Choose a multi-tool type with a sturdy blade, can opener, bottle opener, scissors and screwdriver. Anything else is just additional weight.

Cord

It is always advisable to have some nylon cord for repairs and spare boot laces. It can also be useful for creating emergency shelters.

Walking poles

Walking poles are best used in pairs and can make travelling over uneven terrain easier as you've always got an extra point of contact with the ground. They are also helpful for going up and downhill, as well as crossing rivers. It is advisable to extend the length for downhill and shorten it for uphill. In emergencies they can also be used as splints or poles for impromptu shelters, etc.

When choosing walking poles look for ones with anti-shock features to prevent jarring your arms and shoulders as well as poles that shorten quite small, to make them compact and easy to transport. The disks on the bottom are soil baskets that stop the poles sinking into wet ground; if you go into soft snow you will need snow baskets which are wider.

Water carrier

Hydration systems are available which are flexible plastic containers with drinking tubes and bite valves (you bite to open the valve before you can drink). The containers are placed in your bag with the tube coming out of the bag and attaching to shoulder straps, lapel, etc so you can drink from it easily. These are excellent for hot weather because you don't have to stop for a drink and therefore avoid dehydration.

In cold weather you still need to stay hydrated (dehydration is one of the factors leading to frost bite) but usually not to the same extent as in summer. Hot drinks are essential to keep you warm and stainless steel unbreakable flasks are ideal for this purpose. Remember to "charge" them with hot water for 10 minutes before filling them as this keeps the liquid warmer for longer.

Theory into practice

Research the different type of water carriers and hydration systems available.

Watch

A watch is useful for navigation timings and for telling the time.

Trowel

Lightweight plastic trowels are useful for backpacking trips where you don't expect to encounter many toilets. Always remember a toilet roll as well, wrapped in a plastic bag. Don't go to the toilet near water sources to avoid contamination and always wash your hands afterwards.

Torch

Head torches are best for walking and expeditions as they free up your hands and shine light where you're looking. Don't forget spare batteries and bulbs.

LED bulbs are much more efficient than standard bulbs and therefore last longer (as do the batteries). Some torches are available with two bulbs: a powerful (but energy intensive) halogen for when you need a big light and LED bulbs for normal use. They're more expensive but much more versatile.

Theory into practice

Find out how much burn time LED torches can provide compared to those with standard bulbs. What advantages do LED torches offer on expeditions?

It is also useful to have a spare little torch in your pack for when you need to change the bulb in your main torch.

Food

High-energy foods, such as carbohydrates are the best types of food to carry:

- sandwiches and particularly pitta bread is good because it's flat
- malt loaf is very good expedition food
- fruit
- nuts
- energy bars, biscuits.

Chocolate and sweets tend to give you a sugar rush and then leave you with less energy than they give you. It is best to eat little but often. Drink plenty of water frequently and have warm drinks in winter.

Money

Always carry enough money for extra food and drink, unexpected gifts and emergency 'phone calls etc.

Tissues

Tissues can be used for mopping up spillages, toilet trips, runny noses etc. Don't ignore the value of tissues: even the force's 24-hour ration packs contain a packet of tissues.

Camping equipment

For a camping expedition you'll need all the personal kit discussed but also extra equipment. Some of this is personal, such as sleeping bags, but the majority is group equipment that you can share among the party.

Tents

There are many types of tents available which are suitable for different types of camping. You will need a tent that's big enough for you and whoever you're sharing with and all your equipment, whilst being light and small enough to carry. Like other outdoor gear, tents are graded by season use so make sure you get the right one.

Shape

Backpacking tents come in a range of categories:

1 **Ridge tents** have a triangular cross section and a single ridge running along the top. They tend to be very stable but can be heavy, especially if they have cotton outers. At one time all backpacking tents were ridge design but now they have mostly been replaced by dome tents. Many outdoor pursuit centres and schools still use them however.

A ridge tent

2 **Geodesic dome tents** have flexible poles that are lighter and less bulky than those in ridge tents. They allow the tent to create a dome shape, which is more space efficient. Generally they are lighter than ridge tents but aren't always as stable. There is more variation in suitability for expeditions in this category than most others: some are just suitable for summer valley camping whereas others are made for expeditions in the high mountains. Some domes aren't geodesic. These tend to be 1, 2 or 3 season and not as sturdy.

3 **Hybrid design tents** share some of the shape of the ridge tent (linear or tunnel like) with the flexible poles of the dome tent, although there are countless variations of shape. Most of these tents are suitable for backpacking and are mostly 3 season use.

A hybrid tent

Fabric and poles

The outer of most backpacking tents have flysheets made from nylon with waterproof coatings. This makes them weatherproof and lightweight, but susceptible to damage from the sun's ultra violet rays. Nylon tents also suffer from condensation as they are not as breathable as cotton fabrics.

Inners tend to be of similar fabrics to the flysheet but lighter weight. They will also have some mesh panels for ventilation. The doors of inners should be in 2 parts: a mesh outer door and a fabric inner door. The mesh should be very fine as it's used to keep insects out during the summer while the other doors are open for ventilation.

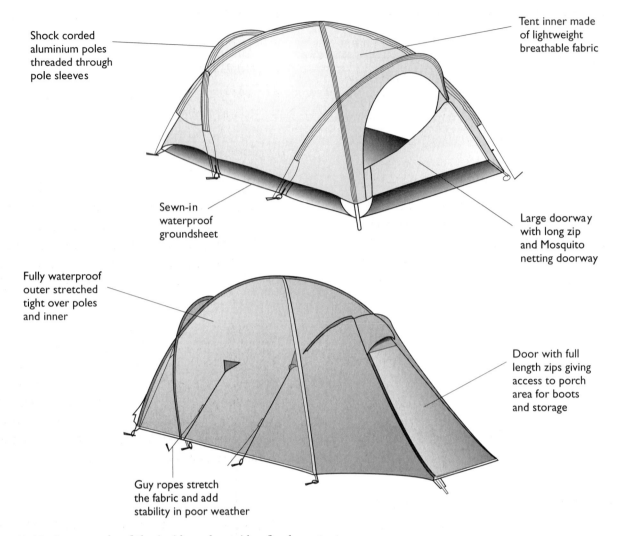

Shock corded aluminium poles threaded through pole sleeves

Tent inner made of lightweight breathable fabric

Sewn-in waterproof groundsheet

Large doorway with long zip and Mosquito netting doorway

Fully waterproof outer stretched tight over poles and inner

Door with full length zips giving access to porch area for boots and storage

Guy ropes stretch the fabric and add stability in poor weather

Figure 11.19 An example of the inside and outside of a dome tent

Poles generally come in 2 main types:

- Fibreglass, which are relatively lightweight and flexible but shatter easily. Once shattered they can be difficult to repair. Less expensive tents have fibreglass poles.

- Metal poles are found in more expensive tents (often it's the pole that is the most expensive part) and are more durable and easier to repair. Alloy poles are the lightest and used in top of the range expedition tents.

Poles for many tents are shock-corded together so that you know which ones are together. Some tents have colour-coded poles and sleeves to make pitching easier.

Care of tents

The following guidelines should be followed when looking after tents:

- After use make sure your tent is dry. If it's stored damp then the fabric could be destroyed.

- Brush any dirt or bits of mud out of the tent or off the base as they can damage the tent when you roll it up.

- Brush any dirt off pegs too and straighten any bent ones.

- Before you use a tent, check that it's all there. Count how many pegs you need and check you have them. Are both the inner and flysheet there? Does anything need replacing or repairing? Is any stitching undone?

- Flysheets eventually need reproofing. To do this, ensure the fabric is clean, put the tent up on a hot day and use a waterproof spray. The heat of the sun should help the process.

- Like waterproofs, tent seams need to be sealed. If they're not or they have come off you can get a seam-sealant stick from camping shops.

- If you can, use a protective sheet under the tent groundsheet to protect it from damage. This is especially important for lightweight tents that use more delicate fabrics. You can buy expensive protective sheets made to fit individual tents or you can use a sheet of plastic.

- Don't leave the tent up in sunlight for weeks on end as this degrades the fabric (even if it has UV inhibitors).

- Sponge any stains; avoid washing machines.

- Keep a repair kit with the tent including needle and thread and a roll of tape. Many tents now come with emergency repair kits.

Theory into practice

Compare a 2 season valley tent with a 5 season mountain tent. What features will they each have to make them suitable for the conditions they are made for? What would be the consequences of using them in different conditions?

Sleeping bags

When camping, you need a sleeping bag. Even in summer it's rare to have a night warm enough not to need a sleeping bag. Sleeping bags are graded by the season rating looked at on page 173–174. The season rating you require will depend upon a number of factors:

- the time of year and weather
- how much you feel the cold
- where you'll be sleeping, for example a valley or in the mountains

- your fitness levels and how tired you are
- whether you'll be in a tent or bivvying
- how much you've eaten
- what you're sleeping on, for example bare ground, airbed or sleeping mat.

Construction

In general, sleeping bags come in 2 styles:

1 Rectangular **caravan** sleeping bags have a long zip down 1 or 2 sides. Usually simply quilted, they are warm enough for valley use although they do come in a variety of filling thicknesses. There is plenty of room (relatively speaking) to move around in the bag.

2 **Mummy** sleeping bags are made for backpacking and other expeditions. They are tapered at the foot to follow the shape of the body better. This means that there is less wasted space filled with dead air that can make you cold but there is also less room to move around in. Mummy sleeping bags are lighter than caravan bags.

Fabrics

The fill of a sleeping bag is very important as it determines how warm the bag will be. Sleeping bags are either filled with down (natural fibres) or synthetics fibres, for example DuPont Hollofil. Each has advantages and disadvantages as shown in Figure 11.20 overleaf.

Outer fabrics are important as they protect both the fill and the user from damage and the elements. For expedition use, outers should be lightweight yet robust, with some weatherproofing. Breathability is also important in sleeping bags. For all of the above reasons, most sleeping bag outers are now made from some form of nylon or polyester.

Liner fabrics should have similar features as well as comfort as they are next to the skin. Breathability and wicking are important to transport away any moisture created by the body. Lightweight expedition sleeping bags tend to have nylon or similar fabrics for linings. Sleeping bags that don't need to be as light can have polycotton or any other comfortable material. These tend to be bulkier as well.

Compression stuff sacks are essential. They have straps down the side that you can tighten when the sleeping bag is inside which compresses the size of the sleeping bag, making it much less bulky.

Some manufacturers make sleeping bag pillows made from similar fabrics to the sleeping bags so that they too are lightweight. Alternatively, you can put clothes inside the stuff sack and use that as a pillow.

Sleeping bag care

Following the guidelines below will ensure your sleeping bag lasts longer:

- Never store your sleeping bag in its stuff sack as this will compress the loft, making it less effective.

- Use a separate detachable liner inside the sleeping bag. This can add a little warmth and prevents the bag from getting sweaty and dirty. After an expedition you only need to wash the liner, not the whole sleeping bag.

- Always use some form of sleeping mat for insulation and to protect the bottom of the bag.

- Air your bag after use as that will get rid of any moisture caused by sleeping in it.

- Ensure that your bag is kept dry. Use a rucksack liner and then keep your sleeping bag in a waterproof bag.

- When packing your sleeping bag into the stuff sack it's better to push the bag in rather than rolling it up as rolling creates creases, which can wear quickly.

- Wash your bag infrequently as this can degrade the filling which stops it being so insulated. If necessary, sponge the outer clean.

Theory into practice

Sleeping bags can come with many features (zip baffles, neck baffles, shoulder baffles, right or left sided zip, pockets, hanging tabs, etc). look through manufacturer's catalogues and websites and describe what these features are for.

Sleeping mats

The ground is very cold and usually damp. If you lie directly on it you will lose heat very quickly so it is advisable to use some form of sleeping mat. These come in four basic forms.

1 **Groundsheet**

   This is the most basic form of sleeping mat and is simply a section of waterproof sheeting placed between your sleeping bag and the ground. Groundsheets ensure that you don't get damp but provide limited protection from

Synthetic features	Down features
Warm when wet	Clumps together when wet
Relatively inexpensive	Expensive
Easy to wash	Requires specialist cleaning
Tends to be bulkier	High compressibility
Tends to be heavier	Low weight
Low to moderate thermal capacity	High thermal capacity
Non-allergenic	Some people are allergic

Figure 11.20 Features of sleeping bags filled with synthetic or down

the cold and no padding. On the plus side they are extremely cheap, lightweight and easy to carry.

2 **Roll mat**

A roll mat is a rectangular piece of polycarbonate foam costing £5 and upwards from camping shops. The more expensive ones are more effective as insulators and are more durable. They form a layer of insulation between you and the ground and offer a degree of comfort, a waterproof layer and good insulation from the cold. However, they are bulky and can be difficult to carry if your tent is already attached to the top of your rucksack.

3 **Airbeds**

Airbeds offer comfort and protection from the damp but can be cold, so it's a good idea to place a blanket under your sleeping bag. They can be bought in most camping shops for around £10. They are heavy and usually require a pump to inflate them.

4 **Self inflating airbeds**

These are the most sophisticated and effective but are also the most expensive option costing anywhere from £45 to £80. They offer the same degree of comfort as a normal airbed but are warmer as they contain less air. They role up smaller than a roll mat and are easy to carry. As their name suggests, they inflate themselves by means of a valve and are quick and easy to deflate the next morning.

Cooking equipment

Cooking equipment comes in many shapes and sizes but the basic requirement is

- stove/burner
- fuel
- lighter/matches
- pans/mess tins
- cutlery
- mug
- pan cleaner
- food
- plates.

Stoves

There are a huge variety of stoves and fuels to choose from:

- **Solid fuel/hexamine**: this is what soldiers are issued with to compliment their ration packs. They consist of a hand-square metal box that breaks open to provide a burning platform and pan stand. Hexamine blocks are placed on the platform and lit and mess tins placed on the pan stand. Many soldiers buy a more sophisticated gas or pressure stove but they are very useful to have as a backup stove.

- **Gas stove**: these are connected to a canister of pressurised gas which flows into a burner and produces a flame when lit. The canister can attach directly to the burner (usually underneath) or can be connected via a tube.

Advantages of hexamine stoves	Disadvantages of hexamine stoves
Inexpensive	Can be difficult to light, especially with matches
Lightweight and compact	No control over the flame (boil, simmer, etc)
Simple, few parts to break	Damages soil/grass
Easy to use	Leaves dirty residue on mess tins
	Low power output

Figure 11.21 Advantages and disadvantages of hexamine stoves

An army hexamine stove

There are several different types of gas and cylinder to choose from. For expedition use you don't want a huge refillable canister: the disposable ones are the best size (but you have to keep the ones you've emptied until you can find a bin to dispose of them).

The simplest form of gas canister used in this country is the blue butane type, which is not resealable; this can be dangerous if it's connected incorrectly and is not very versatile. Butane/propane mix is also available and is more efficient as the canisters tend to be resealable, making them safer. Being removable, they can be switched between stove and gas-powered lantern.

- **Pressure stoves:** these run off liquid fuels such as paraffin and petrol. The more sophisticated are multi-fuel which means they can run off a variety of fuels. Firstly they need pumping to create the pressure required to force the fuel out. After that they need priming which involves pre-heating the burner so that the fuel is vaporised. This can be tricky and requires practice. As the fuels can sometimes be dirty the stoves need regular maintenance. However, they are powerful and fuel is inexpensive and readily available.

- **Meths stoves:** although methelated spirits are liquid, they do not require pressure to burn in a stove. They're simply poured into a receptacle burner and lit. The stoves usually consist of a windshield that the burner sits inside and

Advantages of gas stoves	Disadvantages of gas stoves
Easy to use	Fuel is expensive
Relatively easy to maintain	Loses power as the canister empties
Inexpensive	Not as powerful in the cold
Works at altitude	Some stoves are not very stable
Controllable flame	Empty canisters must be carried out
Moderate power output	Canisters may not be available in some countries

Figure 11.22 Advantages and disadvantages of gas stoves

Advantages of pressure stoves	Disadvantages of pressure stoves
Inexpensive fuels	Stoves are expensive
Easy availability of fuel	Require maintenance and cleaning
High power output	Liquid fuel needs to be carried in separate leak-proof container
Works at altitude and in the cold	May be difficult to control/simmer

Figure 11.23 Advantages and disadvantages of pressure stoves

therefore is well protected from the elements. They also tend to come with a set of pans that fit together as a unit and the whole unit packs away neatly. Meths is not as powerful as gas or pressurised fuel and has a longer cooking time. This means you need to carry more fuel, again in a separate leak-proof container.

> Note: all stoves produce carbon dioxide and should only be used in well-ventilated areas and never inside a tent.

Features of stoves

The following features should be considered when choosing a stove:

1   **Stability**

    Stoves have open flames so care must be taken not to knock them over. Burners that sit on top of the fuel are less stable than those that connect separately, usually with a pipe.

2   **Protection from the wind**

    Wind blows flames out so burners need to be protected with a windshield. Some stoves have them fitted, for others you can buy them separately but be careful where you position them.

3   **Flame control to avoid boiling food away**

    Gas stoves tend to come with fuel regulation but other types may not. Beware that controls are not too near the flame or hot pans. Controls are usually better on stoves with separate fuel supplies.

4   **Compact size**

    This is very important because you need to pack your stove away and stow it in your rucksack. Some stoves have folding parts and others have bits that are made to stack away neatly.

Pans/mess tins/billies

Pans are what you cook in. Most are made of aluminium because of its light weight, but others are available in stainless steel (more robust) and even titanium (tough and lightweight, but expensive). Non-stick coatings can be useful but beware of scratching them with metal utensils.

Most camping pans are round which are easy to stir and clean. However, army mess tins are rectangular as they are generally inexpensive and fold away together compactly. Small items such as pan scrub, herbs, tea towel, cutlery, etc can be stored inside them too.

Decide how many you will be feeding from your pans and that will indicate the size you require. You can travel light with only one pan, but this is less versatile. If you can cope with the extra weight, a kettle is very useful.

The following tips are useful when buying pans

1   Graduated fill lines are useful as they tell you how much liquid to pour in.

2   Lids are essential to keep heat in and therefore save on fuel.

3   Bits and pieces can be stored inside nestled pans.

4   Make sure you have a pan grip so that you can hold the pans. Some have attached handles, others have separate ones.

Advantages of meths stoves	Disadvantages of meths stoves
Easy to use	Flame is invisible: difficult to tell if lit
Low maintenance	Low power output
Comes as a complete set	High fuel consumption
Stable and difficult to knock over	Can be difficult to control flame

Figure 11.24 Advantages and disadvantages of meths stoves

Water purifiers

Extended travel in the countryside can mean that access to clean tap water is not always an option so you need to clean or purify the water. This can be done in a number of ways, but the most common methods are:

- iodine or chlorine sterilisation tablets. Simply add a tablet to 1 litre of suspect water, wait 10 minutes and the water is drinkable.

- water purifiers which filter the water as well as treating it. Several types exist, some with pumps (which tend to be most efficient) and some which allow the water to filter slowly through. They tend to be more effective than tablets but are bigger and heavier to carry as well as being a lot more expensive.

Alternatively, plan your route so that you pass through places where you can fill up with fresh water. This can sometimes be difficult, especially in summer when you can drink much more water than you expect. It is always best to carry some means of purification just in case.

Toiletries

This is your wash kit. Take what you need to wash and groom yourself, but remember it's got to fit in your pack and you have to carry it.

Things like camping towels are worth investigating as they are far lighter and more compact than traditional towels yet can absorb a similar amount of water. They also dry quickly.

Spare clothing

If you're on a short expedition you may not want to take any spare clothing apart from a change of

underwear and something light to sleep in. A pair of soft footwear can also be useful to give your feet a rest from boots. Sandals are good as they let the skin breath, which allows blisters and rubs to heal quicker.

Safety

When you're on an expedition, either on your own or in a small group, safety is very important. If anything goes wrong there is often only one person to immediately help you, and that's yourself, so you need to know how to look after yourself and your friends and how to summon help if you need to.

Summoning help

The emergency distress signal is 6 blasts on a whistle or flashes on a torch, wait a minute and repeat. The answer to the distress call is 3 short blasts/flashes. This does not mean you should stop: carry on so that your rescuers can home in on your position.

Mobile phones are being used more frequently in the outdoors as an emergency means of communication. However, mobile phones do have restrictions:

- some areas have poor coverage, especially where there are few people to use them, such as hill and mountain areas

- large features can block signals. This means that in the valleys or on mountain slopes the phone may be useless

- mobiles use batteries, which can run out (quickly in the cold).

Emergency equipment

The following guidelines outline the emergency equipment you should be carrying on an expedition:

- **Survival bag:** this is usually a large orange bag made of strong plastic which can be used in an emergency when you have to spend the night outside without your camping gear. Once inside a survival bag you have some protection from the elements (wind and rain). Remember to have enough ventilation to breathe, otherwise you will asphyxiate. You will need to insulate yourself from the ground by sitting on your rucksack or lying on your rope. Every member of the group must have at least one survival bag; they are light, compact and cheap and can save your life.

- **Group shelter:** this is a big piece of sewn nylon that everyone gets under and then sits on the edges. It provides some protection from wind and rain and can be useful for emergency first aid, navigation problem solving if lost or having lunch in bad weather. They are available in a range of sizes from 2 person to about 12 person.

- **Personal first aid kit:** small and compact this should contain the basics to help minor injuries or ailments:
  - plasters
  - painkillers – check you're not allergic to them
  - blister dressings/kit
  - safety pins
  - tweezers
  - small wound dressings
  - a bandage
  - any personal medication, for example asthma inhalers
  - sun screen
  - insect repellent
  - waterproof paper, pen and pencil

- **Repair kit:** this is the equivalent of a first aid kit for your clothing and equipment:
  - needle and thread
  - spare buttons
  - safety pins
  - small pair of scissors
  - roll of strong tape
  - any specialised repair kits for tent, stove, airbed, etc.

- **Sunglasses:** it can be bright, even in winter.

- **Survival rations:** high energy food just in case you have to spend an unexpected night on the mountain.

- **Spare clothing:** A spare light fleece or jumper can be useful before you crawl into the survival bag. In winter something more substantial may be needed like an insulated jacket or top: synthetic ones are good as you can put them on top of your outer garments even if it's raining.

- **Rope:** if you are heading into mountainous areas then you may need a rope or two in your party. In experienced hands, ropes can be very useful for safely aiding people up or down steep sections of ground. However, in inexperienced hands they can lead to serious accidents.

- **Flares:** in very remote areas you may also consider flares as a means of summoning help.

Theory into practice

1 Look at your kit list drawn up for the 3-day expedition (see page 192). What safety equipment do you need to add? Take into account the time of year and location of the journey.

2 Sort your kit list into equipment that you personally need to carry and equipment that will be shared among the group. Think of a sensible way to share this equipment out.

Plan and carry out an expedition

This is when you actually get outside to practice and learn camping and expedition skills. If you haven't tried anything like this before then it may be hard. Expeditions can be demanding physically, mentally and emotionally to seasoned outdoor travellers. You will make mistakes, but that's the best way to learn. Next time you will know better and be more prepared.

Planning an expedition

Like anything else, for an expedition to be successful it needs to be well planned.

Aims and objectives

Aims and objectives include the reason for the expedition. Is it to appreciate the Welsh countryside, to kick-start your fitness, to practice navigation and fieldcraft before joining the forces or to tackle some classic mountain routes in the Scottish Highlands?

Once you know *why* you can decide on *where* and *when*. If you're new to navigation then winter in the Scottish mountains may be a bit unrealistic. Consider England or Wales in summer. Other factors that will affect these decisions are: who else is going, fitness levels of the group, how experienced the team is and what equipment is available? Do you actually have a right to go to the chosen destination place or do you need to arrange access?

You also need to know when you have completed your objectives: set specific targets, such as reaching a certain destination or concluding on a certain day.

Planning the route

The route needs to be carefully planned (see page 172) and all of the group should have input in this. When it is complete, everybody needs a copy.

Roles and responsibilities

Once you know what the aim is you can start to assign roles. Decide on who's going to plan the route or will it be a group activity? Is one person best suited to obtaining equipment while another could do the research on the area, routes and weather? This is also a good time to delegate responsibilities such as navigators, person to liaise with campsites, person responsible for money for campsites, transport to the area and food. You must also delegate who will be the responsible person that you leave the route card with and how and when you will contact them to let them know you are well. You all need to agree when this person should start contacting emergency services if you miss a timetabled call.

Timescale

Decide how long you plan to go for ensuring it is a reasonable amount of time to complete your aim. Check it fits with transport timings, access agreements or anticipated weather.

Equipment

Check any equipment you have to ensure it is still in good order or whether it needs repairing/replacing. Ensure it is suitable for the area/activity/time of year and right for the team members (size/height, numbers, etc). If you need new equipment find out where can you get it. Check whether you will need any special equipment in order to fulfil the expedition's objectives.

Menu and food

The menu needs to be planned. This includes all food and should be checked to cover all nutritional requirements for the duration of the expedition. Food should be to the liking of all group members and needs to have as short a cooking time as possible to save on fuel. The number of people going will also affect the type and amount of food chosen, which will also have an effect on the number and size of pans needed and the amount of fuel required.

Food suitable for expeditions includes:

1 Special dehydrated camping meals from outdoor leisure shops

2 Special pre-cooked food in packets from outdoor leisure shops

3 Dehydrated pasta and sauce packet meals (from supermarkets)

4 Packets of noodles

5 Boil in the bag rice

6 Powdered milk

7 Custard powder

8 Fresh food (needs to be eaten quickly, especially in hot weather)

9 Pitta bread and other flat breads.

Theory into practice

Go to the shops and look at the nutritional values of foods, the cooking times of various foods and the pack sizes.

Investigate the nutritional requirements for a 3-day expedition. How much energy will you need to consume to function properly? What other requirements are needed such as vitamins, fats and proteins. Use this information to create a menu for the expedition, stating the energy values for each meal.

Weather

Closer to the time of the expedition you need to regularly check the weather for the area you're going to. It's useful to know what the weather has been like as this can affect the condition of the ground (boggy or stone dry), the size of rivers and streams (dry beds or raging torrents) and can even influence where you can go: in prolonged periods of dry hot weather, access land can be closed due to the risk of fire.

Sources of weather forecasts include:

1 Internet: dedicated weather sites and BBC weather

2 Television weather reports

3 Radio weather reports, especially the shipping forecasts, though they need some interpreting

4 Newspapers

5 Telephone weather lines – some are specific to certain areas and for certain activities, for example mountaineering and walking in the Lake District

Theory into practice

Draw up a detailed list of forecast sources such as website addresses, television programmes and telephone numbers that can be quickly used when you are preparing for your expedition.

Carrying out an expedition

In order to complete your expedition safely and in some comfort, there are a few techniques and skills that are worth knowing and practicing before you go.

Loading a rucksack

There are few hard and fast rules for this; most of it is common sense. However, it's useful to practice packing a rucksack to see how it all fits together. Sometimes you can't fit everything in and have to unpack and start again; experience is the best way to learn.

The following guidelines provide useful tips when packing a rucksack:

- Distribute any shared equipment such as parts of tent, stove, pans, food and maps to ensure that the group has everything it will need.

- Get all your kit together and put it on the floor next to your rucksack. Check that nothing is missing and that everything works and then decide whether everything there is essential.

- Cross items off your checklist as you pack so that you don't miss anything.

- Pack everything in plastic bags to make sure they stay dry and compress any compression sacks for sleeping bags etc.

- Line your rucksack with a waterproof liner before adding anything.

- Light things and items you will not need during the day should be packed at the bottom, for example sleeping bag and extra clothes.

- Items such as pans, food, torch and first aid kit are usually placed in the middle.

- Heavier things such as tents and items you may need on the walk such as waterproofs, hat and gloves, food for the day should be placed at the top.

- Stoves and fuel are often best packed in pockets where they can't contaminate anything else.

- Try to avoid attaching things to the outside of the rucksack. Things like sleeping mat and tent are acceptable as they may be difficult to put inside the bag and are easy and safe to secure. Never attach your sleeping bag to the outside of the rucksack.

Theory into practice

Gather all your expedition equipment together and practice packing your rucksack.

Campsite choice

Many expeditions stay at campsites where flat, reasonably smooth grassy pitches are the norm. If you want to be more adventurous, though, you can try wild camping. In this case, route planning can be trickier as you need to be able to identify spots suitable for campsites from the map and you need to be much more self sufficient.

When choosing a site for camping:

- Look for flat, firm ground, free of bumps and rocks which will make you uncomfortable.

- Check the ground for stones and other debris that could damage your groundsheet and spoil your sleep.

- Avoid hollows as they could be damp and cold collects in them.

- Pitch your tent with its back to the wind.

- Don't camp under trees: sap makes your tent sticky and when it rains you get bigger drops falling.

- A water source nearby is useful such as a stream, river, lake or tarn but don't pitch too near to it because the ground may be boggy, it may flood in rain and will have lots of midges in summer.

- Designate a cooking area some distance from the tent to avoid setting fire to your belongings and spilling food nearby. This area should be flat and preferably sheltered from the wind.

Pitching a tent

There are many different types of tents, each with their own different way of pitching. You should practice putting your tent up several times before you set off on the expedition. You may have to do it at night in heavy rain when you are very tired so experience can be very valuable.

When setting up a tent ensure the following:

- Check the ground for lumps and stones.

- Place a groundsheet protector down and peg it if necessary.

- Lie out the inner groundsheet over the top and peg out opposite corners. This will ensure that it's straight and flat.

- All pegs should go in at a 45 degree angle away from the tent. This prevents them from coming out too easily. Hammer them in with a mallet or stone. Don't stand on them to get them in as you will bend the peg and could hurt yourself.

- Place pegs a short way in to start with, then it's easier to take them out should you need to do some adjustments.

- Assemble poles and attach them to the inner as required.

- Peg out the rest of the inner.

- Place the outer over the inner, pegging corners first.

- Ensure that the outer and inner skins are centimetres apart and peg out the outer.

- Untie the guys and peg them out. Always use the guys as they add lots of stability to your tent.

- Unpack sleeping bags and let them air and inflate sleeping mats.

Theory into practice

Practice putting your tent up at home in the dark.

Looking after your campsite

In many areas, wild camping is illegal and you can be prosecuted for it. It is usually accepted in the mountain areas of the National Parks but it is always best to seek advice from the National Park wardens and/or the landowner first. One of the reasons that wild camping can be frowned upon is the potential that it has for damaging the land and creating an eyesore.

Once you have sought permission and found a suitable site you need to look after it:

- Take a rubbish bag and place any rubbish you create into it. Take this with you when you leave and dispose of it carefully when you return to civilisation. Some bio-degradable substances take a long to degrade such as orange skin and banana peel, so take these with you too.

- Do not be tempted to bury your rubbish.

- Never leave your tent in the same spot for more than one day. If you are staying for longer then move your tent to allow the vegetation to recover.

- If you have to move large stones, replace them when you finish. They are important parts of the environment and provide habitation for numerous creatures and plants.

- Do not start fires. They are highly destructive, damaging soil and vegetation and leave ugly scars. There is also always the risk of causing a larger fire that could tear across the land.

- Leave water sources clean: if using soap or washing up liquid designate an area at least 30 metres away from water and take your own water for rinsing.

- Designate a toilet area, again 30 metres from water and dig a hole to bury it. Do not go to the toilet in buildings, caves, behind huts, etc.

Weather

In the United Kingdom the weather is very unpredictable. One week's expedition in British mountains can encounter hot sunshine, heavy fog, torrential rain, strong winds and lightning storms. This has led to British mountaineers being among the most robust in the world, but does need an understanding of how the weather can affect expeditions.

Hot weather can be debilitating with great heat and dangerous levels of UV radiation, especially at higher altitudes. Protective clothing is essential: peaked hat, sunglasses and loose fitting wicking clothes that protect the skin from sunburn. Cover any exposed skin with sunscreen to prevent burns, peeling or blisters and drink plenty of fluids frequently (it's usually too late when you get thirsty). Afternoons are usually hottest so try to plan your day so that the hardest work is at the start or end, not in the mid-day sun where you'll suffer most. You may want to consider some night walking: clear skies will aid navigation.

Cold weather can be easier to cope with as it's easier to keep warm than cool. Hill and mountain walking are good aerobic activities that keep your body warm. Remember to wrap up when you stop though as you will soon cool down. Hot drinks are good at rest stops too. You can dehydrate in cold weather so you must remember to drink plenty of fluids. Warm hats are important for preventing you from losing too much heat. When camping, have a hot meal before retiring to give you energy and warmth to warm up your sleeping bag. A hot flask prepared the night before provides a warm drink in the morning.

Wind and rain can be harsh and are usually encountered together. Walking can be difficult when the rain is really heavy and everyone puts his or her head down. This can be dangerous as you are unaware of your surroundings and possibly the route. Bearings can be difficult to follow in heavy wind and you may need back up navigators to prevent being blown off course. Communication can also be difficult as the wind blows words away. Keep wrapped up and waterproof, ensure everybody is warm enough while walking and try to maintain morale. Hot drinks are also important.

Lightning storms have obvious hazards. If it looks like a storm is coming, then follow these guidelines:

1 Avoid exposed areas where you're the tallest thing.

2 Do not sit under trees as the electricity travels down and out into the ground.

3 Do not hide by boulders, caves and hollows as you may act like a conduit for electricity.

4 The best thing to do is to find a spot away from the summit, preferably on scree and sit on your rope or rucksack, trying not to touch the ground at all.

Snow and ice are extreme conditions and can require special techniques and skills to operate in. Experience of navigating and surviving in other conditions is essential.

Expedition skills

In this unit we have already covered a large number of skills from map reading to pitching tents. Like any other skills, they take practice and experience to make them worthwhile. The best way to prepare for expeditions is to go out and do them. Your learning curve will be steep at first but

you will be much better prepared for the next time. Many other skills will be picked up along the way, such as the easiest way to walk up and down steep hills (zig zag), route choice and how to spot faint footpaths.

However, some things need to be prepared for before the expedition. Most of these have been covered in expedition planning, but there are a few more to mention.

Fitness

Undertaking an expedition in a remote area carrying your own equipment is a considerable feat if you are unused to physical exercise. Your cardio-vascular system will have to work hard walking up and down hills all day with a heavy rucksack as well as your legs and shoulders having to support extra weight.

Part of your planning therefore should be a training regime starting several weeks before the expedition. This can be in the gym using treadmills and light weights, a progressive outdoor running programme or a schedule of progressive day walks carrying rucksacks. Using the latter you can also practice navigation and other skills too. For more information, look at Unit 8.

First aid

There are a number of common ailments that can occur when walking. It is important that you know how to spot and deal with them as accidents and injuries can become very dangerous in open country. Minor injuries can be dealt with on the trail, but serious accidents require medical aid which could take a long time to arrive.

Minor injuries

1 **Blisters:** caused by rubbing, usually on the heels of the feet but can be anywhere. It is best to stop when you get a "hot spot" and put a blister pad on it. Even better is to tape potential blister spots before you set off by using blister pads or zinc oxide tape. Once you have a blister you need to pop it before you

can dress it. Firstly, wipe the area clean, sterilise a needle (use a flame) then pierce the blister bubble, squeeze the puss out and apply a blister pad. Try to air the feet as much as possible when you stop walking.

2 **Cuts and grazes**: these should be rinsed and covered with a plaster if you want. Although air and time are the best healers, there may be more risk of infection when you're living outdoors. Antiseptic wipes are good for cleaning wounds. If cuts are quite big use steri-strips to hold the edges together, then seek medical attention if you want to avoid scarring.

Serious ailments

1 **Hypothermia**: this is what happens when the body loses too much heat and stops working. This can kill so you need to know the signs and symptoms. It can be brought on by being tired and exhausted in cold conditions, but exasperated by wet and wind.

Early signs may include:

- feeling cold and tired
- possibly numb hands and feet
- some bout of shivering.

If it is not treated, additional signs include:

- increased, uncontrollable shivering
- pale colour
- irrational behaviour and complaints
- lethargy/laziness and not responding to questions and orders
- possible slurred speech and violent outbursts of energy
- stumbling and falling over (uncoordinated movement)
- loss of vision.

Signs in the later stages of hypothermia are:

- shivering stops
- non-responsive

- pulse and breathing weak
- unconsciousness, coma and death.

If hypothermia is spotted early enough, stop for shelter either in a group shelter or tent, change the patient into dry warm clothes and put the patient into a sleeping bag insulated from the floor. Warm drinks and food will help and rest. If you need to get off the mountain ask the patient to subtract 7 from 100 continuing down to 2. If they can't do this they're not well enough to carry on. If they can, pack up and get off the mountain as soon as possible. In more serious situations you may need to obtain help to get the patient to medical aid.

You can avoid hypothermia by staying warm and hydrated, not overdoing it and constantly checking everyone in the group is feeling well.

2 **Fractures**: broken bones, especially legs can result from slips and falls and are clearly serious. Depending on the injury you may need to splint the limb using tent poles or trekking poles. Bandages and slings can be useful to immobilise the injury but don't play with the fracture too much. If the patient can't get up without help, get assistance.

3 **Sprains**: these can be just as bad or worse than fractures and are frequently on ankles. If possible, get the patient to medical aid as soon as possible safely. Treatment for soft tissue injuries is RICE: rest, ice, compression and elevation, though this may be inappropriate depending on the conditions.

Seeking medical aid

In emergences you may need to call Mountain Rescue to help you get the group off the mountain and out of trouble. If you have a mobile phone try it, giving as much information as possible if you get through. If you haven't got one or it doesn't work then you will have to summon help personally. Send 2 people off to the nearest road or source of habitation to call for help. Ensure that they have all the information needed. Someone needs to stay behind and look after the casualty, constantly reassuring him or her. Essential information for the rescue team includes:

- location of party with grid reference and directions

- description of accident

- details of casualty: name, age, sex

- nature of injuries

- what has been done to treat the injuries

- plans of the party (stay put, move to closer location)

- group information: number, experience, ages, sex

- weather/conditions

- equipment available (stove, tent, sleeping bag)

- type of help needed: helicopter, stretcher

- party leader

- contact details.

Hazards

There are several dangers that you could come across when travelling in open country. Some are more prevalent in certain parts of the country or at certain times of year, so good planning should identify them. However, you should be aware of all of them and have some kind of contingency plan:

- rock falls

- river crossing

- streams/rivers in sudden flood

- poisonous/dangerous plants

- barbed wire

- water-borne diseases

- insect-borne diseases

- tetanus

- fires

- poisonous/dangerous animals.

Theory into practice

Research the above hazards and come up with an action plan on how you would deal with them on an expedition? How likely are they to occur in the area of your expedition?

Experiencing outdoor pursuits and access to the countryside

In this section you will learn about other activities that are available in the outdoors and the benefits that they offer to groups and individuals. You will also examine access and conservation of the countryside including the bodies that are responsible for this.

Outdoor pursuits

There are many activities that can be considered outdoor pursuits and Figure 11.25 lists some of them.

Benefits of outdoor pursuits

Outdoor pursuits have been used for many years as tools for the development of both individuals and teams. They are seen to promote confidence and skills that are transferable to many other situations. Organisations (including the public services) and individuals use outdoor activities to develop some or all of the following:

- team-work

- leadership

- individual achievement

- physical achievement

- mental stability

- self reliance

- developing initiative

Activity	Description	Equipment required	Where
Kayaking	Enclosed canoe. Can be difficult to control at first but offers greater speed than open canoes. Usually one person only. Variations include sea kayaking and surf kayaking	Kayak, paddle, buoyancy aid, spray deck (stops water getting inside kayak), wetsuit	Lakes, reservoirs, canals, rivers, etc. Surf kayaking on the coast Sea kayaking on the sea
Canadian canoeing	Open canoe, more stable than a kayak, good for travelling long distances, doesn't cope as well with extreme water but is easier to get in and out. Can be paddled by one or two people.	Canoe, paddles, buoyancy aid, quick drying clothes, wetsuit	Lakes, rivers, canals, reservoirs, etc
Caving	Travelling underground in limestone (usually) caves on a through journey. Can involve tight crawls and sections that are walkable. Pot holing is very similar but vertical and involves complicated ropework.	Robust and water-resistant oversuit, warm when wet clothes underneath, Wellington boots, helmet and headlamp, spare torch, knee pads can be useful. Rope and harness for vertical caves (single rope technique:SRT)	Mostly limestone regions, for example White Peak, Yorkshire Dales, etc. Sometimes in mines too.
Climbing	Ascending rock faces using hands and feet. Rope used as safety measure if climber falls. Variations: single pitch (length of 1 rope), multi pitch (longer than 1 rope length), bouldering (short sections without a rope), winter (climbing on ice and snow or mixed with rock).	Harness, helmet, rope, sticky rubber shoes, belay device (controls the rope), slings and anchors (to attach rope to the rock)	Exposed rock faces, quarries, sea cliffs, boulders, mountains or indoor climbing walls
Mountain biking	Cycling up and down trails, not always in mountains. Often in Forestry Commission woodland	Mountain bike, helmet, bike repair kit, windproof and waterproof clothing	Bridleways in National Parks, some dedicated trails in forests

Figure 11.25 Table showing a range of outdoor pursuits

- problem solving
- building relationships
- improving own performance
- communication
- confidence building
- stress relief
- enjoyment
- inner peace.

Theory into practice

Most people have had some experience of outdoor pursuits at school, college, cadets, etc. Think about some outdoor activities that you have done, either individually or as part of a group. Which of the above benefits did you gain from it?

Access

It has become accepted that footpaths and bridleways are accessible to whoever wants to use them thanks to the Access to Mountains Act 1939 which allowed open access to the high ground of the country. More recently the Countryside and Rights of Way Act 2000 (CROW) has allowed greater access on foot to mountain, moor, heath, down and common land; the act has been called the "right to roam" law as it allows people to wander off footpaths on the specified areas. CROW does not include gardens or crops though and allows areas to be shut off for conservation purposes.

The "right to roam" is just what it says: it only applies to walking, not anything else. Any other activities are not allowed without consent from the landowner. Examples of prohibited activities are:

- camping
- lighting fires
- climbing
- hang-gliding

- using or carrying metal detectors
- taking part in organised games.

Many of these activities are also prohibited by local by-laws in many places.

Rights of way

There are several different types of path open to recreational users, with restrictions as to who can use them:

- **Footpath**: open only to walkers
- **Bridleway**: for walkers, cyclists and horesriders
- **Byway/Byway Open to All Traffic (BOAT)**: open to walkers, cyclists, horesriders and motor vehicles

In addition there are other paths that have no official right of way but are usable so long as they aren't abused such as *permissive paths* which are usually only open to walkers.

Promotion and protection of the countryside

There are various bodies involved in protecting and promoting the countryside. Some are statutory bodies and others are classified as agencies. Statutory bodies have prosecution powers for relevant legislation relating to areas within their remits whereas agencies are bodies that are concerned with given issues or areas but do not hold legal powers.

Statutory bodies

1 **The Countryside Agency**: responsible for conservation of the countryside and its enhancement and to ensure people enjoy the countryside. It advises the government on countryside issues and undertakes its own research.

2 **English Nature**: a government body with responsibility for English wildlife, geology and wild places. They are the protectors of Sites of Special Scientific Interest (SSSI) as well as other environmentally sensitive areas and both

National and Local Nature Reserves. English Nature is concerned with protection of the natural environment and wildlife, rather than the countryside.

3 **Peak District National Park Authority**: this body is responsible for the conservation and promotion of the Peak District National Park. The Peak District is the oldest of the National Parks in this country and is one of the busiest National Parks in the world.

Other organisations

1 **British Mountaineering Council**: the national governing body that represents the interests of climbers and walkers in Britain, including lobbying for access. This body is also involved with conservation relevant to mountaineering, for example nesting birds at crags, litter cleaning at crags, etc

2 **National Trust**: founded in 1895 to be a guardian organisation for the country's threatened coastlands, buildings and countryside. National Trust is a major charity which owns hundreds of buildings and hundreds of acres of land.

Protecting the countryside

As outdoor activities grow more popular, the national governing bodies for the sports have recognised the need for codes of good practice. One of the oldest of these is the Countryside Code from the Countryside Agency. This sets out how to behave when in the countryside and should be followed on all expeditions:

- enjoy the countryside and respect its life and work
- guard against all risk of fire
- fasten all gates
- keep to public paths across farmland
- use gates and stiles to cross fences, hedges and walls
- leave livestock, crops and machinery alone
- take your litter home

- help to keep all water clean
- protect wildlife, plants and trees
- take special care on country roads
- make no unnecessary noise.

Theory into practice

Find out about other codes of practice for outdoor pursuits, for example canoeing, climbing, etc. They may be provided by governing bodies or by individual clubs.

End of unit questions

1 List 4 sources of weather forecasts suitable for expeditions.

2 What does an altimeter do?

3 Who makes maps for walking in the UK?

4 Which 2 scales are used for expedition maps in the UK?

5 Give a 6 figure grid reference for your college.

6 Give a 6 figure grid reference for your best friend's house.

7 How is height shown on maps?

8 Describe how to use an attack point when navigating.

9 What techniques can you use when navigating in poor visibility?

10 List the desirable features for a set of waterproofs.

11 How can you keep a map dry?

12 Write a comparison between down and synthetic sleeping bags.

13 How does the layering system of clothing work?

14 What is the international distress signal?

15 What are the early signs of hypothermia?

16 What effect does the weather have on a backpacker?

17 List the Rights of Way and who can use them.

18 Explain the benefits of outdoor pursuits.

19 What is the Country Code?

20 Describe 2 outdoor pursuits including variants, equipment needed and where they can take place.

Resources

Books

BMC, 1992 *Tread Lightly* (BMC)

Cliff P, 1991 *Mountain Navigation* (Cliff)

HMSO, annually *The Country Code* (HMSO)

Keay W, 1989 *Expedition Guide* (Duke of Edinburgh's Award Scheme)

Langmuir E, 1997 *Mountaincraft and Leadership* (Scottish Sports Council and UKMTB)

Thomas M, 1997 *Weather for Hill Walkers and Climbers* (Alan Sutton)

Magazines

Climber and Hill Walker

High Mountain Sports (BMC)

Summit (BMC)

The Great Outdoors (Newsquest Magazines)

Trail (Emap)

Websites

Bluedome website, portal site for all sorts of outdoor activities: www.bluedome.co.uk

British Mountaineering Council: www.thebmc.co.uk

National Geographic (maps and geography): www.nationalgeographic.com

Duke of Edinburgh's Award Scheme: www.theaward.org

Adventure Activities Licensing Authority, responsible for inspecting outdoor pursuits centres: www.aala.org

Met Office website for weather information: www.meto.gov.uk

Ordnance Survey: www.ordsvy.gov.uk

Harveys Maps: www.harveymaps.co.uk

Ramblers' Association: www.ramblers.org.uk

The Countryside Agency, government agency for the countryside: www.countryside.gov.uk

English Nature, government agency for wildlife conservation: www.english-nature.org.uk

National Trust, private charity for heritage and wildlife: www.nationaltrust.org.uk

Association of National Parks Authority, information on the National Parks: www.anpa.gov.uk

Assessment activities

This section describes what you must do to obtain a pass grade for this unit.

A merit or distinction grade may be awarded if your work demonstrates a deeper understanding of the topics and is of a higher quality. The highlighted sentences indicate the quality of work expected at merit and distinction level.

Assessment methods

A number of assessment strategies may be used in order to achieve the learning outcomes, such as oral presentations, group discussions, written assignments, research projects and role-plays, or a combination of these. It would be a good idea, though it is not essential, to use a variety of methods in order to develop different skills.

It is important that you understand and comply with the key words that may be specified in the grading criteria. For example, if you are asked to 'analyse' something, then make sure that you do not merely describe it. Similarly, if you are asked to 'evaluate' something, then make sure you do not merely summarise it.

Key words

Here are some key words that are often used for grading criteria – make sure you understand the differences between them.

Examine	To look at a subject closely in order to understand it and improve your knowledge
Consider	This means to think about and weigh up a subject
Explain	This means to make something clear and set out the arguments
Analyse	This means to look at a subject closely and interpret or evaluate your findings. Perhaps outlining the pro's and con's of a situation or suggesting changes and improvements
Describe	This means to say what something is like, it is a factual account of how something is or how it appears
Compare	This means to look at the similarities between two or more objects or theories.

Assessment tasks

Using the materials within this unit and your own research, carry out the following tasks.

Task 1

Learning outcome 1 – Demonstrate effective navigation skills in open country

Explain the advantages and disadvantages of a range of suitable maps to be used during an expedition including a full description of the meanings of conventional map symbols.

Produce a complete and accurate route card for open country (which covers at least eight kilometres and five legs) and use this, with some guidance, to complete the eight kilometre journey.

Demonstrate a range of practical navigation skills including knowledge and use of map, compass and techniques (with some guidance).

Suggestions for Task 1: practical exercise followed by report

1 Plan a walking trip of between eight and fifteen kilometres. Complete a route card for the exercise.

2 Complete the route using the route card and other navigation equipment and techniques.

3 Write a report of your route. In your report you must include the route card and explain which maps were used both to plan and carry out the route, including why they were used. In addition, write down all the navigation techniques that were required to complete the route.

A qualified assessor who can aid and assess your navigation abilities and produce a witness statement to testify that you have completed the outcome should accompany you on this journey.

Task 2

Learning outcome 2 – Describe the equipment used in walking and camping and demonstrate an understanding of its uses, properties and care

Describe the equipment and materials taken on an expedition.

Describe and comment upon the effectiveness of a range of different types and designs of personal, group and safety equipment used in walking and camping.

> To obtain a merit grade, you should explain the choice of equipment and materials taken on an expedition and *analyse* and *evaluate* the design and properties of materials used and the selection and care of equipment.

> To obtain a distinction grade, you should *justify* the decisions made in the choice of materials used and the correct selection and care of equipment when taking part in the camping expedition.

Suggestion for Task 2: written assignment

In preparation for the expedition that you must complete, examine the range of equipment available for walking and expeditions. You should look at equipment for the individual, the group and any relevant safety equipment. To be successful you should examine a range of types of equipment and look at properties, fabrics, construction and care.

Following this, you should examine the equipment that you are going to take on your expedition, including the reasons behind your choice of equipment and any special care and use considerations for that equipment.

Task 3

Learning outcome 3 – Plan and carry out an expedition involving an overnight camp

Prepare and carry out a camping and walking expedition of at least 25 kilometres, which includes camping for at least two days and one night.

> To obtain a merit grade, you should demonstrate the use of highly competent, accurate, safe skills when walking, navigating and camping.

> To obtain a distinction grade, you should demonstrate and *evaluate* practical skills used in walking, navigating and camping.

Suggestions for Task 3: practical and written report

1 Properly plan a walking and camping expedition for three days and two nights. Your plans must include the following:

- a detailed route card for each day
- a list of group members, including any necessary medical or dietary information and their responsibilities for the duration of the expedition
- kit list for each member of the group
- a menu for the whole of the expedition, showing the required calorific intake for each meal
- detailed weather report for the location and time of the expedition
- assessment of hazards, for example weather, terrain, fitness, and any other anticipated problems
- a list of safe and environmentally friendly practices for the expedition.

2 Carry out the expedition with a qualified assessor to examine your skills at walking, navigating and camping.

3 Write a report of your expedition including the planning process. Evaluate the expedition including choice and use of equipment and assess your navigation and camping skills.

You should also include a witness statement from your assessor.

Task 4

Learning outcome 4 – Take part in two other outdoor pursuits, be familiar with issues around access to the countryside, its promotion and protection

Experience two other outdoor pursuits and analyse the benefits of outdoor pursuits.

Describe the current issues around access to the countryside, explaining the work of one agency and one statutory body involved in promoting and protecting the countryside.

> To obtain a merit grade, you should *explain* the benefits of outdoor activities and *analyse* the benefits of outdoor activities and the issues around access to the countryside by detailed investigation into the work of one agency and one statutory body involved in the promotion and protection of the countryside.

> To obtain a distinction grade, you should *evaluate* the benefits of outdoor activities and the issues around access to the countryside by detailed investigation into the work of one agency and one statutory body involved in the promotion and protection of the countryside.

Suggestions for Task 4: practical and presentation, case study

1 Take part in a range of outdoor activities (caving, climbing, canoeing, skiing, bouldering, kayaking, etc).

2 Make a presentation about the activities you took part in, explaining what the benefits are in using outdoor pursuits and what benefits you got from your own experiences.

3 Undertake a detailed case study into one agency and one statutory body involved in the promotion and protection of the countryside. Use some of the websites at the end of this unit as a starting point.

UNDERSTANDING DISCIPLINE

Introduction to Unit 14

This unit examines the role of discipline and its function and application in the public services.

It also explores the nature of conformity and obedience in relation to the public services and the various authorities and legislation that govern conduct within the public services.

Assessment

Throughout the unit, activities and tasks will help you to learn and remember information. Case studies are also included to add industry relevance to the topics and learning objectives. At the end of the unit there are assessment activities to help you provide evidence which meets the learning outcomes for the unit. You are reminded that when you are completing activities and tasks, opportunities will be created to enhance your key skills evidence.

After completing this unit, you should have an understanding of the following outcomes.

Outcomes

1 Investigate the **role of discipline** in the public services

2 Explore **conformity and obedience**

3 Examine **self-discipline**

4 Investigate the nature of **authority**

Role of discipline

One definition for the word 'discipline' is: obedience to authority. However, discipline can be used in many different contexts. For example, it may be used as an order, as a deterrent, as a threat, to control or to train and it may or may not have the authority of a written law to reinforce it.

Rules and regulations

For any organisation to operate efficiently there must be a system of rules and regulations in place which are strictly followed particularly if an organisation serves the public. A rule is a principle to which something or someone should conform. Rules may be written laws or they could be customs or codes of conduct that have been adopted by a particular society or culture. Rules are necessary to establish an agreed manner in which to do things so that things run smoothly. A regulation is an authoritative direction given by someone or somebody in authority. For example, there are many regulations that govern the conduct of serving police officers. If the regulations are infringed, then disciplinary action may follow according to the police disciplinary rules.

To ensure that rules are followed correctly, organisations impose a penalty on those who break them. This could take several forms from a verbal reprimand to dismissal. Penalties are usually fixed and written into the rules that govern conduct, in the same way that penalties are fixed by law for certain crimes.

By penalising someone for a breach of the rules is a way of disciplining them. Discipline in this context is a means of ensuring people conform to rules and regulations.

There are rules and regulations which must be followed in prisons

Without discipline it would be impossible for any organisation, including the public services, to function efficiently. Discipline is applicable to all personnel in the uniformed services regardless of rank or status.

It is important to note that discipline does not mean the same as punishment. Although they can mean the same thing in terms of inflicting a penalty for an offence, discipline is a means of producing efficiency, uniformity and order which is meant to bring out the best in someone, whereas punishment is not.

> ### Theory into practice
>
> Identify 3 examples of rules and regulations within your college and explain how they are enforced.

Esprit de corps

To gain acceptance into the public services and Armed Forces is not easy. It requires a certain calibre of person in terms of courage, fitness, determination, integrity and many other special qualities. Once you have been accepted and earned your uniform, you will have a sense of pride and honour knowing that not everyone is fortunate enough to be accepted and you will have a feeling of camaraderie with other colleagues which is

built on mutual trust, loyalty, pride and the interests of that particular service. This is known as 'esprit de corps' and in order to ensure that the esprit de corps is maintained, rules and regulations are introduced. For example, the police discipline regulations ensure that officers have a duty to act in a manner that will not bring the reputation of the police service into disrepute. They must behave in such a manner so as not to discredit the police service or any of its members, whether on or off duty. Any threat to tarnish the reputation of the police service, together with that of its members is an offence under these regulations.

Other professions may also have a sense of esprit de corps, though they may not have the same disciplinary rules for enforcing it as those of the public services.

Following orders

Many important decisions have to be made during the course of normal duty in the public services, some of which might affect people's lives. In order to ensure the efficiency of the public services and

Firefighters can wear their uniform with pride and honour

the elimination of disastrous consequences it is essential that orders are followed. For example, what would happen if the senior officer at the scene of a house-fire ordered a subordinate to arrange the evacuation of the neighbours but the subordinate refused because he or she deemed it unnecessary.

Personnel in positions of authority have earned their position because of valuable knowledge and experience and any refusal to carry out a lawful order not only undermines that authority but it also means the service is less efficient, resulting in disorganisation and confusion.

To avoid this happening, the public services have codes of discipline that ensure lawful orders are obeyed. A lawful order is one that comes from a higher authority. For example, in the fire service a sub-officer may give an order to a firefighter of any rank below sub-officer. In the police service a Superintendent may give an order to a police officer of any rank below Superintendent.

Hierarchy of authority

A hierarchy of authority in relation to the public services means the structure in which the status of authority is ranked one above the other. Depending upon where an officer is ranked, they may give lawful orders to those ranked below and must carry out orders from those ranked above.

Figure 14.1 compares different rank structures in the police and fire services.

Maintaining order

We have already seen how discipline can be used to ensure that rules and regulations are followed and maintaining order is closely related.

Usually there are written rules and regulations that govern orderly conduct, for example rules regarding making a noise after a certain time in barracks. However, where there are no rules governing orderly behaviour then discipline can be used to maintain it.

In the Armed Forces it is not unusual for large numbers of personnel to be transported to a particular area – an area that is strange to the personnel and even those in charge of them. For example, imagine the logistical problems of transporting thousands of troops to Iraq. In this instance, discipline can be used to ensure that order is maintained, even though there are no specific rules to be adhered to.

Uniform approach

In order for organisations to operate smoothly and efficiently there must be in place certain procedures that are standardised and followed. Every member of the organisation should know

Police service	Fire service
Constable	Firefighter
Sergeant	Leading firefighter
Inspector	Sub-officer
Chief Inspector	Assistant Divisional Officer
Superintendent	Divisional Officer
Chief Superintendent	Assistant Chief Fire Officer
Assistant Chief Constable	Deputy Chief Fire Officer
Deputy Chief Constable	Chief Fire Officer
Chief Constable	

Figure 14.1 Rank structures in the police and fire service

Discipline can be used to maintain order when transporting large numbers of troops for active duty

their role and how it fits into the organisation. This can range from the standard of dress to knowing what forms to complete for a particular event. For example, in an organisation like the police service this can include police officers following certain procedures when dealing with reports of theft, missing persons or murder enquiries. Similarly, firefighters follow certain procedures when dealing with different types of hazards.

Without uniformity, efficiency breaks down. If there was no standardisation then there would be no systematic way of doing things. For example, how would the night shift at a fire station know how much petrol was in the fire tender? How would someone who has lost a purse know if it had been handed in?

Loyalty

Loyalty means being true or faithful to something or someone, for example a football team, even though they might not be particularly good in terms of winning competitions.

In the public services you are expected to remain loyal to the interests of the service even though you may sometimes feel that they don't have your best interests at heart. The public services are there

to provide a vital service to the public, not to cater for your every like and dislike as an individual. Unlike civilian life, you cannot ignore someone if you don't care for them, be it a colleague of equal rank or a superior, though you don't have to associate with them when you are off duty. However, whilst on duty as a public service employee you are required to perform your duties to the best of your ability, which includes remaining loyal to the service and taking orders from someone you may not like.

To ensure that you remain loyal, disciplinary codes of conduct state colleagues are to be supported in the execution of their duties.

Theory into practice

There are many rules and regulations governing the conduct of serving police officers. The rules and regulations governing the behaviour of police officers are known as a 'code of conduct,' or a 'discipline code.'

Amongst other things, the police code of conduct states that police officers must:

- obey lawful orders and support their colleagues in the execution of their lawful duties
- behave in such a manner so as not to discredit the police service, whether on or off duty.

Why do you think the above regulations are necessary?

Sense of duty

If you join the public services, you do so because a particular service appeals to you. For example, you might like the prospect of a career that is challenging and varied with good promotion prospects and security or you might choose the Armed Services because of the sense of adventure and travel and the opportunity to use some of the world's most advanced technical equipment. Whatever your reasons for wanting to join the public services, you must not lose sight of the fact that there is a job to do. You must acknowledge that there is a sense of duty and that life within the public services is not one big adventure with no mundane tasks involved.

As a public service employee, the manner in which you carry out your duties can affect many people, sometimes with serious consequences. Whilst it may appear to be a glamorous life some of the time, at other times it may seem tedious and unrewarding. Whatever your role, you must not neglect to perform your duties as failure to do so can have serious effects. For example, you might be on the night shift and in charge of detainees which requires you to make regular checks on their well being every half hour. What would happen if you failed to do those checks and something happened to a detainee whilst under your charge?

Once again, discipline has a role to play in ensuring that public service employees recognise a sense of duty. All the public services have a code of conduct that makes neglect of duty an offence.

Think about it

Discuss what type of behaviour you would expect from firefighters with reference to fire safety advice in the community, emergency response service and other services such as vehicle accidents, trapped animals and storms.

Key concepts

Discipline may be used to:

1 Ensure rules and regulations are followed
2 Maintain esprit de corps
3 Ensure orders are followed
4 Maintain a hierarchy of authority
5 Maintain order
6 Ensure loyalty
7 Ensure a sense of duty.

Case study

Discipline, rules and regulations underpin the purpose of all the police forces within the United Kingdom which is:

- to protect life and property
- to prevent and detect crime
- to prosecute offenders against the peace.

Whilst the wording of the purpose of the police may differ from force to force, it is fundamentally the same throughout the UK. For example, here is the statement of purpose for the West Yorkshire Police.

> The purpose of the West Yorkshire Police is to uphold the law fairly and firmly: to prevent crime; to pursue and bring to justice those who break the law; to keep the Queen's peace; to protect, help and reassure the community: and to be seen to do all this with integrity, common sense and sound judgement.
>
> We must be compassionate, courteous and patient, acting without fear or favour or prejudice to the rights of others. We need to be professional, calm and restrained in the face of violence and apply only that force which is necessary to accomplish our lawful duty.
>
> We must strive to reduce the fears of the public and, so far as we can, to reflect their priorities in the action we take. We must respond to well-founded criticism with a willingness to change.

Conformity and obedience

Conformity

Since the 1930s, psychologists have been interested in the nature of conformity and obedience (what makes us conform and obey). One psychologist, Crutchfield (1955) defined conformity as: "yielding to group pressure". Much later, Zimbardo and Leippe (1991) defined conformity as: "a change in belief or behaviour in response to real or imagined group pressure when there is no direct request to comply with the group nor any reason to justify the behaviour change."

It would seem from these definitions, that conformity is a psychological need for acceptance by others, which means going along with the majority in a group situation and altering your behaviour to that of the group. There is no specific request for you to behave in a certain manner but if you wish to be accepted by a particular group and your behaviour conforms to the others in the group, you may regard yourself as belonging to the group.

Theory into practice

It has now been acknowledged that the following are the main features of conformity:

- there is no explicit requirement to act in a certain way

- it is normally peers or equals who influence us

- the emphasis is on acceptance

- it regulates the behaviour among those of equal status

- behaviour adopted is similar to that of peers

- participants deny conformity as an explanation for their behaviour.

In terms of the points just mentioned, how many times have you conformed? Why did you conform?

Compliance with practices

Compliance is almost the same as conformity, the only difference is that with compliance you are requested, implicitly or explicitly to perform a task – an act of compliance.

However, when we comply with certain practises, which could be practises that we are bound to follow by law or simply practises that have evolved through tradition, we may be said to be conforming.

Think about it

Look at the following examples and decide which of them refers to conformity or compliance (or both)

1 Sally, a visiting professor of psychology from America, was not familiar with British traffic law, so she drove her hire-car on the left side of the road because she noticed that other drivers were doing the same.

2 Jane went to church every Sunday morning with her parents and brothers and sisters. She had done so for as long as she could remember. However, she found the services very boring, though she didn't tell anyone.

3 Steve and Margaret went to the match every Saturday. They would always meet their friends for a drink before the game and then with fifteen minutes to go before the start they would congregate behind the goal with the home crowd and go through the ritual of chanting and singing.

Self-esteem

A person who has a positive self-image including self-respect and a sense of worth has a high self-esteem. Behaviour can be guided by comments such as, "Well done, that was a really good effort" or "Perhaps it would be better if you did it this way." By receiving positive feedback, your self-esteem rises and you gain confidence in your own ability.

Low self-esteem has been described as an illness, whereby people have negative perceptions of themselves and are more likely to feel frustrated and out of control with their lives. This may result in people losing or having a reduced self-awareness – something psychologists have termed 'deindividuation.'

If you lack self-confidence or self-respect then you may be tempted to act in a manner that you wouldn't normally act in order to gain the respect of others. For example, impressionable teenagers might decide to go along with a group and drink alcohol because that is what the members of the group do. Whilst this may harm them physically, it will show the group that they are conforming, which may persuade the group to accept them as a member.

However, this is not to say that all people who conform are suffering from low self-esteem or some kind of anxiety. On the contrary, it is believed by many psychologists that conformity to socially accepted demands is perfectly normal and is one of the main ways in which we develop our character and recognise our role in society.

Theory into practice

Look at the following list and tick those points which you think applies to you:

1 I'm the life and soul of the party

2 I like to be with other people

3 I am quite happy being who I am

4 I'm sure of myself

5 There are many times I'd like to leave home

6 My parents usually consider my feelings

7 I'm happy with life

8 I rarely get discouraged at college

9 I can handle any situation I find myself in

10 I'm doing the best work that I possibly can

11 I'm happy with my friends

12 I wish I were older or younger

13 I can make up my mind and stick to it

14 I'm a lot of fun to be with

If you answered positively to all or most of these questions, according to psychologists you have high self-esteem.

Social norms

According to psychologists Deutsch and Gerard (1955) there are two theories that influence us into adopting social norms: informational social influence (ISI) and normative social influence (NSI).

ISI is the theory that we have a basic need to weigh up information and opinions and when we are in a strange environment we are susceptible as we don't have the information that makes us feel comfortable and in control. Instead, we have to pick up on the thoughts and behaviour of others as a measure of the behaviour that is expected of us in this new environment. In other words, we turn to others for direction and tend to behave according to the majority. For example, if you were waiting to cross the road with a crowd of people at a pedestrian crossing and you couldn't see the lights because someone was obstructing your view you may start to cross the road when the crowd crosses without even checking to see if the lights are in your favour. This is an example of looking to others for guidance on how to behave and conforming according to the behaviour of others. If you are familiar with an environment, then the less you are likely to rely on the behaviour of the majority and the less likely you are to conform.

The NSI theory claims we conform because we have a fundamental need to be accepted by others and we may only be accepted by making a good impression. Usually by saying what the majority want to hear or behaving in a manner that meets their approval. Do you think you would succeed in a job-interview by saying 'no' and frowning, when you ought to be saying 'yes' and smiling?

Closely related to the ISI and NSI theories is the theory of internalisation which is when a private belief or opinion is consistent with public belief and opinion.

Abrams (1990) argues for a social influence known as referential social influence. Social influence occurs when we see ourselves as belonging to a group that possess the same beliefs and characteristics and uncertainty arises when we find ourselves in disagreement with group members. In other words, it is more likely that we will take notice and be influenced by a group to which we have an affinity with than one that we don't. When we categorise ourselves in groups in this way, we are concerned, above anything else, with upholding the norms of the group.

Uniforms

It is generally considered that uniforms are a symbol of unity, pride and authority, especially those worn by public service employees. They are instantly recognisable and members of the public can relate to the personnel who wear them. However, some uniforms can convey power and other uniforms may be used to identify professional authority, such as a doctor's white coat. Powerful institutions, such as the Ministry of Defence and the police invest officers with authority and this may be symbolised in their uniform to indicate the hierarchy of authority to the members of that institution.

Uniforms also offer protection and security to the officers who wear them. For example, firefighters require special personal protective equipment as part of their uniform because of the nature of their work, as do the police when dealing with riots and the armed forces when serving on active duty.

Theory into practice

Think of 4 types of uniform worn by public service employees. What do those uniforms symbolise and how would you describe the way in which the people who wear those uniforms feel?

How do you think members of the public view these employees who wear uniforms?

Uniforms can offer protection and security

Obedience

In some respects, obedience is similar to conformity in that it is a form of compliance. However, it differs in three main ways:

1   With obedience you are ordered or instructed to behave in a particular way and it is irrelevant whether or not you agree with the order or instruction. With conformity there is no requirement to behave in a specific way.

2   With obedience you are ordered to do something by someone in higher authority, whereas with conformity, the influence comes from your peers or equals.

3   Obedience involves social power and status, whereas conformity is generally seen as a psychological need to be accepted by others.

Obedience status

Within the public services, obedience status depends upon rank within the hierarchy of authority. You have to obey those of senior rank, while those of a subordinate rank have to obey you. For example, an inspector in the police service has authority over sergeants and constables but has to be obedient to all other ranks up to Chief Constable. The same principle applies to all the uniformed services, and the higher the rank, the more responsibility you have for making decisions and ensuring your orders are carried out.

It is not only subordinate members of the public services who have a role of obedience to play within the hierarchy of authority – society is organised in such a way that its members also have a certain status. Linton (1945) identifies 5 different social groupings which all have different status and expectations:

1   Age and sex groupings (infant, old, male, female)

2   Family groupings (father, sister, mother)

3   Occupational groupings (teacher, lawyer)

4   Common interest groupings (sports clubs, patrons of certain public houses)

5 Status groupings (manager, team leader).

With these groupings, unlike the public services, there is no law that binds a member of the group to an act of obedience. Instead, the act of obedience has been derived from tradition or culture.

Social contacts

We have all, at some time in our lives, obeyed superiors without questioning their authority. For example, when we were young we never questioned why we had to take tests in school or why our guardians told us to eat our vegetables. Obviously, children are too young to question authority but as we grow older we come to realise that the people we have obeyed have usually had their authority bestowed upon them by society and that appears to make it acceptable. Our social contacts from infancy and through our lives influence our behaviour to accept authority in all its forms.

Proximity

Proximity is the term given to how our behaviour is affected by others. It refers to the regularity and manner with which people interact with each other, which can be determined by how close we live to someone or how close we work with them.

Psychologists believe that the closer and more familiar we are to someone or something, then the less likely we are to obey an order that may do them harm. This is because you have formed an emotional bond or friendly relationship with the person. Furthermore, the further away from you the person *giving* the order is, the less likely you are of carrying out the order where it will do someone harm.

Fear of punishment

One reason why we are obedient is because of fear of being penalised as a consequence of disobeying orders. For example, the financial penalties which may be incurred as a result of breaking the speed limit. In some public services, personnel may incur penalties such as a reduction in rank or suspension from duty.

Some people think that using punishment to control behaviour is wrong and it shows that the authority figure does not understand how to motivate or reward individuals, resulting in resentment and hatred of authority. Even worse, the person being punished may come to accept that aggression is an acceptable means of controlling the behaviour of others.

Think about it

How important is obedience in the public services?

Would you say obedience is always a good thing or should there be a right to question authority?

Psychological studies

Psychologists have conducted a great deal of experimental research into conformity and obedience. Firstly, we will look at three well-known studies of Asch, Milgram and Hofling and then we shall see if the results are applicable to the public services.

The Asch Paradigm

In an experiment, Asch (1951) wanted to show that people do tend to behave according to group pressure, either real or imagined and not because they know the group are right. The experiment, because it is believed to be such a good illustration, has come to be known as 'The Asch Paradigm' (a paradigm is a representative or standard example that is given to explain a theory).

Asch conducted a pilot study in which 36 participants were tested individually in a total of 720 trials. It was found that there were only three mistakes – an error rate of 0.42 per cent and since Asch was happy with the experiment in terms of simplicity, he conducted another experiment but this time the tasks were done as a group as opposed to individually.

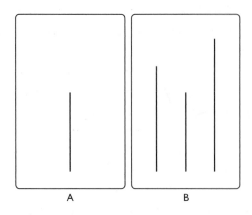

Figure 14.2 The line judgement task

The test was a line judgement task, which involved participants being presented with two cards: one card – a standard card (A) contained a single vertical line and the other card – comparison card (B) contained three vertical lines of varying length. The participants simply had to decide which of the lines on the comparison card matched that on the standard card.

Asch asked some of the participants tested in the pilot study to act as stooges (people who were planted in a group and who knew what role to play but pretended that they were not involved in the experiment) and they were told that the group would contain one participant who was unaware that they were stooges.

Asch commenced several trials, some of which were critical (where the results were monitored) whilst others were not. All the stooges knew when the trials were critical because Asch would indicate this with a secret signal; the other participants (naïve participants) didn't know which were critical and which were neutral.

During the critical trials, of which there were 12, the stooges were all required to unanimously say aloud the incorrect answer, and the experiment was rigged so that the naïve participant was always last, or last but one to give their answer.

The results from the experiments were not overwhelming in favour of conformity being a matter of group pressure, though they were quite remarkable. Asch showed that in 11 out of 12

critical trials one person conformed totally and three quarters conformed at least once. Many similar experiments have subsequently been conducted and the participants, when asked to explain their behaviour, gave the following reasons:

- wanted to act in accordance with the experimenter's wishes and not give an unfavourable impression of themselves, which they might have done had they disagreed with the majority

- doubted the validity of their own judgement because of eye strain or that they could not see the task material properly

- didn't realise they had given the wrong answers and used the stooges as guide posts

- didn't want to appear different

- didn't want to be made to look a fool or inferior, even though they knew the answer they were giving was wrong.

Interestingly, Asch noticed that when the stooges gave their answers verbally and the naïve participants wrote theirs down, conformity was considerably reduced. He concluded that group pressure was responsible for conformity, rather than anything else.

In subsequent Asch-type experiments where there have been more naïve participants than stooges (in some there were 16 naïve participants to a single stooge) and the stooge gave a wrong answer, the participants reacted with laughter and sarcasm, thus giving credence to the theory that people conform because of group or peer pressure.

Milgram's electric shock experiment

Milgram (1974) researched obedience because he was concerned about the serious social problems that have been caused by it in the past. Specifically, the aftermath of the Holocaust and the events leading up to World War II. He wanted to find out whether Eichmann, a high ranking official in the Nazi party, and his accomplices were just following orders and could they be called accomplices.

Milgram used volunteers from all walks of life to participate in the experiments, which involved three people at a time: the experimenter, the learner and the teacher. The experimenter and learner, who were stooges, were to act to a carefully pre-prepared script, whereas the teacher (who was always a naïve participant) only knew that the experiment was concerned with the effects of punishment on learning.

Prior to the commencement of the experiment, all 3 people went into a room where the teacher witnessed the learner being strapped into a chair with his arms attached to electrodes that would, apparently, deliver an electric shock. The teacher was then led into an adjacent room where he was shown a generator, which contained a number of switches, clearly marked with a range of volts from 15 to 450. This equipment was to be used by the teacher to administer an electric shock to the learner if the learner didn't remember a word correctly or refused to respond with an answer. Every time the learner made a mistake, the shocks increased by increments of 15 volts and the learner would respond as if really receiving the shocks.

During the experiments, the teachers showed reluctance to deliver the shocks but after being prompted by the experimenter with phrases such as, "please continue," "please go on," "the experimenter requires that you continue" and finally, "you have no other choice, you must go on," the teachers continued.

Milgram was astonished by the result of his experiments: every teacher administered at least 300 volts and 65 per cent administered 450 volts (a possible lethal amount). He concluded:

"[T]he most fundamental lesson of our study is that ordinary people, simply doing their jobs, and without any particular hostility on their part, can become agents in a terrible destructive process."

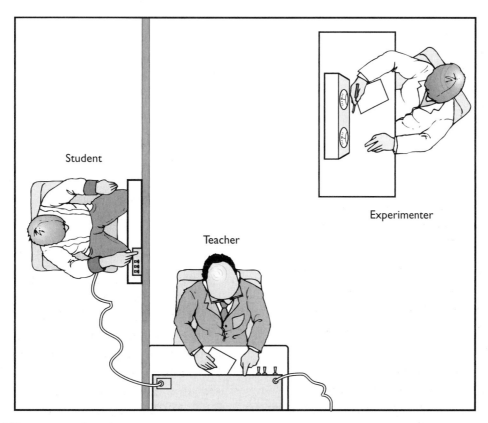

Figure 14.3 The Milgram experiment

Hofling's nurses

In 1966, Hofling and others conducted an experiment with nurses to see if they would intentionally cause harm to a patient if ordered to do so by a doctor. Hofling met with 22 nurses, all from different wards, and warned them of the dangers of a new drug called Astroten which was extremely toxic. Astroten was actually a fictitious drug name made up by the researchers and was nothing more than glucose.

Later, Hofling asked a doctor, who the nurses knew to be on the staff but had never met, to telephone the nurses on each of the wards. The doctor instructed the nurses to administer 20 mg of Astroten to a certain patient. Despite having been told that the maximum dose for this drug was 10mg and the instruction was against hospital policy, which clearly stated drugs couldn't be prescribed over the phone, 21 out of the 22 nurses administered or attempted to administer the drug. Even the fact that the drug was not on the ward stock list to authorise its use, did not prevent the nurses from obeying the doctor's instructions.

Theory into practice

- Explain what each experiment was designed to prove?
- How was Asch's study different to Milgram and Hofling's?
- Did the experiments justify the main reasons for conformity and obedience? For example, in relation to proximity, Milgram concluded that conformity was when the experimenter (authority figure) was in close proximity. However, in Hofling's experiment, the nurses received instruction by telephone and never even saw the doctor.
- Do you think trials are an authentic measure of how people respond to conformity and obedience or do you think that they are contrived in order for the psychologists to prove a point? For instance, you may think it is

significant that two of the three experiments were conducted in universities.
- Which experiment do you find convincing and why?

Relating the studies to the public services

By reflecting on the meaning of conformity and obedience, and the factors that influence them, you should be able to evaluate the application of the studies in the public services.

Personnel in the public services conform to many things including the practice of wearing a uniform, being smart, refraining from alcohol whilst on duty and obeying lawful orders. Conformity in the public services sense means complying with laws and practises rather than, as Asch studied, a change in belief or behaviour in response to group or peer pressure.

One point of Asch's study was that group members would only conform if they identified within the group a member or members with some kind of credibility for influencing a change of behaviour. However, personnel in the public services are guided by discipline and the influencing figures are the higher-ranking officers. The subordinate officers, according to the rules of discipline, must yield to a higher authority.

Subordinate officers must follow the rules of discipline

In institutions such as the public services, where following orders is a matter of routine, Milgram and Hofling's studies seem particularly applicable. However, organisations are more accountable than the participants in Milgram's study were as they had no form of redress and the experimenter (the authoritative figure) was, apparently, unaccountable. Fortunately, public services such as the police service are governed by the Police Complaints Authority (PCA) and other legislation.

Self-discipline

We've already looked at the meaning and the role of discipline. Self-discipline is another form of discipline which is an essential quality for the efficient and effective operation of any of the public services. Self-discipline can be defined as: the ability to apply yourself in the correct manner, including control of yourself and your feelings. Many qualities are needed for self-discipline as outlined below.

Qualities

Personal presentation

Whether or not you agree, people form impressions and opinions about us from the way we appear to them, so if you want to create the right impression then it is important that you are correctly presented.

If you can't be bothered to take a pride in your own appearance, then you will not convey a good message to others. For example, would you like to eat in a restaurant if the waitress had dirty fingernails? In the public services where members of the public may be looking to you for help or guidance, it is particularly important that your appearance is smart.

Punctuality

In order to run efficiently and effectively, organisations have to keep to tight schedules and this means being governed by time. In the public services, punctuality is vital so that at any one time it is known where and when how many people are on duty. At the beginning of a shift, public service personnel are briefed about any major issues that may have arisen, for example a missing child and officers are kept updated. If you are late for a shift and miss the briefing, then you are preventing that organisation from operating efficiently.

Time management

This is a familiar phrase, often used by students who cannot make their assignment deadline. In many cases, it means the assignment has been left to the last minute and unforeseen problems have occurred resulting in an unfinished piece of work. In other words, they have managed their time inappropriately.

In the public services, you have to manage your time by prioritising your workload and ensuring that important reports and other documents are produced on time. For example, if you worked in the police service on the night shift and found a dead body in suspicious circumstances in the early hours of the morning, you would have to inform Her Majesty's Coroner and complete a report as well as protecting the potential scene of crime. Furthermore, you may have to attend the opening of the inquest and a post-mortem examination at the end of your night shift. Meanwhile, all the other administrative tasks normally undertaken would have to take second place as the report on the dead body takes priority.

Reliability

An organisation is only as reliable as those members who make up the organisation. Reliability, as far as the public services are concerned, means that an employee can be depended upon and that they are trustworthy.

Forgetfulness or dishonesty can bring disrepute to the entire service and can destroy public trust and confidence.

Attendance

There may be times when we have to do something that we are not looking forward to – perhaps a presentation in front of class or an important examination. It would be so easy to make excuses and convince ourselves that we are not well enough to perform the task in hand and just not bother to turn up. But isn't this the easy way out? What does it say about your strength of character?

In the public services you are part of a team and by not attending, without good reason, you are letting yourself and the team down. Much of the hard work that has gone before, such as painstaking enquiries and observations, may have all been in vain if you don't attend on the day an arrest is to be made and how can you make plans for a whole team when you know that one of the team has a poor record of attendance?

Composure

Composure is an important quality for working in the public services. If you are a police officer who has been called to the scene of an accident, you will need to keep your composure as you will be the person to whom people will appeal for help, information and attention. You can only give help and bring about order by remaining calm and thinking clearly.

Attitude

Can you show sympathy and understanding even when you feel frustrated and annoyed? Police officers have to be fair, unbiased and courteous and must not allow their personal problems to interfere with their professional responsibilities. People in distress often turn to the police because they see them as someone they believe they can trust to advise and help sort out their problems.

Composure is an important quality in the police force

What would happen if people were reluctant to seek help and advice from the police because they were made to feel that they were being a burden or a nuisance? They would seek help elsewhere, often from unscrupulous characters or they might take the law into their own hands because they felt that going through the normal channels was of no use.

Likewise, if you are discourteous to your colleagues this can affect morale and the efficiency with which you execute your duties.

Performance

You might be happy with just doing enough but members of the public or your colleagues might not be. In the public services, you not only have yourself to think about; you have a duty to perform to the best of your ability at all times. If your performance is perceived as relaxed or carefree in the wrong situation, this may affect the morale of your colleagues. Remember, you have a duty to show *esprit de corps* – you should always be proud and have a high regard for your chosen service.

The performance of public service employees is always monitored in some form by members of the public. It is their performance that instils confidence in the public, knowing that if they needed the public services then they could be relied upon to perform to the best of their ability.

Personality

When we talk about 'personality' in the public services, we mean the distinctive, attractive qualities that make us stand out from others. Just because everyone wears a uniform and has a service number doesn't mean that public service employees don't have personality.

You might think that we can't alter our personalities but this isn't necessarily so. As with many other qualities, we have to work at improving things by practising and then reflecting on what we did right or wrong. Your personality can make a huge difference to your role within the public services: it can make you a popular colleague to work with and it could make you popular with the criminal fraternity when you are trying to illicit important information.

Think about it

Consider the above-mentioned qualities and explain in detail why you think they are necessary for the effective operation of:

● the police service
● the fire service.

Authority

We have already mentioned rules and regulations and obedience to authority. Now we will look at what authority is, the nature and types of authority and various legislation that gives authority its force. Authority, as with discipline, can have different meanings and the meaning of 'authority' is dependent upon the context in which it is used.

Authority may come from a single person or body of people and can mean:

● the power or right to enforce obedience

● delegated power

● a person whose opinion is accepted because of expertise.

Think about it

Consider the following statements:

1 When his friend, Private Johnson, told Private Williams to get a hair cut, he ignored him because he had no authority. However, he didn't ignore the sergeant when he also told him to get a hair cut.

2 Blue watch responded to the authority of sub-officer Bryant because they knew the Divisional Officer was in a meeting.

3 The jury didn't believe Mrs. Chambers' evidence that the deceased died of poisoning but they listened to the authority of the pathologist.

Authority in the public services

Police Complaints Authority

The Police Complaints Authority (PCA) is an independent body which was established by the Government in 1985 to oversee public complaints against police officers in the 43 police forces in England and Wales. It also oversees complaints against officers in the National Crime Squad, National Criminal Intelligence Service, British Transport, Ministry of Defence, Port of Liverpool, Port of Tilbury and Royal Parks police.

The main complaints relate to assault when arrested, incivility, neglect of duty and breaches of the Police and Criminal Evidence (PACE) Codes governing how people are searched, treated in custody and how they are interviewed.

Sphere of authority

When a complaint is received by the PCA, one of its Members (of which there are no less than 8) will consider the suitability of the Investigating Officer, nominated by the police force. The Member will then decide how the enquiry should be conducted, who should be interviewed and what forensic evidence is needed. Throughout the enquiry, the Member will see all of the gathered evidence and will liaise regularly with the Investigating Officer, who will submit their final report for approval before the Member signs off the enquiry as complete.

The PCA also supervises cases that have been voluntary referred from any police force in England and Wales. Police forces, under the Police Act 1996 have the power to refer any serious matter for a supervised investigation voluntarily, even though there has been no complaint. The police service has agreed with the PCA and the Home Office to refer the following:

- all deaths in custody

- all discharges of firearms by police in which a member of the public was injured or killed

- all driving incidents involving police drivers in which a member of the public was killed (and some where serious injuries occurred)

- some serious corruption inquiries.

Ultimately, the PCA has the power to decide whether police officers should face disciplinary hearings as a result of misconduct and it is in this way that it has the right to enforce obedience.

Whilst the PCA supervises more than 400 investigations a year, it is for the chief officer of the force concerned to decide whether a complaint against serving police officers should be recorded and investigated. The PCA has no power to order that a force must record and investigate a particular complaint and the PCA cannot overrule the chief officer.

Nature of authority

Power

Power may be interpreted as the capacity or ability to make a person perform a task that goes against their interests. For example, a serving soldier may be ordered to perform a fatigue (a non-military, mundane task) by the senior officer which is not in the soldier's interest. The soldier would not have performed this task were it not for the power of the senior officer. Hence, for power to be exerted, there must be a conflict of interests before and after the task is completed. Without a conflict of interests there would be no need for power in order to make a person carry out a task.

In the example above, the power of the senior officer came from a legitimate authority but it is possible for an individual or an organisation to have power without authority. For example, a robber with a weapon may have power without authority.

Raven (1965), identified 6 bases of power:

- **Reward power** – we do what we are asked because we desire rewards or benefits, such as praise, a wage increase and promotion.

- **Coercive power** – we do what we are asked because we fear sanctions, such as being made to perform mundane tasks, lack of privileges or even fear of dismissal.

- **Informational power** – we do what we are asked because we are persuaded by the content of a communication (verbal or written) and **not** by any influencing figure.

- **Expert power** – we do what we are asked because we believe that the power-figure has generally greater expertise and knowledge than us.

- **Legitimate power** – we do what we are asked because we believe that the power-figure is authorised by a recognised power structure to command and make decisions.

● **Referent power** – we do what we are asked because we can identify with the source of influence; we may be attracted to them or respect them.

Influence

Influence is different from power in that whilst there will be a conflict of interests before the task is completed but there will be no conflict as the task is being completed. Instead, the person performing the task will have been persuaded by the person requesting it to change their attitude. For example, a senior officer may persuade a soldier on fatigue that meticulously cleaning the camp three times a day is vital to the well being of all the personnel in the company and that the success or failure of the forthcoming operation is dependent upon the pristine condition of the camp. The soldier might come to realise the value of his or her task and readily agree to carry out the task, in which case there is no need for power.

Position

When we talk about someone being in a position of authority we usually mean that they hold a certain rank or status within society or within an organisation such as the public services.

There are several ways in which a person could find himself or herself in a position of authority. For example, a priest has the authority of the church while a mother or father has parental authority over children. In the public services, positions of authority come with promotion to a higher rank and an officer may be promoted to a higher rank because of certain achievements and special attributes, such as experience in the service, good character, knowledge of the job, dedication, self-discipline and respect of one's colleagues.

When a person is placed in a position of authority, they may lawfully command subordinates, who recognise the authority and their duty to obey those legitimate commands.

Think about it

Discuss the dangers of basing authority on fear, reward, power, influence or manipulation?

Status

Status relating to authority is closely related to obedience status, which we have already mentioned on page 216. Many of the reasons why people obey can be applied to why we accept authority. For example, we respect the authority of those people who:

● are experts

● have a higher status

● have power.

In the public services, each officer knows his or her status and the status of their colleagues and where they fit in the hierarchy of authority.

Accountability

At the very beginning of this section we mentioned that one of the uses of discipline was to bring people to account – to answer for their actions. Thankfully, every citizen and every organisation in Britain is accountable for their behaviour including public officials, private companies, employers and individuals. For example, all police officers are accountable to their Chief Constable while all police forces are accountable to their Police Authority.

Think about it

Discuss why we need accountability and who the following people/institutions are accountable to;

● Prime Minister

● your college

● solicitors

● your local authority.

Questioning of orders

The public services and Armed Forces are dependent upon orders being followed for their efficient running. Orders that come from a legitimate source ought to be carried out without question as those people who are in a position of authority have the experience and quality of character to know what is right and what is wrong.

As we have seen in the hierarchy of authority, certain ranks have a right to command subordinate ranks and those subordinate ranks have a duty to carry out those orders. To question a legitimate order instead of carrying it out would seem to be a neglect of duty. However, according to McGinty (2003), since the Nuremberg trials in which Nazi war-criminals were tried for the massacre of 6 million Jews prior to and during the Second World War, there is an argument known as the "Nuremberg defence". This can be used to question an order if a person was asked to do something atrocious, for instance killing defenceless prisoners of war or innocent civilians.

In most cases, it might not be acceptable to question authority as those giving the orders may have the nation's best interest at heart but humans are prone to error, especially in times of extreme stress or extraordinary situations.

Think about it

Can you think of two instances where in retrospect it might have been appropriate to question orders.

Disobedience

Disobedience within the public services and Armed Forces can be an extremely serious charge, depending on the degree of disobedience. For example, serious cases of disobedience in the police and fire services can lead to dishonourable discharge.

The following case study is taken from BBC NEWS/UK, which gives an account of two soldiers who refused to fight in the war with Iraq.

Case study – 'When soldiers will not fight'

Two soldiers serving in Iraq were sent back to their headquarters in Essex after refusing to fight in a war "which involved the death of civilians," and could face a court martial.

The Ministry of Defence has played down the suggestion they were conscientious objectors, a phenomenon that surfaced during World War I when thousands of men refused to join the army after it became over-involved in trench warfare.

Michael McGinty, a defence analyst of the Royal United Services Institute, said, "The soldier effectively says 'I will die for my country, or risk my life for my country but in return I expect my country to do the right thing by me.'"

Justin Hugheston-Roberts, a solicitor with Forces Law, said the case of the two soldiers highlighted a range of issues, not least of which was the possibility the pair could use the new Human Rights Act. He said he understood from the men's solicitor they had been flown back from Kuwait to Colchester but were not being held in custody; they had been returned to their unit and were working with a reserve party. No charges have been brought yet but if charges were brought it would depend on whether they raised their objections before the war began.

However, Mr McGinty said the Armed Forces could not afford to overlook infractions of discipline and the men could expect to face long sentences if found guilty. He said the pair could expect to serve up to two years in Colchester military prison for refusing to fight in Iraq. But he said: "It makes a huge difference if they refused to fight before the war began. Any offence 'in the face of the enemy' is considered much more serious."

Most professional soldiers in the British Armed Forces serve up for at least 12 years.

1   Do you think the soldiers are guilty of disobedience?

2   Could they use the Nuremberg argument?

Blind obedience

Blind obedience means to follow orders unquestioningly and there are many occasions where we should be grateful for the way in which public service personnel obey orders as many lives have been saved and dangerous situations defused.

However, there are some occasions where blind obedience does not leave us with happy memories and feelings of gratitude. We know that during the Second World War, Nazis behaved atrociously but when questioned they insisted that they were merely following orders.

Britain does not escape the accusation of being guilty of war-crimes: An action was filed against the British government in the European Court of Human Rights in Strasbourg by relatives of the 323 Argentineans killed on board the *Belgrano* cruiser in 1982 during the Falklands War. The *Belgrano* was heading away from an exclusion zone but an order was, nonetheless, given to fire on the vessel causing it to sink. A committee of three judges dismissed the action on the grounds that it had been submitted too late.

Positive and negative effects of obedience

The problem with obedience is knowing when to speak out – at which point do you stop obeying and ask yourself if you are doing the right thing by carrying out an order. The question may be answered by balancing the consequences of obedience with the consequences brought about by ignoring an order. Unfortunately, the public services and the Armed Forces do not take into account this kind of moral reasoning. You are not there to act upon your own reasoning; you are there to carry out orders.

This may seem to be a rather sweeping statement but if a person acted upon their reasoning instead of obeying orders and following procedures, then public service organisations would not be as efficient as they ought to be. In a uniformed service, you might be called to do something that goes against what your conscience says you ought to do.

Think about it

- What are the positive effects of blind obedience?
- What are the negative effects of blind obedience?

Think about it

Consider the psychological effects of carrying out an order that you disagree with, yet you feel duty-bound to comply with. Can you think of some examples where this might be the case?

Consider the consequences of a service in which everyone questioned orders. What would that mean for the concept of discipline within that service?

Types of authority

Authoritarian

> "This is what I want you to do and this is the way I want you to do it."

This type of authority is when a leader tells subordinates what task to perform and how to perform it without consultation or advice from other parties. Used appropriately, an authoritarian style of leadership can be effective in bringing about the desired result, though there are many occasions where this type of leadership would not motivate or command respect from those who are carrying out the task.

Dictatorial

> "If you don't do it this way I'll have your house burnt down."

Dictatorial is authority that comes from a dictator, though 'dictatorial' is sometimes used to refer to someone who is domineering and arrogant in the manner in which they give orders.

A dictator is a ruler with unrestricted authority over the state, including that of individuals and has complete power to render current laws invalid and create new laws without the prior consent of the very citizens who will be affected by those laws. Unlike democratically elected leaders, dictators can behave in any manner they see fit without fear of being defeated in elections as the electorate are usually helpless in preventing a dictator from remaining in power.

Dictatorial authority is authority carried out without the consent of the people whom it affects. In order to remain in power, dictatorial regimes rule by intimidation and by instilling in people the fear of brute force.

Consultative

"I'll listen to what you have to say but the final decision will be mine, whether you agree or not."

Consultative authority, also known as collective authority, is where a leader might share a problem with several members of a team either individually or in a group with a view to hearing ideas and suggestions. The leader will then make a decision but not necessarily a decision that is influenced by suggestions and ideas from the group.

Participative (democratic)

"This is what we have so far and this is what we need to do – I think we ought to do it this way but do you have any suggestions?"

With this type of authority, the leader includes one or more employees in the decision making process. However, the leader maintains the final decision-making authority. Using this style is not a sign of weakness, it is a sign of strength that employees respect.

Think about it

Which type of authority do you think would be applicable in 3 chosen public services? Explain why.

Legislation

Members of the public services and Armed Forces are not only subject to the laws of the land, they also have to abide by codes of conduct and disciplinary rules and regulations relating to their particular service. These rules and regulations are written into Acts of Parliament.

The rules and regulations are not solely for enforcing discipline. They are also there to protect the rights of serving officers who may have broken a rule and to make sure procedures for dealing with disciplinary hearings are standardised. Furthermore, they are there to protect members of the public from such things as harassment and victimisation by clearly stating, for example police powers of arrest and search.

Armed Forces Discipline Act 2000

This Act provides the statutory framework for discipline procedures for our three Armed Forces. The basis for this statutory framework stems from the Army Act 1955, the Air Force Act 1955 and the Naval Discipline Act 1957 which are renewed by Parliament every five years and are known collectively as the Service Discipline Acts (SDAs). Essentially, the Armed Forces have their own legal system and it applies to personnel wherever in the world they are based, whether in peacetime or conflict. However, the Act does not apply only to service personnel: it may apply to civil servants and their dependants, as well as the civilian dependants of service personnel.

The Act deals with the processing and punishment of personnel who have been charged, or are likely to be charged, under disciplinary regulations. This legislation makes provision for:

- the right for an accused to apply for bail pending trial

- the trial judge to direct the accused's commanding officer to give orders for the accused's arrest

- the right to appeal against the summary award of the commanding officer

- appeals against a conviction by way of a fresh hearing

- appeals against sentence by way of a fresh hearing but only the evidence relevant to sentencing will be reheard

- the punishment from a Summary Appeals Court cannot be more severe than that which was initially awarded by commanding officer

- appeals must be brought within fourteen days beginning with the date on which the punishment was awarded or within such longer period as the court may allow

- accused's right to elect trial by court-martial

- where accused elects trial, the court cannot award any punishment which could not have been awarded by the commanding officer or appropriate superior authority had the election for trial not been made.

Armed Forces Act 2001

As mentioned previously, the Armed Forces Discipline Act which provides the statutory framework for discipline for our 3 Armed Forces, is reviewed by Parliament every five years. The Armed Forces Act 2001 enables the reviewing process to continue. The last Armed Forces Act was dated 1996 and the next one will be in 2006.

The main purpose of this Act is twofold:

- It makes amendments to previous outdated legislation to ensure the military system is a modern and fair system

- It gives certain rights to service police (military police) to deal with service personnel in the same way that civilian police are empowered to deal with civilians

The key aspects covered by this legislation are:

- statutory powers of search and seizure (of premises too), including stop and search for the service police

- judicial officers empowered to issue search warrants and to issue warrants for the arrest of persons who may fail to comply

- a right for the Crown to ask the Attorney General to refer a sentence to the Court-Martial Appeal Court where it is considered unduly lenient

- the power for courts to make wasted costs orders against either the Crown or defence for improper, unreasonable or negligent action of a representative resulting in the other party incurring costs. There is also a section dealing with the recovery by the Services of travel and accommodation costs of witnesses who are unreasonably required by the defence to attend a hearing

- a power for the Secretary of State to make orders applying changes in civilian criminal justice legislation to the armed forces

- protection of children in families with the armed forces abroad

- the categories of civilians who are subject to Service law whilst overseas are set out in the Service Discipline Acts.

- removal of references to the death penalty from the three Service Acts and, where these relate to specific offences, replacement with references to a penalty of imprisonment or any less punishment authorised by the Act

- mandatory sentences in circumstances where an accused is repeatedly convicted of certain offences.

Police Discipline Regulations 1995

These regulations, which amend the previous regulations of 1985, set out offences which might be committed by serving police officers under a discipline code and the manner in which the offences are to be dealt. The regulations were amended mainly because the old regulations made provision for the Chief Constable to delegate disciplinary hearings to the Deputy Chief Constable but this rank has now been abolished. Instead, the Assistant Chief Constable, in the absence of the Chief Constable, may preside over disciplinary hearings.

Police (Discipline) Regulations 1985 (SI No. 518)

These regulations state 17 offences that could be committed by serving police officers. Whilst the regulations were amended in 1995, 1997 and 2003, the offences remain the same. As well as having to abide by discipline regulations, serving police officers also have to adhere to a code of conduct, which is covered by the Police (Conduct) Regulations 1999.

A Statutory Instrument has the force of law and the Secretary of State creates them, under the authority of the Police Act 1964. Each time a regulation is made under a Statutory Instrument it is given a number and the number for these regulations is 518. Each time a regulation is amended it will be allocated a different Statutory Instrument number.

Below, are 3 rules that come under the Police (Conduct) Regulations:

1 **Honesty and integrity** – officers should not be inappropriately indebted to any person or institution, and should be reliable in the discharge of their duties.

2 **Fairness and impartiality** – police officers have a particular responsibility to act with fairness and impartiality in all their dealings with the public and their colleagues.

3 **Politeness and tolerance** - officers should treat members of the public and colleagues with courtesy and respect, avoiding abusive or deriding attitudes or behaviour. In particular, officers must avoid: favouritism of an individual or group; all forms of harassment,

victimisation or unreasonable discrimination and overbearing conduct to a colleague, particularly to one junior in rank or service.

Think about it

How many more rules can you think of, which might apply to the conduct of police officers? Visit the website:
http://www.homeoffice.gov.uk/docs2/mg6b.pdf
and compare your answers with Police (Discipline) Regulations 1985 and Police Conduct Regulations 1999.

Police And Criminal Evidence Act 1984

This is the main Act of Parliament dealing with the law on police powers. It sets out the rules that the police must follow in relation to searching, arresting or detaining people.

If the police do not follow the codes of practice, then any evidence they obtain as a result may not be able to be used in court as it can potentially be regarded as unreliable or unsafe.

The codes of practice, as well as the rules governing conduct can be changed from time to time without the main law being altered by Parliament. The authority to do this is known as a 'Statutory Instrument.'

Besides standardising procedures for gathering evidence, the Police and Criminal Evidence Act also legislates the procedure for dealing with complaints. For example, section 84 of the Act places a burden on the Chief Constable to take steps to obtain and preserve evidence relating to a police complaint. Furthermore, the Chief Constable must decide upon the appropriate authority to deal with the complaint such as the Chief of Police of the force area concerned and if the officer who is subject of the complaint is a senior officer, then the Police Authority for that force must be informed.

End of unit questions

1 Would it be true to say that discipline is a form of punishment? If not, then what is it?

2 Give 3 reasons why discipline is required in the public services.

3 What does 'hierarchy of authority' mean?

4 What is meant by '*esprit de corps*?'

5 Briefly explain the main differences between conformity and obedience and give an example of each.

6 Why would low self-esteem be a bad thing in the public services?

7 Is the wearing of uniforms always a good thing?

8 Is obedience to a command, irrespective of its nature, a good thing?

9 Regarding proximity, what did you find odd about the findings of Milgram's experiment compared to Hofling's?

10 Do you think obedience is related to fear? If so, give an example and relate it to the public services.

11 Briefly explain why self-discipline is important in the public services.

12 In the public services, is there any time when it would be appropriate to question an order?

13 What is meant by a 'moral dilemma?'

14 When we say "someone has power over someone else," what is meant by 'power'?

15 Briefly explain what the Police Complaints Authority does.

16 What is meant by the Nuremberg defence'?

17 What is meant by 'blind obedience'?

18 What is 'dictatorial authority'?

19 What is the main purpose of the Army Act 1955?

20 What is the purpose of the Police and Criminal Evidence Act 1984?

Resources

Websites

The Trial of Adolph Eichmann – 1961: http://www.usd.edu/honors/HWB/1999/1999d/Eichmann.htm

Conformity and Obedience – Dr. C. George Boeree: http://www.ship.edu/~cgboeree/conformity.html

Self-esteem: http://www.timesonline.co.uk/article/0,,2–552622,00.html

Socialisation and the Individual: http://infotrain.magill.unisa.edu.au/epub/People/nette/socialis.htm

Police Discipline Regulations: http://www.homeoffice.gov.uk/docs2/mg6b.pdf

Discipline and Military Law: Discipline and Military Law Reference Library

Armed Forces Act: http://web.onetel.com/~aspals/aspalsafa01.html

The Police (Discipline) (Amendment No. 2) Regulations 1995: http://www.hmso.gov.uk/si/si1995/Uksi_19952517_en_1.htm

Suggested reading

Gross, R & McIlveen, R (1998): *Psychology A New Introduction*: Hodder & Stoughton: London

Assessment activities

This section describes what you must do to obtain a pass grade for this unit.

A merit or distinction grade may be awarded if your work demonstrates a deeper understanding of the topics and is of a higher quality. The highlighted sentences indicate the quality of work expected at merit and distinction level.

Assessment methods

A number of assessment strategies may be used in order to achieve the learning outcomes, such as oral presentations, group discussions, written assignments, research projects, role-plays or a combination of these. It is a good idea, though it is not essential, to use a variety of methods in order to develop different skills.

It is important that you understand and comply with the key words specified in the grading criteria. For example, if you are asked to 'analyse' something, then make sure that you do not merely describe it. Similarly, if you are asked to 'evaluate' something, then make sure you do not merely summarise it.

Key words

Here are some key words that are often used for grading criteria – make sure you understand the differences between them.

Examine	To look at a subject closely in order to understand it and improve your knowledge
Consider	This means to think about and weigh up a subject
Explain	This means to make something clear and set out the arguments
Analyse	This means to look at a subject closely and interpret or evaluate your findings. Perhaps outlining the pro's and con's of a situation or suggesting changes and improvements
Describe	This means to say what something is like, it is a factual account of how something is or how it appears.
Compare	This means to look at the similarities between two or more objects or theories.

Assessment tasks

Using the materials within this unit and your own research, carry out the following tasks.

Task 1

Learning outcome 1 – Investigate the role of discipline in the public services

Explain the need for discipline in at least two public services.

> To obtain a merit grade, you should *analyse* the role of discipline in public services.

> To obtain a distinction grade, you should *evaluate* the application of the role of discipline in the public services.

Suggestion for Task 1: group role-play (3 parts)

1st part: In groups of four, outline a simulated breach of discipline for the police or fire service where a senior officer (or peer) intervenes and reports the offender(s).

2nd part: The offending officer(s) is then brought before his/her respective chiefs on disciplinary charges. After the charges are read out, the chief explains the severity of breaches of discipline (by way of analysing the role of discipline within that service).

3rd part: The offending officer(s) has an advocate (representative), who pleads for the officers (by way of an evaluation of the application of the role of discipline) and asks that they be given the least sentence.

The role-plays may be recorded and supplemented with an assessor's testimony.

Task 2

Learning outcome 2 – Explore conformity and obedience

Describe the main features of conformity and obedience.

Identity and explain three factors which influence conformity and three factors which influence obedience.

> To obtain a merit grade, you should *analyse* two conformity and obedience studies and *evaluate* their application in the public services.

> To obtain a distinction grade, you should *analyse* two conformity and obedience studies and *evaluate* their application in the public services.

Suggestion for Task 2: small-group presentation

Using the information contained within this unit, describe the features and influencing factors of conformity and obedience. The audience could be involved and reference can be made to peers and other students within college, regarding fashion, music, mobile phones and so on.

Analyse the studies of Milgram and Asch and try to relate the experiments to life in the public services today. The audience could be involved to provide a consensus of opinion as to the value of such studies in relation to the public services.

Task 3

Learning outcome 3 – Examine self-discipline

Describe the qualities needed for self-discipline in a given public service.

Explore the possible effects of lack of self-discipline in a given public service.

> To obtain a merit grade, you should *explain* in detail how these qualities are necessary for the effective operation of a given public service.

Suggestion for Task 3: report

Using the information contained within this unit, write a report under the various headings as outlined under the learning outcome. Try to include examples that you have researched in your report.

Task 4

Learning outcome 4 – Investigate the nature of authority

Explain the meaning of authority in relation to the public services.

Identify and explain four types of authority.

> To obtain a merit grade, you should *analyse* the positive and negative effects of blind obedience.

Suggestions for Task 4: presentation, role-play or discussion

This outcome could be met by a presentation, role-play or discussion. If a presentation is used as the assessment, case studies could be included such as the Hillsborough Disaster of 1989 or the My Lai Massacre of 1968 to analyse the negative and positive effects of blind obedience.

A role-play could be used to meet all outcomes and this could be combined with a group discussion, which could be recorded and supplemented with an assessor's observation report.

SIGNALS AND COMMUNICATION

Introduction to Unit 22

This is a practical unit, which looks at written and transmitted communication in the public services. It will help you to understand the types of equipment used and identify the skills required in the world of public services signals and communication. You will also develop some of these skills for yourself.

You will explore the range of forms of communication transmission including how the different public service groups use radios, Morse code and semaphore. You will also have the opportunity to practice some of these techniques.

Assessment

Throughout the unit, activities and tasks will help you to learn and remember information. Case studies are also included to add industry relevance to the topics and learning objectives. At the end of the unit there are assessment activitities to help you provide evidence which meets the learning outcomes for the unit. You are reminded that when you are completing activities and tasks, opportunities will be created to enhance your key skills evidence.

After completing this unit you should have an understanding of the following outcomes.

Outcomes

1   Investigate the types of **formal written communication used in the public services**

2   Investigate and compare **radios and radio communication in public services work**

3   Explore **other forms of communication transmission in public services work**

4   Demonstrate **practical signalling and communication skills**

Written communication

Each branch of the public services has developed its own specific procedures for written communication in the form of: content, format and language. These procedures are often updated on a regular basis so it is important that you are sensitive to this when completing your own research. Always check that you are looking at the most recent information.

Although most of the information surrounding these documents is confidential there are constants and similarities and these are covered below.

Letters

The vast majority of letters sent inside the public services will be of a formal nature, particularly letters that relay official information such as orders or schedules. The language of formal letters is straight to the point and the information is often numbered. Demi formal letters are used when communicating on a person to person basis, for example to officially thank someone for a job well done or for hospitality shown on a visit. Figure 22.1 is an example of a formal letter set out in the standard format used by the Army.

RESTRICTED (i)

S/TGB/121 (iv)

2LI
AN Army Barracks
Soldierville   (ii)
Armyshire

AN Army Barracks ext 222

5 Sep 2003 (iii)

Internal Information (v)
Captain BE Alert

Training Ammunition

Reference our telephone conversation of 4 Sep 2003.

1   The allotment of training ammunition for 51mm mortars has been delayed until 20 Sep 2003
2   Your unit will now use Field Firing Range 2 on 22 Sep 2003 instead of Field Firing Range 1 on 16 Sep 2003. (vi)

Captain S. N. A. Glass

Distribution
External: (vii)
Internal: (viii)
Captain BE Alert
Action: (ix)
QM
Wpn Trg Offr
Information: (x)
2IC
RSM

Key

i.   Security classification

ii.   Recipient's address

iii.   Date

iv.   Reference code

v.   Sender

vi.   Information which is being communicated. Note the brevity of the language.

vii.   External recipients (none in this case)

viii.   Internal recipients

ix.   Who will action the letter, in this case the Quarter Master and Weapons Training Officer. Note the use of abbreviations

x.   Who will receive a copy of this letter for information, in this case the 2nd in command and the Regimental Sergeant Major

Figure 22.1 An example of a formal letter sent out by the Army

Memos

Memos are most often sent internally within organisations or branches, for example between stations within a regional Fire Brigade. They are a quick method of passing on information or updating staff of new initiatives or procedures. Each of the public services has its own standard format. These come in the form of pre printed (often self carbonating) memo pads for hand-written memos or preset formats for word processing.

In today's electronic age, e-mail is rapidly taking over and is being used more and more by the public services as it is a quicker and often more reliable method of communicating. For example, in the Ambulance Service information about new drugs that paramedics could use are sent by e-mail and paramedics can simply print off the information and add it to the aide memoir that they keep in their pocket.

Reports

Reports are often used to communicate the findings of specific investigations or reviews. For example, a report may be written on the findings of an investigation into the reaction times of the Ambulance service. Reports are always presented in a formal manner and follow a similar format whatever the public service:

- a statement detailing the purpose of the investigation
- details of the persons carrying out the investigation
- name of the person(s) responsible for writing the report
- date of both the investigation and publication of the report
- status of the report, for example final findings, draft
- summary of the main findings

- detailed description of the findings
- proposals including a timeline
- appendices (often in the form of data, charts or graphs).

Think it over

Why is it important to have specific formats for written communications and why is it important for language to be brief and clear?

Theory into practice

Collect examples of letters written by the Army, Royal Navy, Royal Marines, Royal Air Force, Police, Fire and Ambulance Services and Customs and Excise and compare the formats. What similarities and differences are there?

If you send a written request for information, you should receive a written response.

Format of written communication

Check latest standards/procedures

As already stated, the services update their procedures regularly, so it important for the writer to check that they are familiar with the latest standards set. This is particularly important for those new to a specific role or for those whose role does not require them to produce written communications on a regular basis.

Accuracy

Spelling, punctuation and facts should always be checked for accuracy and any opinions stated should be clearly identified as such, for example 'It is the opinion of this group that . . .'

Language

The language used should be clear and unambiguous. The reader should not be left to ponder the meaning as mistakes in the public services can be costly or even fatal.

Communications should be brief, giving the reader the information needed in the shortest and clearest possible way. Abbreviations specific to each public service may be used.

Format

The writer should follow the set procedures for the format of each different type of communication, for example letters, memos, reports:

- All written communications should be dated and if relevant also include a time. During battle or times of national crisis this becomes essential.

- Pages should be numbered. If a document is dropped it is easier to organise it again and stops any mistakes occurring.

- When reference is made to another document, the title, author and date of that publication should be noted for cross-referencing.

- Longer documents, especially reports, often have appendices. These contain the detailed evidence used to support the findings and more often than not come in the form of data presented by means of charts and graphs. They are placed at the back of the document but are referenced at the relevant points.

Identification

Each document should clearly identify the sender and/or the group they represent. Usually a reference code is also used. Communications should also clearly state their destination.

The security classification or status of the document should be written clearly and centrally, often at the top of the first page. The Army for example uses: Top Secret, Secret, Confidential and Restricted with each of these classifications having a defined audience. Copies should be made and given to the relevant people using their correct rank or title or simply filed.

Radios and radio communication

Communication is vital to all of the public services and has been an essential part of their make up since their earliest days. For example, beacons were used as a means of communicating the presence of enemy forces long before telecommunications were even considered. Police officers have been using whistles for centuries to attract attention to criminals and request aid. The Army even has its own unit dedicated to communications called the Royal Corps of Signals.

The Armed Forces have been at the forefront of communications use and research. This is because keeping in touch with friendly forces in war is essential, as is denying the enemy from your messages. Problems arise for the British forces because there are three forces, each one with its own standard and traditional ways of transmitting information. Trying to coordinate between all three forces is an enormous undertaking, but one which is essential in this age of Joint Forces.

Military communication becomes even more difficult when you add the presence of foreign friendly forces. Shortly before the Second Gulf War, American forces were issued with a communications system that allowed transmissions across all of their services to avoid blue on blue engagements (friendly fire). Blue on blue fire happened much more than it should in the First Gulf War. Bringing all forces onto the same communication network is a technical nightmare, but a tactical necessity on today's battlefield.

Communications therefore are very important to the public services and they have to be used correctly. Many protocols have been set up to ensure that information is transmitted effectively and efficiently.

Radio is one of the most important forms of communication in the public services. It enables communication in the form of words and codes to be sent over vast distances and is not reliant on cables.

The most common types of radios used across the public services are the two-way or the smaller hand held version, the walkie-talkie. Simply speaking, this type of radio is made up of a transmitter and a receiver. The transmitter converts sounds into electromagnetic waves which travel through the air. These are then picked up by a receiver and converted back into identifiable sounds.

However, it should also be noted that the use of mobile phones is now on the increase. In time they may take over from the radio as the main means of verbal communication.

Walkie-talkies

The biggest advantage of a walkie-talkie is its small size. Which is useful for communicating quickly when in the field. The downside is the relatively short distance that many are able to send and receive messages. The larger the unit the greater the wattage, which enables a message to be sent and received further. An average retail model can usually manage 1 to 3 miles. The more sophisticated versions used by many of the domestic public services work over 6 to 8 miles. The armed forces, however, use more powerful, but more bulky versions, which cover far greater distances.

Within each public service, different types of radios are used. This is often to stop information being transmitted across regions which could cause confusion. The choice of radios used often comes down to the cost. Some of the types of radio currently in use are PFX, ICOM, Clansman, PYE, RACAL and Motorola.

There are many problems associated with the use of walkie-talkies, for example picking up transmission from outside individuals such as taxi firms, messages being listened in on by members of the public and short battery life. The first two problems are virtually impossible to eradicate as the airwaves are open to all. Frequency ranges are allocated by the government in line with

Public service	Radios used for:
Army	Base to unit contact. Person to person contact in the field.
Royal Navy	Ship to shore contact.
Royal Air Force	Ground to air contact. Contacting other mobile vehicles, for example when refuelling tankers, ambulances, fire engines.
Police	Contacting officers in vehicles, on horses or on the beat. Communication between officers when pursuing suspects.
Fire	Contacting officers when out with vehicles. Officer to officer contact when fighting fires.
Coast Guards	Ship to shore contact. Ship to ship contact when out searching for a lost craft/person.
Ambulance	Base to ambulance personnel providing details of locations. Ambulance personnel to hospitals providing details of a patient's condition and estimated time of arrival at A&E.

Figure 22.2 Radios are used in the public services across a range of areas

international agreements to different groups such as the police, ambulance, fire, commercial users and amateur radio enthusiasts but this cannot stop other users from picking them up either intentionally or not.

Theory into practice

Find out what other uses the public services have for walkie-talkie radios.

Radio specifications

The main differences between the types of radio used are:

- battery life/power supply
- weight
- number of channels
- frequency range (directly related to the number of available channels).

The choice of radio used by each public service and even within the public service is a balance between the 4. For example, not all roles require a battery life of 24 hours therefore it is unwise to have a battery life of more than 12 hours as the extra weight is an unnecessary burden. An army platoon, however, may be away from base for some days and would need the extra battery life, regardless of the extra weight. Figure 22.3 looks at the differences between 2 types of walkie-talkie used by the public services. The first is a Motorola, which can be purchased on the high street, the second is the Clansman UK/PRC 349 used by the Army at section and platoon level.

A Motorola walkie-talkie

	Motorola	Clansman UK/PRC 349
Frequency range	UHF 462.5625–467.7125	37–46.975 MHz
Channels	14	400
Power supply	3 AA alkaline batteries	12v primary battery 12v re-chargeable battery
Range	Up to 3 km	1.5 km
Range countryside		2–2.8 km
Range woodland		1.2–1.5 km
Built up areas		0.3–0.5 km
Antenna	Fixed 7cm	0.5 or 1 m whip
Weight	200 gms	1.4 kg
Facilities	Volume control. Battery low indicator.	Whisper mode using a throat mike. Battery low warning.

Figure 22.3 A comparison of Motorola and Clansman UK/PRC 349 walkie-talkies

Think it over

1 Discuss the main advantages/disadvantages of each type of radio listed in Figure 22.3?

2 Why do you think the Army use the UK/PRC 349 rather than the Motorola?

Theory into practice

Find out the specifications of other walkie-talkies used by the public services and compare them in a chart similar to Figure 22.3.

The use of radios in the public services

Radio discipline

The following rules for **radio discipline** are common throughout the public services, only phrased differently.

1 Use correct voice procedures.

2 Be alert continually for communications.

3 The radio must not be switched off unless the person at base says so.

4 Ensure you are using the correct frequency.

5 Answer calls immediately.

6 Listen before transmitting.

7 Press the button before you start to speak.

8 Release the button immediately you have finished.

Voice procedures

The purpose of voice procedure is to ensure that messages are sent and received accurately and that callers cannot be identified by anyone who does not have authorisation to be listening in.

Call signs

Call signs are used to identify individuals or groups communicating over the airwaves. They are code names aimed at making the communication more secure and ensuring that individuals are identified accurately, for example 'Hello this is Papa one zero'. If a number of units are taking part in one activity a common call sign is often used but with a different number, for example papa one, papa two, papa three. In the Army the commander (of a section, platoon or battalion) is always called 'Sunray'.

Code words

Code words are used to serve two main purposes: speed of transmission and security of information. The police, fire and ambulance services often use code words or abbreviations when transmitting information to speed up communication time as lives may be at risk, for example RTA for road traffic accident, DOA for dead on arrival, or IC1 for Caucasian male. The Armed Forces also use codes often known as TLAs which are three letter abbreviations, for example 2ic for second in command and RMS for Regimental Sergeant Major. This type of communication is used routinely in ordinary conversation as well as via the radio.

Codes which are used for security reasons are often associated with a specific operation. For example, a large-scale police operation to catch a gang of drug dealers may be given the codename 'Tiger's Eye'.

A soldier operating a walkie-talkie

This would be known only to the officers involved and used throughout the operation. As police radio signals can be easily be listened in by criminals, such code words do not allow them to identify the current stage of the operation.

The ambulance service may use a code name to describe a specific type of incident, for example a problem at a football match. These code names are restricted to keep the information away from the press or to avoid panic which may cause problems on the roads and deny ambulance access.

Security of information is extremely important to the Army. If the enemy can intercept radio communication then operations can be compromised and lives put at risk. In order to lessen this risk the Army uses a form of coding called BATCO (battalion code). This consists of a numerical code that is used once and then discarded, reducing the risk of enemy decoding.

Phonetic alphabet

An example of an internationally recognised voice procedure/protocol is the phonetic alphabet used by NATO (see Figure 22.4). It is important that a standard coding is used so that different armed forces and countries within NATO can communicate. It is also routinely used by all British public services.

When transmitting individual letters, for example a car number plate or spelling out the name of a location, this system aims to solve the problem of mishearing such letters as m/n, b/d/p. f/s. The quality of sound received via a radio is prone to interference and an unexpected crackle could mean the difference between an ambulance arriving at the right location in time to save a life or not. As a result, the accuracy of the information transmitted is vital.

Once again, to avoid confusion, numbers are pronounced one at a time, for example 36 is pronounced three six, not thirty six.

A	Alfa
B	Bravo
C	Charlie
D	Delta
E	Echo
F	Foxtrot
G	Golf
H	Hotel
I	India
J	Juliet
K	Kilo
L	Lima
M	Mike
N	November
O	Oscar
P	Pap
Q	Quebec
R	Romeo
S	Sierra
T	Tango
U	Uniform
V	Victor
W	Whiskey
X	X-ray
Y	Yankee
Z	Zulu

Figure 22.4 The phonetic alphabet

Theory into practice

1 Work out the following words being spelt letter by letter:

   i   romeo alpha delta india oscar

   ii charlie alpha mike papa

   iii sierra echo romeo victor india charlie echo sierra

2 Work out a short message and transmit it to a partner using walkie-talkies and the phonetic alphabet. Did the message come through intact?

Prowords

Prowords are common words and phrases used when transmitting messages. Prowords are easily pronounceable words or phrases. By keeping to a common protocol and a limited number of phrases it avoids confusion for the person receiving the message. For example, in the English language alone there are numerous ways of greeting someone but only 'hello' is used when transmitting messages. This cuts out confusion and allows the person listening to the message to concentrate on the information being communicated instead of trying to fathom what is essentially unimportant. A simple 'hello' at the beginning of a message also indicates that nothing has gone before and has been missed. Using prowords also saves time as one or two words often stand in the place of many.

Tips for preventing confusion when transmitting messages

1 Keep the microphone close to but not touching your mouth

2 Avoid talking quickly

3 Don't shout

4 Use short easily recognisable words

5 Keep conversations short

6 Listen before you speak

7 Think about what you are going to say before you start the communication

8 Don't make unnecessary transmissions

Examples of prowords	
I spell	I am about to spell out a word or group of letters using the phonetic alphabet.
Figures	I am going to send you a number figure by figure.
Hello	The greeting used at the beginning of a communication.
This is	Used to introduce the speaker.
Send	Go ahead with your transmission.
Message	I am about to send you an important communication. You will need to write this down.
Over	This is the end of my transmission. A reply is required and you are free to transmit.
Out	This is the end of my transmission. No reply is expected.
Wait out	Your transmission has been received and a further transmission on the same subject will follow later.
Long message	Used at the beginning of a message, which is longer than 20 seconds. The message is broken up into 20 second chunks with a pause between each. The person receiving the message replies '**Roger so far**' after each chunk. There is also a pause of 5 seconds after each chunk to allow other radio users to transmit urgent messages. The phrase '**long message**' not only tells the person receiving the message to expect the information in chunks but also advises other radio users that this frequency will be in use for some time.
Roger	Your message has been received satisfactorily.
Wrong	What has been said is incorrect, the correct version is . . .
Radio check	This phrase is used to establish whether or not all radio users can hear.
Say again	Please repeat your last transmission.
	In the Armed Forces, the proword '**repeat**' is a command to tell an artillery battery to fire again, so '**say again**' is used when a message is not understood.
I say again	I am repeating my last transmission.

Figure 22.5 Examples of common words and phrases used when sending messages

Types of communication

One to one

Radios are designed to transmit one message at a time. As a result, the most common form of communication is in the form of one radio holder speaking to another. However, this feature only applies to transmitting messages as any number of radio holders using the same frequency can listen in on a conversation.

Radio net

A group of radio holders working on the same frequency with a view to communicating with each other has one radio holder, normally at the control base serving as the control. The other radio holders are known as substations and often have a common coding system as shown in the diagram below.

In Figure 22.6 below, the control has the call sign 'zero four'. The substations use the call signs 'alpha one four' 'bravo two four' 'charlie three four' and 'delta four four'.

The substations reply alphabetically but the control always goes first.

In a radio net there are 4 main types of call as shown in Figure 22.7 below.

Rebro

Rebro is radio broadcast which is used to relay messages between radio users who are out of range and therefore unable to communicate with each other. The rebro consists of two radios: one receives the messages and the other passes them on to other users.

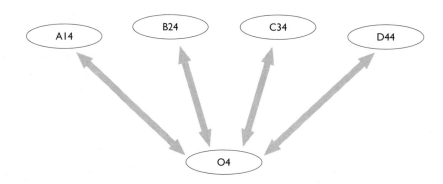

Figure 22.6 A group of radio holders communicating with each other

1	Single call	From one station to another, for example 'hello B24, this is A14.'
2	Multiple calls	From one station to two or more stations, for example 'hello 04. A14 and B24, this is C34' In this example 04 would respond first followed by A14 and B24 in that order.
3	All stations call	From one station to all stations, for example 'Hello all stations, this is D44
4	Collective call	A call which is designed to be received by 2 or more pre-selected stations, for example Hello Echo Echo 1 this is 04 The stations A14 and D44 have been given this call sign collectively.

Figure 22.7 The 4 main types of call in a radio net

Other forms of communication transmission in public services work

The word transmit, although generally used in conjunction with radio and telecommunications actually means to send information from one point to another. Long before walkie-talkies and other long range radios were invented, information was being transmitted over long distances by the armed forces using Morse code, semaphore, heliographs and field telephones. The latest development in communication, especially within the Armed Forces is SATCOM (Satellite communications)

Morse code

This is a system for sending messages using combinations of short and long sounds to represent the different letters of the alphabet, for example the letter 'A' is represented by · - (dit dah) in morse code. The short sound is known as a dit and the long sound a dah. Between each sound there is a pause as long as one dit, between each letter is a pause as long as 3 dits and between each word is a pause the length of seven. When written down it is shown in the form of dots and dashes. It was invented by Samuel Morse in 1840 and was used by telecommunication companies to send telegrams by wire. An operator would tap out the message which would then be transmitted by wire to a receiver at the other end. The receiver would then translate it back into words. This was a highly skilled task requiring not only good control but also a quick memory.

Today it is used by amateur and maritime radio operators or by the military when other forms of signal are too weak to receive.

Advantages of morse code

- Can be used visually or aurally: more versatile than many other types of communication.

- Doesn't require a very strong signal.

- Does not necessarily require expensive or delicate equipment and can be easily maintained.

- Universal use: can be used between different units and services as it isn't force specific.

Disadvantages of morse code

- Requires trained operatives to make sense of messages.

- Universal use means that it can easily be intercepted and understood by other trained personnel, necessitating encryption for secure messages.

- Time consuming to send, receive and translate messages – not as quick as spoken communication.

Theory into practice

1 Find out the Morse code signs for the alphabet and then try writing out the following phrases using 'dit' and 'dah'. Remember to put a space between each letter and a longer space between each word:

I am in location

Send reinforcements

2 Try tapping out a word to a partner for them to translate.

Semaphore

Used predominantly by the Navies around the world this is a form of communication which uses flags as a means of communicating letters. The signaller holds two flags to spell out the message and different combinations of positions indicate letters and numbers.

Advantages of semaphore

- Useful if radio and other technical communications are compromised.

● Does not require expensive equipment: only requires flags and a pair of binoculars.

Disadvantages of semaphore

● Requires trained operatives to use and translate.

● Requires line of sight.

● Time consuming to send, receive and translate messages.

> **Theory into practice**
>
> Find out the semaphore signs used for the alphabet and using flags or simply your arms, send a quick message to a partner for them to translate.

Other communications using flags

Maritime Signal Flags have an international flag code which uses over 40 different flags. Unlike in semaphore, the flags used are simply hoisted, often in groups, above a ship or boat. The flags can represent either letters to spell out words or actual messages.

For example, the word kick is shown below by the following flags:

However, the same flag which signifies K also gives the message 'I wish to communicate with you'. Each ship must carry a codebook to identify what each flag means in 9 different languages. Captains can then understand messages sent ship to ship. Warships often use secret codes however in an attempt to confuse the enemy.

> **Theory into practice**
>
> Use the Internet to find meanings of the Maritime Signal Flags and complete the following tasks:
>
> 1 Which flags would you use to give the message 'My vessel has stopped and is making no way through the water. I require a tug'?
>
> 2 Spell out the words ship and caution using maritime flags.

Heliograph

This is a system of communication using light as a means of transmission. Using the same basic coding as Morse code, messages are sent using short and long flashes of light. This is achieved either by a special button on a torch or lamp or by simply turning it on and off. In emergency situations, a mirror can be used to catch the light from the sun.

Other forms of visual communication

In tactical situations, talking can alert the enemy to your presence and radio communications may be intercepted. At other times, there may be too much noise to allow speech to be heard. This is where visual signals are essential. Infantry soldiers and tactical police units will use a range of gestures to communicate orders and information between their team. Such a method is clearly only useful if the person you are communicating with is alert and looking for such signals and can understand them.

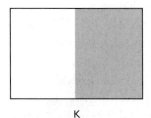

K

I

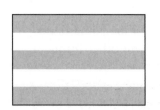

C

K

Figure 22.8 Communication using Maritime Signal Flags

The growing number of public services using helicopters has meant that many operatives now have to learn the international gestures for communicating with pilots and other crew.

> ### Theory into practice
> Find out some of the gestures used in the public services when visual signals are essential.

Field telephones

Field telephones are portable telephone systems, but much more like land lines than mobile telephones. They typically come in a box with a standard telephone handset and are connected to other telephones in the system, similar to a radio net except that they are connected by wires and a switchboard. They were first introduced in the First World War and were invaluable for military communications. Despite the advent of sophisticated radio systems they are still in use and offer some advantages over radio:

- they are a connected system and therefore not limited to range of sight as are many radios

- they tend to be easier to use than radios as mostly they don't require buttons to be pressed before speaking and usually provide clearer communications

- they are a closed system and are therefore much easier to keep secure

- modern developments in telephony allow digital connections, conferencing and other useful features.

SATCOM

SATCOM stands for satellite communication. It is a more powerful form of radio which can cover far wider distances and can communicate words, pictures and other forms of information.

Information transmitted in this way is more secure than via a radio but can still be intercepted by determined parties. It is used by the armed forces to coordinate large-scale manoeuvres over long distances.

Advantages of SATCOM

- Secure means of communicating.

- Enables communication of pictures as well as sounds.

- Clear reception.

- Wider range than other forms of communication.

Disadvantages of SATCOM

- Highly technical system – many links where a problem can occur which requires specialists to fix.

- Can be intercepted by sophisticated enemies.

- Relies on satellites which could become targets in full scale wars and can be damaged by meteorites, solar disturbances etc.

- Operatives need special training to set up and use the equipment.

- Expensive.

Digital communication

Digital is one of the fastest growing communications systems worldwide. Public services organisations are developing these technologies and new systems are constantly being brought on line.

The mainstay of the Army's digital communications is called PTARMIGAN. Making use of civilian and military satellites, it forms a comprehensive network connecting field operations to central command and provides exceptional quality voice and data services. Its software enables interconnectivity between British and allied tactical systems. On a smaller scale it allows individual users, via mobile units, to access all its facilities in the same way that mobile phones allow access to the Internet and network specific software facilities. Other digital systems used by the Army include EUROMUX, compatible with systems used by NATO allies and TRIFFID. The nest few years will see the introduction of:

- CORMORANT which will provide high-speed digital communications in the field of a quality never before seen.

- FALCON, a replacement system for PTARMIGAN

- PROMINA, uses cormorant's technology but can adapt to different forms of transmission including satellite, radio waves, microwaves and line services to provide such facilities as video conferencing, synchronous and non synchronous data services and digital or analogue voice communication. Its biggest asset is its ability to adapt quickly to the changing environment whilst being deployed which means if radio waves can't get the message through effectively it will switch to a method that will, mid communication with no loss of information.

Key concepts

1 Morse code is used by all of the forces when other forms of communication are not secure. It can be used with codes.

2 Semaphore is used mostly by Navies to communicate ship to ship without using radio, which can be intercepted.

3 Heliographs (lights) are another visual form of communication and are often combined with Morse code.

4 Visual signals are used by many public services when spoken communication is not appropriate.

5 SATCOM satellite communication and digital systems allow greater range, flexibility and security.

Practical signalling and communications skills

This section assesses your ability to use 4 or more of the methods of communication covered in this unit by choosing a variety of tasks from the list below to demonstrate your skills in communication. Your course tutor can tell you which combination of tasks is the most suitable for you.

Theory into practice

1 From your investigations into the written formats used by different public services, **choose ONE given format** and produce either a letter or memo.

2 Devise and pass simple messages using a **radio net** and **one standard voice** procedure, for example prowords or the phonetic alphabet.

3 Send a simple message using **2 forms** of transmission from: Morse code, semaphore, International Signal Flags or heliographs.

4 Imagine you are the radio controller for the ambulance service. Devise and transmit a radio communication using **standard voice procedures** giving the exact location and approximate casualty situation of a road traffic accident.

5 Imagine you are a member of the Paratroop regiment, injured and separated from your unit whilst on patrol behind enemy lines. Your radio's battery life is low and the reception is weak. Choose an appropriate method of transmitting a request for immediate evacuation. You will need to give details of your medical condition, your location and that of the enemy as well as the risk they pose to your rescuers.

6 Devise a message to send to a partner using semaphore. The message should be no shorter that 20 words and should include numbers as well as letters.

7 Pass a message over a distance of no shorter than 200 metres using heliographs. The message should be no shorter than 20 words.

End of unit questions

1 What is the difference between letters and memos?

2 List the security classifications used by the Army.

3 What information should be included in all forms of written communication?

4 Name the branch of the Army responsible for communications.

5 List the problems associated with radio use encountered by the public services.

6 What are the main differences between types of radio?

7 What are the rules for radio discipline?

8 What is BATCO and why is it used?

9 Explain the following prowords: Roger, Wait out, Radio check.

10 What does 'rebro' mean?

11 Give two advantages and two disadvantages for Morse code.

12 Which public service makes most use of signalling flags? Why?

13 What is a heliograph?

14 What is 'satcom'?

15 In what kind of situations would the public services use hand signals?

16 What form of communication is taking over from memos in many situations?

17 How many types of communication do you use to communicate with people?

18 What is a radio net?

19 What is the phonetic alphabet?

20 Explain the differences between a walkie-talkie and a field telephone.

Resources

Websites

Radiocommunications Agency: government agency responsible for non-military radio communications: http://www.radio.gov.uk/

Advice on radio usage from UNHCR: http://www.reliefweb.int/telecoms/training/unhcrradio.html

Website of the Royal Corps of Signals, the Army's specialists in communications: http://www.army.mod.uk/royalsignals/

Police Information Technology Organisation – provides the police with IT and communications equipment: http://www.pito.org.uk/index.htm

Motorola, manufacturer of many popular radio systems: http://www.motorola.com/

Radio manufacturer: http://www.racalcomm.com/

Radio manufacturer: http://www.icomamerica.com/

How Stornoway Coastguard use communications: http://www.barvasmoor.freeserve.co.uk/communications.htm

Website of the Maritime and Coastguard Agency: http://www.mcga.gov.uk/c4mca/mcga-home.htm

West Sussex Fire Brigade's communications history: http://www.wsfb.co.uk/firecomms.html

Assessment activities

This section describes what you must do to obtain a pass grade for this unit.

A merit or distinction grade may be awarded if your work demonstrates a deeper understanding of the topics and is of a higher quality. The highlighted sentences indicate the quality of work expected at merit and distinction level.

Assessment methods

A number of assessment strategies may be used in order to achieve the learning outcomes, such as oral presentations, group discussions, written assignments, research projects and role-plays, or a combination of these. It is a good idea, though it is not essential, to use a variety of methods in order to develop different skills.

What is important, however, is that you understand and comply with the key words specified in the grading criteria. For example, if you are asked to 'analyse' something, then make sure that you do not merely describe it. Similarly, if you are asked to 'evaluate' something, then make sure you do not merely summarise it.

Key words

Here are some key words that are often used for grading criteria – make sure you understand the differences between them.

Examine	To look at a subject closely in order to understand it and improve your knowledge
Consider	This means to think about and weigh up a subject
Explain	This means to make something clear and set out the arguments
Analyse	This means to look at a subject closely and interpret or evaluate your findings. Perhaps outlining the pro's and con's of a situation or suggesting changes and improvements
Describe	This means to say what something is like, it is a factual account of how something is or how it appears.
Compare	This means to look at the similarities between two or more objects or theories.

Assessment tasks

Using the materials within this unit and your own research, carry out the following tasks.

Task 1

Learning outcome 1 – Investigate types of formal written investigation used in the public services

Investigate the formal written formats of communication used in the public services.

Explain how and why reports are used.

To obtain a merit grade, you should *analyse* the use of reports in signals and communication.

To obtain a distinction grade, you should *justify* the use of different types of formal written communications signals and other forms of communication transmission.

Suggestion for Task 1: written assignment

Research and evaluate the various forms of formal written communication used in the public services. You should use the content of this chapter and contact a local public service of your choice for further information. Include any letters or other forms of written communication within this service as they will be valuable reference material for the assignment.

Include a bibliography and acknowledgements section detailing where your information came from.

Task 2

Learning outcome 2 – Investigate and compare radios and radio communication in public service work

Suggestion for Task 2: presentation

Research radios and the way in which they are used in two public services. You need to look at the details of the radios themselves (manufacturer and specifications) and the way in which they are used (as part of a radio net; for secure communications; ease of use, etc).

Present your findings to your group using visual aids, for example PowerPoint over head projectors.

Obtain a witness testament from your assessor to prove that you have completed the outcome.

Task 3

Learning outcome 3 – Explain other forms of communication transmission in public service work

Identify and explain other forms of transmitted communications and then the need for other forms of transmitted communication.

Compare the advantages and disadvantages of other forms of communications transmission.

To otain a merit grade you should *analyse* the need for other forms of transmitted communications and their advantages and disadvantages.

Suggestion for Task 3: leaflet

Create a leaflet for new recruits in a public service of your choice, detailing various types of communication used in that service other than formal written or by radio. You must describe these other forms of communication, using diagrams where appropriate and investigate why they are used.

Your leaflet should be three to six pages long and be relevant to the topic and its intended audience.

Task 4

Learning outcome 4 – Demonstrate practical signalling and communications skills

Produce written forms of formal communication using the correct format.

Pass simple messages on a radio net using a standard voice procedure and using at least two forms of transmitted communications.

> To obtain a merit, you should use correct voice procedure when using at least one radio communications system and demonstrate skills required to send a complex message using two other forms of transmitted communications.

> To obtain a distinction, you should demonstrate competent and confident voice procedure usage when using at least one radio communication system and competence in two other forms of transmitted communication.

Suggestion for Task 4: practical assessment

Scenario: you are part of a search and rescue team operating behind enemy lines in an urban environment. In order to liberate some prisoners of war, your group has split up to search the area.

You have seen two of the POWs and have assessed their location and enemy security. You must pass this information on to the other members of your team as well as your base. Unfortunately, there are some problems with your radio communications associated with a recent solar flare. Consequently, some of your mobile radios are not working and you must use alternative forms of communication to pass on your information to the team. You can still communicate with base via radio, though.

You must transmit the following information:

1 Objective discovered.
2 Two prisoners are located in an office on the second floor of the college building.
3 Two guards are outside the door and there are no windows to the office.
4 One of the prisoners has trouble walking.

All of the messages must be transmitted to base via radio.

You must send two messages to your team-mates using alternatives forms of communication (such as morse code or semaphore).

Following your practical communications exercise, you must produce a report of the operation using the correct format.

Produce a memo to a Royal Electrical and Mechanical Engineer (REME) technician informing them of your team's problems with the radios.

MAJOR INCIDENTS

Introduction to Unit 24

This chapter aims to help you understand the effects on individuals, communities and organisations of major incidents and disasters. It will consider how public service organisations plan for and deal with such incidents and the impact of an incident on the environment and on the physical and social well being of the people involved.

In addition, this chapter will consider how multiple public services work together to deal with major incidents and the problems that can arise with inter-agency cooperation and communication. It will examine how public service responses to major incidents are reviewed and the potential long-term policy and procedural implications of disasters and major incidents.

Assessment

Throughout the unit, activities and tasks will help you to learn and remember information. Case studies are also included to add industry relevance to the topics and learning objectives. At the end of the unit there are assessment activities to help you provide evidence which meets the learning outcomes for the unit. You are reminded that when you are completing activities and tasks, opportunities will be created to enhance your key skills evidence.

After completing this unit you should have an understanding of the following outcomes.

Outcomes

1 Examine the **effects of disaster and major incident situations**

2 Investigate **disaster planning and prevention**

3 Investigate **inter-agency cooperation** between services

4 Analyse the **impact** of a specified disaster or major incident situation on individuals and communities

Effects of disaster and major incident situations

Dealing with disasters and attending major incidents has always been a key role of the public services but in today's climate of increased global and national terrorist threats it has become even more important. The impact of events such as the destruction of the World Trade Centre have become global media events and the heroism of the men and women of New York's pubic services has become legendary. However, not all major incidents capture public interest or outrage in this way or are considered particularly newsworthy by the media. Major incidents happen on a daily basis around the world and it is the responsibility of all public services to work together to plan for and deal with the consequences of them.

The consequences of major incidents are wide ranging and involve effects on the individual such as death, injury, disability, psychological trauma and the loss of loved ones. This includes incidents such as the sinking of the Herald of Free Enterprise and the Southall rail crash amongst others. An incident may also have dramatic effects on the communities involved, destroying its social infrastructure and its physical surroundings leaving communities homeless and fractured, such as the Gujerat and Kobe earthquakes. The environmental effects of major incidents can also be disastrous for the long term health and well being of individuals and communities. Disasters can leave environmental pollution and chemical contamination in their wake such as happened at the Chernobyl nuclear power plant.

Aspects of major incidents

'Disaster' is a term used to describe a catastrophic event in which there is large-scale loss of life or property. It is a term often used by the media to capture and retain public interest and is a highly emotive term bringing to mind notions of widespread destruction and death.

The public services prefer the term 'major incident' to describe such an event. In technical terms a major incident is an occurrence which requires the implementation of special arrangements by one or more public services. According to the Association of Chief Police Officers (ACPO) Emergency Procedures Manual, major incidents may involve many aspects (see Figure 24.1 below).

Many types of major incidents may occur which require a combined public service response. In the UK, different government departments are responsible for different types of major incidents. This means that although the public services carry out their duties according to a major incident plan (this will be discussed in more detail later) a different government ministry will lead the strategic review and enquiry depending upon the nature of the major incident as shown in Figure 24.2 overleaf.

It is clear to see from the range of possible incidents shown in the table that the modern public services must be able and ready to attend a variety of major incidents each with its own risks and consequences and each with a different government department at its head. They must be equipped to liaise with a variety of other public services and differing lead government departments.

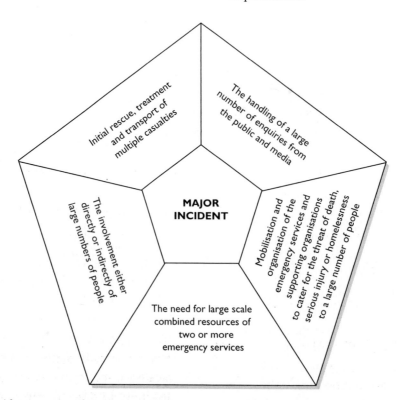

Figure 24.1 A major incident can involve many aspects

Major incident	Example	Lead government body dealing with the incident
Flooding	River bursts its banks	Department of Environment, Food and Rural Affairs (Defra)
Marine/coastal pollution	Spills from oil tankers	Defra
Radiation hazards in UK	Leaks from nuclear power plant	Department of Trade and Industry
Radiation hazards outside UK	A leak from a foreign nuclear reactor such as the Chernobyl incident in 1986	Defra
Satellite incidents	Satellites re-entering the atmosphere	Home Office
Emergencies on offshore installations	An oil terminal explosion such as the one faced by the Piper Alpha rig in the North Sea in 1989	Defra
Disasters overseas	A situation where UK aid is sought such as the Gujerat Earthquake in 2001	Foreign and Commonwealth Office
Search and rescue	The sinking of a ship and rescue of survivors such as the Herald of Free Enterprise ferry in 1987	Civil Ships – Department for Transport, Local Government and Regions (Coastguard Agency) Military Ships – Ministry of Defence (MOD)
Severe storms	Hurricanes such as the one which hit the South Coast in 1987	Home Office
Sports grounds accidents	Deaths or injuries at football or other sporting venues. Examples of this include the Bradford Fire in 1985 and the Hillsborough Disaster in 1989	Dept of Culture, Media and Sport
Major explosions or structural failures	Disasters caused by gas explosions, dam breaches or the collapse of buildings	Defra
Unexpected bombs	Suspect packages or unexploded World War II ordnance	Home Office

Figure 24.2 Table showing the different government bodies dealing with major incidents

Think about it

Look at Figure 24.2, identify one disaster and consider:

- what impact it might have on the individuals concerned?

- what wider impact it might have on a community?

Types of disasters and major incidents

Although there are many types of disasters ranging from flooding to explosions to transport incidents, the causes of these incidents can generally be divided into 3 broad categories:

1 Human causes

2 Technological causes

3 Natural causes

These categories cover the vast range of major incidents that a member of a public service could possibly expect to encounter in day-to-day operations.

Human causes

The human causes of major incidents are due to the mistakes or deliberate acts of some of the individuals involved. Examples of human causes are factors such as:

- pilot error
- driver error
- intoxication/drugs
- speeding
- terrorist acts
- sabotage
- incompetence.

Examples of major incidents with identified human causes are found all over the world. Two examples in the UK are the sinking of The Herald of Free Enterprise where the large bow doors of a passenger and freight ferry were left open by accident and the Kegworth Air Disaster in which pilot error was blamed.

Theory into practice

Research the Kegworth air disaster and describe the human causes of the incident.

Case study – The Herald of Free Enterprise

The Herald of Free Enterprise sank on 6th March 1987 only minutes after leaving the port of Zeebrugge in Belgium en route to its destination in Dover. Of the 530 or so crew and passengers, 189 lost their lives. It became the worst peacetime disaster for maritime Britain since the sinking of the Titanic in 1912.

The Herald of Free Enterprise was a large modern car passenger ferry of a type commonly called a roll on/roll off (ro/ro). It was a system which allowed cars to roll on or enter at one end of the ship and drive straight off at the other end of the ship when reaching the destination port.

These type of ferries must have large doors allowing cars and lorries to enter at both the bow and stern of the ship. In addition, the deck space for vehicles is large and open containing no watertight bulkheads. This means that if water enters the deck it is free to go wherever gravity and the movement of the ship takes it. These were crucial factors in the sinking.

The ferry had set sail from Zeebrugge with the bow doors open and as she picked up speed water began to spill over the open doors at a rate of up to 200 tons per minute. This volume of water in open deck space almost immediately rendered the ship unstable causing a 30-degree list to port which then forced the rest of the flood to the same place. The speed of the capsize was astonishing and left no time for the crew and passengers to escape. The capsize took around 90 seconds.

The sequence of events which led to the bow doors being left open points directly to human and organisational error. The assistant bosun whose responsibility it had been to close the doors was relieved of duties by the bosun and went to bed. The bosun did not supervise the closing of the doors as it was not part of his job. To compound matters the bow doors were of a clam shell design, which opened and closed on a horizontal plane meaning the bridge crew could not visually observe the status of the doors. In addition, the bridge had no warning lights or alarms which would indicate that all was not well.

The rescue operation began immediately. A nearby vessel that had seen the lights of the ferry disappear radioed port control at Zeebrugge who activated their major incident plan.

The Herald of Free Enterprise

The port arranged civilian crisis centres to register and treat survivors and all of the local hospitals. Although the rescue operation was swift it was not without its problems. Lorin and Norberg (1989) note that there was 'no coordination' between the military and civilian rescue operations. In major incident scenarios effective communication between all parties involved is a crucial element in effective search and rescue and can enhance the operational effectiveness of the response. In addition, there was substantial confusion in processing the survivors and the bodies of the deceased and many were double counted giving inaccurate data to the rescue teams, the public and the media.

The effects of this disaster were to change the way ro/ro ferries were operated with the introduction of new maritime safety regulations, which included the installation of bulkheads, additional flotation devices in the hulls of ferries and the mandatory installation of bow door warning lights.

1   Do the advantages of large bow doors outweigh the disadvantages of them?

2   In your opinion who is ultimately responsible for the sinking of The Herald?

3   Can you think of some recommendations that would help the public services work together in incidents such as this?

Technological causes

Technological causes of major incidents are also relatively common and relate to the failure of equipment or structures which are not fit for their purpose usually due to age, overuse and lack of maintenance. Examples of technological causes are as follows:

- metal fatigue
- faulty wiring
- design faults
- extreme physical stress which the technology was not designed to cope with
- insufficient maintenance
- equipment failure
- inappropriate equipment used.

Examples of major incidents in which the technological causes take primary responsibility are the explosion of Air France Concorde flight 4590 in 2000 in which a burst tyre on take off led to the rupture of a fuel tank and the fire in the Station Nightclub in Rhode Island, USA in which a pyrotechnic display used on stage caused a fire which killed over 95 people in February 2003.

Theory into practice

Research and describe the technological causes of two major incidents, one UK based, the other international.

Case study – The explosion of Air France flight 4590

On 25th July 2000, Air France flight 4590 crashed into a hotel in the town of Gonesse just outside Paris with the loss of all on board and several fatalities on the ground. What makes this incident so memorable is that flight 4590 was a Concorde, the world's only supersonic aircraft.

Flight 4590 began its take off at Charles de Gaulle Airport at 4.44pm (local time) and exploded 2 minutes later as the pilot desperately tried to turn the plane to make an emergency landing at Le Bourget Airport just one minute away. The French Accident Investigation Bureau concluded that the explosion was caused by a strip of metal which fell off a Continental Airlines DC-10, which had just taken off from the same runway. The metal fragment punctured one of the tyres on Concorde's landing gears shooting heavy pieces of rubber in the direction of the under wing fuel tanks.

Air France flight 4590 with underwing fire visible at take off

The fuel in the tanks ignited leading to a fire which caused a loss of engine power. It was too late to abort take off and Concorde began its assent with its wing engulfed in flames. The black box account of the final 2 minutes of the flight indicate clearly that the crew fought to stabilise the aircraft but it went into an 'airframe stall' which is a loss of control due to a lack of speed and lift. In total, 110 passengers and crew were killed and 4 people were killed in Gonesse as a result of the impact.

The emergency response had begun even before Concorde crashed. The emergency crews at Charles de Gaulle airport had been scrambled as soon as the fire on the wing was spotted. A local network alarm system notified fire response teams at the neighbouring Le Bourget Airport and these were the first to arrive on the scene at Gonesse. The high speed impact of the fuel laden aircraft ensured there would be no survivors on board and the main job of the response crews was to establish cordons, contain the fires and ensure that any ground based casualties received prompt rescue and treatment.

The technological factors here are crucial in understanding the causes of the incident. Firstly, there is the 40 cm metal strip which fell from the DC-10 aircraft on take off. Pieces of aircraft do not routinely fall off and it is an unusual occurrence for it to do so, but more startling is the fact that this piece of metal could cause a tyre to blow out on Concorde leaving 114 people dead. Aviation companies operate a safety rule which states that no one equipment failure on an aircraft should be sufficient to cause a crash. Clearly the damage caused by an exploding tyre should not be sufficient to cause such a catastrophe.

All remaining French Concorde aircraft had their flight certification suspended until necessary modifications could be made to ensure that the same event could not occur again. The British fleet of Concordes were temporarily grounded, but resumed normal flights within days. Air France Concorde flights resumed again in November 2001.

1 Why was there no possibility of survivors from the plane?
2 Do you think Continental Airlines are responsible for the incident?
3 What do you think was the impact of the crash on the town of Gonesse?
4 Was Air France right to ground its Concorde fleet after the incident?

Case study – The Gujerat earthquake 2001

On 26th January 2001 the most devastating earthquake to hit India in 50 years struck the North West state of Gujerat. Earthquakes are caused by sudden movements in the Earth's crust, which lead to violent shaking of the ground and the consequent destruction of life and property. Earthquakes are measured by their magnitude on the Richter scale. The earthquake which struck Gujerat, measured 7.9 on the Richter scale and had a devastating impact across a 100 km radius.

The Gujerat earthquake 2001

Estimates put the number of dead at around 20,000 and injured at 170,000. Up to 300,000 people were left homeless and in some towns the earthquake rendered 95% of the structures uninhabitable. In an accident such as this, major incident plans (if they exist) are often of no use as the public service infrastructure including police, fire and hospitals are destroyed along with everything else.

Generally aid has to come from outside the affected area and this can take time and cost lives. The initial impact of the Gujerat earthquake on the people and communities involved was only the beginning. Many other difficulties were caused by the earthquake bringing hardship to survivors and creating challenges which hampered response teams including:

- road destruction cutting off routes of entry to the incident zone
- widespread power failure
- widespread communications failure
- disruption to and pollution of water supplies
- the threat of aftershocks
- unstable structures
- health threats posed by thousands of decaying or buried corpses
- loss of public service professionals in the affected area
- loss of airports and ports to facilitate transport.

In events such as this, the remainder of the country's military and civilian forces combine with specialist overseas aid agencies and foreign public service representatives to deal with the situation.

The effects of an incident on this scale include:

- deaths, human suffering and injury
- billions of pounds of property and capital investment destroyed
- destruction of the public service infrastructure leading to possible violence, looting and gang culture
- destruction of the healthcare infrastructure leading to injured survivors dying and other survivors without healthcare
- widespread risk of epidemics from diseases such as cholera
- widespread damage to the environment affecting traditional industries such as farming and fishing
- environmental effects such as floods and mudslides.

1   Why was the devastation caused by the earthquake more severe in India than it would have been in a nation like the USA?

2   What overseas aid agencies became involved in the rescue and recovery effort?

3   Why is a combined public services response difficult in natural disasters?

4   What impact does a delayed public service response have on the situation?

Natural causes

The natural causes of major incidents are not very common in the UK but other parts of the world are not as fortunate as we are and they may have to deal with a whole range of major incidents and emergencies which would seem alien to our own public services. Causes of natural disasters include conditions such as:

- earthquakes
- mudslides
- floods
- volcanoes
- hurricanes
- tornadoes
- drought and famine
- forest fires
- disease epidemics.

Examples of large-scale natural disasters which have killed many thousands of people are not difficult to find throughout human history, for example the biblical accounts of Noah's flood, the destruction of Pompeii by the volcano Vesuvius, the bubonic plague epidemics in the 17th century and the droughts and famines in Africa in the late twentieth century. Recent examples are the Gujerat Earthquake in India in 2001 which killed an estimated 20,000 people and the floods/mudslides which hit Venezuela in 1999 which killed thousands and left up to 100,000 people homeless.

Theory into practice

Research the last time the UK was hit by an earthquake. Identify its magnitude on the Richter scale and describe the damage it did and the response of the public services to it.

Multiple causes of disasters

Many disasters may have multiple causes, for example flooding in Venezuela in 1999 (see Figure 24.3). It can often be very difficult to establish which factor was actually the real cause of a disaster situation, which is why teams of experts are often commissioned to research the causal factors in a major incident. If you can understand why an incident has happened you are on the first step of the ladder to reducing the risk of it happening again and being better prepared to deal with it if it does.

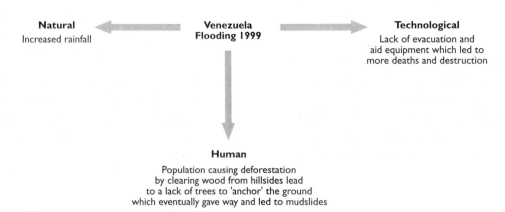

Natural
Increased rainfall

Venezuela Flooding 1999

Technological
Lack of evacuation and aid equipment which led to more deaths and destruction

Human
Population causing deforestation by clearing wood from hillsides lead to a lack of trees to 'anchor' the ground which eventually gave way and led to mudslides

Figure 24.3 Some disasters may have multiple causes

Potters Bar rail crash

Theory into practice

Examine the famines that occurred in Ethiopia throughout the 1980s and explain the range of causal factors behind it including human, technological and natural factors.

British major incident – Potters Bar rail crash

One example of a British major incident is the Potters Bar rail crash which happened on the 10th May 2002 when a WAGN service running from London to Kings Lynn crashed at Potters Bar in Hertfordshire. 5 people died at the scene and 2 died later in hospital. Over 70 people were injured, 11 of them critically.

The train was travelling at around 100 mph when the train derailed and crashed into the station. One of the carriages mounted the station platform and ploughed across it, stopping only when it hit and destroyed a bridge.

The Health and Safety Executive (HSE) report on the incident blamed missing nuts in a set of points which led to a point's failure. This point's failure 'squeezed' the wheels of the rear coach causing the wheels to climb the rails and become derailed. The train was carrying over 150 people at the time and it is remarkable that so few people died. Within 2 minutes of the crash, Hertfordshire's major incident plan had been implemented and within 5 minutes emergency vehicles were arriving at the scene.

In total, 19 ambulances were deployed and 11 fire engines from both Hertfordshire and London. The police established and maintained cordons and co-ordinated the rescue and recovery. Local hospitals cancelled planned surgery lists as they prepared to take in large numbers of seriously wounded survivors. A local branch of Sainsbury's was used as an emergency treatment centre caring for the less severely injured until they could receive hospital treatment.

The investigation of the incident was lead by the British Transport Police in conjunction with the Health and Safety Executive (HSE). The HSE report made several key recommendations to Railtrack, the owners of the faulty points.

● carry out a review of points to see if any modifications are required

● consider replacing the existing points system with one that is designed to be safer

● review the procedures for installing, settling, adjusting, maintenance, inspection and testing of points

● ensure all those working with points understand the relevant standards which need to be implemented if they are to be safe

● review the arrangements for reporting, recording, reviewing and acting upon deficiencies found with the safety of points

● where contractors and sub-contractors are used their staff should be reviewed to ensure competency, training, qualifications and experience when engaged in safety related work.

International major incident – Chernobyl

One example of a major international incident occurred on 25th April 1986 at the Chernobyl power plant in the former USSR (now Ukraine). The nuclear power station had 4 reactors and it was tests being conducted on reactor number 4 which led to the disaster. The test concerned the capability of the plant equipment to support the reactor cooling system and emergency equipment; it was not considered a risk as it concerned a non-nuclear part of the power plant's systems.

This lack of awareness of risk led to a lack of communication and cooperation between the team operating the test and the team responsible for reactor safety. Consequently, insufficient safety precautions were employed in the test and the plant operators took a number of actions that were contrary to established safety procedures.

Chernobyl power plant

A resulting power surge caused a sudden increase in temperature within the reactor causing part of the nuclear fuel to rupture and fuel particles to react with water coolant causing an explosion, which destroyed the reactor.

The effects of the Chernobyl incident were widespread and are still ongoing today. They include factors such as:

Health effects – 30 people died and 140 people who were on site or involved in the fire fighting operation suffered radiation sickness or radiation induced health problems. One of the most striking health effects is the rise in the incidence of thyroid cancer in children and babies who were exposed to radioactive particles at the time of the incident. In the 10 years after the explosion childhood thyroid cancer incidents rose by a factor of 8 from 4–6 incidences per million prior to the accident to 45 incidences per million after. There were also significant psychological health effects as the population dealt with the fear of the effects of the radiation coupled with the destruction of communities and social networks due to enforced relocation.

Agricultural/environmental effects – The release of radioactive particles into the atmosphere and their resultant return to Earth has left large tracts of agricultural land unstable inside the Ukraine. In other areas of contamination, farming is subject to strict safety and monitoring protocols. It is estimated that it could take up to 300 years for all of the radioactive particles to completely decay. The problem was not as drastic in other nations although there are still restrictions today on some UK sheep, Scandinavian reindeer and fish from some Swedish lakes.

The nuclear reactor at Chernobyl is still highly radioactive and has the potential to cause tremendous damage. Is it currently encased in a concrete shell, but this cannot be a permanent solution and eventually the concrete will deteriorate. The question about what could be done with it still remains unanswered. The

Chernobyl incident, although 17 years old has left a legacy, which may continue for many generations. The incident focused the minds of all those who work in the nuclear industry on safety and incident management which may go some way to helping prevent another disastrous incident like Chernobyl.

Theory into practice

1 Why didn't the USSR have a major incident plan to cover the eventuality of a nuclear accident like Chernobyl?

2 What were the communications problems which led to the Chernobyl incident?

3 What are the long-term effects of the disaster for the local area?

4 What are the long term effects of this incident globally?

Terrorist incident – the Omagh bombing

On the 15th August 1998 at 3.10pm a 500 lb car bomb exploded in the busy shopping district of the Northern Ireland town of Omagh. This appalling act of terror marked the single worst atrocity in the 30-year history of the recent troubles. It claimed the lives of 29 people including a 20-month-old baby girl and a woman heavily pregnant with twins. Many more were injured, 311 received hospital care and 129 were admitted to hospital for more severe injuries.

The Royal Ulster Constabulary announced their suspicions that the Real Irish Republican Army (RIRA) was responsible for the attack and within days these suspicions were confirmed when the RIRA admitted responsibility. The RIRA is a splinter faction of the Provisional IRA who separated in 1997 due to objections about ongoing peace negotiations.

The blast devastated the shopping centre of Omagh. Close to the blast, buildings were destroyed and people were killed. Further away, flying metal, glass and masonry caused many injuries, the blast wave tore the limbs from several people and the intense heat caused burns. A water main under the blast burst and added to the carnage and confusion.

Many police were already in Omagh centre searching for a potential bomb due to telephone warnings that had been received earlier. In addition, the Northern Irish public services are sadly used to dealing with the aftermath of terrorist incidents. Both of these factors led to an almost immediate public service response. The Royal Ulster Constabulary (RUC) immediately set up cordons and began coordinating the disaster response. They put appeals out on local radio for all medical personnel to go to local hospitals to help the rescue effort.

A large fleet of ambulances ferried the injured to a total of 8 hospitals. The Army were brought in to supplement the 50 or so firefighters who were at the site of the blast to search for buried survivors under the devastated wreckage of the town centre. Communications were put under intense strain due to hundreds of members of the public phoning the public services, hospitals and local voluntary organisations trying to get news of dead or injured relatives. This was further exacerbated by the damage to communications systems caused by the bomb blast itself.

The success of the Omagh major incident response was helped by the fact that 2 months before the bombing all of the local agencies involved in emergency response planning had taken part in a large-scale major incident simulation of a road accident. This simulation tested many of the actions and routes used subsequently in Omagh. The benefits of major incident simulations will be discussed later in this chapter.

The effects on individuals involved in the Omagh bombing are both short and long term and have much in common with the effects of other major incidents:

- death
- severe injury
- minor injury
- permanent disability
- post traumatic stress disorder
- loss of loved ones
- loss of businesses and livelihoods
- psychological trauma.

Theory into practice

1 Why was the public service response able to be implemented so quickly in the case of the Omagh bombing?

2 What was the role of the Army in the rescue and recovery operation?

3 List and describe the communications difficulties posed by the Omagh bombing.

Disaster planning and prevention

The broad nature of the types of disaster that can occur and the varying scales of the sizes of major incidents make effective planning and prevention strategies a key aspect of the public services response.

As a result, most local authorities produce major incident plans in conjunction with the local emergency services. There is currently no legal obligation for local authorities to undertake emergency planning but almost all do in order to ensure the safety of the public and to protect itself from the legal consequences of victims and survivors of major incidents suing them for breach of care.

A major incident plan is a document which sets out the roles, responsibilities and possible responses of the public services to a range of possible major incidents, such as flooding, terrorist attack or transport accidents. There are 3 types of incident plans:

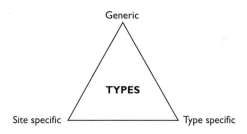

Figure 24.4 There are 3 types of incident plans used in the public services

1 **Generic plans** – These are general plans which do not apply to a specific situation but which could be adapted to cover a variety of eventualities.

2 **Type specific plans** – These are plans drawn up for a specific kind of major incident such as a flood management plan or a plan for a biological terrorist attack. They are developed when it is considered likely that a major incident will happen in a specific region. For example, some areas are more prone to flooding than others and so a type specific flooding plan would be of use to these areas.

3 **Site specific plans** – These are disaster plans which cater to a specific location or site such as town centre evacuation plans, shopping centre evacuations or chemical plant responses. They are produced when a particular site may become the scene of a major incident. For instance, if a chemical plant is located near a highly populated area it is sensible to plan for a chemical leak or explosion. Site specific plans can include very detailed information such as who is responsible for specific actions and which buildings/locations are designated for which purposes.

Once the plans are drawn up they are 'exercised' or simulated to ensure that they actually do what they are intended to do. This is very important as the potential for confusion, lack of communication and repetition of acts such as counting the dead and injured is very high. It is vital to ensure that the roles and responsibilities of each attending service do not cross over, but rather that they run easily side-by-side. When a major incident plan has been successfully tested it is circulated to all of the agencies who may be called upon to provide a response. This ensures that all agencies work to the same plan.

Think about it

What would be the implications of a major incident occurring without a major incident plan being in place to the following groups:

- the public services
- the health service.

Key features of a major incident plan

An effective major incident plan will seek to address the following factors.

- To establish what constitutes a major incident and what stages are likely to occur in an emergency. This allows all parties involved to share an accurate definition of what a major incident is so that a situation is not wrongly classified. If a minor incident is classed as a major one by mistake it will cost a tremendous amount financially and also in terms of human and technological resources to scramble the appropriate personnel and equipment. Equally, if there is delay in confirming a situation as a major incident then the response plan will not be swiftly implemented and public safety may be compromised.

- It will highlight and clarify the roles and responsibilities of the attending services. Although the public services perform different functions there can be overlap between their duties in normal operational life. For example, a firefighter can also be a trained paramedic. This overlap can cause confusion at the scene of a major incident and may cause errors to be made which misinform the public or compromise safety. In the Herald of Free

Enterprise incident the number of casualties and missing were initially unclear due to double counting and confusion over whose role it was to complete a count. If this were to happen in a major incident today, rescuers would not know how many people remained to be recovered and they might abandon rescue plans prematurely.

- Major incident plans must also identify the necessary coordinated arrangements with existing public, health and voluntary services who may be called upon to participate in a major incident. When disasters are considered, many individuals will recognise that the 3 emergency services are likely to be involved but may not understand the breadth of organisations which may be called upon to give assistance. All of these organisations must coordinate with each other and the local authority to ensure that plans are adequate and realistic and that specialist knowledge is in evidence.

- Building on the last point of coordination, a major incident plan must identify the communications systems and resources available to respond in the event of a large emergency. Most public services use communications which operate on different frequencies to avoid operational confusion in day to day life, but in a major incident effective cross service communications need to be present if a rescue and recovery operation is to be effective. All levels of a command structure need to be able to communicate with each other and be aware of what is going on in the surrounding area.

Organisations involved in emergency planning and response

There are 2 main groups of individuals involved in emergency planning and responding to major incidents:

- public services
- voluntary agencies.

Public services are those groups who usually provide the first response to a major incident and voluntary agencies act as support for the public services. Some of the organisations involved are shown in Figure 24.5. It is not possible in the scope of this chapter to examine all of these agencies so only a selection of public services and voluntary organisations will be discussed.

Emergency response from public services

The police service

The police service plays a key role in emergency response at the scene of major incidents as it is their role to coordinate the activities of all of the other responding agencies. They must ensure that the scene is protected from unnecessary interference and must collect evidence which might be needed for a criminal prosecution to be taken against those individuals or organisations which caused the incident.

In addition to coordinating the scene, they also have a role in helping and supporting the other public services in their roles. For instance, the police establish and maintain cordons which are protective perimeters around the work of the other services. Usually in a major incident 3 types of cordon might be deployed.

- **Inner:** around the disaster site itself.
- **Outer:** contains command centres, body holding areas, ambulance points.
- **Traffic:** to divert traffic away from the surrounding area enabling public service vehicles to move freely and preventing the disaster site becoming a public spectacle.

It is also the responsibility of the police at the scene of a major incident to collect and process information about casualties and arrange for the dead to be identified and removed until such time as the relatives come forward to claim them. They work very closely with Her Majesty's Coroner who ultimately establishes the cause of death via an autopsy.

The police have primary responsibility for conducting any criminal investigation based on

Public services	Voluntary agencies
The Police Service	British Red Cross
The Fire Service	St John Ambulance Brigade
The Ambulance Service	Womens Royal Voluntary Service (WRVS)
The RAF	Radio Amateur Emergency Network (RAYNET)
The Army	RSPCA
The Royal Navy	Citizens Advice Bureau
Local Authorities	Churches
Health Authorities	Salvation Army
HM Coroner	Cruse (Bereavement care)
Local hospitals	Victim Support
HM Coastguard	Mountain Rescue/Cave Rescue
The Environment Agency	Royal National Lifeboat Institution

Figure 24.5 Organisations involved in emergency planning and responding to major incidents

Cordons provide protective perimeters

the evidence they have gathered. In the case of a rail disaster this duty falls to the British Transport Police. In common with all of the public services the police will also undertake rescue work and the savings of lives at an incident.

The fire service

One of the main roles of the fire service at the scene of a disaster is to coordinate and conduct the rescue and recovery operation. This involves finding people trapped in wreckage or under debris with the use of specialist equipment such as hydraulic cutting equipment or thermal imaging cameras. Another one of their roles is to prevent the spread of any fires, put out existing blazes and taking preventative action to stop fire starting. This may include neutralising fire accelerants such as fuel and removing flammable objects from the inner cordon if possible. The fire service is also required to deal with chemical or hazardous waste at the scene of a major incident to ensure there is minimum contamination and injury to the environment, ordinary citizens and public service rescue workers.

This duty of care is extended in that the fire service has direct responsibility for all public service workers within the inner cordon regardless of which service they belong to. This means that the fire service must ensure that all inner cordon workers are fully briefed on the dangers and hazards which will be present and are adequately equipped and trained to perform their role. This

ensures that public service casualties and injuries are kept to a minimum. The fire service along with other public services is also responsible for assisting paramedics in the treatment and removal of casualties. Although the police have primary coordination responsibilities, the actual disaster site itself is the province of the fire service.

Case study – train derailment

A local passenger train has derailed on the approach to a major town. Several carriages have left the tracks and one of them is on fire. It appears that there are multiple seriously injured casualties and several fatalities. The major incident plan has been implemented and the public services scrambled.

1   Which service has the primary command and coordination role in the event of a rail crash?

2   Which service is responsible for the safety of those within the inner cordon?

3   What are the potential communications issues in this scenario?

4   What are the potential command problems in this scenario?

5   Draw a diagram of the crash site demonstrating how cordons might be situated.

The ambulance service

The ambulance service has primary responsibility for the treatment and transport of casualties at the scene of a major incident. They decide which individuals are most in need of immediate treatment and prioritise their response accordingly. This is a process known as 'triage'. Paramedics also decide which hospital to take casualties to. This is very important, particular when large numbers of people are injured and local hospitals might easily become overwhelmed. The ambulance service also has primary responsibility for the decontamination of casualties and public service personnel in the case of a chemical or biological incident.

Case study – road traffic incident

This morning there was a major road traffic incident on the main arterial road between 2 large towns. The conditions involved dense fog and slippery road surfaces. The incident involved 15 vehicles including a tanker carrying toxic chemicals and a car transporter. The first agencies at the scene are reporting multiple casualties and at least 3 fatalities. The chemical tanker is in danger of breaching and causing extensive contamination to the area.

1 How will the ambulance service decide on how to prioritise the treatment of casualties?

2 What will be the primary responsibilities of the police service at the scene?

3 What will be the role of the local hospitals?

4 Which agency takes primary responsibility for protecting the environment from potential toxic spills?

5 Which agency has primary responsibility for the decontamination of casualties?

The Armed Services

The Home Office publication 'Dealing with Disaster' describes 3 broad categories of military aid which is available to help support the emergency services during a major incident:

Category A: Assistance in dealing with a natural disaster or major accident

Category B: Short term routine assistance on special projects

Category C: The full time attachment of military personnel to the civilian public services for a specified period

The responsibility for dealing with major incidents lies squarely with civilian public services and the Armed Services are under no obligation to have personnel equipped and ready to respond. If the Armed Services do respond there are several ways in which they can be utilised:

- helicopter reconnaissance of a disaster site
- search and rescue
- deployment of medical personnel and field hospitals
- building structures such as temporary bridges
- specialised equipment and expertise to maintain essential services such as water and electricity
- manpower in activities such as emergency flood prevention.

Civil authorities must be prepared to meet the financial costs of requesting an armed service response if the Army, Navy or RAF decides to levy a charge.

Case study – flooding

Following 2 weeks of heavy rains, the River Timble has risen substantially and is threatening to breach specially prepared flood defences and overwhelm the small village of Timble which has 700 inhabitants. The local authority has activated its emergency flood prevention plan and in addition to the usual services the local army detachment has been called in to support the civilian efforts. Another issue causing considerable concern is the location of Timble sewage processing plant which is a sizable facility that processes the waste water and sewage of several local communities. The plant is directly in the path of the impending flood and there is a substantial risk of contamination of the local water supply and the possible spread of disease.

1 In this scenario what duties would be likely to be allocated to the Army?

2 Whose responsibility would it be to protect the water supply and deal with any water contamination?

3 In the event of a major flood in Timble which service would coordinate the evacuation of the local population?

4 Which service would take the responsibility of protecting businesses and homes left behind in an evacuation from the possibility of looting and burglary?

Think about it

In what kind of real-life situation might the civilian services call for military assistance.

Local authorities

The primary role of the local authority in the area where a major incident occurs is to support the emergency services in the operation of their duties. This must be balanced against maintaining local authority services to the wider community such as healthcare, education and utilities. In the aftermath of a disaster or major incident when the initial rescue response is complete, the role of the local authority becomes much more prominent as they take the lead role in the recovery and rebuilding phase of the incident.

Another major role which many local authorities undertake is the creation and implementation of the disaster plan which will contain arrangements on how to deal with a major incident should it occur.

HM Coastguard

This agency has primary responsibility for the organisation and conduct of maritime search and rescue. It aims to rescue individuals in danger at sea and wherever possible it also seeks to prevent or limit damage to the environment by maritime disasters such as chemical or oil spills.

Think about it

Which other agencies would HM Coastguard work closely with in the case of a maritime disaster?

Combined objectives

Government guidelines in the Home Office publication; 'Dealing with Disaster' state clearly that regardless of any specific responsibilities that the emergency services, Armed services or other public services might have they must all work together in achieving the common combined objectives which follow:

- to save life
- to prevent escalation of disaster
- to relieve suffering
- to safeguard the environment
- to protect property
- to facilitate criminal investigation and judicial, public, technical or other enquiries
- to continue to maintain normal services at an appropriate level
- to inform the public
- to promote self help and recovery
- to restore normality as soon as possible
- to evaluate the response and identify lessons to be learned.

Emergency response from voluntary organisations

In addition to the many public services which may be involved in a major incident response, there are also a number of voluntary organisations who can offer support and aid to the public services and the civilian causalities.

The British Red Cross

As with many voluntary organisations, the Red Cross have only a small staff of full time employees, relying instead on trained volunteers who may be equipped or trained to assist the ambulance service in stretcher bearing and ambulance transport duties as well as welfare and counselling services. They may also be required to perform nursing auxiliary duties at local hospitals in the event of large numbers of casualties overwhelming existing hospital facilities. Another organisation which provides similar services to the Red Cross is the St John Ambulance Brigade.

Womens Royal Voluntary Service (WRVS)

The type of duties performed by the WRVS revolve around welfare issues such as the staffing of reception and rest centres and the provision of food and clothing to parties involved in a major incident.

Radio Amateur Emergency Network (RAYNET)

RAYNET is a crucial source of back up for emergency services communications provision. It consists of licensed amateur radio operators who are willing and able to assist the emergency services if required. RAYNET is capable of providing a self contained emergency communications system in many parts of the country. In addition, they can call upon neighbouring RAYNET groups in adjacent areas or countries in order to extend their provision as far as is required by the emergency services.

Mountain/cave rescue

These services operate on a voluntary basis in many areas of the UK where there is substantial risk to members of the public who hill walk, climb mountains or enjoy caving. These are areas such as Snowdonia in Wales, The Lake District and the Cairngorms in Scotland. Conditions on hills and mountains can be very unpredictable and can leave groups of hikers trapped in freezing conditions. Mountain rescue teams comprise of local individuals with extensive experience in navigating the local terrain who are trained in rescue techniques and first aid. They have obvious advantages over other full time public services in situations such as this because they are closer to the incident and have specialist expertise and local knowledge. Similarly, if a party is trapped underground these volunteers may be the best-equipped and trained service to rescue them.

Think about it

Describe the roles of the following voluntary services and list how they might assist emergency services at the scene of a major incident.

- RSPCA
- Citizens' Advice Bureau
- The Salvation Army
- The Clergy

Case study – terrorist attack

A large explosive device detonates in a busy shopping centre. There are many hundreds of casualties who require varying levels of treatment. There is also extensive property damage to the shopping centre. The local authority has activated its major incident plan which is site specific and the emergency services are already in attendance.

There are several immediate problems which require action such as dealing with frantic relatives, the treatment of individuals with minor injuries and the distribution of blankets and comfort stations for the wounded. These problems are taking emergency service workers away from other duties.

1 Which voluntary services would the local authority call on to assist in this incident?

2 Which volunteer services would be best equipped to help deal with the large numbers of minor injuries?

3 Which service would be best equipped to organise reception and rest centres?

4 In the event of an emergency service communications failure which voluntary group could help?

5 Which voluntary services could offer counselling to victims?

Simulations and exercises

In order to ensure that a disaster plan runs smoothly it is necessary to run periodic simulations which evaluate how effective a combined emergency and voluntary service response is.

Exercises and simulations should not be seen as being separate from the major incident plan. They should be seen as a vital integrated section of the plan which ensures the plans efficiency in times of disaster. They provide a unique opportunity for a variety of public services and voluntary agencies to come together and practice a combined response to a major incident.

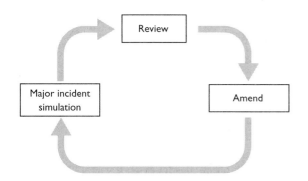

Figure 24.6 The simulation cycle in preparing for major incidents

A simulation or exercise is a recreation of the scene of a major incident which allows the agencies involved to practice their roles and responsibilities in a safe environment. All kinds of incidents may be exercised such as simulated air crashes, terrorist incidents, chemical spillages or public order disturbances. The benefits of these simulations are numerous:

- they provide training opportunities for the services and personnel who may be called to a real incident

- they allow public service organisations to identify and address any operational weaknesses which may emerge during an exercise

- they allow a variety of services to work together and gain an understanding of each others roles and responsibilities which creates a sense of teamwork and professional respect

- the exercising of a response allows the public services to learn from their mistakes before attending a real incident

- businesses, communities and individuals are more likely to survive a major incident

- the response in a real incident is likely to be swift and confident

- the social, financial and legal consequences of a major incident are likely to be minimised

- they allow for contingency plans to be tested

- they reassure the general public that the services are an effective team who are able to respond to any emergency.

There are some disadvantages to exercising disaster plans such as the financial cost, the extensive planning and preparation and the drain on manpower. However, many of these drawbacks can be minimised depending on the type of simulation used.

Generally simulations and exercises fall into four main categories each with their own advantages and disadvantages as shown in Figure 24.7:

1 Seminar

2 Table top

3 Control post

4 Live

Think about it

Is the financial cost of exercises outweighed by the benefits of them?

Seminar

A seminar is a discussion based exercise which is designed to outline to all the agencies involved exactly what their roles and responsibilities are and what the procedures would be in dealing with a particular major incident. This can be done as part of a large group or can break down into smaller groups to discuss one particular aspect of the emergency response or focus on the responsibilities of one particular service.

Table top

This is similar in nature to a seminar exercise but it generally involves fewer individuals. The public services and any other agencies talk through their responses to a specified major incident in the order in which they would occur if the incident were real. They generally conduct these exercises around a conference table, hence the name of the exercise. Table top exercises are effective in testing major incident plans as they highlight any weaknesses in a safe environment where lives are not at risk.

Control post

Control post exercises are designed to test communication systems. Each attending public service will operate from the control room they would use if the incident were real. This includes static control rooms and mobile communications systems. Control post exercises are useful in determining room layouts, staffing and the overcoming of communications difficulties.

Live

Live exercises can test a small part of a major incident plan such as an evacuation or it can test a full-scale major incident response. The exercise is carried out as realistically as possible including fake casualties and a simulated media response. This provides all the agencies involved with an opportunity to get to grips with the problems arising from a major disaster and attempt to solve them in real time just as they would need to do in a real incident.

Think about it

Which method of exercising do you think is most effective. Explain your reasons.

Computer simulations

Computer simulations can be very effective tools in aiding the exercising of a major incident. Systems such as Minerva, which is a team based command simulator developed and used by the Metropolitan police can be used effectively for multi-agency training with each public service receiving command information in visual and audio format.

Minerva also allows command teams to communicate with front line personnel via pager, radio and phone or even face-to-face. Minerva style systems have several advantages over traditional tabletop exercises. They provide significant realism via video link and they allow the command teams of different agencies to work together in coordinating their particular aspect of a response separately from other command teams. This means that effective channels of communication must be opened and maintained just as with a real incident.

Simulation analysis

The key to a successful simulation lies in the debrief and analysis which occurs after the event. Whatever style of exercise is used, it is of vital importance to review the response of the organisations involved so that the success can be built upon and the failures identified and overcome.

The process of analysis is part of an ongoing training procedure which reviews performance at all levels so that training needs can be met. This means that responses to future disasters will be quicker, coordinated and more efficient, saving both lives and money. They can also help in the process of disaster prevention.

Advantages and disadvantages of methods of exercising		
Type	**Advantages**	**Disadvantages**
Seminar	• Low cost • Brings services together • Applicable to old and new staff • Informs agencies of new developments • Less labour intensive	• Not very realistic • Emphasis on problem solving, not decision making • Usually used for small aspects of a response rather than the whole response
Table top	• Low cost • Less labour intensive • Ensures all plans 'dovetail' • More realistic • Agencies can interact and get to know each other	• Lacks elements of realism • Only a few individuals involved, usually senior staff
Control post	• Ensures difficulties with communications are ironed out • Cost effective and efficient • More realistic than seminar and table top	• Only a few individuals are involved, usually team leaders • Less realistic than live exercises
Live	• Tests part or all of a plan • Very realistic • Ensures all services and communications operate effectively • Allows for responses to media to be tested • Involves personnel at all levels	• Labour intensive • Very expensive • May cause disruption to the area where it is held

Figure 24.7 Advantages and disadvantages of methods of exercising

Prevention

An exercise may also highlight ways to assist in preventing a major incident in the first place and The Health and Safety Executive (HSE) plays a key role in this area. The HSE was established in 1988 after the Piper Alpha Oil Platform in the North Sea suffered a major incident which led to the loss of 167 oil workers. The HSE's mission is to ensure breaches of safety legislation do not cause further disasters and they have substantial powers to ensure companies and corporations operating in the UK do not put the health of their employees, the public or the environment at risk by engaging in dangerous practices or being negligent in their duty of care. The HSE has sixteen divisions:

• Chemical hazardous installations division

• Directorate of science and technology

• Electrical equipment certification service

- Field operations directorate
- Health and safety laboratory
- HSE information services
- HSE language services
- Local authority unit
- Mines inspectorate
- Nuclear safety directorate
- Offshore safety division
- Policy unit
- HM railway inspectorate
- Safety policy directorate

The main piece of legislation, which provides the HSE with its powers, is the Health and Safety at Work Act etc (1974) which allows them to:

- enter any work premises without notice and talk to employees and safety representatives
- collect samples or take photographs
- impound dangerous equipment and substances
- give advice/warnings
- serve improvement/prohibition notices
- prosecute in the criminal courts of England/Wales.

The HSE is another of the many organisations which must co-operate with each other if the response to a major incident is to be effective.

Inter-agency cooperation

We have already examined issues of effective exercising and the benefits of various simulation techniques. We have also identified the roles and responsibilities of various statutory and voluntary agencies at the scene of a major incident. The focus of the next section will focus primarily on the role of effective communications and commands in promoting inter-agency cooperation.

Inter-agency cooperation revolves around several key issues:

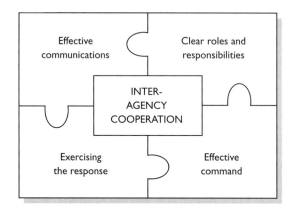

Figure 24.8 Inter-agency cooperation is important when dealing with major incident simulations

Chains of command

In a typical major incident, the coordinated inter-agency response has three levels of command as shown in Figure 24.9:

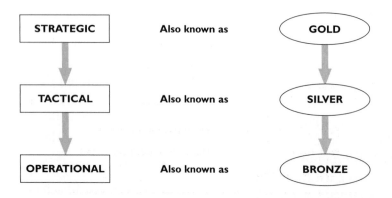

Figure 24.9 There are three levels of command in a coordinated inter-agency response

An example of a major incident command structure for a typical major incident such as a chemical spillage or flood evacuation would look similar to Figure 24.10.

The services involved at each level obviously depends on the type of incident; a maritime incident may contain a variety of different services such as HM Coastguard, Royal Air Force and the Royal Navy. However, the structure detailed above highlights the relative positions of the personnel involved in a response. Each level of the hierarchy has its own particular responsibilities in coordinating a response.

Think about it

Why are 3 levels of command advantageous?

Strategic – gold

This section of the hierarchy consists of chief officers of various agencies who are located away from the scene of the incident, usually at the Police Service Headquarters. This command group is in overall strategic command of an incident and deals with issues such as implementing established policies and plans and providing the media response to an incident.

In addition, gold command organises and provides resources such as labour and equipment, which silver command can deploy as required. Gold/strategic command must also determine the prioritisation of requests from silver command and decide which requests are most important. This command also determines and reviews contingency plans for a swift return to normality once the incident is brought under control.

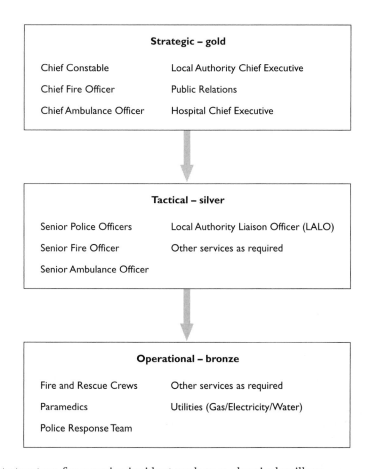

Figure 24.10 Major incident structure for a major incident such as a chemical spillage

This structure allows for a greater degree of centralised coordination and the integration of management processes across agency boundaries. The location of gold command away from the scene of the disaster minimises issues of risk and distraction to senior officers and also facilitates liaison with other agencies such as the lead government department ultimately responsible and the local authority who will take a lead role in the rebuilding of the incident.

Tactical – silver

Silver command consists of senior public service officers based at the scene of the incident or as close as is safe to be. Their primary responsibility is to receive the directives of gold command and formulate them into a workable strategy to be used at the disaster site itself. This involves determining the resources required and planning and coordinating when certain tasks will be undertaken.

The role of tactical/silver command is not to be involved at the scene, but is more of a general management role of the overall situation. It provides a pivotal link between the theoretical strategy of gold command distant from the incident and bronze command who are directly at the scene dealing with the incident. Inter-agency cooperation is crucial at this level and extensive liaison between the silver commanders of various public service agencies occurs at tactical headquarters.

Operational – bronze

Bronze command is wholly concerned with gaining control at the scene and the coordination of life and property saving measures. Generally, bronze command is the first level in the hierarchy to be activated as the emergency services may be on the scene of an incident within 5 minutes. They will concentrate on their own role until directed otherwise after the establishment of silver and gold command.

This level has responsibility for ensuring silver and gold command is fully appraised of the situation at the scene. The accuracy of this information is vital if gold and silver levels are to implement appropriate policy and strategy and provide the media with accurate and up to date information.

Methods of communication

Clearly this major incident command structure requires extensive inter-agency liaison if it is to be effective in responding to a complex and dangerous situation. This is yet another area where the use of high quality simulations and exercises can pay dividends. Exercises provide opportunities for gold, silver and bronze to practice their respective roles and responsibilities ensuring that commanders know each other and have worked with each other before. This minimises conflicts of command and helps to highlight effective methods of communication which can later be deployed in a major incident. Figure 24.11 highlights the complexity of command arrangements at a disaster site. Further informatin of communications systems can be found in Unit 22 Signals and Communications.

There have been many occasions in which problems with communications systems have had a direct impact on the effectiveness of a major incident response as shown in the following case studies.

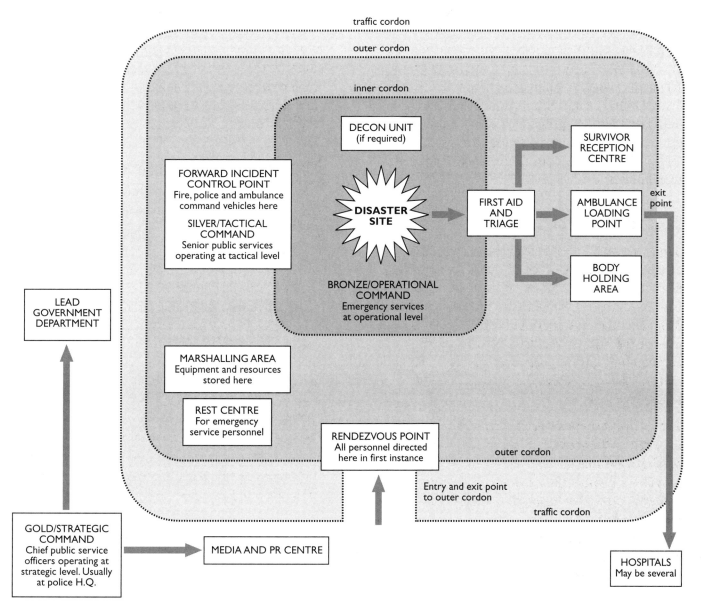

Figure 24.11 A major incident scene

Case study – The Kings Cross fire

Kings Cross is a major station on the London underground. In November 1987 a fire began under an escalator at the station, probably due to a dropped match or cigarette. The ensuing blaze killed 31 people and many more required medical treatment. The public services in attendance had several communications issues to overcome. Firstly, communications underground were not as effective as they could have been, leading to broken and missed transmissions which compromised safety and affected the efficiency of the response.

Another difficulty with communications in this combined response was the incompatibility of the radio systems of the Fire Brigade and British Transport Police which hampered the effective exchange of communications. The Fennell Report into the disaster published in 1988 highlighted these issues and several more and made recommendations including increased compatibility between radio networks of the attending agencies and improved communications provisions for an underground emergency response.

Case study – The Hillsborough disaster

In April 1989, 96 people died as a result of a crush inside a football ground caused by overcrowding. The football game was an FA Cup semi-final and the turnstiles at the ground could not cope with the extremely large volume of spectators. To relieve overcrowding outside the turnstiles, several additional gates were opened but this simply transferred the overcrowding inside and spectators were crushed against metal barriers designed to stop pitch invasions.

The police were already in attendance but there were several significant communications issues which delayed an effective response and contributed to the scale of the loss of life. Firstly, the communications systems used by the police became overwhelmed by the communications traffic. Each radio user had equal priority on the system, but the volume of officers who were all trying to contact base at the same time to give intelligence or to call for assistance or request direction made the system unusable. This in turn meant a delay in opening the pitch invasion barriers, which might have saved the lives of those being crushed against it. It also meant that many officers did not know a disaster was occurring until it was too late.

The Hillsborough disaster of 1989

The enquiry into the disaster by Lord Justice Taylor held the police largely to blame for the incident, although no officers were charged or disciplined over the incident by the government. The Taylor report recommended that police control rooms be adequately staffed to ensure all transmissions can be received and acted upon if required. In addition, other communications channels should be used as and when required to ensure that particular channels are not overcrowded and that there is a command channel dedicated solely for the use of the police commander so that he/she may contact other senior officers at the disaster site.

Think about it

What are the advantages of having a dedicated communications channel for senior commanders?

Theory into practice

Research the Lockerbie air crash and identify communications issues which may have affected the response of the public services.

Solutions to communications problems

The following procedures should be followed to ensure effective communication methods at a major incident:

- use of dedicated command channels on radio frequencies

- increased use of mobile phones at major incident scenes if technically appropriate to do so

- implementation of the telephone preference scheme which gives certain phone numbers such as police or local authority numbers preference in being connected if phone lines are overwhelmed

● designated inter agency multi channel UHF radios distributed to silver commanders by the police at the scene of a major incident

● rigorous testing and exercising of major incident plans

● adequate control room staff to interpret and evaluate transmissions

● effective command structures.

Impacts of major incidents

In the aftermath of a major incident many questions are likely to be asked regarding what were the causes and how can such events be avoided in the future. The public services go through a similar procedure, questioning and evaluating their own performance and the effectiveness of their major incident plan. This procedure is called a debrief and it provides all of the organisations and agencies involved with an opportunity to discuss and comment on various aspects of the combined response and the overall operation.

Debriefings may occur at individual agency level, for example the police holding their own single service debrief or at multi-agency level, for example silver commanders from the 3 emergency services coming together to evaluate silver command's combined response. Ultimately, every organisation who had involvement in the incident should have the opportunity to contribute to the debrief and help improve the response for the next time. An effective debrief is not about apportioning blame, instead it should revolve around ensuring the services are aware of any weaknesses so that they do not reoccur at the next major incident. To assist in this procedure the services sometimes appoint a neutral individual to coordinate the debrief. This ensures that a non-threatening environment is created and the co-ordinator does not have a bias towards one service or another.

Function	Detail
Collect evidence for an enquiry	Major incidents are often caused by criminal or neglectful actions. Evidence must be gathered which establishes the causes of the incident and where responsibility for the disaster lies. Debriefings can highlight some of these issues.
Improve combined response	Debriefings allow the services to review their response to an incident and evaluate their individual and collective performance in order to improve their response for the next time.
Identify staff development needs	A debriefing identifies areas for development of staff skills. It may be that some staff need equipment training, while others may require increased competence in public relations. The debrief highlights these needs and then the agencies concerned can address them.
Improve future training and exercising	The debrief of a major incident will allow future training and exercising to be improved on the basis of accurate experience in the field. Senior officers will know which aspects of a disaster need to be exercised and identify areas in which efficiency could be improved.

Figure 24.12 Debriefings after major incidents perform many useful functions

Case study – The Hatfield train derailment

On the 17th October 2000 a GNER train travelling from London to Leeds was derailed one mile outside Hatfield train station in Hertfordshire. The incident killed 4 people and injured many others. All of the subsequent debriefings conducted by the services were pulled together by Hertfordshire Emergency Services Major Incidents Committee (HESMIC) into one debriefing report, which could then be widely circulated and have its recommendations acted upon. Some of the issues and concerns raised in the debrief are described below:

- There was confusion in communication between the emergency services and Railtrack over the safety of power lines which was not resolved for over an hour into the incident.

- There were many people milling around in the inner and outer cordons who had no role to perform. They were not challenged on their legitimacy to be present.

- A helicopter was used, but the noise of its rotors meant that safety instructions could not be easily heard by emergency services on the ground.

- The identification of silver/tactical commanders was difficult as many individuals were wearing similar high visibility tabards.

- Some survivors of the derailment had to complete their onward journey by train.

- Although the clergy were put on standby to help survivors in the reception centres, they were not deployed.

- The Queen Elizabeth II hospital was put on standby but it was never given the signal to activate its major incident response. The hospital made the decision to activate the plan itself when casualties began to arrive.

These are just some of the issues raised by the Hatfield debriefs. It is clear that there is no such thing as a perfect incident response and there are always lessons to be learned in an ongoing cycle of development.

1. Why is it inappropriate for a major incident survivor to continue their onward journey on the same form of transport that was involved in the incident?

2. Examine the points made in the HESMIC debriefs regarding combined operations at the Hatfield rail crash and create a list of recommendations detailing how the problems encountered could be overcome in time for the next major incident.

Public enquiries

Occasionally, if a major incident is severe or costs many lives, a public enquiry is called. A public enquiry is an official and open government investigation which considers all the evidence and establishes the causes and consequences of an incident before making recommendations on how future incidents of a similar type may be avoided. A public enquiry is commissioned by the government after a catastrophic incident and is usually conducted by a leading barrister or judge who is impartial to the proceedings. Enquiries can take a long time to complete and often the

Types of debriefing	
Hot	**Cold**
This takes place immediately after a major incident response has been completed. It has the advantage of capturing the immediate impressions and reactions of those involved, but the disadvantage is that emotions may be running high among those participating and this may colour their input	This takes place a period of time after the incident. It has the advantage of allowing the agencies involved to reflect on their own performance and the performance of others which will bring more elements of discussion to the table. The disadvantage is that the immediate impressions of those involved are lost.

Figure 24.13 Types of debriefing after a major incident

findings will not be published for months or even years.

The following major incidents are examples of where a public enquiry was commissioned and who conducted the enquiry:

- Piper Alpha disaster – Lord Justice Cullen

- Hillsborough Stadium disaster – Lord Justice Taylor

- Herald of Free Enterprise sinking – Lord Justice Sheen

- Kings Cross underground fire – Desmond Fennel QC

The recommendations made by public enquiries can have a tremendous impact on the operation of the public services, the operations of companies and corporations and the legal system. Often new legislation is created after a major incident has occurred which is designed to prevent by law the safety breaches which caused an incident in the first place. An example of a major incident which had a great impact on safety legislation is the Piper Alpha disaster.

Think about it

What are the implications of choosing not to hold a public enquiry?

Case study – Piper Alpha

Piper Alpha was an oil rig in the North Sea which exploded on July 6th 1988 and burned with the loss of 167 lives. The incident occurred due to failures in communication and safety procedures – a primary condensate pump failed and control room staff made the decision to switch to a secondary pump. However, the secondary pump was undergoing routine maintenance and was missing a valve. The hole left by the missing valve allowed high pressure North Sea gas to explode through it and ignite. The platform contained large amounts of stored oil and gas which proceeded to ignite and explode virtually destroying the platform structure.

The explosions rendered emergency evacuation procedures such as lifeboats inoperative and helicopter evacuation was unsafe due to heat, smoke and the risk of further explosions. The personnel on board had to either remain on the burning platform or jump over one hundred feet into an icy cold North Sea covered in oil fires. Around 62 men were saved after making such a jump. The majority of the others who had not died immediately as a consequence of the explosions congregated in the accommodation block which was further away from the flames, but this area was not smoke proofed and carbon monoxide and other noxious fumes given off by the blaze proved fatal for them.

Piper Alpha oil rig

The government immediately announced a public enquiry to be headed by the Hon. Lord William Douglas Cullen, a renowned Scottish Judge. The objectives of the enquiry were twofold; firstly it had to establish the causes and circumstances of the disaster and secondly it had to make recommendations about how such a catastrophe could be avoided in future. As a direct result of Lord Cullen's recommendations, the Piper Alpha incident saw several new types of safety technology being developed and implemented both in the UK and installations world wide.

These included innovations in both active and passive fire protection systems and an interlocking fireproof panel system which can now be used on offshore installations to offer protection from heat and flames for up to 2 hours. Another form of safety offered on board rigs since Piper Alpha is the establishment of a temporary safe refuge (TSR) which contains command and communications facilities in addition to offering physical protection for workers. Other innovations include:

- increased use of highly sensitive early warning alarm systems designed to detect smoke, gas leaks and fire.

- the development of freefall lifeboats which are enclosed capsules designed to withstand over 100ft drops from offshore installations into the sea. They are also specially designed to withstand extremely high temperatures such as those which occurred in the oil fires on the North Sea surface below Piper Alpha.

- immersion suits which provide flotation and thermal insulation in the case of an offshore worker being forced to evacuate directly into the sea.

- the development of dry transfer systems which resemble cable cars. Cables connect the rescue ships with the rig and a sealed capsule can travel up and down it carrying people away from the rig in safety.

Post traumatic stress disorder

Major incidents such as Piper Alpha described above or any one of the disasters described throughout this chapter can have long term effects on the psychological and emotional well being of those involved. This applies not only to survivors of major incidents, but also to members of the public services involved in the disaster rescue and recovery operation. The sights seen by public services at major incidents are traumatic and emotionally shattering.

Over the last twenty years or so it has become widely acknowledged that the psychological

Figure 24.14 Common psychological effects of a major incident on individuals involved

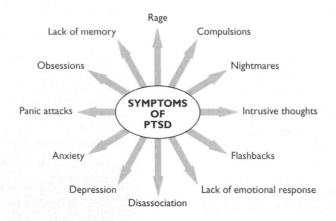

Figure 24.15 Symptoms of traumatic stress disorder

impact of wars, conflict and major incidents can have long term effects. There are many common psychological problems which survivors and rescue workers might experience after being involved in a disaster (see Figure 24.14). These effects can be short term lasting for hours or days or longer term spanning months and years.

Most people involved in major incidents experience mild stress symptoms which gradually dissipate over a short period of time. However, some individuals will experience more severe stress symptoms which may lead to post traumatic stress disorder (PTSD). These more severe symptoms include those described in Figure 24.15.

These symptoms can significantly impair an individuals ability to function in everyday life which can lead to occupational, social, marital and parenting problems. The Armed Forces are particularly at risk of PTSD following active service. In the US, where a great deal of work has been done on PTSD, it is estimated that 30% of the veterans of any conflict will experience the disorder at some point. A clear example of PTSD in UK disaster survivors comes from The Royal College of Psychiatrists who conducted a long term follow up study of the survivors of Piper Alpha. They discovered the following findings:

- after 10 years 21% of survivors still had PTSD

- 97% had experienced PTSD symptoms within 3 months of the incident

- 64% of survivors claimed to have psychological problems 10 years on

- 70% experienced acute survivor guilt (I should not have survived).

Think about it

Is enough done in the UK to support survivors of a disaster? In pairs, discuss how the government, public services and voluntary agencies could support survivors more effectively.

The trauma experienced during a major incident can last for many years. However, a controversial element of PTSD is whether or not rescue workers such as the police or paramedics should be able to claim compensation if they develop PTSD in the course of attending a major incident as part of their required duties. This issue has had major media attention recently when a South Yorkshire police officer who was on duty during the Hillsborough football disaster received an estimated £330,000 from South Yorkshire police in an out of court settlement. The officer, who had been involved directly in the rescue effort had suffered a breakdown and delayed onset PTSD. The families of those who died at Hillsborough received around 100 times less than the former police officer received.

Think about it

Should emergency workers and Armed Service personnel have a right to be compensated for PTSD when attending major incidents is a part of the job they signed up for. Explain your reasons.

Case study

You are a fire brigade station officer whose team is called out to attend a major road traffic incident involving 17 vehicles which have collided in heavy fog on a major motorway. Tragically the incident claims the life of 5 individuals, amongst them are 5-year-old twin girls who were trapped in a car and had to be cut free. In the weeks that follow the incident you begin to notice that one of your firefighters is behaving uncharacteristically. She is late for work, uncommunicative and edgy. You know that this firefighter has a 5 year-old daughter herself.

1　What might be wrong with the firefighter?

2　What other symptoms might you expect to appear?

3　What could you do personally to help this officer?

4　What support mechanisms are available in the fire service to help firefighters who suffer psychological stress?

5　Why might this particular firefighter be more likely to be disturbed by the traffic incident than others?

There is no definitive cure for PTSD but it often responds to a combination of counselling and drug therapy. One of the most often used techniques in PTSD treatment is called 'exposure therapy'. This is where the victim relives the experience over and over again in controlled conditions until the frightening memories lose their impact. The best known drug therapies associated with PTSD are also treatments for depression, such as Prozac.

Decontamination procedures

The world after September 11th is a much more cautious place. Individuals and organisations are much more aware of the terrorist potential of biological and chemical agents and the public services must be equipped to deal with them at the scene of a major incident. In addition, many major incidents which occur accidentally have the potential to release noxious chemicals or hazardous materials (HazMat) into the environment.

The role of the services in decontamination procedures for chemical, biological, radiological and nuclear (CBRN) attacks and HazMat incidents are outlined in the government's Strategic National Guidance on decontamination issues which was published in draft form for the first time in February 2003. Briefly, their roles are shown in Figure 24.16 below.

If the decision is taken to decontaminate then the casualties will normally be moved away from the area of greatest contamination to a safer area where on site decontamination can begin. Ideally, casualties will remove all contaminated clothing, but if they are unable to do this themselves then

Police
- be responsible for the overall co-ordination of the incident response (the same as with other major incidents)
- determine the boundaries of the cordons in association with the fire service, based on scientific data
- ensure unprotected people do not enter the cordons
- collect and store evidence in the case of a CBRN attack.

Fire service
- to assess the level of hazard
- work with the ambulance service to provide mass decontamination
- assist the ambulance service with casualty decontamination
- minimise risk to the environment
- supply personal protective equipment (PPE) to individuals involved in the rescue and recovery.

Ambulance service
- primary responsibility for casualty decontamination
- co-ordination with fire service if mass decontamination is required
- notify hospitals.

The Armed services
- assist in dealing with unexploded CBRN ordnance
- provide safety advice.

Figure 24.16 The roles of the services in decontamination procedures

their clothing may be removed by emergency service workers. This prevents contaminated clothing further contaminating the body of the individual concerned.

Mass decontamination procedures include low-pressure water spray from a fire service hose and portable showers, but can depend on the type of hazardous material that has been encountered. Mass decontamination normally takes place at the inner cordon, although if victims are trapped at the disaster site they can be decontaminated as they wait to be freed.

Another method of decontamination which may be used is the 'rinse-wipe-rinse' method described below. The rinse–wipe–rinse method can take up to 5 minutes per casualty. Clearly this may not be a viable option in some incidents. These methods of decontamination would also be used for the attending public services at the scene of the incident.

Think about it

What cultural issues need to be considered during the decontamination process?

Case study

A terrorist organisation has released a small amount of a suspected biological agent into a busy airport. There are several hundred people with possible contamination and many more who are panicking and are rushing to leave the scene, possibly spreading the contamination outside the airport. You are the senior ambulance officer in attendance and you have several key decisions to make.

1 Which services should you liaise with and why?

2 Should you choose individual decontamination or mass decontamination?

3 Which other agency could assist you in the decontamination procedure?

4 Where could casualties normally be moved to?

5 Who has responsibility for the safe storage of the clothes and possessions of the casualties while they undergo decontamination?

6 The group of casualties are mixed gender. What are the issues if you ask them to undress for mass decontamination and how could these issues be addressed?

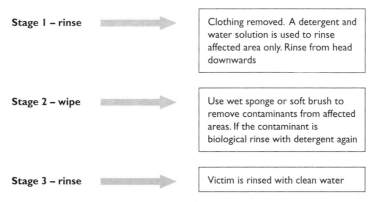

Stage 1 – rinse → Clothing removed. A detergent and water solution is used to rinse affected area only. Rinse from head downwards

Stage 2 – wipe → Use wet sponge or soft brush to remove contaminants from affected areas. If the contaminant is biological rinse with detergent again

Stage 3 – rinse → Victim is rinsed with clean water

Figure 24.17 Rinse-wipe-rinse method of decontamination

End of unit questions

1 What is the definition of a major incident?

2 Which is the lead government body for flooding incidents?

3 Identify and describe the 3 main categories of major incident.

4 What caused the Herald of Free Enterprise to sink?

5 What caused the explosion of Air France Concorde, flight 4590?

6 What scale is used to measure the magnitude of earthquakes?

7 Which terrorist group claimed responsibility in the Omagh bombing?

8 What does HSE stand for?

9 What were the long-term health impacts of individuals contaminated with radiation from Chernobyl?

10 What does PSTD stand for?

11 What is a major incident plan?

12 Describe 3 types of major incident plan.

13 What are the main features of an incident plan?

14 What is the role of the ambulance service at the scene of a major incident?

15 Identify and describe the 3 types of cordon used at a major incident site.

16 Identify and describe the 3 levels of command employed at a major incident.

17 Describe 2 methods of decontamination.

18 What communications issues can occur at a major incident site?

19 How can major incidents force a change in the law?

20 What is risk analysis?

Resources

Home Office 'The Decontamination of People Exposed to Chemical, Biological, Radiological or Nuclear (CBRN) Substances or Material' Strategic National Guidance First Edition: Feb 2003.

HM Fire Service Inspectorate, 'Fire Service Manual Vol 2 Fire service Operations: Incident Command' HMSO 2002

The Hon Lord Cullen, 'The Public Enquiry into the Piper Alpha Disaster' cm 1310 HMSO 1990

The Hon Lord Cullen, 'Enquiry into the Shootings at Dunblane Primary School' cm 3386 HMSO 1996

Fennell D 'Investigation into the Kings Cross Underground Fire' cm 499 HMSO 1988

Hidden A, 'Investigation into the Clapham Junction Railway Accident' cm 820 HMSO 1989

Lord Justice Taylor, 'The Hillsborough Stadium Disaster, 15th April enquiry interim report' cm 765 HMSO 1989

Assessment activities

This section describes what you must do to obtain a pass grade for this unit.

A merit or distinction grade may be awarded if your work demonstrates a deeper understanding of the topics and is of a higher quality. The highlighted sentences indicate the quality of work expected at merit and distinction level.

Assessment methods

A number of assessment strategies may be used in order to achieve the learning outcomes, such as oral presentations, group discussions, written assignments, research projects and role-plays or a combination of these. It is a good idea, though it is not essential, to use a variety of methods in order to develop different skills.

It is important that you understand and comply with the key words specified in the grading criteria. For example, if you are asked to 'analyse' something, then make sure that you do not merely describe it. Similarly, if you are asked to 'evaluate' something, then make sure you do not merely summarise it.

Key words

Here are some key words that are often used for grading criteria – make sure you understand the differences between them.

Examine	To look at a subject closely in order to understand it and improve your knowledge
Consider	This means to think about and weigh up a subject
Explain	This means to make something clear and set out the arguments
Analyse	This means to look at a subject closely and interpret or evaluate your findings. This can include an outline of the pro's and con's of a situation or suggestions for changes and improvements
Describe	This means to say what something is like – it is a factual account of how something is or how it appears.
Compare	This means to look at the similarities between two or more objects or theories.

Assessment tasks

Using the materials within this unit and your own research, carry out the following tasks.

Task 1

Learning outcome 1 – Examine the effects of disaster and major incident situations

Describe in detail three recent disasters or major incidents and, with examples, the three main ways in which disasters or major incidents are caused.

Suggestion for Task 1: report

This is an ideal task to do as a report. Using the information contained in this chapter and your own research select three recent disasters and discuss them in detail and then discuss the human, technological and natural causes of disasters and major incidents.

Task 2

Learning outcome 2 – Investigate disaster planning and prevention

Describe the main features of a major incident plan detailing the organisations involved in major incident planning in Britain.

Explain the nature and value of disaster simulations.

> To obtain a merit grade, you should *analyse* the role played by the emergency and other public services in a recent disaster.

> To obtain a distinction grade, you should *evaluate* how the emergency services review their response to a given disaster scenario.

Suggestion for Task 2: role play activity

This task would work very well as a role play divided into several parts.

Part 1 – In small groups design a major incident plan highlighting and incorporating the key features you would find in professional major incident plans. Each person takes on the role of one of the public services to contribute to the plan.

Part 2 – Engage in a major incident role play and fulfil the public services role assigned to you, analysing your role and others within the disaster. Feedback to the group on your findings from the role play.

Part 3 – The original panel who developed the disaster plan reconvene after the simulation and review the response of each of their services. Make notes during your discussion on the nature and value of disaster simulations.

Task 3

Learning outcome 3 – Investigate inter-agency cooperation between public services

Explain the role of three emergency services and three organisations outside the emergency services in a given disaster scenario outlining possible command and communications problems which may arise between agencies, giving possible solutions.

Suggestion for Task 3: individual presentation

This task could be completed as a presentation which fulfils the requirements of the criteria outlined above.

Task 4

Learning outcome 4 – Analyse the impact of a specified disaster or major incident situation on individuals and communities

Describe a range of long term environmental or health problems which could follow three given types of disaster.

Explain the roles of three organisations dealing with these situations.

> To obtain a merit grade, you should *analyse* the enviromental or health problems following one recent disaster.

> To obtain a distinction grade you should *critically analyse* the impact on processes, procedures, communications, legislation, roles and responsibilities of one disaster.

Suggestion for Task 4: report

Using the information provided in this chapter and your own research write a report which outlines the long term health and environmental impact of one human disaster, one technological disaster and one natural disaster. In addition, include how three public service organisations would help deal with these consequences.

If you want to achieve a higher grade, you should ensure you analyse the environmental and health problems rather than just discuss them. In addition, you should critically analyse how disasters and the public service response to them can change things in future disaster responses. For example, the Piper Alpha disaster changed safety legislation on oil platforms, the Kings Cross Underground fire highlighted problems with communications which needed to be resolved as did the Hillsborough football disaster.

INTEGRATED VOCATIONAL ASSIGNMENT (IVA)

What is an IVA?

The IVA is an assignment set by your awarding body EDEXCEL. It is not an examination, it is a normal assignment and is likely to resemble the ones you are used to doing throughout your National Award/Certificate/Diploma.

It is set externally to ensure that your qualification has equivalency with other level three qualifications such as A-levels which have external tests. It is marked by your tutors and then checked by specialist practitioners at EDEXCEL to ensure that your tutors are marking in accordance with a strict marking grid. You should not have to worry about an IVA any more than you would worry about another assignment.

You must remember that your IVA is a compulsory part of your course and if you do not complete it you may not be eligible to pass your course.

Which subjects are covered by IVA?

If you are completing the National Award in Public Services then Unit 3 Leadership will be covered by your IVA.

If you are completing the National Certificate or Diploma in Public Services your IVA will cover Unit 3 Leadership and Unit 4 Citizenship and Contemporary Issues.

How will I get my IVA?

A new IVA is produced every year which will be issued by your college or school at a time they choose. However, the IVA is released into the public domain on the EDEXCEL website earlier than many centres may give it to you. This means that you can go to the EDXCEL website www.edexcel.org.uk and print it off from there if you want to have extra time to consider it. Be careful to ensure you are downloading the latest version.

How long will I get to complete my IVA?

Completion time for the IVA is at the discretion of your centre. The final deadline for submission of your work is usually at the end of March but EDEXCEL does not specify a time that it should be given to you. This means that your tutors may provide you with the IVA at any point from September onwards. If you want to get a head start then there is nothing to stop you accessing the assignment direct from the website.

What help will my tutors give me?

Your tutor should help and guide you in exactly the same way that they would for other units on your course. This means that they may point you in the direction of useful resources, such as books, journals or websites. They may give you guidance on structure and presentation of your work and some tutors may be happy to check your notes or draft for spelling and grammar errors. It is important to remember that all the work you submit should be your own. Your tutors cannot and will not complete the work for you.

What does the IVA consist of?

Your IVA consists of:

- A set of general instructions – this is a list of around ten bullet points which provide you with guidance on how to complete the IVA. It would make good sense to read them thoroughly as they will help you approach your assignment in the correct way.

- Your assignment scenario and tasks – These should be similar to assignments you already complete. The scenario will consist of a hypothetical but realistic situation involving the public services followed by a series of tasks or questions you must complete which are based on the scenario. The work you have done in class should help you address these tasks, as will this book and your own research.

- A summary of your tasks and what you should hand in. This is a description of what should be in you final package of work. Checking that you comply with this ensures that you don't forget sections or parts of your assignment.

- The assessment criteria for the unit – always reference your answers to this set of criteria as it will provide you with as much guidance on what the assignment requires as the assignment brief itself. Look at the criteria and make sure that your assignment answers the set criteria as well as the assessment tasks.

- Your IVA coversheet – this is the front cover of your assignment which must be placed at the start of your assignment.

What happens if my IVA is late?

It is your responsibility to ensure you plan your academic workload sufficiently well so that none of your assignments are late and this is especially true for the IVA. Each college makes a decision as to whether it will accept late work and the grounds on which they will permit extensions. Your centre can submit your late work for re-marking but it may delay your achievement.

You cannot resit your IVA but if you take your IVA in the first year of your course and wish to improve your grade in year two of your course, you can choose to complete the following year's IVA but you must pay a supplementary remarking fee. Your centre is the best place to arrange this.

There may be some occasions where a student is eligible for an extension to allow more time for work to be completed, such as bereavement or a serious illness. If you feel you qualify and would like to be awarded an extension you should speak to your tutors as soon as you become aware of the situation. Equally, you may feel your work should receive special consideration because of your personal circumstances and in this instance your college has an EDEXCEL form which they can complete on your behalf. Speak to you tutors as soon as you can about this if you feel it applies to you.

How can I do well on my IVA?

You can achieve a high grade on your IVA in much the same way that you would achieve a high grade on any other assignment. The following points will help you work towards a successful outcome for all of your work, including the IVA.

1   Make sure you start your assignment as soon as you get it. This is true of all your

assignments, but it is particularly important in the IVA as it is a double unit assignment on the National Certificate and Diploma courses, which means you will need double the length of time to complete it. Don't underestimate the length of time you will need to understand, research and write your work. It is likely that you will need several months to be able to do a creditable job of it.

2   Read your assignment thoroughly and ensure you understand what is required of you. If you just skim the assignment it is highly likely you will miss many relevant points which could have improved your grade. If you don't understand a question you must always ask your tutor for clarification.

3   Do not be tempted to take the easy way out and simply reproduce work you have found in textbooks or on the Internet. All of your work must be your own. You may not copy anything you find and if you do use work from external sources you must reference it within the body of your work and again in the bibliography. It is wholly unacceptable for you to submit copied work.

4   If you complete any aspect of your assignment as part of a group you must record your achievement individually. This means all of your contribution to the group task must be identified and your individual contribution must show that you have met all the outcomes.

5   It is important that you use a wide variety of resources in order to complete your work. Using one or two sources of information will not provide you with the depth and detail required for a high grade. Remember that you may use textbooks, journals, magazines, newspapers, Internet, first hand accounts from public services officers or other professionals, your own primary research and public service promotional information to name but a few. The more sources you use the fuller your answers are likely to be and this will be reflected in your grade.

6   Try to produce work as professionally as possible. It is extremely difficult to mark work where the writing is illegible, so if you know your handwriting is poor then it is in your interests to word process it. If your spelling and grammar is poor then have a dictionary handy or use the spelling and grammar checker on your computer. Your work should be focused and well organised with each task clearly signposted.

7   Pay attention to the key words in your tasks, such as analyse, explain or describe. These key words mean different things and it is important to know what these words mean and how to interpret them in your assignment (see page vii in the Introduction).

8   Consider creating an action plan which details your plan of how you will approach your assignment with timescales (there is an example of an action plan at the end of the Leadership chapter). This will help you monitor how well you are doing and whether you are falling behind schedule in producing your work.

9   If you are having any kind of difficulty with the assignment such as problems managing part-time work and study, health problems or home life difficulties you should tell your tutor immediately so that they can offer you the support you need.

10 Before you hand your work in, check that you have included everything and not left any parts out by accident. This last check and read through may pick up other mistakes on your assignment you didn't spot while you were writing it.

11 If you use a word processor you should ensure you back up your work onto a hard drive or the college network if you are allowed access to your own network area. Don't just rely on a floppy disk to save your work as they can be damaged very easily and the data may be lost.

INDEX

 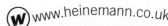